A Resource Guide for Elementary School Teaching

Planning for Competence

SIXTH EDITION

PATRICIA L. ROBERTS

RICHARD D. KELLOUGH

KAY MOORE

California State University, Sacramento

Upper Saddle River, New Jersey
Columbus, Ohio

Library of Congress Cataloging-in-Publication Data

Roberts, Patricia
   A resource guide for elementary school teaching: planning for competence / Patricia L.
   Roberts, Richard D. Kellough, Kay Moore. — 6th ed.
      p. cm.
   Rev. ed. of: A resource guide for elementary school teaching / Richard D. Kellough,
   Patricia L. Roberts. 5th ed. c2002.
   Includes bibliographical references and index.
   ISBN 0-13-119612-X
   1. Elementary school teaching. 2. Competence based education. I. Kellough, Richard D.
   (Richard Dean). II. Moore, Kay. III. Kellough, Richard D. (Richard Dean). Resource guide
   for elementary school teaching. IV. Title.

LB1555.K39 2006
372.1102—dc22   2004065551

Vice President and Executive Publisher: Jeffrey W. Johnston
Executive Editor: Debra A. Stollenwerk
Associate Editor: Ben M. Stephen
Senior Editorial Assistant: Mary Morrill
Production Editor: Kris Roach
Production Coordination: Amy Gehl, Carlisle Publishers Services
Photo Coordinator: Monica Merkel
Design Coordinator: Diane C. Lorenzo
Cover Designer: Jason Moore
Cover Image: Corbis
Production Manager: Susan Hannahs
Director of Marketing: Ann Castel Davis
Marketing Manager: Darcy Betts Prybella
Marketing Coordinator: Brian Mounts

This book was set in Garamond by Carlisle Communications, Ltd. It was printed and bound by Banta Book Group/ Harrisonburg. The cover was printed by Coral Graphic Services, Inc.

Photo Credits: Charles Gupton/Corbis/Bettmann, p. 1; Courtesy of Martin Luther King, Jr. School, Phoenix, AZ, p. 2; Derke/O'Hara/Getty Images Inc.–Stone Allstock, p. 16; Silver Burdett Ginn, p. 28; Scott Cunningham/Merrill, pp. 48, 78, 150, 158; Anthony Magnacca/Merrill, pp. 124, 187, 234, 271; Karen Mancinelli/Pearson Learning Photo Studio, pp. 101, 212; Pearson Learning Photo Studio, p. 102; David Mager/Pearson Learning Photo Studio, p. 262.

Pearson Education Ltd.
Pearson Education Singapore Pte. Ltd.
Pearson Education Canada, Ltd.
Pearson Education—Japan

Pearson Education Australia Pty. Limited
Pearson Education North Asia Ltd.
Pearson Educación de Mexico, S.A. de C.V.
Pearson Education Malaysia Pte. Ltd.

10 9 8 7 6 5 4 3 2 1
ISBN: 0-13-119612-X

Preface

Welcome to the sixth edition of *A Resource Guide for Elementary School Teaching: Planning for Competence*. We have kept the original purpose of this resource guide, which is to provide a practical and concise guide for college or university students who are preparing to become competent elementary schoolteachers, and the core of the purpose is reflected in the subtitle, *Planning for Competence*. Other readers who may find this guide useful are experienced teachers who want to continue developing their teaching skills and curriculum specialists and school administrators who want a current, practical, and concise text of methods, guidelines, and resources for teaching in the elementary school.

NEW TO THIS EDITION

Currently, because of all the interest in education, state and interstate standards, national standards, high-stakes testing, state teacher tests, and the No Child Left Behind Act, the research and preparation for this sixth edition were quite demanding. This edition provides the following new materials:

- An inside front cover presentation titled *Strategies and Materials You Can Use in Classroom Teaching.* The list offers teacher-friendly materials found in the chapters.
- Scenarios titled **Looking at Teachers** as chapter openers and related **Praxis Warm-Ups** at the end of each chapter and on the Companion Website. All chapters begin with instructional scenarios titled *Looking at Teachers.* These scenarios provide insights into different grade levels in the elementary school. They also serve as additional springboards for thinking about elementary school teaching and learning and class discussion. These openers are the basis for the **Praxis Warm-Ups**—short constructed response-type questions that will help precredentialed and prelicensed teachers prepare to take the Praxis II tests and other teacher tests. All chapters close with *About*

Praxis and Other Teacher Tests boxes that serve as additional informational sources for precredentialed elementary teachers who are getting ready to take upcoming Praxis tests or other teacher licensing exams.
- Visual chapter organizers and overviews. In all of the chapters, the visual chapter organizers serve as an advance organizer that is documented by research for its value in meaningful learning, and is a part of each chapter's introduction and overview.
- The use of technology is explored in a recurring feature called *Technology Tips for the Classroom.* Here, readers will find strategies for integrating technology in the elementary classroom. Related Web links can be found on the *Web Destinations* module of the Companion Website.
- All chapters end with a section titled *Extending My Professional Competency.* This section features:
  - *Praxis Warm-Up.* This component allows precredentialed and prelicensed teachers to respond to constructed response-type questions based on the chapter-opening vignettes. Hints for successfully answering these can be found in the Appendix. Additional constructed response-type questions for each chapter are in the *Praxis Warm-Up* module on the Companion Website.
  - *For Your Discussion.* This component invites precredentialed and prelicensed teachers to read and respond to discussion questions so that they can actively rehearse/practice their responses to questions that might be asked of them by a colleague, a parent, or a community member. Through the questions, they might be asked to explain content, theory, a related research, or to identify techniques or strategies; they might be asked to connect a topic to another topic in this text or be asked to relate an experience that they have had to a topic in the chapter. Additionally, they might be asked to react to the subject matter or to situations or explain a point of view about a current trend or issue, or explain their reactions to a problem happening in education.

- *Online Portfolio Activities.* This component invites precredentialed teachers to begin an online portfolio to assist them in self-evaluation, in assessing their teaching, in self-reflection, in continuing professional growth and development, and, if appropriate for their state, in documenting their competence for certification and licensing regulations. A user can go to the *Online Portfolio Activities* module for any chapter on this book's Companion Website.
- **Core subject matter for Praxis identified in subject index.** We have added an asterisk by selected word entries in the subject index to identify the core subject matter we suggest reviewing to prepare for taking the Praxis II exam or other teacher licensing exams.

UNIQUE FEATURES

With all of this in mind, the sixth edition also has several unique features:

- **Perforated Application Exercises in every chapter.** The exercises emphasize the beginning teacher working cooperatively and collaboratively with others in a group just as he or she would work with other members of a faculty team.
- **Chapter objectives.** Precredentialed (and credentialed) teachers are asked to consider the chapter objectives at the front of each chapter to get a description of what the teacher should be able to do on completing the reading of the chapter and after completing the related application exercises, the end-of-the chapter activities, and reading and interacting with the supporting Companion Website material.
- **Key terms in bold.** Definitions of key terms are found in the glossary in the resource guide.
- **Exemplary schools and programs featured.** So readers can learn and read about or visit exemplary schools and programs, some are recognized and identified by name throughout this text. These schools are supported by thousands of committed teachers, administrators, parents, and community representatives who struggle daily, year after year, to provide children with quality education. When clicked on the Companion Website, the names of these schools and programs link a reader to the websites.
- At the end of each chapter, readers will find a **Summary; For Further Reading** lists references, both classic and current; and **Notes** documents the chapter sources. At the end of the text, there is an **Appendix** with hints for the *Praxis Warm-Ups.* There is also a **Glossary; Children's Literature Index; Name Index;** and **Subject Index.**

- **Inside back cover matrix correlates text material with the INTASC principles, the NBPTS Standards, and Praxis II.** All chapters, with added illustrations, contain material that connects with the subject matter on which precredentialed teachers are usually tested through Praxis II and other teacher tests—these are the areas of management, assessment of learning, curriculum and instruction, assessment of teaching, and professional development.

OUR BELIEFS: HOW AND WHERE THEY ARE REFLECTED IN THIS RESOURCE GUIDE

In the preparation of this text, we saw our task *not* as making the teaching job easier for you—effective teaching is never easy—but as improving your teaching effectiveness and providing relevant guidelines and current resources. You may choose from these resources and build on what works best for you. Nobody can tell you what will work with your students; you will know them best. We do share what we believe to be the best of practices, the most useful of recent research findings, and the richest of experiences. The highlighted statements that follow present our beliefs and explain how they are included in this resource guide.

The best learning occurs when the learner actively participates in the process, which includes having ownership in both the process and the product of the learning. Consequently, this resource guide is designed to engage you in "hands-on" and "minds-on" learning about effective teaching. For example, rather than simply finding a chapter devoted to an exposition of the important topic of cooperative learning, in each chapter you will become involved in cooperative and collaborative learning. In essence, via the application exercises found in every chapter (and those found on this book's Companion Website), you will practice cooperative and collaborative learning, talk about it, practice it some more, and, finally, through the process of doing it, learn a great deal about it. This resource guide *involves* you in it.

The best strategies for learning about teaching are those that model the strategies used in exemplary teaching of children. As you will learn, integrated learning is the cornerstone of effective teaching for the 21st century, and that is a premise on which this resource guide continues to be designed.

To be most effective, any teacher, regardless of grade level and subject, must use an eclectic style in teaching. Rather than focusing your attention on particular models of teaching, we emphasize the importance of an eclectic model—that is, one in which you select and integrate the best from various instructional approaches. For example, there are times when you will want to use a systematic explicit expository approach, perhaps by lecturing; there are many more times when you will want to use an implicit, social-interactive, or student-centered approach, perhaps through project-based learning. This resource guide provides guidelines that will help you not only to decide which approach to use at a particular time, but also ways to develop your skill in using specific approaches.

Learning should be active, pleasant, fun, meaningful, and productive. Our desire is, as it always has been, to present this text in an enthusiastic, positive, and cognitive-humanistic way, in part by providing rich experiences in cooperative and collaborative learning. How this is done is perhaps best exemplified by the active application exercises found throughout this book and also on the Companion Website. Some application exercises have been rewritten from previous editions, others have been deleted, and still others have been moved to the Companion Website. Some new application exercises have been added to ensure that you become an active participant in learning the methods and procedures that are most appropriate in facilitating the learning of the actively responsible children present in today's elementary schools.

Teaching skills can be learned. You realize that in medicine, certain knowledge and skills must be learned and developed before the student physician is licensed to practice alone with patients. In law, certain knowledge and skills must be learned and developed before the law student is licensed to practice in a courtroom. So it is in education: In teacher preparation, knowledge and skills must be learned and developed before the teacher candidate is granted a certificate and is licensed to practice the art and science of teaching children. We would never consider allowing just any person to treat our child's illness or to defend us in a legal case; the professional education of teachers is no less important! Receiving professional education in how to reach children is absolutely necessary, and certain aspects of that education must precede any interaction with children if teachers are to become truly accomplished professionals.

TEXT ORGANIZATION

Competent elementary school teaching is a kaleidoscopic, multifaceted, eclectic process. When preparing and writing a resource guide for use in elementary teacher preparation, by necessity, one must separate that total kaleidoscopic view into separate views, which is not always possible to do in a way that makes the most sense to everyone using the book. We believe that there are *developmental components involved in becoming a competent teacher.* This book is organized around those components:

(a) why, (b) what, and (c) how and how well. Each of the three parts of this resource guide clearly reflects one of these three components. Each part is introduced with the chapters of that part. The visual graphic shown here illustrates how these three developmental elements are divided.

Why? Elementary School Teaching and Learning Part I	What? Planning for Curriculum and Instruction Part II

Planning for Competency

How and How Well?
Effective Instruction, Teacher Assessment,
and Professional Development
Part III

These components match the major subject material that the Praxis II Principles of Learning and Teaching tests and other teacher tests contain:

Resource Guide Components	Teacher Tests
Who?	Planning for Management
What?	Planning for Curriculum and Instruction
How and How Well?	Planning for Effective Instruction; Planning for Teacher Assessment and Professional Development

Part I: Elementary School Teaching and Learning

To better reflect the *why* component—the reality and challenge of elementary school teaching today—Part I underwent substantial reorganization and updates for this edition. It has four chapters. Chapter 1 presents an important overview of the reality and the challenge of teaching in an elementary school today. It mentions high-stakes testing (more about high-stakes testing in Chapter 5) and the No Child Left Behind Act. As in all chapters, it has included technology, information about teacher tests, and access to the Companion Website. In this edition, Chapters 1 and 2 are, we believe, better organized with figures and more focused in the overview of elementary schools and elementary learners today. Chapter 2 is about students and considers the developments in cognitive learning theory that enhance and celebrate the differences of students and their styles of learning. *Regardless of gender, social or physical abilities, and ethnic or cultural characteristics, all students must have equal opportunity to participate and learn in the classroom.* This belief is reflected throughout this resource guide.

Chapter 3 relates mainly to the topic of management and is devoted to the behaviors of a classroom teacher. This chapter reflects the expectations, responsibilities, and classroom behaviors that are characteristic of competent elementary schoolteachers. Chapter 4 is about the learning environment, specifically the classroom, and is stronger in this edition with added illustrations and new organization. Because a teacher must have the students' attention to effectively implement any instructional plan, guidelines for establishing and maintaining a supportive environment for learning are also presented in Chapter 4.

Part II: Planning for Curriculum and Instruction

To reflect the planning, or *what,* component, Part II includes three chapters that are stronger chapters than in the previous edition because of their added illustrations and new organization. *Effective teaching is performance based and criterion referenced.* Related to this, Chapter 5, about the rationale for planning and selecting the content of the curriculum, contains information about the standards that have been developed for different subject areas of the elementary school curriculum and about the high-stakes testing that often accompanies curriculum standards. The section on preparing and using instructional objectives emphasizes the relationship of objectives to assessing learning and planning instruction. Chapter 5 also has updated material about controversial issues related to a teacher's rationale for selecting materials, district material selection, and reconsideration policies, and the difference between a challenge and censorship; it includes a five-part action plan related to censorship.

Chapter 6 is about assessing what students know or think they know before, during, and after the instruction to assist teachers in further planning of instruction. In addition to the use of portfolios, scoring guides, rubrics, checklists, performance assessment, and student self-assessments, the chapter provides practical guidelines for parent–teacher collaboration and for marking and grading. Emphasis is placed on how a teacher can interpret test results, ways to report results, and ways to communicate results to parents or guardians interested in the student's achievement.

Chapter 7 presents instructional planning as a three-level and multi-step process, and introduces the topics of activity planning, lesson planning, and unit planning. Also, to link the primary topic of this chapter about instructional planning to the strategies introduced in this part, this chapter provides the theoretical considerations for the selection of instructional strategies. Some classic references, including G. Polya's method of problem solving, are included in the references in this resource guide or on the Companion Website.

Part III: Effective Instruction, Teacher Assessment, and Professional Development

For this edition, the *how* and *how well* component now includes four chapters. Chapter 8 provides guidelines and resources for the use of teacher talk and questioning, with enhanced emphasis on the encouragement and use of children's questions. Chapter 9 provides guidelines and resources for the use of demonstrations, teaching of thinking, use of inquiry learning, and educational games. Chapter 10 emphasizes various ways of grouping children for instruction, using assignments, ensuring equity in the classroom, using project-centered teaching, and writing across the curriculum. Chapter 11 focuses your attention on the *how well* component and mainly reflects how the teacher is doing. You'll recall that the *how well* component for assessing students' learning is discussed in Chapter 6. Chapter 11, traditionally considered an important chapter by the readers, emphasizes *how well the teacher is doing*— the assessment of teaching effectiveness and guidelines for ongoing professional development. Also in Chapter 11 are other items that have been popular with precredentialed teachers, such as E-Teaching (Emergency Teaching Kit—a Multicultural Friendship Kit), a Teachalogue (guidelines for student teaching), and support in finding a teaching position, writing the résumé, and continued professional development.

Part III also contains three peer teaching application exercises: the first of these, A Cooperative Learning and Peer Teaching Exercise in the use of Questioning—Peer Teaching, is in the *Additional Application Exercises* module for Chapter 8 on the Companion Website. In Chapter 9, the second peer teaching application exercise is titled Developing a Lesson Plan Using Different Approaches: Inquiry Learning Level II, Thinking Skill Development, a Demonstration, or an Interactive Lecture–Peer Teaching. Chapter 11 contains the third and most sophisticated of the three peer teaching application exercises, Pulling It All Together Peer Teaching. This exercise, in essence, is a performance assessment-type final examination for the course or program for which this resource guide is being used.

SUPPLEMENTARY MATERIALS

The following ancillaries are available to instructors who adopt this text. To request information, please contact your local Prentice Hall representative. If you do not know how to contact your sales representative, please call faculty service at 1-800-526-0485 for assistance.

For the Instructor

- **The Online Instructor's Manual** provides instructors with a variety of useful resources, such as assessments, chapter overviews, teaching strategies, ideas for classroom activities, and discussions.
- Every Companion Website integrates **Syllabus Manager™,** an online syllabus creation and management utility.
  - **Syllabus Manager™** provides you, the instructor, with an easy, step-by-step process to create and revise syllabi, with direct links into Companion Website and other online content without having to learn HTML.
  - Students may logon to your syllabus during any study session. All they need to know is the web address for the Companion Website and the password you've assigned to your syllabus.
  - After you have created a syllabus using **Syllabus Manager™,** students may enter the syllabus for their course section from any point in the Companion Website.
  - Clicking on a date, the student is shown the list of activities for the assignment. The activities for each assignment are linked directly to actual content, saving time for students.
  - Adding assignments consists of clicking on the desired due date, then filling in the details of the assignment–name of the assignment, instructions, and whether or not it is a one-time or repeating assignment.
  - In addition, links to other activities can be created easily. If the activity is online, a URL can be entered in the space provided, and it will be linked automatically in the final syllabus.
  - Your completed syllabus is hosted on our servers, allowing convenient updates from any computer on the Internet. Changes you make to your syllabus are immediately available to your students at their next logon.

To take advantage of the many available resources, please visit the text's Companion Website at **www.prenhall.com/roberts.**

For the Student

- **The Companion Website (www.prenhall.com/roberts)** contains additional information for students (and instructors) to use in an online environment. To support a student teacher's preparation for competency in elementary school teaching, the Companion Website has several useful modules:
  - *Objectives Module* (to review your criteria base for each content area/chapter)
  - *Additional Content Module* (to broaden your knowledge base about content expanding each chapter)
  - *Self-Check Module* (to measure your understanding of chapter content and prepare for course exams)
  - *For Your Discussion Module* (to broaden your background knowledge and response skills as a future member of an elementary school faculty)
  - *Web Destinations Module* (to further support your preparation for elementary school teaching by leading you to suggested educational websites)
  - *Praxis Warm-Up Module* (to prepare for the Praxis II exams related to elementary education)
  - *Online Portfolio Activities Module* (to develop a professional teaching portfolio)
  - *Additional Application Exercises Module* (to broaden your application skills related to the content of each chapter)
  - *Other Teacher Tests Module* (to provide information to teachers who are in states that do not offer the Praxis tests)
- In terms of the *Self-Check* module on the Companion Website, content for Chapter 6 also includes a *mid-point self-evaluation* for precredentialed teachers that relates to the content and competency development addressed in the first six chapters. Content for Chapter 11 on the Companion Website has a *final self-evaluation* related to the content and competency development reflected in the remaining chapters of this resource guide. The self-checks and the self-evaluations are a valuable basis for a prelicensed teacher's self-evaluation, self-reflection, and continued professional growth and development.

**Additional Application Exercises and Additional Content Module found on the Companion Website at
www.prenhall.com/roberts**

	Additional Application Exercises **Module**	*Additional Content* **Module**
Chapter 1	• A Second Reflection on My Own Elementary School Experience	• First Day Jitters: Resources
Chapter 2	• Obtaining Personal Insight Regarding Whole-Part Content for the Grade I Want to Teach	• Developmental Characteristics of Children of Particular Age Groups • Guidelines for Working with Students with Special Needs • Teaching Toward Positive Character Development • Selected Resources on Character Education • Additional Readings About Elementary Learners
Chapter 3	• The Preactive Phase of Instruction • Web Destinations of Use to Elementary Schoolteachers	• Virtual Field Trip • Resources for Free and Inexpensive Printed Materials • Infringing Copyright Law and the Internet • Professional Journals and Periodicals • The ERIC Information Network • Safety Rules and Guidelines for the Elementary Schoolteacher and Classroom • Basic Teacher Behaviors That Facilitate Students' Learning • More Readings About Expectations, Responsibilities, and Facilitating Teacher Behaviors
Chapter 4	• Sending a Positive Message Home • Teachers' Behavior Management Systems • Observations and Analysis of How Experienced Teachers Open Their Class Meetings or the School Day • Selecting Measures of Control	• Plan for Effective Organization and Administration of Activities and Materials • Classroom Procedures and Guidelines for Acceptable Behavior • Starting the School Year Well • Emphasizing Procedures Rather than Rules • The First Day: Meeting Students • What Students Need to Understand from the Start • Time-Out Procedures • Managing Class Meetings • Opening Activities • Smooth Implementation of the Lesson • Transitions: A Difficult Skill for Beginning Teachers • Student Misbehavior • Types of Student Misbehavior • No Short-Term Solutions to Major Problems • Teacher Response to Student Misbehavior • Order of Behavior Intervention Strategies • Scenarios for Case Study Review • Common Mistakes to Avoid During First Years of Teaching • More Readings on Managing an Effective and Safe Learning Environment

	***Additional Application Exercises* Module**	***Additional Content* Module**
Chapter 5	• Examining State Standards and Other Curriculum Documents • Examining Local Curriculum Documents • Examining Student Textbooks and Accompanying Teachers' Editions • Preparing a Content Outline • Recognizing Verbs That Are Acceptable for Overt Objectives • Recognizing the Parts of Criterion-Referenced Instructional Objectives • Recognizing Objectives That Are Measurable • Assessing Objectives According to Domain	• Curriculum and Instruction: Clarification of Terms • Components of an Instructional Plan • Benefit of Student Textbooks to Student Learning • Problems with Reliance on a Single Textbook • Guidelines for Textbook Use • More on Classroom Activities and Children's Literature Related to a Multitext Guide and America's Revolutionary Times • A Community's Conflict Resolution Using the Book, *Mahatma Ghandi's Way* • More on Planning for Learning Outcomes • More on Planning with Objectives: Overt and Covert Performance Outcomes • Balance of Behaviorism and Constructivism • Teaching Toward Multiple Objectives, Understandings, and Appreciations • Four Key Components: ABCDs • Classifying Instructional Objectives • Cognitive Domain Hierarchy • Affective Domain Hierarchy • Psychomotor Domain Hierarchy • Learning That Is Observable and Not Observable • Definition of Integrated Curriculum • Spectrum of Integrated Curriculum • Integrated Thematic Unit • Further Readings About Planning and Selecting Content
Chapter 6	• Evaluating Written Teacher Comments • Teacher–Parent Conferences	• Guidelines for Assessing What a Student Says and Does • Guidelines for Assessing What a Student Writes • Assessment for Affective and Psychomotor Domain Learning • Guidelines for Using Portfolios for Assessment • Frequency of Testing • Test Construction • Administering Tests • Teacher Review of Publisher-Created Tests Before Administering to Children and Screening Tests • Controlling Cheating • Determining the Time Needed to Take a Test • More on Preparing Assessment Items • Classification of Assessment Items • General Guidelines for Preparing Assessments

	Additional Application *Exercises* **Module**	*Additional Content* **Module**
		• Attaining Content Validity
		• Arrangement Item, More Guidelines for Using Multiple-Choice Items, Completion Drawing
		• Meaning of Key Directive Verbs for Essay Responses
		• Completion Statement
		• Correction
		• Grouping
		• Identification
		• Matching
		• Short Explanation
		• True–False Statements
		• Criterion-Referenced vs. Norm-Referenced Grading
		• Determining Grades
		• Reporting Student Achievement
		• The Grade Report
		• Teacher–Parent/Guardian Communications
		• Contacting Parents/Guardians
		• Progress Reporting to Parents/Guardians
		• Further Readings about Assessing and Reporting Student Achievement
Chapter 7	• Obtaining Personal Insight Regarding the Connection of Units to Unit Parts	• Questions for Lesson Self-Reflection
	• Connecting Questions and Activities for a Unit	• A Continual Process
	• Planning Curriculum Activities	• Well-Planned, But Open to Last-Minute Change
	• Self- and Peer-Assessment of My Lesson Plan	• Implementation of Today's Lesson May Necessitate Changes in Tomorrow's Plan
	• Analysis of a Lesson That Failed	• The Problem of Time
	• Generating Ideas for Interdisciplinary Units	• About the Daily Planning Book
	• Integrating the Topics	• Timetable
	• Initiating an ITU with a Question Map	• Assignments
	• Connecting Questions and Activities for an ITU	• Benefits of Coached Practice
		• Special Notes and Reminders
		• Materials and Equipment to Be Used
		• The Common Thread
		• Interdisciplinary Thematic Unit (ITU)
		• More Readings About Preparing Activities, Lessons, and Units
Chapter 8	• Identifying the Cognitive Levels of Questions	• Experience Related to Personal Response Question
	• Wait Time and the Art of Questioning	• Artwork Response Question
	• Examining Materials for Levels of Questioning	• More About Implementing Questioning
	• Observing the Cognitive Levels of Classroom Verbal Interaction	• Further Readings About Teacher Talk and Questioning
	• Practice in Creating Cognitive Questions	
	• A Cooperative Learning and Peer Teaching Exercise in the Use of Questioning	
Chapter 9	• A Study of Inquiry and Strategy Integration	• Printed Materials, Visual Displays, and the Internet
	• More Internet Sites of Use to Elementary Schoolteachers	• The Internet History
		• More Professional Journals and Periodicals

Additional Application *Exercises* **Module**	Additional Content **Module**
	• Copying Printed Materials
	• The Classroom Writing Board
	• The Classroom Bulletin Board
	• The Felt/Flannel Board
	• Media Tools
	• When Equipment Malfunctions
	• Multimedia Program
	• Television, Videos, and CD-ROMS; Digital Cameras
	• Placement and Use of Computers: The Online Classroom
	• Selecting Computer Software
	• Sources of Free and Inexpensive Audiovisual Materials
	• Using Copyrighted and Multimedia Programs
	• Further Readings About Demonstrations, Thinking, Inquiry Learning, and Games
Chapter 10	• Whole-Class Discussion as a Teaching Strategy: What Do I Already Know? • Teacher Interaction with Students According to Student Gender or Other Personal Characteristics	• What the Internet Looks Like • Selecting CD-ROM Materials • Teachers May Advertise Values in Homework • Guidelines for Constructing a Learning Center • Guidelines for Using Assignments (Work and Homework): A Checklist • For Further Readings on Grouping and Assignments to Promote Positive Interaction and Quality Learning
Chapter 11	• A Professional Résumé	• More Suggestions for E-teaching • Student Teaching from the Mentor Teacher's Point of View • What to Do Before an Observation • What to Do During an Observation • What to Do After an Observation • A Checklist for a Letter of Recommendation • Resources for Locating Teaching or Substitute Teaching Jobs • Further Readings About Assessing Teaching Effectiveness and Continuing Professional Development

ACKNOWLEDGMENTS

We would never have been able to complete this edition had it not been for the valued help of numerous people: former and current students and teachers in our classes who have shared their experiences with us, administrators and colleagues who have debated with us about important issues in education, and authors and publishers who have graciously granted permission to reprint materials. To each, we offer our warmest thanks.

Although we take full responsibility for any errors or omissions in this resource guide, we are deeply appreciative to others for their recent cogent reviews and educational insight in the development of this edition. We also express our special appreciation to the following individuals for their contributions to this text: Michael Lewis, Dean, College of Education, California State University–Sacramento; Janet Bicknese, Director, Sykview School, Prescott, Arizona; Thomas A. Ford, Principal, Sierra Oaks Elementary School, Sacramento, California; Lisa A. Packard, teacher, Prescott, Arizona, for her valuable feedback and activities related to characteristics of a competent teacher, alliterative name game, long-term planning, and others.

We continue to respond to the reviewers and users of this resource guide and have made changes as a result of their feedback. Those who have provided reviews for this edition, for which we are deeply grateful, are as follows: Douglas M. Brooks, Miami University, Ohio; Karen Harris, Fayetteville Technical Community University; Gae R. Johnson, Northern Arizona University; and Colleen Hardy, Evangel University.

Further, we want to express our deepest admiration and appreciation to the highly competent professionals at Merrill/Prentice Hall with whom we have had a professional relationship for many years. We especially thank Mary Morrill, Senior Editorial Assistant, for her valuable assistance, technical expertise, and ongoing cheerfulness, and Executive Editor Debbie Stollenwerk, who maintained her confidence in our ability and kept her positive attitude—all of which helped make writing this sixth edition enjoyable.

Although it is very difficult to predict what the children of today will really need to know to be productive citizens in the middle of this century, we do believe they will always need to know how to learn, how to read, how to communicate effectively, and how to think productively. We believe that young people need skills in how to gain knowledge and how to process information, and they need learning experiences that foster effective communication and productive, cooperative behaviors. We hope all children will feel good about themselves, about others, and about their teachers, schools, and communities. This resource guide continues to emphasize the importance of helping students to develop these skills, feelings, and attitudes.

The appropriate teaching methods for reaching these goals are those that incorporate thoughtful planning, acceptance of the uniqueness of each individual, honesty, trust, sharing, risking, collaboration, communication, and cooperation. Also, we believe children best learn these skills and values from teachers who model the same. This resource guide continues to be faithful to that hope and to that end.

We are indeed indebted and grateful to all the people in our lives, now and in the past, who have interacted with us and reinforced what we have known since we began our careers as teachers: Teaching is the most rewarding profession of all.

P. L. R.
R. D. K.
K. M.

About the Authors

Patricia L. Roberts joined the faculty of the School of Education at California State University, Sacramento, where she taught courses in children's literature, reading, and language arts, and served as coordinator of a Teacher Education Center in Elementary Education and Associate Chair and Chair of the Department of Teacher Education. In addition, Dr. Roberts is the author and coauthor of more than 20 teacher resource books and texts, including a *Guide to Developing Interdisciplinary Thematic Units,* 3rd Edition (with R. D. Kellough). She writes for journals and is a member of the National Council of Research on the Teaching of English and other professional groups. Her current research centers on teaching curriculum content with children's literature and family values found in fiction for children. Dr. Roberts, an invited biographee in *Who's Who in America* and *Who's Who in the World,* is the recipient of the Distinguished Alumnus of the Year Award from the University of the Pacific and the California State University's Award for Merit for Teaching. The Award of Merit is given for a superior teaching record and outstanding service to the institution and to the community. Additional recognitions include listings in *International Who's Who of Intellectuals, Who's Who in American Education, Two Thousand Notable American Women, The World Who's Who of Women, The Director of Distinguished Americans, International Directory of Distinguished Leadership,* and *The International Who's Who of Contemporary Achievement.*

Richard D. Kellough is author and coauthor of more than 40 textbooks, including *A Resource Guide for Teaching K–12, Teaching Young Adolescents: A Guide to Methods and Resources, Secondary School Teaching: A Guide to Methods and Resources,* and *Your First Year of Teaching,* as well as numerous jour-

nal articles. A member of several prominent organizations, Dr. Kellough has been elected to the Phi Sigma Society, the Botanical Society of America, the American Bryological Society, and was the recipient of the Outstanding Biology Teacher Recognition Award from the National Biology Teachers Association, State of California. His many recognitions include being named a National Science Foundation Research Fellow at the University of California, Davis, as well as listings in *The International Authors* and *Writers Who's Who, Leaders in Eco Education, Men of Achievement* (Volume 1), *Dictionary of International Biography,* and *Leaders in Education.*

Kay Moore is a professor at California State University, Sacramento, in the Department of Teacher Education who is currently serving as the Director of the Liberal Studies program. In the department, Professor Moore teaches courses in literacy and social studies for preservice teachers and undergraduate and graduate classes in juvenile literature. A former elementary classroom teacher for 10 years, she was honored as El Dorado County (California) "Teacher of the Year" for 1985. Professor Moore was president of the California Reading Association (CRA) from 1994 to 1995 and received the John Martin Award for exemplary service to that organization. She is the author of two juvenile books published by Scholastic, *If You Lived at the Time of the Civil War* (1994) and *If You Lived at the Time of the American Revolution* (1997). She is a contributor to CRA's publication, *A Taste of Literacy,* and with Linda Wells, created the story coloring book, *The Night Before Christmas, 1849.* Kay also contributed to the CRA publication *Building Literacy: Making Every Child a Reader* and for the last five years has designed activities for the California Young Reader Medal activities book for the middle/junior high/high school books.

Brief Contents

Contents

*To assist the precredentialed teacher in preparing for taking a Praxis II Principles of Learning and Teaching exam or other teacher test, we have placed asterisks by selected word entries in the subject index. The asterisks indicate the subject matter that we suggest be reviewed in preparation for taking a teacher test. The asterisks stand for Target Topics for Teacher Tests and provide a reference for content areas for review.

NOTE: Every effort has been made to provide accurate and current Internet information in this text. However, the Internet and information on it are constantly changing, so it is inevitable that some of the Internet addresses listed in this book will change.

EDUCATOR LEARNING CENTER: AN INVALUABLE ONLINE RESOURCE

Merrill Education and the Association for Supervision and Curriculum Development (ASCD) invite you to take advantage of a new online resource, one that provides access to the top research and proven strategies associated with ASCD and Merrill—the Educator Learning Center. At **www.educatorlearningcenter. com,** you will find resources that will enhance your students' understanding of course topics and of current educational issues, in addition to being invaluable for further research.

How the Educator Learning Center Will Help Your Students Become Better Teachers

With the combined resources of Merrill Education and ASCD, you and your students will find a wealth of tools and materials to better prepare them for the classroom.

Research

- More than 600 articles from the ASCD journal Educational Leadership discuss everyday issues faced by practicing teachers.
- A direct link on the site to Research Navigator™ gives students access to many of the leading education journals, as well as extensive content detailing the research process.
- Excerpts from Merrill Education texts give your students insights on important topics of instructional methods, diverse populations, assessment, classroom management, technology, and refining classroom practice.

Classroom Practice

- Hundreds of lesson plans and teaching strategies are categorized by content area and age range.
- Case studies and classroom video footage provide virtual field experience for student reflection.
- Computer simulations and other electronic tools keep your students abreast of today's classrooms and current technologies.
- The Educator's Learning Center is a joint website with the Association for Supervision and Curriculum Development (ASCD) and Merrill Education. The site offers a link to Research Navigator for educational journals, articles from the ASCD journal *Educational Leadership,* lesson plans and teaching strategies categorized by content area and age range, excerpts from Merrill education texts on important topics, as well as classroom videos, case studies, and computer simulations. See *www. EducatorLearningCenter.com.*

Look into the Value of Educator Learning Center Yourself

A four-month subscription to Educator Learning Center is $25 but is **FREE** when packaged with any Merrill Education text. In order for your students to have access to this site, you must use this special value-pack ISBN number **WHEN** placing your textbook order with the bookstore: 0-13-168670-4. Your students will then receive a copy of the text packaged with a free ASCD pincode. To preview the value of this website to you and your students, please go to **www.educatorlearningcenter.com** and click on "Demo."

ELEMENTARY SCHOOL TEACHING AND LEARNING

What Do I Need to Know About Today's Elementary Schools?

1

Visual Chapter Organizer and Overview

The Elementary School: Getting to Know It

- Primary and Elemiddle Schools
- Magnet Schools and Charter Schools
- Orientation Meetings for Teachers
- School Schedules
- Subjects of the Curriculum
- Team Teaching
- Looping

The Fundamental Characteristic of Exemplary Elementary School Education

- Teachers and Commitment
- Teachers and Reflective Decision Making
- The Effective Principal
- Commitment to Helping All Children Succeed in School

Ways to Connect with Home, Community, and School

- Home and School Connections
- Service Learning and Place-Based Education
- Telecommunications Networks
- Professional Resources File

The Emergent Overall Picture

- Key Trends and Practices Today
- No Child Left Behind Act
- Curriculum Standards and High-Stakes Testing
- Problems and Issues That Trouble the Nation's Schools

🔍 Looking at Teachers

Rachael is a fifth-grade teacher in a low socioeconomic school within a moderately large city on the East Coast of the United States. The 34 students in her class include 10 English language learners and 10 with identified learning problems. Some of the children have skills equivalent to those of first graders. In any given week, Rachael recycles newspapers and sells snacks to help pay for field trips because the school and the children cannot. On a typical school day recently, Rachael began her work at 7:10 A.M. with three parent conferences. The children arrived and school began at 8:15 and ran until 2:45 P.M. Rachel then tutored children until 3:30, conducted four more parent conferences, straightened her classroom and readied a few things for the next day, went home at 6:30 P.M., had dinner, and then planned lessons and read and marked papers for 2 hours before retiring for the night.

For your reaction and discussion with your group, this is the first elementary teacher's schedule to consider in this chapter.

First day of school jitters ever in your thoughts? Or just interested in what the first day of school might be like for students and teachers alike? If so, read about Sarah Jane Hartwell saying "I hate my new school" in *First Day Jitters* (Watertown, MA: Charlesbridge Publishing, 2000) written by Julie Danneberg and illustrated by Judy Love. It is the first day of school and Sarah does not want to go. She says that she doesn't know anybody and that school will be hard and she hides in her bed under her bluish-purple bedcovers. The family's white cat and brown terrier are by her bedside and look concerned when she says she feels sick. Mr. Hartwell cajoles Sarah into eating breakfast, gives her a lunchbox, and drives her to her new school where Mrs. Burton, the school principal, meets Sarah at the car and walks with her to her classroom. There, Mrs. Burton introduces her to the students in the class as their . . . new teacher, Mrs. Sarah Jane Hartwell. At the end of this story, a reader or a listener is surprised to learn that the one who is concerned and has the jitters is the teacher! If this story appeals to you, why not take time to browse the children's book section in the local library or bookstore for this book or similar ones to read to your class on the first day of school?

Putting first-day apprehensions aside for the moment—at which we are sure you'll be successful because you are intent on developing your competencies—we want to welcome you to the exciting world of elementary school teaching. Whether you are starting your first career or beginning a new and different career, this resource guide is for you—it is written for anyone interested in elementary school teaching and in starting the journey toward becoming a professional teacher of children in kindergarten through grade six.

If you are currently in a teacher preparation program, then it is possible that near the completion of the program you will be offered your first teaching contract. When that happens, you will be excited—eager to sign the contract and to begin your new career. But after the initial excitement, you will have time to reflect. Many questions will then begin to surface: "What grade(s) will I have?" "What preparations will I need to make?" "Will I be a member of a teaching team?"

Other questions may come to your mind: How can I prepare for students I have never met? What school and district policies do I need to learn? What support services will I have? What standardized tests are given, when will they be given, and how shall I prepare students for them? What reading, mathematics, social studies, and science programs will I be using? Where and how do I obtain classroom supplies? What are my extracurricular responsibilities? Is there a school dress code for the students? How shall I contact parents? How often will I be evaluated and by whom? Will there be an orientation for new teachers? And—how do I get answers to my questions?

To guide you through this initial experience, and to help answer some of the questions you might have now and in the future, the information presented in this book about schools, students, teachers, administrators, and parents and guardians offers a basic glimpse into today's world of elementary school teaching. This active world is so complex that few authors can say everything that needs to be said to every teacher. But we must begin somewhere and this chapter, with the visual chapter organizer that serves as a preview before reading the text, is our beginning.

CHAPTER OBJECTIVES

Specifically, on completion of this first chapter, you should be able to:

1. Describe two or more essential characteristics of exemplary elementary school education.
2. Describe two or more current trends, problems, and issues in American public elementary school education.

3. Describe the significance of home, school, and community connections to a child's education and of efforts being made by elementary school educators to enhance the connections among the home, school, and local and global communities.

4. Reflect on your own elementary school experiences and reflect on which experiences would help you make certain decisions as a teacher in your classroom.

5. Identify one or more reasons other teacher candidates have selected teaching as a career goal and identify one or more personal/professional characteristics that make an effective teacher.

THE ELEMENTARY SCHOOL: GETTING TO KNOW IT

The elementary school usually enrolls children between the ages of 5 and 11; converting these ages to what traditionally have been known as "grades," we get grades kindergarten through 6 (K–6).

Primary and Elemiddle Schools

In some places, the elementary school is a primary school, with grades K–3 or K–4, followed by a middle school, and then a high school with grades 9–12. In other places, the elementary school grade ranges are K–8. Because it houses children of both elementary and middle school age, a K–8 school is sometimes referred to as an *elemiddle school*. The K–8 elementary schools ordinarily are followed by a 4-year high school. The K–6 elementary schools are usually followed by a 3–year junior high school or a middle school followed by a 3-year senior high school. However, a K–6 elementary school with a 2-year middle school and a 4-year high school is not uncommon.

Magnet Schools and Charter Schools

Whatever elementary grade you are being hired to teach, you will want to know more information: What will the students be like? What will their parents or guardians be like? If it is a multiple school district, to which school will I be assigned? Will it be a traditional school or a magnet school, that is, a school that focuses on a particular academic or philosophical area? For example, Capitol Hill Magnet School (St. Paul, Minnesota) provides a program for gifted and talented children in grades 1–8; at High Peaks Core Knowledge Elementary School (Boulder, Colorado), the Core Knowledge Curriculum is the center of fo-

cus,[1] and at Irwin Avenue Elementary School (Charlotte, North Carolina), the focus is on the philosophy of open education.[2]

Here are some of the other possibilities. The school you are assigned to could be a **charter school,** an autonomous educational entity operating under a charter or contract, that has been negotiated between the organizers, who create and operate the school, and a sponsor, who oversees the provisions of the charter.[3] As an example of a recent charter school, a state teachers' union and the district's teachers' association have created the Humane Education Charter School (Sacramento, California) that aims to reduce violence through the teaching of respect, compassion, responsibility, and community service for children in grades K–6. Further, the school you are assigned to could be a **full-service community school,** a school that serves as a center for education and also provides various health, social, and cultural services under one roof.[4]

Orientation Meetings for Teachers

As a beginning teacher, you will be expected to participate in an orientation meeting for teachers. Some school districts start the academic year with a district-wide orientation, and others schedule on-site orientations at each school. Many school districts do both, with perhaps a district-wide meeting in the morning followed by on-site meetings in the afternoon. Of course, the scheduling and planning of orientation meetings will vary district by district and school by school. The objectives for all orientation meetings, however, should be similar. As a new teacher, you will be encouraged by district personnel to meet several responsibilities that are found on the orientation checklist in our Companion Website's **(www.prenhall.com/roberts)** *Additional Content* module for this chapter. 🖉 For example, you will be asked to become familiar with the district's or school's written statement of its unique beliefs and goals—its **statement of mission** (or philosophy or vision)—and what that statement means to the people affiliated with the school or district. Sample statements are shown in Figure 1.1.

School Schedules

School schedules vary from state to state, from district to district, and from school to school. Many school years begin in late August or early September and continue through late May or mid-June. Other schools operate on a year-round schedule with the school year beginning in August and ending in June or July.[5] In a school with year-round education (YRE), a

Figure 1.1
Sample elementary school mission statements
(*Source:* Reprinted by permission.)

- The mission of Julian Harris Elementary School (Decatur, Alabama; grades K–5; available online at www.ptc. dcs.edu/schools/elem/jh/jh.html, January 15, 2005) is to prepare each child for the future by encouraging them to be excited about learning. The staff will challenge all students to reach their maximum potential.

- The mission of Sierra Oaks Elementary School (a California Distinguished School; Sacramento, California; grades K–5; available online at www.sanjuan.edu/services/r&e/sarc-current/sierra.pdf, January 15, 2005), which has students who have a variety of ethnic, religious, and linguistic backgrounds, is as follows: The teachers, administrators and parents of Sierra Oaks Elementary School are dedicated to providing all students with an environment that will create a desire to continue the learning process throughout their entire lives. We want the students to develop a sense of responsibility and respect for themselves and others in the community. It is our goal that they will be able to function independently while at the same time developing a moral and ethical behavior that will allow them to be tolerant of others and work cooperatively with those around them. Students at Sierra Oaks will demonstrate a high degree of competence in communication and literacy skills which includes reading, writing, speaking, and listening. In addition, the students will be encouraged to be critical and creative in their thinking process and to demonstrate a high degree of competence in all that they do.

- The mission of Skyview School (Prescott, Arizona; grades K–8; available online at www.skyviewschool.org, January 15, 2005), a charter school, is to enrich the lives of students and to ensure that future generations are well prepared to live their lives with meaning, dignity, and the ability to work together for a better world. Respect and responsibility toward self, others, and the natural environment are the guiding principles. The staff believes that children possess a blend of multiple intelligences and, drawing on the best practices in education, celebrates each child's uniqueness and tailors education to develop the fullest potential of each learner. Encouraging a sense of competence and self-motivation, classroom life is interwoven with community life through practical experiences.[6]

- Whittier School (Chicago, Illinois; grades K–6; available online at www.whittier.cps.k12.il.us, January 15, 2005) is a community of learners who desire healthy bodies, emotional strength, confidence, ambition, and integrity. We hope always to respect and appreciate the work of others, experience the rich heritage of diverse cultures as well as our own, and be participating citizens in a democracy.

- The staff of Woodland Hills Elementary School (Lawton, Oklahoma; grades K–6; available online at www.lawtonps.org/woodlandhills/whs%20other/handbook0405/a.htm#phil, January 15, 2005) holds high expectations for student success and is dedicated to providing an education setting in which all students can learn and develop to their full intellectual, social, physical, and emotional potential. The staff seeks to instill in students an appreciation of their American heritage, a positive attitude, and the responsibility for lifelong learning skills through cooperation and support of parents and the community.

teacher might teach for 3 consecutive months followed by a month off, then for another 3 months on and then a month off, and so on, throughout the year, or might teach in a 45/15 program, which refers to a yearlong schedule of 9 weeks (45 days) of school followed by 3 weeks (15 days) off. Another example of an alternative schedule is the modified year-round schedule, which involves teaching for 9 weeks, then being off for 2 weeks.

In most places in the United States the school year is still approximately 180 days out of a 365-day calendar year. Some schools, however, such as the Brooks Global Studies Extended-Year Magnet Elementary School in Greensboro, North Carolina, have extended their school year to a longer time such as 210 days and are called **extended-year schools.**

Not to be confused with the extended-year school is the **extended-day school.** Fremont Magnet Elementary School (Bakersfield, California), for example, provides for its 1,000 students a regular (mandatory) school program from 8:00 A.M. until 2:10 P.M. each day, Monday through Friday, followed by an optional magnet program until 5:00 P.M.

Some schools are in session less than 5 days per week, such as 4 days.[7] Most schools that are on a 4-day week are small rural schools, often including grades K–12, where the children spend several hours each day riding the school bus. Schools on a 4-day week usually go longer each day, such as from 8 A.M. until 4 P.M., with Monday or Friday off. Still other schools have a 4-day week with only teachers attending on Fridays for preparation time.

After being assigned to a school and becoming familiar with the campus, you should turn your attention to all of the available school schedules for playground duty, lunch, bus duty, the library, special programs, and special days. The school day usually begins at about 8:00 A.M. and lasts until about 3:00 P.M. In schools that are crowded, beginning and ending times may be staggered, and some students and teachers may start as early as 7:30 A.M. and leave at 2:30 P.M. Others may begin at 9:00 A.M. and continue until 4:00 P.M. District and state laws vary, but they generally require that teachers be in the classroom no less than 15 minutes prior to the start of the school and remain in the classroom no less than 15 minutes after the dismissal of the children.

Subjects of the Curriculum

The time spent daily on each subject taught will vary with grade level and may be dictated by adopted program, state law, or district policy, but for each grade, the curriculum plans should include lessons for multiple subjects: English/reading/language arts (also known as **literacy**), mathematics, science, social science/history/geography—the four subject areas of the **core curriculum**—and art, music, physical education, health, and, sometimes, foreign language. In some schools and in some grades, not all of these subjects are taught every day, nor are they necessarily all taught in one classroom by just one teacher.

Although studies demonstrate that the early study of a second language provides cognitive benefits, gains in academic achievement, and positive attitudes toward diversity, the study of a second or foreign language, unfortunately, is not a part of the curriculum for very many elementary schools.[8] In some elementary schools, however, such as Sunset Elementary School (Miami, Florida), foreign language study is a significant component of the core curriculum.[9]

The choice of language offered by elementary schools varies, of course, depending to some extent on the community, the availability of teachers, and the extent to which the program can be sustained for several years.[10] Generally, elementary school foreign language programs fall within a spectrum of types. At one end are **total immersion programs,** in which all of the classroom instruction is in the target foreign language. At the other end of the spectrum are foreign language experience (FLEX) programs, where classes may meet only a few times a week, and the goal is to introduce children to one or more foreign languages and cultures rather than to develop proficiency in the use of a target foreign language.

Somewhere in the middle on the spectrum are what are known as foreign language in the elementary school (FLES) programs, which focus mostly on cultural awareness and developing listening and speaking skills in a target foreign language. FLES programs follow the natural sequence of language learning: understanding, speaking, reading, and writing. For young children, a typical FLES lesson would include physical activities such as songs, rhymes, games, and playacting with puppets.[11]

In addition to the specialized skills of the subjects mentioned previously, students learn other, more general skills as components of the elementary school curriculum. These include critical thinking skills, socialization skills, and organizational and study skills.

Team Teaching

Traditionally, elementary schoolteachers have taught their groups of children in their self-contained classrooms for most of the school day while fairly isolated from other teachers and school activities—not unlike the parallel play of preschool children, that is, playing side by side but not together. In some schools, that is still the case. Increasingly, however, elementary school teachers are finding themselves members of a collaborative **teaching team** in which several teachers work together to reflect, plan, and implement a curriculum for a common cohort of students. This type of team teaching may comprise only a few teachers, for example, all second-grade teachers of a particular elementary school, or the teachers who teach the same cohort of sixth-grade children in English/reading/language arts and in social studies/history/geography at the same or another school. They may meet periodically to plan a curriculum and learning activities around a common theme.

Sometimes, teaching teams comprise one teacher each from the four areas of the core curriculum. In addition to teachers of the core subjects, specialty-area teachers may be part of the team, including teachers of foreign language, physical education, the arts, and even special education teachers, school counselors, and specialty personnel who work with at-risk students. Because the core and specialty subjects cross disciplines of study, these teams are commonly called interdisciplinary teaching teams, or simply **interdisciplinary teams.**

Looping

In some schools, a teacher or a team of teachers remains with the same cohort of elementary children for

Figure 1.2a
A kindergarten class schedule*
(*Source:* Courtesy of Lynne Baker and Connie Thomas,
kindergarten teachers, Sierra Oaks School, San Juan Unified
School District, Carmichael, California)

This is the A.M. schedule shared by the two
teachers; the schedule is repeated in the afternoon
when a second group of children arrive at 12:05
and are dismissed at 3:25.

9:10–9:25	Opening
	Attendance
	Weather
	Calendar
	Message
9:25–10:25	Language Arts
10:25–10:40	Snack/Recess
10:40–10:50	Music and Movement
10:50–11:50	Math
11:50–12:15	Free Choice Learning Centers
12:15–12:30	Review, Story, Dismissal

Note: This schedule creates a unique learning environment
involving the strengths of three teachers. Each teacher has a
homeroom class for spelling and reading. For science and social studies, math, and language arts, the students are divided into three groups, each of which includes one third of
the children from each teacher's assigned class. These groups
are changed each quarter, thus providing children with the
opportunity to work cooperatively with many different peers
throughout the school year. This helps them to develop the
life skills needed to work with and to adjust to new situations. The groups are created randomly, maintaining a balance of females and males. The three teachers maintain
control of the scheduling of students who attend special
classes for learning disabilities, speech, counseling, and tutoring. By changing the schedule every quarter, the teachers
also have control of placing students with behavior problems
and children with personality conflicts, thus creating a more
effective learning environment for all.

Figure 1.2b
A first-grade class schedule
(*Source:* Courtesy of Teri Schuddeboom, first-grade teacher,
Hemlock Elementary School, Vacaville Unified School
District, Vacaville, California)

8:25–8:55	Community circle
	Attendance
	Flag salute
	Patriotic song
	Community song
	Calendar process
	Weather graph
	Lost tooth chart
	Appreciations
	Share a sentence
8:55–9:15	Spelling activities
9:15–10:05	Reading activities
10:05–10:20	Recess and snack time
10:20–10:50	Reading continued
10:50–11:15	English/handwriting
11:15–12:00	Lunch/recess
12:00–12:10	Semisilent sustained reading
12:10–12:20	Read aloud to class
12:20–12:35	Community circle (math oriented)
	Number line
	Make the date in cents
	Add one straw each day to straw
	box and group into tens
	Clock work
12:35–1:05	Math (or library one day a week)
1:05–1:35	Social studies, science, or health
1:35–2:15	Art, music, physical education, or
	journal writing
2:15–2:25	Room cleanup
2:25	Dismissal

two or more years, a practice known as **looping**
(also referred to as *multiyear grouping, multiyear instruction, multiyear placement, persistent teams,* and
teacher–student progression). Although the practice
of looping is not new, in recent years there has been
renewed interest in it because of the positive findings
related to young children from recent research studies. Positive findings indicate that the benefits of looping include improved student–teacher relationships,
more efficient instruction, better learning, improved
attendance, fewer referrals to special education programs, and improved student behavior.[12] Perhaps the
positive findings can be summarized as being the result of an effective teacher (or teaching team) getting
to know a group of children well and being able to

remain with that group longer than one school year,
rather than starting all over again in a year with an entirely different group of children.

Inside your own busy classroom, you will be
learning the names of your students, making decisions, following your detailed instructional plans, and
keeping one eye on the clock for a day or two—a behavior that helps you observe the schedule for recess,
lunch, coordination with other teachers, and dismissal at the end of the school day. You will find that
the changes in scheduling may vary from year to year
at a particular school. Figures 1.2a, 1.2b, 1.2c, and
1.2d present sample teacher schedules that reflect
some of the variety you will find for different grades
at different schools.

Figure 1.2c
A third-grade class schedule
(*Source:* Courtesy of Gloria Morrill, third-grade teacher, Sierra Oaks Elementary School, San Juan Unified School District, Carmichael, California)

9:10–10:35	Classroom Business
	Math Block
10:35–10:45	Recess
10:45–12:10	Language Arts Block (Reading, Writing, Grammar, Speaking, Listening, Spelling)
	Physical Education (Friday 11:30–12:10)
	Computer/Library (Wed. 11:00–12:05)
12:10–12:50	Lunch
12:50–1:45	Language Arts continued (Independent reading, Teacher read-aloud, Cursive)
	Math Carousel (Friday)
1:45–2:00	Recess
2:00–3:25	Integrating Social Studies
	Science
	Art
	Physical Education (Thursday, 2:00–2:40)

Figure 1.2d
A fifth-grade schedule for a "house" of three teachers*
(*Source:* Courtesy of Stephanie Rice, Deana Romero, and Teri Catron, fifth-grade teachers, Hugh Bish Elementary School, Lawton, Oklahoma)

8:45–9:00	Whole school assembly (flag salute, birthdays, announcements, songs, and sharing)
9:00–9:20	Spelling in homeroom class
9:20–10:00	Music, art, and physical education (alternating every third day)
10:00–10:10	Bathroom break, class change
10:10–11:10	Group 1—Language arts; Group 2— Math; Group 3— Science and social studies
11:10–11:15	Class change
11:15–12:15	Group 1—Math; Group 2—Science and social studies; Group 3— Language arts
12:15–12:20	Change back to homeroom class
12:20–12:45	Oral and silent reading in homeroom class
12:45–1:10	Lunch
1:10–1:30	Recess
1:30–1:35	Class change
1:35–2:35	Group 1—Science and social studies; Group 2—Language arts; Group 3—Math
2:35–3:20	Reading in homeroom class
3:20–3:25	Cleanup and dismissal

*Refer to note on page 7.

THE FUNDAMENTAL CHARACTERISTIC OF EXEMPLARY ELEMENTARY SCHOOL EDUCATION

Wherever and however the students are housed, whatever the schedules, and regardless of other practices, in the end, it is the dedication and commitment to students and the involved adults' understanding of students that is the incisive element. Thus, it is everyone at school—the teachers, administrators, office staff, bus drivers, cooks, grounds crew, security staff, custodial staff, and support personnel—who reflect the fundamental characteristic of exemplary elementary school education. This characteristic, as we see it, is to celebrate and build on the diverse characteristics and needs of students. That, in fact, is the essence of Chapter 2.

Teachers and Commitment

Elementary schoolteachers represent myriad individual personalities that are perhaps impossible to capture in generalizations. Let us imagine that a teaching colleague mentions that Charles Burger, in Room 17, is a "fantastic teacher," "one of the best teachers in the district," "super," and "magnificent." What might be some of the characteristics you would expect to see in Charles' teaching behaviors? (Teacher responsibilities and behaviors are the topic of Chapter 3.)

You can expect Charles to (a) be understanding of the school's stated mission and committed to it; (b) know the curriculum and how best to teach it; (c) be enthusiastic, motivated, and well organized; (d) show effective communication and interpresonal skills; (e) be willing to listen to the students and to risk trying their ideas, and (f) be warm, caring, accepting, and nurturing toward all students.

Elementary school students need teachers who are well organized and who know how to establish and manage an active and supportive learning environment (the topic of Chapter 4), even with its multiple instructional demands. Students respond best to teachers who provide leadership and who enjoy their function as role models, advisers, mentors, and reflective decision makers.

Teachers and Reflective Decision Making

During any school day, whether you are a teacher of kindergarten children or a teacher of sixth graders, you will make hundreds of nontrivial decisions.

Some of the decisions are made instantaneously. Other decisions are made in preparation for the teaching day. During one school year, a teacher literally makes thousands of decisions—some of which can and will affect the lives of that teacher's students for years to come. This is, indeed, an awesome responsibility.

Initially, of course, you will make errors in judgment, but you will also learn that children can be amazingly resilient and that there are experts available who can guide you to help ensure that the children are not damaged by your mistakes. You can learn from your errors. Keep in mind that the sheer number of decisions you make each day will mean that not all will be the best decisions that could have been made had you had more time and better resources for planning.

Good Teaching Is as Much an Art as It Is a Science

Although pedagogy is based on scientific principles, good classroom teaching is as much an art as it is a science. Few rules apply to every teaching situation. In fact, decisions about the selection of content, instructional objectives and materials, teaching strategies, a teacher's response to student misbehavior, and the selection of techniques for assessment of the learning experiences are all the result of subjective judgments. While many decisions are made at a somewhat unhurried pace when you are planning for your instruction, many others will be made intuitively and quickly. Once the school day has begun, there is rarely time for making carefully thought-out judgments. At your best, you base your decisions on your teaching style, which, in turn, is based on your knowledge of school policies, pedagogical research, the curriculum, and the unique characteristics of the students in your charge. You will also base your decisions on common sense and reflective judgment. The better your understanding and experience with the students, the curriculum, and the school's environment and policies, and the more time you give for thoughtful reflection, the more likely it will be that your decisions will result in the students meeting the learning targets and educational goals. (Learning targets and educational goals are discussed in Chapter 5.)

You will reflect on, conceptualize, and apply understandings from one teaching experience to the next. As your understanding about your classroom experiences accumulates, your teaching will become more routine, predictable, and refined. The topic of reflective decision making is presented more fully in Chapter 3; for now, to extend your awareness of the reality of elementary school teaching with others in a cooperative and collaborative way, do Application Exercise 1.1 and Application Exercise 1.2.

The Effective Principal

The principal can make a difference. As a new or visiting member of the faculty, one of your tasks is to become familiar with the administrative organization of your school and district. One person significantly responsible for the success of any school is the principal. From your point of view, what are the characteristics of an effective elementary school principal? Perhaps foremost are the principal's vision of what a quality school is and the drive to bring that vision to life—school improvement is the effective principal's constant theme.

Through personal skills in instructional leadership, the principal establishes a climate in which teachers and students share the responsibility for determining the appropriate use of time and facilities. Because exemplary elementary school educators believe in the innate potential of every child, instead of dumbing down standards and expectations, they modify the key variables of time, grouping, and instructional strategies to help each child achieve quality learning (as you'll see in Chapter 8), a task nearly impossible to do without a supportive, knowledgeable, positive, and forward-thinking school principal.[13]

In addition to the school principal, there sometimes is an assistant or vice principal, especially for larger schools. This person has specific responsibilities and oversight functions, such as student activities, school discipline and security, transition programs, and curriculum and instruction. Sometimes teachers who are mentors, grade-level leaders or department chairs, or designated team leaders may also serve administrative functions. But the principal is (or should be) the person with the final responsibility for everything that happens at the school. Whereas principals used to debate whether they were leaders or managers, today there is no debate—to be most effective, the principal must be both.[14]

Commitment to Helping All Children Succeed in School

In any school there are students who have a high probability of dropping out. *At risk* is the term used by educators when referring to those students. Researchers have identified five categories of indicators that cause a child to be at risk: (a) academic failure—exemplified by low marks and grades, absences from school, low self-esteem; (b) family instability—identified by moving, separation, divorce;

(c) family socioeconomic situation—exemplified by low income, negativism, lack of education; (d) family tragedy—identified by parent/guardian illness or death, health problems; and (e) personal pain—exemplified by drugs, physical and psychological abuse, or suspension from school.[15] Many children, at any one time, have risk factors from more than one of these categories. Although some schools have a higher percentage of children at risk than do others, it has been estimated that by year 2020 the majority of students in the public schools in the United States will be at risk.[16]

APPLICATION EXERCISE 1.1 REFLECTING ON MY OWN ELEMENTARY SCHOOL EXPERIENCES*

Instructions: The purpose of this application exercise is to help you recall and reflect on your own elementary school experiences and explore which experiences might help you make certain decisions as a teacher in your classroom. When you have completed the application, share your reflections and ideas about decision making with others in your group.

Name(s), location(s), and approximate dates of elementary school(s) attended: _____

_____

_____

_____

Public or private? _____

1. What do you remember most from your elementary school years? _____

_____

_____

_____

_____

2. What do you recall about your teachers? _____

_____

_____

_____

_____

3. Which teacher do you remember most clearly? Why? _____

_____

_____

_____

4. To what extent did you feel your school had a safe, supportive learning environment? _____

_____

_____

_____

5. What one grade or class do you recall with special fondness? Explain why. _____

_____

_____

_____

6. Is there any one grade or class that you particularly would like to forget? If so, explain why.

_____

_____

_____

_____

APPLICATION EXERCISE 1.1 *(continued)*

7. What do you recall about peer, teacher, or parental pressures during your elementary school years? _____

_____

_____

_____

8. What do you recall about your own strengths and weaknesses? Which teacher touched on your own strengths and how? _____

_____

_____

_____

9. What do you recall, if anything, about being in the earliest grades (K–3)? Is there any other aspect of your life during elementary school that you wish to share? _____

_____

_____

_____

10. Which reflections about one of these experiences would influence you in making a certain decision as a teacher in your classroom? _____

_____

_____

_____

*On this application exercise and the other application exercises that follow in this text, we suggest that you rehearse/practice/use the manuscript or cursive handwriting that you expect to model for elementary students in your classroom. In our current technology-centered era, elementary students will need, in addition to their skills on a keyboard, skills in handwriting to communicate with others. The students will benefit from seeing your legible and efficient handwriting as a model that allows them to communicate with others and to quickly take notes about something important to them.

APPLICATION EXERCISE 1.2 DIALOGUE WITH A TEACHER CANDIDATE: "SOLE" MATES

Instructions: The purpose of this activity, one that we call *Sole Mates*, is to identify reasons other teacher candidates have selected teaching as a career goal and to identify one or more personal/professional characteristics that make an effective teacher. Select one teacher candidate, and on the back of the page of questions (see the outline of two feet), record that person's responses to the following questions on one of the outlines, while that person records your responses to the same questions on the other outline. Use some of the information to introduce your Sole Mate to the group. Share other responses with your group. (*Note to instructor:* This application could be used during the first week of your school term as an icebreaker.)

Date of interview _____   Name of interviewee _____

Questions to ask:

1. Why and when did you select elementary school teaching as a career?

2. What do you plan to do during the summer when you are free from teaching in a 9-month school?

3. Why would you like to teach/not teach in a year-round school?

4. What other teachers are there in your family?

5. What is your favorite grade level? Favorite subject?

6. To what extent do you plan to help your school have a safe, supportive learning environment?

7. What are your future plans? A lifetime career as a classroom teacher? Moving into a specialty or an administrative position?

8. How would you describe your current feelings about being an elementary teacher? What specifically are you most looking forward to during this program of teacher preparation?

9. What personal and professional characteristics do you feel you have that would make you an effective teacher?

10. What else would you like to say about yourself and your feelings concerning the program so far?

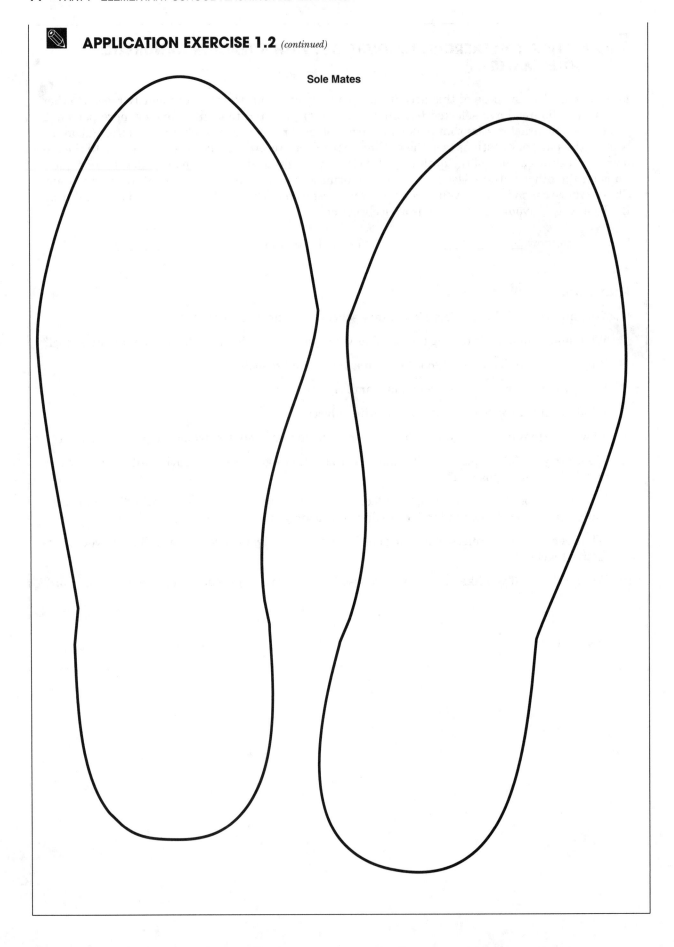

APPLICATION EXERCISE 1.2 *(continued)*

Sole Mates

I pledge allegiance to myself
and who I want to be
I can make my dreams come true
If I believe in me
    I pledge to stay in school and learn
    the things I need to know
    to make the world a better place
    for kids like me to grow
        I promise to keep my dreams alive
        and be all that I can be
        I know I can, and that's because
        I pledge to stay alcohol, tobacco, and drug
free.

(Source unknown)

Today's movement to transform schools into caring and responsive learning environments has as its sole purpose that of helping all children, especially those at risk, make the transitions necessary to succeed in school and in life. The future of our nation and, indeed, our world, might rest heavily on the success of this movement.

Responsive Practices for Helping All Children Succeed in School

Because of the enormous diversity of students in the classroom, the advantage of using a combination of practices concurrently is usually greater in helping all children succeed in school than is the gain from using any singular practice by itself. The reorganization of schools (such as moving sixth graders to a middle-level school) and the restructuring of school schedules (such as YRE and extended school days), then, represent only two aspects of efforts to help all students to make successful transitions.

Other important responsive practices (including attitudes) are (a) sharing with all teachers and staff the perception that all children can learn when they are given adequate support, although not all students need the same amount of time to learn the same thing; (b) maintaining high, although not necessarily identical, expectations for all students; (c) paying personalized attention, being an adult advocate, and creating scheduling and learning plans to help students learn in the manner by which they best learn—research clearly points out that achievement increases, students learn more, and students enjoy learning and remember more of what they have learned when individual learning styles and capacities are identified and accommodated; learning style traits are known that significantly discriminate among students who are at risk of dropping out of school

and students who perform well, as discussed in Chapter 2; (d) engaging parents and guardians as partners in their child's education; (e) spending extra time and guided attention on basic skills, such as those of thinking, writing, and reading, rather than on rote memory; (f) using specialist teachers, smaller student cohorts, and smaller classes; (g) engaging in **peer tutoring** and **cross-age coaching;** and (h) paying particular attention to the development of coping skills. These responsive practices are repeated and discussed throughout this resource guide. Another responsive practice in promoting the success of all children is making connections among the home, school, and local and global communities, as discussed next.

WAYS TO CONNECT WITH HOME, COMMUNITY, AND SCHOOL

It is well known that family members' involvement in and support for their child's education can have a positive impact on that child's achievement at school. For example, when parents, guardians, or siblings of at-risk students get involved, the child benefits from more consistent attendance at school, more positive attitudes and actions, better grades, and higher test scores.[17] In recognition of the positive effect that parent and family involvement has on student achievement and success, the National PTA, in 1997, published National Standards for Parent/Family Involvement Programs.[18]

Home and School Connections

At times, teachers develop their own personal family-involvement programs.[19] At other times, schools have adopted formal policies about home and community connections. These policies usually emphasize that parents and guardians should be included as partners in the educational program and that teachers and administrators will inform parents and guardians about their child's progress, about the school's family involvement policy, and about any programs in which family members can participate. Some schools are members of the **National Network of Partnership 2000 Schools.** Efforts to foster family and community involvement are as varied as the schools and people who participate, and include (a) student–teacher–parent/guardian contracts and assignment calendars, sometimes available via the school's web page on the Internet; (b) home visitation programs; (c) involvement of community leaders in the classroom as mentors, aides, and role models;[20] (d) electronic hardware and software for family members to help their children, along with newsletters and workshops;[21] (e) homework hotlines; (f) personal notes home and regular phone calls about a student's progress, both expressing concern and praising students;[22] and (g) involvement of students in service learning.[23] One of your tasks as a visiting or new teacher will be to discover the extent and nature of your school's efforts to involve family and community representatives in the education of the children. Educators increasingly are looking at service learning and place-based education, discussed next, as means of helping young people connect learning with life.

Service Learning and Place-Based Education

In service learning, students learn and develop their social skills in active participation linked to place-based education and thoughtfully organized and curriculum-connected experiences that meet community needs.[24]

In support of place-based learning, community members, geographic features, buildings, monuments, historic sites, and other places in a school's geographic area constitute some of the richest instructional laboratories that can be imagined. To take advantage of this accumulated wealth of resources, as well as to build school–community partnerships for service learning, you are advised to begin your file of community resources once you are hired by a school district. For instance, you might include files about the skills of the students' parents, guardians, or other family members, noting which ones could be resources for the study occurring in your classroom. You might also include files about various resource people who could speak to the students and about what other communities of teachers, students, and adult helpers have done.

Telecommunications Networks

Teachers who want to guide their students toward becoming autonomous thinkers, effective decision makers, and lifelong learners and to make their classrooms more student-centered, collaborative, interdisciplinary, and interactive are increasingly turning to telecommunication networks and the global community. Webs of connected computers allow teachers and students from around the world to teach each other directly and gain access to quantities of information previously unimaginable. Students using distance learning and networks learn and develop new inquiry and analytical skills in a stimulating environment and gain an increased appreciation of their role as world citizens. Sample websites and addresses are shown in the accompanying *Technology Tips for the Classroom* feature found in every chapter throughout this resource guide.

Companion Website

To broaden your knowledge base and to prepare yourself for your first year as a teacher, go to our Companion Website at **www.prenhall.com/roberts** and click on the *Additional Content* module for Chapter 1.

Professional Resources File

Now is a good time to start your professional resources file and then maintain it throughout your career. For your file, many resource ideas and sources are mentioned and listed throughout this resource guide.

THE EMERGENT OVERALL PICTURE

Certainly, no facet of education receives more attention from the media, causes more concern among parents, guardians, and teachers, or gets larger headlines than that of a decline—either factual or fanciful—in students' achievement in the public schools. Reports are issued, polls taken, debates organized, and blue ribbon commissions formed. Community members write letters to local editors about it, news editors de-

vote editorial space to it, television anchors comment about it, politicians use it, and documentaries and specials focus on it in full color. We read headlines such as "Students Play Catch-Up on Basic Skills," "U.S. Students Lag Behind Other Nations," and so on. We are not positive about this, but we think this current interest has never been matched in its political interest and participation, and it has affected and continues to affect both the public schools and the programs in higher education that are directly or indirectly related to teacher preparation and certification.[25] In the words of Mark Clayton, "Teachers are being asked to teach more and achieve better results—all with a population that has never been more diverse and demanding."[26]

In response to this interest, educators, corporations and local businesspersons, and politicians have acted. Around the nation, their actions have resulted in the following:

- The No Child Left Behind Act, which emphasizes high standards and accountability for all student groups, high standards in programs to improve school safety and reduce drug use; high quality of effective teachers; and increased interaction with parents and development of innovative programs
- High-stakes testing, (which is covered in more detail in later chapters)
- Development of curriculum standards (see Chapter 5)
- Emphasis on education for cultural diversity and for ways of teaching language-minority students
- Emphasis on helping students make effective transitions from one level of schooling to the next and from school to life, with an increased focus on helping students connect what is being learned with real life as well as one making connections between subjects in the curriculum and between academics and vocations
- Emphasis on raising test scores, reducing school dropout rates, increasing instructional time, and changing curricula
- Formation of school–home–community connections
- New requirements for high school graduation
- School restructuring to provide more meaningful curriculum options
- Changes in standards for teacher certification.

With regard to changes in standards, model standards describing what prospective teachers should know and be able to do to receive a teaching license were prepared and released in 1992 by the Interstate New Teacher Assessment and Support Consortium (INTASC), a project of the Council of Chief State School Officers (CCSSO), in a document titled *Model Standards for Beginning Teacher Licensing and Development.* Representatives of at least 36 states and professional associations—including the National Education Association (NEA), the American Federation of Teachers (AFT), the American Association of Colleges for Teacher Education (AACTE), and the National Council for the Accreditation of Teacher Education (NCATE)—comprise the group. The standards are performance-based and revolve around a common core of principles of knowledge and skills that cut across disciplines.

The INTASC standards[27] were developed to be compatible with those of the National Board for Professional Teaching Standards (NBPTS). Specifically addressing standards for certification as an early childhood generalist (ages 3–8) are the following eight categories of NBPTS standards:

1. Understanding young children
2. Promoting child development and learning
3. Knowledge of integrated curriculum
4. Multiple teaching strategies for meaningful learning
5. Assessment
6. Reflective practice
7. Family partnerships
8. Professional partnerships.[28]

Technology Tips for the Classroom

- Meet with other teachers who are technology friendly to consider activities involving desktop publishing, video production, and web design, as appropriate, for your students.
- If finances, budget concerns, and materials are available, consider an arrangement in at least one classroom (that could be shared) where video projection equipment can be suspended from the ceiling. Use a handheld remote to show subject content from the Internet, television, or recorded content/information that is sent to a screen at the front of the class.
- Find a checklist, such as that found on the Internet at www.infopeople.org/bkmk/select.html. Then review with your students examples of materials that meet and do not meet the criteria on the checklist for class use; by doing this, you and your students can develop skill in assessing materials and information found on the Internet.
- Consider allowing each student or teams of students to become experts on specific sites during particular units of study. It might be useful to start a chronicle of student-recorded log entries about particular websites to provide comprehensive long-term data about those sites.
- When students use information from the Internet, require that they print copies of sources of citations and materials so you can check for accuracy. These copies may be maintained in their portfolios.

Figure 1.3
Key trends and practices
in today's elementary
schools

- Measurable school goals, including basic skills and essential knowledge; students involved in goal setting
- Standards to improve safety in the schools and decrease use of drugs
- Facilitating students' social skills as they interact, relate to one another, solve meaningful problems, learn conflict resolution, and develop relationships and peaceful friendships
- Facilitating the development of students' values as related to their families, the community, and their school
- Federal funds for after-school learning opportunities and drug- and violence-prevention activities
- Integrating the curriculum, especially with reading and the language arts, and using the Internet in the classroom as a communication tool and learning resource
- Parent information program about the quality of their child's teacher, as defined by the state; involving parents and guardians in school decision making
- More flexible teacher quality grants to states and local districts and funding for professional development
- Promotion of innovative programs such as reforming teacher certification or licensure requirements, alternative certification, tenure reform, and merit-based teacher performance systems
- Differential and bonus pay for teachers in high-need subject areas such as reading, math, and science, high-poverty schools and districts; mentoring programs
- Funding to support alternative approaches that promote school choice
- Funding for charter schools
- Assessment that emphasizes instruction and testing in areas where each student needs it most; use of heterogeneous grouping, cooperative learning, peer coaching, and cross-age tutoring as significant instructional strategies

Companion Website

To find links to sites that support your elementary school teaching, go to our Companion Website at **www.prenhall.com/roberts** and click on the *Web Destinations* module for Chapter 1.

Key Trends and Practices Today

We discuss key features of the No Child Left Behind Act in the following section. However, other key trends and practices current in today's educational scene are listed in Figure 1.3.

No Child Left Behind Act

Related to today's elementary schools, some teachers, both precredentialed and credentialed, are wondering about the No Child Left Behind (NCLB) initiative and what it means for their classrooms. Some wonder how it will be implemented in their schools, districts, and states. The NCLB act is a legislative act that requires, among many things, the states to test students'

level of mastery of basic educational skills (i.e., third-grade students should demonstrate their abilities to read), and educators are feeling more pressure than ever before to raise students' scores on tests. From our point of view, the key word that describes the emphasis in the NCLB act is *high:* high standards and accountability for all student groups, high standards in programs to improve school safety and reduce drug use, high quality of effective teachers, and increased interaction with parents and innovative programs. The NCLB act also stresses accountability.

- **High standards for all student groups.** NCLB changes current law by requiring that states, school districts, and schools ensure that students in all student groups (e.g., students with learning disabilities, English language learning economically disadvantaged, American Indian, black, Asian, Hispanic, white) meet high standards. Schools must have clear, measurable goals focused on basic skills and essential knowledge.
- **High standards in programs to improve school safety and reduce drug use.** Under the

NCLB act, states are held accountable for using effective programs to improve school safety and drug use. Teachers will be empowered by the states to remove violent or persistently disruptive students from the classroom. In addition, the act ensures that parents will know whether their child attends a safe school. School districts will be able to use federal dollars on after-school learning opportunities and drug- and violence-prevention activities. Emphasis will be placed on preventing drug use and violence among youth and ensuring that schools use funds for programs that have demonstrated proven effectiveness in making schools safer. Funds may be used for after-school programs; to provide students with safety and anti-substance abuse activities before, during, and after school; and to educate students about the dangers of drugs, especially newly emerging drugs.

- **High quality of effective teachers.** Under the NCLB act, states will be accountable for ensuring that all children are taught by effective teachers and for developing a plan to ensure this goal will be met. Local districts, on request, will be required to disclose to parents information about the quality of their child's teacher, as defined by the state. To assist states in their efforts to prepare, recruit, and train high-quality teachers, the Eisenhower Professional Development Program and the Class Size Reduction Program will be consolidated into more flexible teacher quality grants to states and local districts. In addition to funding professional development, states and school districts will be free to use their funds to promote innovative programs such as reforming teacher certification or licensure requirements, alternative certification, tenure reform, and merit-based teacher performance systems; differential and bonus pay for teachers in high-need subject areas such as reading, math, and science, and in high-poverty schools and districts; and mentoring programs.

- **Increased interaction with parents and innovative programs.** The NCLB act seeks to increase parental options and influence in the belief that competition can be the stimulus a bureaucracy needs in order to change, and that parents, armed with options and choice, can ensure that parents, armed with options and choice, can ensure that their children get the best, most effective education possible. A school choice fund will be created to demonstrate, develop, implement, evaluate, and disseminate information on innovative approaches that promote school choice, and funding will be provided to assist charter schools. Funds may be used for local innovative programs, as well as to provide choice to students in persistently failing or dangerous schools so they can attend adequate, safe schools of choice.

- **Accountability.** The major push of the No Child Left Behind initiative and accompanying 21st century skills has led to a different type of assessment in today's classrooms. Currently, at some grade levels, artificial intelligence software presents students with problems, keeps track of their responses, and designs an individualized learning program that emphasizes instruction and testing in areas where each student needs it most. Here are two examples:
Example 1: Lightspan, Inc. (*www.lightspan.com*) has a series of testing software, *EduTest*, that helps teachers design assessments based on the statewide basic skills demanded by the No Child Left Behind Act. In the state of Florida as an example, the Department of Education requires the Florida Comprehensive Assessment Test (FCAT). This test has been failed by tens of thousands of students. To offset this, Florida made available Lightspan's *EduTest* tutorial software to prepare for the FCAT in schools in at-risk areas. The software has easy-to-read profiles so teachers can see who is making progress and who needs immediate help and this makes a difference in test preparation. In support of this, a principal at one elementary school (Jacksonville) reported that the software pushed the school's scores up and out of the at-risk range and thus made a difference in the students' FCAT scores.
Example 2: *READ 180* (*http://teacher.scholastic. com/products/read180/*) is reading software for students in grades 4–12 who are reading below grade level. The software assesses the students' reading skills while creating exercises that reinforce those skills. To accompany the software, the teachers teach group reading and skills lessons and introduce high-interest, low-reading-level books. The students then rotate through three computer learning stations with computer lessons, and the software calculates each student's skill levels in decoding, vocabulary, and other reading areas. The lessons help the students learn basic reading skills by providing each student with an individualized set of lessons that emphasize some needed skills.

For more information about the NCLB act, go to *www.ed.gov/nclb/landing.ihtml?re=pb*.

Curriculum Standards and High-Stakes Testing

Curriculum standards define what students should know and be able to do. High-stakes testing is the result of test developers using both state and national standards, accessible on the Internet (*www. statestandards.com*), for guidance in developing standardized tests for students. High-stakes testing also refers to the tests being used at various grade levels to determine student achievement, promotion, and

Figure 1.4
National professional
associations for teachers

AAE: Association of American Educators, 25201 Paseo de Alicia, Suite 104, Laguna Hills, CA 92653 (www.aaeteachers.org/)

AFT: American Federation of Teachers, AFL-CIO, 555 New Jersey Avenue, NW, Washington, DC 20001 (www.aft.org)

NAPE: National Association of Professional Educators, Suite 300, 900 17th Street, Washington, DC 20006 (www.teacherspet.com/napeindx.htm)

NEA: National Education Association, 1201 16th Street, NW Washington, DC 20036-3290 (www.nea.org)

Figure 1.5
Problems and issues that trouble the nation's teachers and schools

Related to Achievement
- A demand for test scores and statistics that can be used to judge schools, with a concomitant controversy over the concept of grading schools and publishing the reports
- Continuing controversy over standardized norm-referenced testing[29]
- Controversy over the inclusion/exclusion of certain children from state mandatory testing

Related to Content
- Continuing disputes over books and their content
- Continuing, long-running arguments about values, morality, and sexuality education
- Controversy created by the concept of teaching less content but teaching it better
- Dispute over the need for the development of a national curriculum with national assessment[30]
- Identification and development of programs that recognize, develop, and nurture talents in all youth at all levels of education[31]
- Teaching and assessing for higher order thinking skills

Related to Grouping
- Continued disagreement over use of traditional ability grouping or curriculum tracking

Related to Schools and Teachers
- Low teacher salaries when compared with other college-educated workers[32]
- Retention in grade versus social promotion[33]
- Scarcity of teachers of color to serve as role models for minority children[34]
- School security and the related problems of crime, drugs, violence, and weapons on school campuses and in school neighborhoods[35]
- School populations that are too large[36]
- Sexual harassment of students[37]
- Shortage of male teachers, especially in the elementary schools[38]
- School buildings that are old and desperately in need of repair and updating

Related to Students At Risk and Teachers
- Shortage of qualified teachers, especially in certain disciplines and in schools with high percentages of children at risk
- The number of students at risk of dropping out of school
- The education of teachers to work effectively with children who may be too overwhelmed by personal problems to focus on learning and to succeed in school[39]
- The expectation that teachers should teach more and with improved results to a population of students, some at risk, that has never been more diverse or demanding

rewards to schools and even to individual teachers and students. In about half of the 50 states, some tests may be a requirement from high school. More will be said about this when standards are discussed in Chapter 5.

You may be interested to know that students with access to computers can practice and prepare online for the state-mandated standardized tests. In schools with the required computer technology and with the appropriate number of computers to provide access time to individual students, selected software programs can help students prepare for the tests. Two such programs are *Homeroom* (*www.homeroom.*

comfaq/about.asp) and, as mentioned previously, *EduTest* (*www.eduTest.com*). Proponents of such on-line preparation argue that a major advantage is the immediate scoring of practice testing with feedback about each student's areas of weakness, thereby providing the teacher with information necessary for immediate remediation. If their arguments are accurate, then it would seem that students of such technology-rich schools would clearly be at an advantage over students in schools where this technology is not available. It would follow that district and government agencies that mandate the standards and specific assessment practices should provide avenues and tools to ensure equity and success for all students toward reaching the expected learning outcomes within the designated learning time. To keep up to date with information about this issue of high-stakes testing and others, use your national professional associations as sources. For Internet addresses, see Figure 1.4.

Problems and Issues That Trouble the Nation's Schools

Major problems and issues plague our nation's schools, some of which are mentioned in Figure 1.5. Some of these are discussed in subsequent chapters (see index for topic locations). Perhaps you and members of your class can identify other issues and problems faced by our nation's schools.

One example of a problem/issue is that of traditional instruction versus dialogue and exploring ideas with students. When compared with traditional instruction—one of the characteristics of exemplary instruction in today's classrooms—the teacher's encouragement of dialogue, discussion, and exploring ideas among students will be discussed throughout this guide and especially in Chapter 7. As mentioned in the preface to this book, modeling the very behaviors we expect of teachers and students in the classroom is a constant theme throughout this text.

About Praxis and Other Teacher Tests

Before we present facts about the Praxis II Principles of Learning and Teaching™ and other teacher tests, we want to point out that studies indicate that teacher certification or licensing relates directly to student learning in a positive way. Consider these advantages:

- Fully credentialed teachers have a positive, statistically significant effect on student test scores when compared to teachers who are uncertified in their subject areas (exceptions are mathematics and science teachers with emergency certificates).[40]
- Mathematics and science teachers, even those who have emergency certificates, benefit from more teacher education training, and such training appears to increase student achievement.[41]
- In a study in one state, school districts with higher percentages of licensed teachers perform significantly better on state achievement tests, even when holding constant some characteristics related to teachers, schools, and the family backgrounds of students.[42]

About Praxis Teacher Tests. As a prospective teacher, you are probably aware that most state departments of education, and some colleges and universities, now require precredentialed candidates to take teacher tests before they are licensed/credentialed to enter the classroom. Tests for teacher credentialing and licensing vary in different states. As one example, the Praxis II Principles of Learning and Teaching tests, which cover educational tasks and skills, are required in more than 30 states and are required of beginning teachers. There are three levels of testing (assessment):

Praxis I: This level includes an Academic Skills Assessment (multiple-choice questions) that precredentialed teachers take early in career preparation to measure reading, writing, and math skills; a computer-based Academic Skills Assessment, with a range of question types, multiple choice, constructed response/essay); and a Listening Skills Test (multiple choice with recorded segments).

Praxis II: This level has Subject Assessments/Speciality Area Tests that precredentialed teachers usually take when graduating from a college or university and when entering the teaching profession to measure one's knowledge of the subject(s) in which one is seeking certification as well as to measure one's general teaching knowledge and skills. This resource guide supports the following tests: the Praxis II Elementary Education: Content Area Exercises Assessment (constructed response-type questions) and Elementary Education: Curriculum, Instruction, and Assessment (multiple-choice questions). Further, the inside back cover of this guide presents a matrix of the content of this resource guide and how it connects with the Praxis II Principles of Teaching and Learning tests, the INTASC principles, and the NBPTS standards, and the teaching standards of a selected state. In addition, the subject index of this resource guide has a symbol (*) by the subject entries that we suggest be reviewed carefully before taking a teacher test.

(continued)

Here are some of the categories of content that you can expect to find in the Praxis II Elementary Education: Content Area Exercises Assessment:

- Knowledge of children's personal, social, and emotional development; developmentally appropriate instruction; language and communication
- Knowledge of learning theories
- Knowledge of instructional principles, i.e., planning, motivation, supportive learning environment, diversity, enrichment, reteaching, procedural skills, and conferencing
- Knowledge of class management, i.e., organization, procedures, learner responsibility, interventions, and discipline
- Knowledge of evaluation of effectiveness of instruction and progress of students; explanation of assessments that increase learning and motivation; assessments that are authentic or traditional; analysis of results; effective assessment practices; and measurement
- Self-knowledge that includes professional development, reflective teaching, collaboration, and partnerships with colleagues, parents, and community members.

Praxis III: At this assessment level, Classroom Performance Assessments are used to evaluate aspects of the beginning teacher's classroom performance, usually during the first year of teaching. These occur in the teacher's own classroom by local observers who use validated criteria.

To support your professional interest in preparing for Praxis II Principles of Learning and Teaching tests and some of the other teacher tests, all application exercises in this chapter offer opportunities for you to reflect generally on the content about today's elementary schools. In this chapter, prelicensed teachers are asked to participate cooperatively and collaboratively (much as they would do when working together as a faculty of an elementary school) and to do the following:

- Recall their own elementary school experience (Application Exercise 1.1).
- Identify reasons other teacher candidates have selected teaching as a career goal (Application Exercise 1.2).
- Turn to our Companion Website (**www.prenhall.com/roberts**) and click on the *Additional Application Exercise* module to complete an additional application exercise, namely, A Second Reflection on My Own Elementary School Experiences.

If you want to respond to a constructed response-type question similar to those found on the Praxis II Elementary Education tests, turn to the Praxis Warm-Up in the end-of-chapter material. This warm-up takes another look at the classroom vignette found in the Looking at Teachers section at the beginning of this chapter.

Some teacher tests in other states are published by the Educational Testing Services or other agencies and companies. These credentialing tests are used by states, colleges, and universities and are developed by advisory groups made up of teachers, teacher educators, administrators, and representatives from professional organizations.

 Other Teacher Tests. For those of you who will be teaching in states that do not administer the Praxis II Principles of Learning and Teaching tests, go to our Companion Website at **www.prenhall. com/roberts** and click on the *Other Teacher Tests* module for Chapter 1 to access information about teacher tests other than the Praxis.

SUMMARY

In beginning to plan for developing your teaching competencies, you have read an overview about the characteristics of education in today's elementary school, including the similarities and differences in schools that have grades K–6, the characteristics of some of the adults who work there, and some of the trends and practices, such as those exemplified by current national and state standards as well as the No Child Left Behind Act. You realize that there are prob-

lems and issues that continue to concern our nation's schools. This knowledge will be useful in your assimilation of the content explored in the chapters that follow, beginning in the next chapter with the characteristics of elementary schoolchildren, how they learn, and strategies to work effectively with them.

What's to Come. Despite the many blue ribbon commissions, writers, and politicians who vilify facets of public school education, thousands of dedicated teachers, administrators, parents, and members of the community struggle daily, year after year, to provide students with a quality education.[43] Throughout the chapters of this text, many exemplary schools and school programs are recognized and identified by name.

EXTENDING MY PROFESSIONAL COMPETENCY

Praxis Warm-Up: A Constructed Response-Type Question

Referring back to the chapter vignette, consider Rachael and her class of students. You'll recall that Rachael is a fifth-grade teacher in a low socioeconomic school in a large city on the East Coast. The 34 students in her class include 10 English language learners and 10 with identified learning problems. Some of the children have skills equivalent to those of first graders. In any given week, Rachael recycles newspapers and sells snacks to help pay for field trips because the school and the children cannot support those things financially. At times with the students, Rachael reviews what money has been made from selling the snacks to help pay for the group's field trips. During these reviews, she has observed that some of her students with learning problems do not understand the place-value arrangement in counting money from pennies to dimes to dollars.

Describe two (2) activities that you would use to help Rachael's students with learning problems who do not understand the ones, tens, and hundreds place-value arrangement in mathematics. Give examples of what the children would be doing during the activity. Explain how you, as the teacher, would assess the children's understanding of the ones, tens, and hundreds place-value arrangement after they have completed the activity.

Hints for responding to Praxis Warm-Ups are found in the Appendix.

Praxis. To do another Praxis Warm-Up with a constructed response-type question, go to our Companion Website at **www.prenhall.com/roberts** and click on the *Praxis Warm-Up* module for Chapter 1. Constructed response-type questions are designed to help you prepare for the Praxis II Principles of Learning and Teaching tests.

For Your Discussion

1. **An Exemplary Elementary School.** How would I be able to explain a way to recognize an exemplary elementary school? What does school size have to do with an exemplary elementary school? **To do:** Briefly research the topic of exemplary schools and see K. Cotton, School Size, School Climate, and Student Performance, *Close-Up Number 20* (Portland, OR: Northwest Regional Educational Laboratory, May 1996); Retrieved December 15, 2004, from *www.nwrel.org/scpd/sirs/10/c020.html.* After your research, describe at least three characteristics you would expect to find in an exemplary school. Explain why you have selected those particular characteristics.

2. **Involving Parents.** How can I involve parents in their child's learning? **To do:** Form groups with no more than five people per group. Select a particular age group (5–6, 7–8, 9–14) for your group. In a period of time, such as 15 minutes, help your group members brainstorm and list as many ways as they can that an elementary schoolteacher could involve parents and guardians and other family members in their children's learning. Help your group share its results with the entire class.

3. **Social Influences on Today's Children.** What would I say if a parent asked me what societal influences affected the children of today? How would I explain the effects, if any, of crimes, gangs, drugs, and images of professional athletes and musicians among those influences? **To do:** Research and identify what specifically, if anything, the elementary school classroom teacher should know to be able to effectively deal with the effects mentioned.

4. **School Dress Codes.** What is my opinion of a program of school dress codes? **To do:** Discuss with others your thoughts and opinions about the topic. To start the discussion, give your reactions to the following: Some schools and districts have implemented uniform dress code policies. The theory is that a uniform dress code will reduce distractions and disruptions caused by variations in clothing and make economic disparities among the children less obvious. Might it erase the dangers caused by gang influence? Can it be economically advantageous to parents and guardians?

5. **Student Success in School.** What specific techniques would I discuss with someone who wanted to know about some of the techniques that are used to help children succeed in school? **To do:** Join with a small group (two or three of you per group). Assist your group in assuming the responsibility for one or two of the techniques, finding out as much as possible about the technique, such as the extent to which it is being used, its history, successes, limitations, and so forth. Establish guidelines and a date for reporting results to the entire class later in the semester.

Online Portfolio Activities

Supporting Principle 5 of INTASC and Standards 3 and 4 of NBPTS: At the Companion Website **(www.prenhall.com/roberts),** click on the *Online Portfolio Activities* module to start an online portfolio.

Companion Website

Also on the Companion Website at **www.prenhall.com/roberts,** you can measure your understanding of chapter content in the *Objectives* and *Self-Check* modules and apply concepts in the *For Your Discussion* module.

FOR FURTHER READING

Battista, M. T. (1999). The Mathematical Miseducation of America's Youth: Ignoring Research and Scientific Study in Education. *Phi Delta Kappan, 80*(6), 425–433.

Brandt, R. S. (Ed.). (2000). *Education in a New Era.* Alexandria, VA: Association for Supervision and Curriculum Development.

Buckley, F. J. (2000). *Team Teaching: What, Why, and How?* Thousand Oaks, CA: Sage.

Cawelti, G. (2000). Portrait of a Benchmark School. *Educational Leadership, 57*(5), 42–44.

Cooper, R. (1999). Success for All Schools, One at a Time. *Principal, 78* (3), 28–32.

Costa, A. L., and Garmston, R. J. (2002). *Cognitive Coaching: A Foundation for Renaissance Schools.* Norwood, MA: Christopher-Gordon.

Cotton, K. (1996, May). *School Size, School Climate, and Student Performance* (Close-Up Number 20). Portland, OR: Northwest Regional Educational Laboratory.

Danna, S. (2003, April/May). Pursuing National Board Certification, Part 2. *Pi Lambda Theta Newsletter 47*(6), 5.

Darling-Hammond, L. (2000). Teacher Quality and Student Achievement: A Review of State Policy Evidence. *Education Policy Analysis Archives, 8,* 555–565.

Darling-Hammond, L., Berry, B., and Thoreson, A. (2001). Does Teacher Certification Matter?: Evaluating the Evidence. *Educational Evaluation and Policy Analysis, 23,* 566–577.

Freidman, T. (2000). *The Lexus and the Olive Tree: Understanding Globalization.* New York: Anchor Books.

Fuller, E. J. (1999). *Does Teacher Certification Matter? A Comparison of TAAS Performance in 1997 between schools with Low and High Percentages of Certified Teachers.* Austin, TX: Charles A. Dana Center, University of Texas at Austin.

Goldhaber, M., and Brewer, D. (2000). Does Teacher Certification Matter? High School Certification Status and Student Achievement. *Educational Evaluation and Policy Analysis, 22,* 129–145.

Good, T. L. (1999). The Purposes of Schooling in America, Introduction. *Elementary School Journal, 99*(5), 237–241.

Goodlad, J. I. (1999). Teachers as Moral Stewards of Our Schools. *Journal for a Just and Caring Education, 5*(3), 237–241.

Hall, G. E., and Hord, S. M. (2001). *Implementing Change: Patterns, Principles, and Potholes.* Boston: Allyn & Bacon.

Manno, B. V., Finn, C. E., Jr., and Vanourek, G. (2000). Beyond the Schoolhouse Door: How Charter Schools Are Transforming U.S. Public Education. *Phi Delta Kappan, 81*(10), 736–744.

Pelton, J. (2000). *E-Sphere: The Rise of the Worldwide Mind.* Westport, CT: Quorum Books.

Powell, W. (2000). Recruiting Educators for an Inclusive School. In W. Powell and O. Powell (Eds.), *Count Me In: Developing Inclusive International Schools.* Washington, DC: Overseas Advisory Council.

Ray, P., and Anderson, S. (2000). *The Cultural Creatives: How 50 Million People Are Changing the World.* New York: Crown.

Schank, R. C. (2000). A Vision of Education for the 21st Century. *T*H*E Journal, 27*(6), 42–45.

Senge, P., Cambron-McCabe, N., Lucas, T., Smith, B., Dutton, J., and Kleiner, A. (2000). *Schools That Learn: A Fifth Discipline Fieldbook for Educators, Parents and Everyone Who Cares about Education.* New York: Doubleday.

NOTES

1. For further information on the Core Knowledge Curriculum, see T. A. Mackey, *Uncommon Sense: Core Knowledge in the Classroom* (Alexandria, VA: Association for Supervision and Curriculum Development, 1999), or contact the Core Knowledge Foundation, 801 E. High Street, Charlottesville, VA 22902, (800) 238–3233. Visit the High Peaks Core Knowledge Elementary School at *www.highpeaks.org/.*

2. See M. A. Dunn, Staying the Course of Open Education, *Educational Leadership, 57*(7), 20–24 (April 2000).

3. L. A. Mulholland and L. A. Bierlein, *Understanding Charter Schools (Fastback 383).* (Bloomington, IN: Phi Delta Kappa Educational Foundation, 1995), p. 7. Connect to the charter school home page via the United States Charter School website at *www.uscharterschools.org/pub/uscs_docs/index.htm.* For additional information and for a copy of the National Charter School Directory, contact the Center for Educational Reform, at (202) 822–9000, e-mail to cer@edreform.com, or go to the website at *http://edreform.com/.*

4. See, for example, S. Maguire, A Community School, *Educational Leadership, 57*(6), 18–21 (March 2000); H. Raham, Full-Service Schools, *School Business Affairs, 64*(6), 24–28 (June 1998); and D. MacKenzie and V. Rogers, The Full-Service School: A Management and Organizational Structure for 21st Century Schools, *Community Education Journal, 25*(3–4), 9–11 (Spring/Summer 1997).

5. K. Rasmussen, Year-Round Education, *Education Update, 42*(2), 1, 3–5 (March 2000).

6. The mission statements of the Sierra Oaks Elementary School and Skyview School are reprinted by permission of, respectively, Thomas Ford, Principal, Sierra

Oaks Schools, Sacramento, California, and Janet Bicknese, Director, Skyview School, Prescott, Arizona.

The mission statement for Sierra Oaks Elementary School evolved collaboratively from an analysis of disaggregated assessment data from the Standardized Testing and Reporting (STAR) System completed by the school staff and the School Site Council, a site-based parent survey developed by the School Site Council, and a teacher survey that asked for a quantitative assessment of curricular programs, school climate and educational environment, instructional practices, and other areas. An annual report is given in the School Accountability Report Card (SARC), which is distributed to the parent community and is available at the San Juan Unified District website, *www.sanjuan.edu/service*. Further, the Academic Performance Index (API) is reported through the school's weekly newsletter that is given to all students and parents.

The Skyview School community of learners includes families with a deep commitment to children, education, leadership, and service. The school was founded by parents seeking an innovative educational environment for their children; they spent years researching educational models and developed a program that combined the values of respect and responsibility with cognitive research that supports inquiry, application, and real-life contextual learning.

7. See K. Reeves, The Four-Day School Week, *School Administrator, 56*(3), 30–34 (March 1999).

8. M. H. Rosenbusch, *Guidelines for Starting an Elementary School Foreign Language Program* (Washington, DC: ERIC Clearinghouse on Assessment and Evaluation, 1995), ED 383227.

9. Sunset Elementary School is an international studies magnet school with language/culture programs of study in cooperation with the Spain and other countries. See the school's website at *http://sunsetdadeschools.net*. In contrast, a charter school could be an international baccalaureate school with a curriculum approved by the International Baccalaureate Organization (IBO). Since 1997, IBO has offered a Primary Years program for children ages 3–12; since 1992, a Middle Years program for students 11–16 years old; and since 1967, a diploma program for students who are in their final 2 years of secondary school. See IBO's website at *www.ibo.org*. For more about charter schools, see J. Zimmerman (Ed.), The Comer School Development Program. Education Research Consumer Guide, No. 6 (Washington, DC: Office of Educational Research and Development, 1993); J. Comer, *Waiting for a Miracle* (New York: Dutton, 1997); and D. W. Woodruff et al., Collaborating for Success: Merritt Elementary Extended School, *Journal of Education for Students Placed at Risk, 3*(1), 11–22 (1998).

10. To see how one school in the state of Washington added Spanish instruction for all its children in grades K–5, see G. Ernst-Slavit and A. O. Pierce, Introducing Foreign Languages in Elementary School, *Principal, 77*(3), 31–33 (1998).

11. J. Reeves, *Elementary School Foreign Language Programs* (Washington, DC: ERIC Clearinghouse on Assessment and Evaluation, September 1989), ED 309652.

12. See D. L. Burke, *Looping: Adding Time, Strengthening Relationships* (Champaign, IL: ERIC Clearinghouse on Elementary and Early Childhood Education, 1977), ED 414098; C. Forsten, J. Grant, and I. Richardson, Multiage and Looping: Borrowing from the Past, *Principal, 78*(4), 15–16, 18 (March 1999); and J. Grant, I. Richardson, and C. Pforsten, In the Loop, *The School Administrator, 56*(1), 30–33 (January 2000).

13. B. J. Omotani and L. Omotani, Expect the Best, *Executive Educator, 18*(8), 27, 31 (March 1996).

14. J. L. Doud and E. P. Keller, *The K–8 principal in 1998: A 10-Year Study of the National Association of Elementary School Principals* (Alexandria, VA: NAESP, 1998).

15. P. L. Tiedt and I. M. Tiedt, *Multicultural Teaching: A Handbook of Activities, Information, and Resources*, 6th ed. (Boston: Allyn & Bacon, 2002).

16. R. J. Rossi and S. C. Stringfield, What We Must Do for Students Placed at Risk, *Phi Delta Kappan, 77*(1), 73–76 (September 1995). See also the several related articles in the theme issue titled. The Changing Lives of Children, *Educational Leadership, 54*(7) (April 1997). Visit the home page of the National Institute on Education of At-Risk Students at *www.ed.gov/offices/OERI/At-Risk*.

17. A. V. Shaver and R. T. Walls, Effect of Title I Parent Involvement on Student Reading and Mathematics Achievement, *Journal of Research and Development in Education, 31*(2), 90–97 (Winter 1998).

18. P. Sullivan, The PTA's National Standards, *Educational Leadership, 55*(8), 43–44 (May 1998). For a copy of the standards, contact the National PTA, 541 N. Fairbanks Court, Suite 1300, Chicago, IL 60611–3396; phone: (312)670–6782; (800)307–4PTA; fax: (312)670–6783;

19. See R. J. Nistler and A. Maiers, Stopping the Silence: Hearing Parents' Voices in an Urban First-Grade Family Literacy Program, *The Reading Teacher, 53*(8), 670–680 (May 2000).

20. See "Community Leaders Return to the Classroom" at *www.eurekacityschools.org/scrapbook2/commleaders.html/*.

21. T. Whiteford, Math for Moms and Dads, *Educational Leadership, 55*(8), 64–66 (May 1998).

22. See C. Gustafson, Phone Home, *Educational Leadership, 56*(2), 31–32 (October 1998).

23. See C. Bodinger-deUriarte et al., *A Guide to Promising Practices in Educational Partnerships* (Washington, DC: U.S. Government Printing Office, 1996), ED 392980, and the articles in the May 1998 theme issue about engaging parents and the community in school in *Educational Leadership, 55*(8).

24. See P. Sullivan, Big Help Gets Big Hand in Chicago, *Our Children, 24*(1), 21 (August/September 1998); T. M. Prosser and J. A. Levesque, Supporting Literacy through Service Learning, *The Reading Teacher, 51*(1), 32–38 (September 1997); S. H. Billig, Research on K–12 School-Based Service Learning: The Evidence Builds, *Phi Delta Kappan, 81*(9), 658–664 (May 2000).

25. For more about what businesses are doing to promote education, see L. Sosniak, The 9% Challenge: Education in School and Society, *Teachers College Record*; retrieved January 15, 2005, from *www.tcrecord.org*; ID number 10756. See also G. I. Maeroff (Ed.), *Imaging Education: The Media and School in America* (New York: Teachers College Press, 1998) and the article by G. J. Cizek, Give Us This Day Our Daily Dread: Manufacturing Crises in Education; retrieved from the Phi Delta Kappa International website at *www.pdkintl.org*.

26. M. Clayton, The Goal: Great Teachers. The Plan: A Work in Progress, *The Christian Science Monitor Electronic Edition*; retrieved March 8, 2005, from *http://csmonitor.com/cgi-bin/durableRedirect.pl?/durable/1999/04/20/*

p14s1.htm. Note that the classroom teacher to whom you are assigned during your field experiences is referred to variously as the *cooperating teacher,* the *student-teaching supervising teacher,* or the *host, mentor,* or *master teacher.* Throughout this resource guide, the term *cooperating teacher* or *collaborating teacher* is used.

27. For copies of the INTASC document, contact CCSSO, One Massachusetts Avenue, NW, Suite 700, Washington, DC 2000; phone: (202)336–7000; *www.ccsso.org.*

28. Access the standards via the Internet at *www.nbpts. org/standards/stdsoverviews.cfm.* You may want to review C. Danielson's "Framework for Teaching" in J. Cooper's *Classroom Teaching Skills,* 7th ed. (New York: Houghton-Mifflin, 2003). You can also compare the standards with the competencies that are identified in Chapter 3 of this resource guide and with the components of professional practice in C. Danielson, *Enhancing Professional Practice: A Framework for Teaching* (Alexandria, VA: Association for Supervision and Curriculum Development, 1996).

29. A. Kohn, Raising the Scores, Ruining the Schools, *American School Board Journal, 186*(10), 31–34 (October 1999).

30. S. Ohanian, *One Size Fits All: The Folly of Educational Standards* (Portsmouth, NH: Heinemann, 1999), and S. Ohanian, Goals 2000: What's in a Name? *Phi Delta Kappan, 81*(5), 233–255 (January 2000).

31. See J. Fulkerson and M. Horvich, *Talent Development: Two Perspectives,* and J. Van Tassel-Baska, *The Development of Academic Talent,* both in *Phi Delta Kappan, 79*(10), 756–759 and 760–763, respectively (June 1998).

32. See D. J. Hoff, International Report Finds U. S. Teacher Salaries Lagging, and J. Blair, Honored Teachers Want More Pay and Respect, *Education Week, 19*(36), 5 and 11, respectively (May 17, 2000).

33. K. Kelly, Retention vs. Social Promotion: Schools Search for Alternatives, *The Harvard Educational Letter, 15*(1), 1–3 (January/February 1999).

34. See "The Need for Minority Teachers" in P. R. Rettig and M. Khodavandi, Recruiting Minority Teachers: The UTOP Program (Fastback 436). (Bloomington, IN: Phi Delta Kappan Educational Foundation, 1998); see also R. M. Ingersoll, The Teacher Shortage: Myth or Reality? *Phi Lambda Theta Educational Horizons, 81*(3), 146–152 (Spring, 2003).

35. Intended to alert teachers and parents to the warning signs exhibited by troubled children is *Early Warning-Time Response: A Guide to Safe Schools.* Written by the National Association of School Psychologists and released in August 1998, the guide is available free by calling (877)4ED-PUBS or from the Internet at *www.ed.gov/about/offices/list/osers/osep/gtss.html.*

36. Research repeatedly indicates that small schools (less than 400 students for an elementary school) are at least equal to, and often superior to large ones on most measures. See K. Cotton, School Size, School Climate, and Student Performance (Close-Up Number 20), (Portland, OR: Northwest Regional Educational Laboratory, 1996); retrieved December 15, 2004, from *www.nwrel.org/scpd/sirs/10/c020.html.*

37. A useful document for schools is L. A. Brown et al., *Student–Student Sexual Harassment: A Legal Guide for Schools* (Alexandria, VA: Council of School Attorneys, National Schools Boards Association, 1998); also see the two texts by N. Cambron-McCabe et al., *Public School Law: Teacher's and Student's Rights,* 5th ed., and *Legal Rights of Teachers and Students* (both Boston: Allyn & Bacon, 2004).

38. See K. Vail, A Few Good Men, *American School Board Journal, 186*(10), 28–30 (October 1999). Also see J. Shen, G. L. Wegenke, and V. E. Cooley, Has the Public Teaching Force Become More Diversified? National and Longitudinal Perspectives on Gender, Race, and Ethnicity, *Phi Lambda Theta Educational Horizons,* pp. 112–129 (Spring 2003) for a review of the Schools and Staffing Survey (SASS) from K–12 education in the United States from the National Center for Educational Statistics (NCES) during the years 1987–1988, 1990–1991, and 1999–2000. It determined the overall trend of gender, race, and ethnicity in the public teaching force. It seems that teaching is still a profession of female teachers, whose numbers have increased slightly since 1987–1988. The number of male teachers has actually been going down since that time period. The percentage of minority teachers who are American Indian, Alaskan Native, Asian or Pacific Islander, or African American has increased slightly, whereas the percentage of Hispanic teachers has had an 86% increase since 1987–1988.

39. You can read many positive findings in *Do You Know the Good News about American Education?* published in 2000 by the Center on Education Policy (CEP) and the American Youth Policy Forum. The document can be downloaded from AYPF's website at *www.aypf.org/ publications/Good_News.pdf.*

40. Goldhaber, M., & Brewer, D, (2000). Does Teacher Certification Matter? High School Certification Status and Student Achievement. *Educational Evaluation and Policy Analysis, 22,* 129–145.

41. L. Darling-Hammond, B. Berry, and A. Thoreson, Does Teacher Certification Matter?: Evaluating the Evidence, *Educational Evaluation and Policy Analysis 23,* 566–577 (2001).

42. L. Darling-Hammond, Teacher Quality and Student Achievement: A Review of State Policy Evidence, *Education Policy Analysis Archives, 8,* 146–157 (2000).

43. For example, you can read many positive findings in *Do You Know the Good News About American Education?* published in 2000 by the Center on Education Policy (CEP) and the American Youth Policy Forum.

The Nature of the Challenge: What Do I Need to Know About Elementary Learners?

Visual Chapter Organizer and Overview

Dimensions of the Challenge	Meeting the Challenge: Recognizing and Providing for Student Differences
The Classroom in a Nation of Diversity	Instructional Practices That Provide for Student Differences: General Guidelines Developmental Characteristics of Children of Particular Age Groups Recognizing and Working with Students with Special Needs
Supporting the Challenge: Learning Modalities, Learning Styles, Learning Capacities, and Implications for Teaching	
Learning Modalities Learning Styles The Three-Phase Learning Cycle Learning Capacities: The Theory of Multiple Intelligences	

Looking at Teachers

Given the diverse nature of elementary learners, teachers often ask "What can be done to put the theory of multiple intelligences and multilevel instruction (a theory discussed further in this chapter) into practice?" Here is what one teacher did: In one fourth-grade classroom, during one week of a 6-week thematic unit on weather, the students were concentrating on learning about the water cycle. As part of this study of the water cycle, the teacher asked, "What do you think makes clouds? What might happen when cool water vapor meets dust or smoke particles in the air?" To help the students demonstrate that the meeting of particles and cool water vapor in the air makes a cloud, the teacher had a student volunteer select a clear 1-liter plastic bottle with a cap, put a drop of water from the water faucet into the bottle, and then the teacher lit a small match (with the principal's knowledge) and dropped it into the bottle. The teacher quickly put on the cap and the student started squeezing and releasing the sides of the plastic bottle. After a few squeezes and releases by various students, a white cloud started to appear in the clear plastic bottle and the group talked about what was going on. They observed that some of the water had evaporated and, evidently, turned into water vapor that they could not see. When the students squeezed the plastic bottle, the vapor warmed up and when the students released the bottle, the vapor cooled down. When the vapor cooled down enough, the vapor condensed into a cloud of visible drops that was created from the particles of dust and smoke from the match.

With the students' further help, the teacher divided the class into several groups of three to five students per group to continue working on projects. The groups worked on six projects simultaneously to learn about the water cycle:

- One group of students designed, conducted, and repeated an experiment to discover the number of drops of water that can be held on one side of a new one-cent coin versus the number that can be held on one side of a worn one-cent coin.
- Working in part with the first group, a second group designed and prepared graphs to illustrate the results of the experiments of the first group.
- A third group of students created and composed the words and music for a song about the water cycle.
- A fourth group incorporated their combined interests in mathematics and art to design, collect the necessary materials, and create a colorful and interactive bulletin board about the water cycle.
- A fifth group read about the water cycle in materials they researched from the Internet and various libraries. One source was *Where Does Water Come From?* (Hauppauge, NY: Barron's, 1992) by C. Vance Cost and illustrated by Sue Wilkinson.
- A sixth group created a puppet show about the water cycle.

At the end of the week, the groups shared their projects with the class. Later on, you will read more about the theory of multiple intelligences to help you put this theory into practice in your classroom.

The bell rings, and the children enter your classroom, a kaleidoscope of personalities, all idiosyncratic, each a packet of energy, with different focuses, experiences, dispositions, learning capacities, and differing proficiencies in the verbal and written use of the English language; in other words, all different challenges. One of the challenges you will understand is the reason why young students in the early grades sympathize with Leo, a baby tiger, and with what the young tiger is going through in the story *Leo, the Late Bloomer* (New York: Windmill, 1971) written by Robert Kraus and illustrated by Jose Arugeo. It seems that the young tiger can't do anything right—he can't read, write, draw, or talk. His mother tells his father that Leo is a late bloomer but his father isn't so sure and watches him constantly to see if Leo shows any signs of blooming. Eventually, Mother Tiger is right, and Leo blooms. Indeed, Leo's blooming (any child's blooming) is just one part of the challenge of elementary school teaching: to understand and to teach 30 or so unique individuals, all at once, and to do it for 6 hours a day, 5 days a week, 180 or more days a year! What a challenge it is today, to be a teacher, whether you are teaching 5-year-olds in kindergarten or 11- or 12-year-olds in the sixth grade.

To prepare yourself for this challenge, consider the information provided in this chapter about the diverse characteristics and needs of elementary schoolchildren—because it is well known that for them, their academic achievement is greatly dependent on how well their other developmental needs are understood and satisfied.

CHAPTER OBJECTIVES

On the completion of this second chapter, you should be able to:

1. Explain one or more examples of children's diversity and their learning modalities, learning styles, and learning capacities (multiple intelligences).
2. Explain the importance of multicultural education and providing for student differences.
3. Give one or more examples of developmental characteristics of children in different age

groups, some implications for instruction, and how positive character development could impact the classroom.

4. Give examples of working with special needs students, that is, English language learners, gifted students, children who take more time but are willing to try, recalcitrant learners, and abused children, and identify one or more key characteristics of productive teaching for them.

5. Generate thoughts about the grade or age level at which you might prefer to teach.

DIMENSIONS OF THE CHALLENGE

At any age, children differ in many ways: physical characteristics, interests, home life, intellectual ability, learning capacities, motor ability, social skills, aptitudes and talents, language skills, experience, ideals, attitudes, needs, ambitions, hopes, and dreams. Having long recognized the importance of these individual differences, educators have made many attempts to develop systematic programs of individualized, differentiated, and personalized instruction. For instance, in the 1920s, teachers used the programmed workbooks of the Winetka Plan. The 1960s brought a multitude of plans, such as IPI (Individually Prescribed Instruction), IGE (Individually Guided Education), and PLAN (Program for Learning in Accordance with Needs). Later, the 1970s saw the development and growth in popularity of individual learning packages and the individualized education program (IEP) for students with special needs. Although some of these efforts did not survive the test of time, others met with more success; some have been refined and are still being used. Today, for example, some schools report success using personalized learning plans and differentiated instruction for all students, not only those with specific needs.[1]

Personalized learning reflects the point of view that all persons learn in their own ways and at individual rates and are influenced by learning styles and learning capacities, modality preferences, information-processing habits, motivational factors, and physiological factors. Also, interests, background, innate and acquired abilities, and a myriad of other influences shape how and what a person will learn. From any particular learning experience, no two people ever learn exactly the same thing. Within the concept of personalized learning, however, is the teacher's insight in selecting developmentally appropriate strategies and adjusting instruction accordingly to meet the needs of individual students. This selection of adjusting strategies and instruction is referred to as **differentiated** or **tiered instruction.**

The Classroom in a Nation of Diversity

Central to the challenge of adjusting instruction to the individual is the concept of multicultural education, the recognition and acceptance of students from a variety of backgrounds. The goal of this concept is to provide schooling so that all children—male and female students, students with special needs, and students who are members of diverse racial, ethnic, and cultural groups—have equal opportunity to achieve academically. In the words of James A. Banks,

> Schools should be model communities that mirror the kind of democratic society we envision. In democratic schools, the curriculum reflects the cultures of the diverse groups within society, the languages and dialects that students speak are respected and valued, cooperation rather than competition is fostered among students and students from diverse racial, ethnic and social-class groups are given equal status in the school.[2]

The variety of individual differences among students requires that teachers use teaching strategies and tactics that accommodate those differences. To most effectively teach a diverse group of students, you need the skills shown in Figure 2.1. The last two topics are discussed in this chapter.

To help you meet the challenge, a wealth of information is available. As a licensed teacher, you are expected to know it all—or at least to know where you can find the necessary information and to review it when needed. Certain information you have stored in memory will surface and become useful at the most unexpected times. While concerned about all students' safety and physical well-being, you will want to remain sensitive to each child's attitudes, values, social adjustment, emotional well-being, and intellectual development. You must be prepared not only to teach one or more subjects but also to do it effectively with children of different cultural backgrounds, diverse linguistic abilities, and different learning styles, as well as with students who have been identified as having special needs because of handicapping conditions. It is, indeed, a challenge! The statements that follow make this challenge even more clear:

• The United States has an increasing ethnic, cultural, and linguistic diversity that is affecting schools all across the country, not only in the large urban areas but also in suburbs and small rural communities.

• The United States truly is a multilingual, multiethnic, multicultural nation. Of children ages 5 to 7, approximately one out of every six speaks a lan-

Figure 2.1
Effective teaching in a
diverse classroom

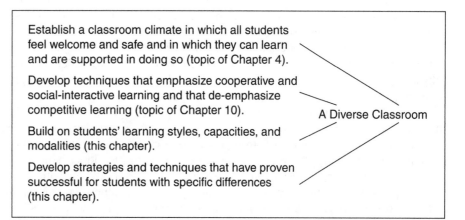

Establish a classroom climate in which all students feel welcome and safe and in which they can learn and are supported in doing so (topic of Chapter 4).

Develop techniques that emphasize cooperative and social-interactive learning and that de-emphasize competitive learning (topic of Chapter 10).

Build on students' learning styles, capacities, and modalities (this chapter).

Develop strategies and techniques that have proven successful for students with specific differences (this chapter).

A Diverse Classroom

guage other than English at home. Many of those children have only limited proficiency in the English language (i.e., conversational speaking ability only).

- In many large school districts, as many as 100 languages are represented with as many as 20 or more different primary languages found in some classrooms.
- The traditional two-parent, two-child family now constitutes only about 6% of U.S. households. Approximately one half of the children in the United States will spend some years being raised by a single parent. Many children go home after school to places devoid of any adult supervision. And, on any given day, tens of thousands of children are homeless, that is, they have no place at all to call home.
- By the middle of this century, the nation's population is predicted to reach 383 million (from 2000's approximately 282 million), a population boom that will be led by Latinos and Asian Americans.
- Also by midcentury, minority youths in the school-age population throughout the United States will average close to 40%; a steady increase in interracial marriages and interracial babies may challenge the traditional conceptions of multiculturalism and race.[3]

The overall picture that emerges is that of a rapidly changing, diverse student population that challenges teaching skills. Teachers who traditionally have used direct instruction (see Chapter 7) as the dominant mode of instruction have done so with the assumption that their students were relatively homogeneous in terms of experience, background, knowledge, motivation, and facility with the English language. However, no such assumption can be made today. As a classroom teacher for the 21st century, you must be knowledgeable and skilled in using teaching strategies that recognize, celebrate, and build on the cultural, ethnic, and linguistic diversity of the classroom,

the community, and the nation. The emerging picture of education you face is your challenge.

SUPPORTING THE CHALLENGE: LEARNING MODALITIES, LEARNING STYLES, LEARNING CAPACITIES, AND IMPLICATIONS FOR TEACHING

Classroom teachers who are most effective are those who adapt their teaching styles and methods to their students, using approaches that interest the children, that are neither too easy nor too difficult, that match the students' learning styles and learning capacities, and that are relevant to the children's lives. This adaptation process is further complicated because each child is different from every other one. All do not have the same interests, abilities, backgrounds, or learning styles and capacities. As a matter of fact, not only do children differ from one another, but each child also can change to some extent from one day to the next. What appeals to a child today may not have the same appeal tomorrow.

Therefore, as the teacher, you need to consider both the nature of children in general (for example, methods appropriate for a particular group of children in kindergarten are unlikely to be the same as those that work best for a group of sixth graders) and each child in particular. As a student of a teacher preparation program, you probably have already experienced a recent course in the psychology of learning; what follows is merely a brief synopsis of knowledge about today's teaching and learning and its relevancy.

Learning Modalities

The phrase **learning modality** refers to the *sensory portal* (or input channel) by which a person prefers to receive sensory reception (modality preference), or the actual way a person learns best (modality adeptness).

Some children prefer learning by seeing (a *visual modality*); others prefer learning through instruction from others (through dialogue), an *auditory modality;* whereas still others prefer learning by doing and being physically involved, the *kinesthetic modality,* and by touching objects or using manipulatives, the *tactile modality.* A person's modality preference is not always that person's modality strength.

Although primary modality strength can be determined by observing children, it can also be mixed and it can change as the result of experience and intellectual maturity. The way a child learned best when in the first grade, for example, is not necessarily the child's modality strength now that the same child is in the fourth grade. As one might suspect, modality integration (i.e., engaging more of the sensory input channels, using several modalities at once or staggered) has been found to contribute to better achievement in student learning. We return to this concept in Part II of this resource guide.

Because many children have neither a preference nor a strength for auditory reception, elementary schoolteachers should severely limit their use of the lecture method of instruction, that is, of placing too much reliance on formal teacher talk (discussed in Chapter 8). Furthermore, instruction that uses a singular approach, such as auditory (e.g., talking to students), deprives students who learn better another way—the kinesthetic and visual learners. If a teacher's verbal communication conflicts with the teacher's nonverbal messages, children can become confused, and this, too, can affect their learning. And when there is a discrepancy between what the teacher says and what that teacher does, the teacher's nonverbal signal will send the strongest message every time. Actions do speak louder than words![4] For example, a teacher who has just finished a lesson on the conservation of energy and does not turn off the room lights on leaving the classroom for lunch has, by inappropriate modeling behavior, created cognitive dissonance (disequilibrium) and sabotaged the real purpose for the lesson. For another example, cognitive dissonance (disequilibrium) is created by a teacher who asks children not to interrupt others when they are on task but who repeatedly interrupts children when they are on task. The teacher's contradictory words and behavior confuse children. A teacher's job is not that of confusing children.

As a general rule, most elementary school students prefer and learn best by touching objects, by feeling shapes and textures, by interacting with each other, and by moving things around. In contrast, learning by sitting and listening is difficult for many of them.

Learning modality traits are known that significantly discriminate between students who are underachieving and at risk of not finishing school (discussed in Chapter 1) and students who perform well. Students who are underachieving and at risk need (a) frequent opportunities for mobility; (b) options and choices; (c) a variety of instructional resources, environments, and sociological groupings; (d) learning opportunities during late morning and afternoon, rather than in the early morning; (e) informal seating rather than wooden, steel, or plastic chairs; (f) low illumination; and (g) tactile/visual introductory resources reinforced by kinesthetic (e.g., direct experiences and whole-body activities)/visual resources, or introductory kinesthetic/visual resources reinforced by tactile/visual resources.[5]

As an example, at one problem school, after discovering that nearly two thirds of its students were either tactile or kinesthetic learners, teachers and administrators grouped the students according to their modality strengths and altered the reading instruction schedules every 3 weeks so that each group of students had opportunities to learn at the best time of day. As a result, student behavior, learning achievement, and attitudes improved considerably.[6]

Regardless of grade level and subject(s) you intend to teach, you are advised to use strategies that integrate the modalities. Well-designed, thematic units (discussed in Chapter 7) and project-based learning incorporate modality integration.

In conclusion, when teaching any group of students of mixed learning abilities, mixed modality strengths, mixed language proficiency, and mixed cultural backgrounds, for the most successful teaching the integration of learning modalities is a must.

Learning Styles

Related to learning modality is **learning style,** which can be defined as independent forms of knowing and processing information. Although some elementary schoolchildren may be comfortable with beginning their learning of a new idea in the abstract form (e.g., visual or verbal symbolization), most need to begin with the concrete approach (e.g., learning by actually doing it and using manipulatives as shown by the Learning Experiences Ladder later in this text). Many students prosper while working in groups, whereas others do not and prefer to work alone. Some are quick in their studies, whereas others are slow and methodical and cautious and meticulous. Some can sustain attention on a single topic for a long time, becoming more absorbed in their study as time passes. Others are slower starters and more casual in their pursuits, but are capable of shifting with ease from topic to topic and from subject to subject. Some can study in the midst of music, noise, or movement, whereas others need quiet, solitude, and a desk or table.

The point is this: Learners vary not only in their skills and preferences in the way knowledge is received, but also in how they mentally process that information once it has been received. The latter is a person's style of learning. Learning style is not an indicator of intelligence, but rather an indicator of how a person learns.

Classifications of Learning Styles

Although there are probably as many types of learning styles as there are individuals, two major differences in how people learn are in how they perceive situations and how they process information.[7] On the basis of perceiving and processing and earlier work by Carl Jung on psychological types,[8] Bernice McCarthy identifies four major learning styles, as presented next:[9]

1. The *analytic learner* perceives information abstractly and processes it reflectively. The analytic learner prefers sequential things, needs details, and values what experts have to offer. Analytic learners do well in traditional classrooms.

2. The *commonsense learner* perceives information abstractly and processes it actively. Commonsense learners are pragmatic and enjoy hands-on learning. They sometimes find school frustrating unless they can see an immediate use for what is being learned. In the traditional classroom, the commonsense learner is likely to be a learner who is at risk of not completing school, of dropping out.

3. The *dynamic learner* perceives information concretely and processes it actively. Dynamic learners also prefer hands-on learning and are excited by anything new. They are risk takers and are frustrated by learning if they see it as being tedious. In a traditional classroom, the dynamic learner also is likely to be an at-risk student.

4. The *imaginative learner* perceives information concretely and processes it reflectively. Imaginative learners learn well by listening and sharing with others, by integrating the ideas of others with their own experiences. They often have difficulty adjusting to traditional teaching, which depends on classroom interactions and students' sharing and connecting of their prior experiences. In a traditional classroom, the imaginative learner is likely to be an at-risk student.

The Three-Phase Learning Cycle

To understand conceptual development and change, researchers in the 1960s developed a Piaget-based theory of learning in which students are guided from concrete, hands-on learning experiences to the ab-

stract formulations of concepts and their formal applications. Their theory became known as the *three-phase learning cycle.*[10] Long a popular strategy for teaching science, the learning cycle can be useful in language arts and other disciplines as well.[11]

The three phases of the learning cycle are as follows:

1. The *exploratory hands-on phase,* in which students can explore ideas and experience assimilation and disequilibrium that lead to their own questions and tentative answers.

2. The *invention* or *concept development phase,* in which, under the guidance of the teacher, students invent concepts and principles that help them answer their questions and reorganize their ideas; that is, the students revise their thinking to allow the new information to fit.

3. The *expansion* or *concept application phase,* another hands-on phase in which the students try out their new ideas by applying them to situations that are relevant and meaningful to them. During application of a concept, the learner may discover new information that causes a change in the learner's understanding of the concept being applied. Thus, as discussed further in Chapter 9, the process of learning is cyclical.[12]

More recent interpretations or modifications of the three-phase cycle include McCarthy's 4MAT.[13] With the 4MAT system, teachers employ a learning cycle of instructional strategies to try and teach to each student's learning style. As stated by McCarthy, in the cycle, learners

> sense and feel, they experience, then they watch, they reflect, then they think, they develop theories, then they try out theories, they experiment. Finally, they evaluate and synthesize what they have learned in order to apply it to their next similar experience. They get smarter. They apply experience to experiences.[14]

And, during this process, they are likely to be using all four learning modalities.

The *constructivist learning theory* suggests that learning is a process involving the active engagement of learners who adapt the educative event to fit and expand their individual world view (as opposed to the behaviorist pedagogical assumption that learning is something done *to* learners)[15] and to accentuate the importance of student self-assessment. In support of that theory, some variations of the learning cycle include a fourth phase of assessment. However, because we believe that assessment of what students know or think they know should be a continual process, permeating all three phases of the learning cycle, we reject any treatment of assessment as a self-standing phase.

Learning Capacities: The Theory of Multiple Intelligences

In contrast to the concept of learning styles, Gardner introduced what he calls *learning capacities* exhibited by individuals in differing ways.[16] Originally (and sometimes still), referred to as *multiple intelligences,* or ways of knowing, capacities thus far identified are:

- **Bodily/kinesthetic.** Ability to control and maneuver one's body in such events as athletics, dance, and drama
- **Interpersonal.** Ability to understand people and relationships
- **Intrapersonal.** Ability to assess one's emotional life as a means to understand oneself and others
- **Logical/mathematical.** Ability to handle chains of reasoning and to recognize patterns and orders, to work with numbers
- **Musical.** Ability to perceive pitch, rhythm, sounds, tones, and variations of these; the ability to sing or play a musical instrument
- **Naturalist.** Ability to draw on materials and features of the natural environment to solve problems or fashion products
- **Verbal/linguistic.** Ability to learn and recognize distinctions among words, sounds, and language
- **Visual/spatial.** Ability to perceive images and to manipulate the nature of space, such as through architecture, mime, or sculpture.

As discussed earlier, and as implied in the earlier presentation of McCarthy's four types of learners, many educators believe that many students who are at risk of not completing school are those who may be dominant in a cognitive learning style that is not in sync with traditional teaching methods. Traditional methods are largely of McCarthy's analytic style: Information is presented in a logical, linear, sequential fashion. Traditional methods also reflect three of the Gardner types: verbal/linguistics, logical/ mathematical, and intrapersonal. Consequently, to better synchronize methods of instruction with learning styles, some teachers and schools, such as Essex Modern Languages Elementary Magnet School (Akron, Ohio), have restructured the curriculum, instruction, and assessment around Gardner's learning capacities[17] or around Sternberg's triarchic theory.[18] Sternberg identifies six metaphors for the mind and intelligence (anthropological, biological, computation, epistemological, sociological, and systems) and proposes a theory of intelligence consisting of three elements: analytical, creative, and practical.[19]

The classroom vignette in the *Looking at Teachers* section at the beginning of this chapter shows one way to put the theory of multiple intelligences and multilevel instruction into practice in a classroom.

Also, sources on learning style assessment are given in the accompanying *Technology Tips for the Classroom* feature.

From the preceding information about learning styles you must realize at least two facts:

1. **Intelligence is not a fixed or static reality, but can be learned, taught, and developed.** Both you and your students must understand that intelligence is not a fixed entity, but a set of characteristics that, through a feeling of "I can" and with proper coaching, can be developed. When children understand that intelligence is incremental, something that is developed through use over time, they tend to be more motivated to work at learning than when they believe intelligence is a fixed entity.[20]
2. **Not all children learn and respond to learning situations in the same way.** A child may learn differently according to the situation or according to the child's ethnicity, cultural background, or socioeconomic status.[21] A teacher who, for all students, uses only one style of teaching, or who teaches to only one or a few styles of learning, day after day, is shortchanging those students who learn better another way. As emphasized by Rita Dunn, when children do not learn the way we teach them, then we must teach them the way they learn.[22]

MEETING THE CHALLENGE: RECOGNIZING AND PROVIDING FOR STUDENT DIFFERENCES

As a part of the expectations, responsibilities, and facilitating behaviors of an elementary schoolteacher, what measures could be taken to improve learning assistance for children in your classroom who will need special support in their educational activities? One of your concerns related to this may be a realization that your district may not have all of the funds needed to purchase special technology for the students and another may be to determine ways to provide those students, in the best way that you can, with some ability and instruction to seek and retrieve information. In some areas, there might be an adaptive center for special needs students in your school or district or a special education resource teacher that you can meet with to discuss your concerns.

Interest in improving learning assistance for special needs students was a focus of the 1997 President's Committee of Advisors on Science and Technology on the Use of Technology to Strengthen K–12 Education in the United States. This committee recommended that special attention be given to the use of technology by students who have special needs. In support of this interest, you may first want to review some of the information about available assistive technologies for special needs students by reading a current source on technologies for adaptive assistance that has been recommended to you or by reading *Adaptive Technology for the Internet: Making Electronic Resources Accessible to All* by Barbara Mates.[23] Second, you may want to assist your students in becoming productive members of the learning process regardless of their special needs or impediments by finding lessons and activities in the special education section (with downloads of freeware) through one of your favorite sites or through the Education World website at *http://educationworld.com/a_curr/curr139.shtml.* Third, you may want to become familiar with some of the current technology. Related to current technology, here are some additional resources to review or discuss with a special education resource teacher in your district:

- To provide learning services to students who are deaf or hearing impaired, consider a program that translates text into American Sign Language characters on a computer screen that the resource teacher recommends or a program called *Signing Avatar.*
- To assist students who are challenged physically, you may want to become familiar with a multisensory approach to reading similar to the *Kurzweill Scan and Read* program. To do this, research any zoom text-screen magnification program, any screen reader for the blind that is designed to read the web, any keyboard with large print and raised keys, and the use of track balls, joysticks, and voice recognition computers.
- For students with visual impairments, investigate the value of *pwWebSpeak,* a web browser for those who want to access the Internet in a nonvisual or combined auditory/visual way, and the value of a speech output system interfaced with a screen reader and a Braille display.

From research and practical experience have come a variety of instructional techniques that make a difference. First consider the following general guidelines, most of which are discussed in further detail in later chapters in this text.

Companion Website

To find links to resources about learning styles and the use of technology in the classroom, go to our Companion Website at **www.prenhall.com/roberts** and click on the *Web Destinations* module for Chapter 2.

Technology Tips for the Classroom

- Keep informed about the plan that the U.S. Department of Education is advocating for teaching technology in America's schools. It is called the National Education Technology Plan and will emphasize the requirements of the No Child Left Behind Act. It will also take advantage of the use of the Internet, identify sites that link to problems that teachers are facing, and provide learning opportunities that students can use. To keep informed, visit www.nationaledtechplan.org/
- The National Education Technology Plan also ensures that technology is being used effectively in the schools, looks at models in which education can be more customized and personalized for students, and makes laptops more affordable for schools. Further, the plan will identify ways in which technology can be integrated further into the curriculum, will support the purchase of assistive technologies for students with disabilities, and will encourage use of distance learning and virtual schools. There also is a focus on data-driven decision making, accountability, and professional development.

Instructional Practices That Provide for Student Differences: General Guidelines

To provide learning experiences that are consistent with what is known about ways of learning and knowing, consider the recommendations that follow and refer to them during the planning or preactive phase of your instruction:

- As frequently as is appropriate, and especially for skills development, plan the learning activities so they follow a step-by-step sequence from concrete to abstract.
- Collaboratively plan with students challenging and engaging classroom learning activities and assignments.
- Concentrate on using student-centered instruction by using project-centered learning, discover and inquiry strategies, simulations, and role playing.
- Maintain high, but not necessarily identical expectations for every student; establish high standards and teach toward them without wavering.
- Make learning meaningful by integrating learning with life, helping each child successfully make the transitions from one level of learning to the next and from one level of schooling to the next.

- Provide a structured learning environment with regular and understood procedures.
- Provide ongoing and frequent monitoring of individual student learning.
- Provide variations in meaningful assignments that are based on individual student abilities and interests.
- Use explicit instruction to teach the development of skills for thinking and learning.
- Use reciprocal peer coaching and cross-age tutoring.
- Use multilevel instruction.
- Use interactive computer programs and multimedia.
- Use small-group and cooperative learning strategies.

Developmental Characteristics of Children of Particular Age Groups

After many years of experience and research, specialists have come to accept certain precepts about children of particular ages, regardless of their individual genetic or cultural differences. Before going further, turn to our Companion Website supporting this chapter at **www.prenhall.com/roberts** on the *Additional Content* module for more information about children's developmental characteristics.[24–25] Then, return to this resource guide to begin Application Exercises 2.1 and 2.2.

APPLICATION EXERCISE 2.1 OBTAINING PERSONAL INSIGHT REGARDING THE AGE OR GRADE LEVEL THAT I MIGHT PREFER TO TEACH

Instructions: Because of the age and developmental diversity of children in grades K–6, the purpose of this exercise is to challenge you to begin thinking about the grade or age level at which you might prefer to teach. However, we realize that the best way to fairly decide on an optimum grade level is to actually experience teaching it. Though a grade level may look challenging on paper in this exercise, we want to point out that the grade level may actually be a good classroom experience for you.

1. Print the list of developmental characteristics from the *Additional Content* module on our Companion Website at **www.prenhall.com/roberts.** As you read through it, after each numbered item mark a plus or a minus sign, depending on the extent to which that item matters to you, where a plus (+) means it matters a lot and a minus (–) means it does not matter to you.

2. After reading and marking all items with either a plus or a minus, for each category identify the percentage of minus signs for the category. Complete the calculations as follows: Dividing the number of plus signs that you gave for these items by the total number provides the percentage of plus signs given for that category. Subtracting that percentage number from 100 provides the percentage of minus signs for the category. Continue for each of the other two categories, ages 7–8, and ages 9–14. Place the percentages in the blanks:

   Ages 5–6 percentage plus signs = _____

   Ages 7–8 percentage plus signs = _____

   Ages 9–14 percentage plus signs = _____

3. The category that received your highest percentage of plus signs is ages _____.
   Would you concur that you have a preference toward teaching at this level? Yes or no? (circle one) Explain why or why not.

4. Compare and discuss your results for this exercise with those of your classmates. What generalizations, if any, can be made from your individual results and collective discussion?

For Your Notes

✎ APPLICATION EXERCISE 2.2 CONVERSATION WITH A CLASSROOM TEACHER

Instructions: The purpose of this exercise is to interview one or more elementary schoolteachers, perhaps one who is relatively new to the classroom and one who has been teaching for 10 years or more, to identify one or more characteristics of productive teaching. Use the following questions. You may duplicate blank copies of this form. Share the results with others in your class.

1. Name and location of school _____

   _____

2. Grade span of school _____

3. Date of interview _____

4. Name and grade level (and/or subject) of interviewee _____

   _____

5. In which area(s) of the school's curriculum do you work?_____

   _____

6. Why did you select teaching as a career? _____

   _____

   _____

   _____

7. Why are you teaching at this grade level? _____

   _____

   _____

   _____

8. What preparation or training did you have? _____

   _____

   _____

   _____

   _____

9. What advice about preparation can you offer? _____

   _____

   _____

   _____

   _____

   _____

   _____

10. What do you like most about teaching? _____

   _____

   _____

   _____

APPLICATION EXERCISE 2.2 *(continued)*

11. What do you like least about teaching? _____

_____

_____

_____

12. What is the most important thing to know to be an effective classroom teacher (i.e., what is the key characteristic of productive teaching)? _____

_____

_____

_____

13. What other specific advice do you have for those of us entering teaching at this level?

_____

_____

_____

_____

_____

_____

_____

_____

_____

_____

_____

_____

_____

_____

_____

_____

_____

_____

_____

_____

_____

Recognizing and Working with Students with Special Needs

Special needs students (also referred to as **exceptional students** and *students with disabilities*) include those with disabling conditions or impairments in any one or more of the following categories: autism, emotional, hearing, language or speech, mental retardation, orthopedic, traumatic brain injury, visual, other health impairment, or specific learning disabilities. To the extent possible, students with disabilities must be educated with their peers in the regular classroom. Public Law 94-142, the Education for All Handicapped Children Act of 1975, mandates that all children have the right to a free and appropriate education and to nondiscriminatory assessment. Recent amendments to this act include a name change to Individuals with Disabilities Education Act (IDEA, PL 101-476, 1990), and normalizing of the educational environment for students with disabilities that requires provision for the *least restrictive environment* that is as normal as possible for these students (PL 105-17, 1997).

Students identified as having special needs may be placed in the regular classroom for the entire school day, called **full inclusion** (as is the trend).[27] Those students may also be in a regular classroom for the greater part of the school day, called *partial inclusion,* or only for designated periods. While there is no single, universally accepted definition of the term, *inclusion* is the concept that students with special needs should be integrated into general education classrooms regardless of the extent to which they can meet traditional academic standards.[28] The term **inclusion** has largely replaced the use of an earlier and similar term, **mainstreaming.** As a classroom teacher, you will need information and skills specific to teaching learners with special needs in your classroom.

Generally speaking, teaching students who have special needs requires more care, better diagnosis, greater skills, more attention to individual needs, and an even greater understanding of the students. The challenges of teaching students with special needs in the regular classroom are great enough that to do it well, you will need specialized education beyond the general guidelines presented here. At some point in your teacher preparation, you should take one or more courses in working with the learner with disabling conditions who is included in the regular classroom.

When a child with special needs is placed in your classroom, your task is to deal directly with the differences between this student and other students in your classroom. To do this, you should develop an understanding of the general characteristics of different types of special needs learners, identify the child's

Figure 2.2

Multiple pathways to success: Productive ways of attending to student differences, of providing a more challenging learning environment, and of stimulating the talents and motivation of each learner

- Adult advocacy relationships for every student
- Allowing a student to skip a traditional grade level, thereby accelerating a student's passage through the grades
- Cooperative learning activities
- Curriculum compacting
- Extra efforts to provide academic and personal help
- High expectations for all students
- Individualized educational programs and instruction
- Integrating modern technologies into the curriculum
- Interdisciplinary learning and thematic instruction
- Looping
- Low (no higher than 17:1) teacher–student ratio
- Multiage grouping and midyear promotions
- Multidisciplinary, student-centered, project-based learning
- Peer and cross-age teaching
- Problem-centered learning
- Second opportunity recovery strategies
- Service learning
- Specialized schools and nontraditional schedules

unique needs relative to your classroom, and design lessons that teach to different needs at the same time, called **multilevel instruction,** or **multitasking,** as exemplified in the chapter's opening vignette and in Figure 2.2.[29] Remember that just because a student has been identified as having one or more special needs does not preclude that person from being gifted or talented.

Congress stipulated in PL 94-142 that an individualized education program (IEP) be devised annually for each special needs child. According to that law, an IEP is developed for each student each year by a team that includes special education teachers, the child's parents or guardians, and the regular education classroom teachers. The IEP contains a statement of the student's present educational levels, the educational goals for the year, specifications for the services to be provided, the extent to which the student should be expected to take part in the regular education program, and the evaluative criteria for the services to be provided. Consultation by special and skilled support personnel is essential in all IEP models. A consultant works directly with teachers or with students and parents or guardians. As a regular education teacher, you may play an active role in preparing the specifications for the special needs students assigned to your classroom, as well as have a major responsibility for implementing the program.

Although the guidelines given in Table 2.1 are important for teaching all students, they are especially important for working with special needs students.

The trend today is to provide sufficient curriculum options, or multiple pathways, so each student can reach his or her potential. Because the advantage gained from using a combination of responsive practices concurrently is seemingly greater than is the gain from using any single practice by itself, in many instances in a given school, the practices overlap and are used simultaneously. These practices are shown in Figure 2.1 and are discussed in numerous places in this text. Please check the index for topic locations.

Companion Website

To broaden your knowledge base about the developmental characteristics of children of particular age groups and about teaching diverse types of students, go to our Companion Website at **www.prenhall.com/roberts** and click on the *Additional Content* module for Chapter 2.

Table 2.1
Basic guidelines for special needs students

Although guidelines represented by the information that follows are important for teaching all students, they are especially important for working with special needs students.

1. Familiarize yourself with exactly what the special needs of each learner are. Privately ask the special needs learner whether there is anything the student would like for you to know and what you can specifically do to facilitate the student's learning while in your classroom.

2. Adapt and modify materials and procedures to the special needs of each student. For example, a child who has extreme difficulty sitting still for more than a few minutes will need planned changes in learning activities. When establishing student-seating arrangements in the classroom, give consideration to students according to their special needs.

3. Try to incorporate into lessons activities that engage all learning modalities: visual, auditory, tactile, and kinesthetic. For the visual approach, a child can tell a story while the teacher writes down the words and says them (auditory). This writing later serves as the material the child learns to read. Next, the child repeats a word (auditory) and, finally, the child traces the word (kinesthetic and tactual). Also try simple and straightforward teaching techniques such as these: For prereading each paragraph, read aloud questions about the main ideas in the paragraph to the students, provide students with printed copies of the questions and the paragraph that the students are reading, and discuss what the students can recall about the ideas.

4. Provide high structure and clear expectations by defining the learning objectives in behavioral terms. Teach children the correct procedures for everything. Break complex learning into simpler components, moving from the most concrete to the abstract, rather than the other way around. Check frequently for student understanding of instructions and procedures and for skill development and the comprehension of content.

5. Use computers and other self-correcting materials for practice and for provision of immediate and private feedback to the student.

6. Develop your with-itness, steadily monitoring children for signs of restlessness, frustration, anxiety, and off-task behaviors. Be ready to reassign individual learners to different activities as the situation warrants. Established classroom learning centers can be a big help.

7. Have all students maintain assignments for a week or some other period of time in an assignment book or in a folder that is kept in their notebooks. Post assignments in a special place in the classroom and frequently remind the students of assignments and deadlines. One assignment might be to have students ask themselves the prereading question "What am I reading and studying this paragraph for?" Then have the students find the main idea in the paragraph and underline it. Next, have each student think of a question about the main idea and write it. Individually, or as a group, look back at the questions and answers and talk about how this information provides the students with more information.

Table 2.1

Basic guidelines for special needs students *(continued)*

8. Maintain consistency in your expectations and in your responses. Special needs students, in particular, can become frustrated when they do not understand a teacher's expectations and when they cannot depend on a teacher's reactions.

9. Plan an interesting variety of activities to bridge learning, activities that help the children connect what is being learned with their world. Learning the connection of what is being learned with the real world helps motivate students and keeps them on task.

10. Plan questions and questioning sequences and write them into your lesson plans. Plan questions that you will ask the special needs students so that they are most likely to answer them with confidence. Use signals to let students know that you are likely to call on them in class (e.g., prolonged eye contact or mentioning your intention to the student before class begins). After asking a question, give the student adequate time to think and respond. Then, after the student responds, build on the student's response to indicate that the child's contribution was accepted as being important.

11. Provide for and teach toward student success. Provide activities and experiences that ensure each student's success and mastery at some level. Use of student portfolios can give evidence of progress and help build student confidence and self-esteem.

12. Provide time in class for children to work on assignments (responsibility papers) and projects. During this time, you can monitor the work of each child while looking for misconceptions and misunderstandings, thus ensuring that students get started on the right track.

13. Provide help in the organization of student learning. For example, give instruction in the organization of notes and notebooks. Have a three-hole punch available in the classroom so students can put papers into their notebooks immediately, thus avoiding disorganization and loss of papers. During class presentations, use an overhead projector with transparencies; students who need more time can then copy material from the transparencies. Ask students to read their notes aloud to each other in small groups, thereby aiding their recall and understanding and encouraging them to take notes for meaning rather than for rote learning. Encourage and provide for peer support, peer tutoring or coaching, and cross-age teaching. Ensure that the special needs learner is included in all class activities to the fullest extent possible.[30]

14. Use collaborative and cooperative learning,[31] and select specially designed programs for English language learners;[32] consider language and cultural differences,[33] and use simplified vocabulary;[34] introduce response journals for students to record their responses to what they are reading and studying;[35] and work toward being parent friendly, that is, welcome parents and guardians in a variety of innovative ways.[36]

15. Communicate with all parents in a positive manner. For instance, terminology and information can be shared when appropriate: A child with exceptional ability in one or more of the visual or performing arts is termed *talented*;[37] *gifted* students are often unrecognized[38] and are sometimes at risk of dropping out of school;[39] it is estimated that between 10% and 20% of school dropouts are intelligent students who are in the range of being gifted.[40] A list of indicators of superior intelligence ranges from ability to extrapolate knowledge to a different circumstance to resiliency to understanding one's cultural heritage.[41] Gifted students can have problems such as low self-esteem and being indifferent, hostile, and critical of themselves.[42] When possible, provide multiple pathways (options such as curriculum compacting) so achievement increases and students learn more because individual learning capacities, styles, and modalities are identified and accommodated.[43, 44]

16. You are legally mandated to report any suspicion of child abuse, a grave matter of pressing national concern. Some characteristics of children who are abused or neglected are sudden changes in behavior, crying, unexplained lacerations and bruises, and withdrawal from adult content and peer interaction.[45]

17. Consider character education as part of the district's developing curricula with the goal of developing "mature adults capable of responsible citizenship and moral actions."[46, 47] A specific aspect of the curriculum might include having the students do research and present a particular stance on a controversial issue.[48]

About Praxis and Other Teacher Tests

About Praxis Teacher Tests. We want to point out that this resource guide is compatible with the Praxis II Principles of Learning and Teaching tests, i.e., Elementary Education: Content Area Exercises Assessment (which has constructed response-type questions) and Elementary Education: Curriculum, Instruction, and Assessment (which has multiple-choice response-type questions). Of further interest, the inside back cover of this text presents a matrix of the connections between the Praxis II Assessment Tests for elementary teaching and learning, and the content in this text.

To continue to support your interest in preparing for the Praxis II Principles of Learning and Teaching tests and some of the other teacher tests, all application exercises in this chapter offer opportunities for you to reflect generally on elementary schoolchildren. Specifically, you are asked to participate cooperatively and collaboratively and to do the following:

- Begin thinking about the grade level and age of students that you might wish to teach (Application Exercise 2.1).
- Meet and interview a teacher who can share his or her experience (Application Exercise 2.2).
- Turn to our Companion Website (**www.prenhall.com/roberts**) and click on the *Additional Application Exercise* module to complete an additional application exercise, namely, Obtaining Personal Insight Regarding Whole-Part Content for the Grade I want to Teach.

In this exercise, you are asked to look at a reading text or other student text, a teacher's edition, or curriculum overview for the age or grade level that you think you might like to teach and to identify a unit of study so you can then determine how the unit of study is divided into parts.

If you want to respond to a constructed response-type question similar to those found on the Praxis II Elementary Education tests, turn to the Praxis Warm-Up in the end-of-chapter material. This warm-up takes another look at the classroom vignette found in the Looking at Teachers section at the beginning of this chapter.

 Other Teacher Tests. For those of you who will be teaching in states that do not administer the Praxis II Principles of Learning and Teaching tests, go to our Companion Website at **www.prenhall. com/roberts** and click on the *Other Teacher Tests* module for Chapter 2 to access information about teacher tests other than the Praxis.

SUMMARY

As a classroom teacher, you must acknowledge that the students in your classroom have different ways of receiving information and different ways of processing that information—different ways of knowing and of constructing their knowledge. These differences are unique and important and, as you will learn in Part II of this text, are central considerations in curriculum development, instructional practice, and the assessment of learning.

You should try to learn as much as you can about how each student learns and processes information. But because you can never know everything about each student, the more you dialogue with members of the child's family and your colleagues, vary your teaching strategies, and assist students in integrating their learning, the more likely you are to reach more of the students more of the time.

What's to Come. In short, the chapters to come will help you be an effective elementary school classroom teacher. You should (a) learn as much about your stu-

dents and their preferred styles of learning as you can; (b) develop an eclectic style of teaching, one that is flexible and adaptable; and (c) integrate the disciplines, thereby helping children make bridges or connections between their lives and all that is being learned.

EXTENDING MY PROFESSIONAL COMPETENCY

Praxis Warm-Up: A Constructed Response-Type Question

Given the diverse nature of elementary learners, teachers often ask "What can be done to put the theory of multiple intelligence and multilevel instruction (a theory discussed further in this chapter), into practice?" To respond to this question, you'll recall from the vignette at the beginning of the chapter what one fourth-grade teacher did: The teacher divided the class into several groups of three to five students per group and the groups worked on six projects simultaneously to learn about the water cycle. The teacher's objective for one group was to have them design and prepare graphs to illustrate the results of the experiments of another group, but then the teacher discovered that some of the students in the group did not know how to design and prepare a graph. The teacher realized that the other fourth-grade students knew graphs very well and would probably be bored by a lesson in which she retaught basic graphing.

Describe two different activities that would help the students who need help in designing and preparing graphs. The activities should be ones to help the students understand the concept of graphs as well as the usefulness of graphs to relate facts in a concise form. Give examples of what the students should be able to do during the activities you select, and justify your selection of activities by explaining what is known about how students of this age learn.

Hints for responding to Praxis Warm-Ups are found in the Appendix.

Praxis. To do another Praxis Warm-Up with a constructed response-type question, go to our Companion Website at **www.prenhall.com/roberts** and click on the *Praxis Warm-Up* module for Chapter 2. Constructed response-type questions are designed to help you prepare for the Praxis II Principles of Learning and Teaching tests.

For Your Discussion

1. **Classroom Management.** How would I describe what a teacher should plan to do as a result of learning style information about his or her students? **To do:** Here is a class scenario to respond to: Brian, a social studies teacher, has a class of 33 sixth graders who during his expository teaching (lecture, teacher-led discussion, and recitation lessons) are restless and inattentive, which results in classroom management problems. At Brian's invitation, the school psychologist tests the students for learning modality and finds that of the 33 students, 29 are predominantly kinesthetic learners. What guidance did this information give Brian? What should Brian plan to do as a result of this information?

2. **Diversity in Learning and Teaching.** How will I explain why knowledge of learning styles, learning capacities, and teaching styles is or should be important to a classroom teacher? **To do:** Role play your explanation with a listening colleague; trade roles.

3. **Economic Diversity.** What will I say when asked what concerns me most about the estimate that 20% of all children ages 6 to 11 in the United

States are living in poverty? **To do:** Access any Internet educational sites to see what is currently being done to address this concern. Meet with a colleague and discuss a plan that could be implemented in your class, school, or district to ameliorate your concern.

4. **Educational Practice.** What would I say to identify one specific example of educational practice that seems contradictory to exemplary practice or theory as presented in this chapter? **To do:** Meet with the whole group and, as a class, list the discrepancies. Ask volunteers for explanations for the discrepancies.

5. **Learning Style.** How would I describe my learning style? **To do:** Meet with a colleague and do the following: (a) Classify a learning style for each of you, i.e., an imaginative learner, analytic learner, commonsense learner, or a dynamic learner; and (b) tell how your learning style has changed as you have gotten older. Include any information you have about the developmental characteristics of young people that might have affected the changes in your learning style. Also include any information you have about the content areas of the elementary school curriculum (i.e., mathematics, social studies, science, writing) that might have affected changes in your learning style. Discuss your point of view about the idea that some ages and/or content areas might be more compatible with certain learning styles.

Online Portfolio Activities

Supporting Principles 2 and 3 of INTASC and Standards 1, 2, 3, 4, and 7 of NBPTS: At the Companion Website (**www.prenhall.com/roberts**), click on the *Online Portfolio Activities* module to continue your online portfolio supporting knowledge of students.

Companion Website
Also on the Companion Website at **www.prenhall. com/roberts,** you can measure your understanding of chapter content in the *Objectives* and *Self-Check* modules and apply concepts in the *For Your Discussion* module.

FOR FURTHER READING

Armstrong, T. (1998). *Awakening Genius in the Classroom.* Alexandria, VA: Association for Supervision and Curriculum Development.

Armstrong, T. (2000). *Multiple Intelligences in the Classroom* (2nd ed.) Alexandria, VA: Association for Supervision and Curriculum Development.

Baker, J. C., and Martin, F. G. (1998). *A Neural Network Guide to Teaching* (Fastback 431). Bloomington, IN: Phi Delta Kappa Educational Foundation.

Beaumont, C. J. (1999). Dilemmas of Peer Assistance in a Bilingual Full Inclusion Classroom. *Elementary School Journal, 99*(3), 233–254.

Benson, A. C., and Fodemski, L. M. (1999). *Connecting Kids and the Internet: A Handbook for Librarians, Teachers, and Parents* (2nd ed.). New York: Neal-Schuman.

Brandt, R. (1998). *Powerful Learning*. Alexandria, VA: Association for Supervision and Curriculum Development.

Brisk, M. E., and Harrington, M. M. (2000). *Literacy and Bilingualism: A Handbook for ALL Teachers*. Mahwah, NJ: Lawrence Erlbaum.

Brock, B. L., and Grady, M. L. (1997). *From First-Year to First-Rate: Principals Guiding Beginning Teachers*. Thousand Oaks, CA: Corwin Press.

Buzzelli, C. A., and B. Johnston (2002). *The Moral Dimensions of Teaching: Language, Power, and Culture in Classroom Interaction*. New York: Routledge Falmer.

Cavigliole, O., and Harris, I. (2003). *Thinking Visually: Step-by-Step Exercises That Promote Visual, Auditory, and Kinesthetic Learning*. New York: Pembrooke.

Choate, J. S., and Rakes, T. A. (1998). *Inclusive Instruction for Struggling Readers* (Fastback 434). Bloomington, IN: Phi Delta Kappa Educational Foundation.

Clark, G., and Zimmerman, E. (1998). Nuturing the Arts in Programs for Gifted and Talented Children. *Phi Delta Kappan, 79*(10), 747–751.

Cooper, J. (2003). *Classroom Teaching Skills* (7th ed.). Boston: Houghton Mifflin.

Council for Exceptional Children. (2000). *Bright Futures for Exceptional Learners: An Action Agenda to Achieve Quality Conditions for Teaching and Learning*. Reston, VA: Council for Exceptional Children.

Crane, B. (2000). *Teaching with the Internet: Strategies and Models for the K–12 Curricula*. New York: Neal-Schuman.

Dickinson, T. S. (2001). *Reinventing the Middle School*. New York: RoutledgeFalmer.

Dougherty, E. (2001). *Shifting Gears: Standards, Assessment, Curriculum, and Instruction*. Golden, CO: Fulcrum Resources.

Ford, D. Y., and Harris III, J. J. (1999). *Multicultural Gifted Education*. New York: Teachers College Press.

Franklin, J. (2001, May). Trying Too Hard? How Accountability and Testing Are Affecting Constructivist Teaching. *Education Update, 42*(3), 1–8.

Gibb, G. S., and Dyches, T. T. (2000). *Guide to Writing Quality Individualized Education Programs: What's Best for Students with Disabilities?* Needham Heights, MA: Allyn & Bacon.

Goldman, L. (2000). *Helping the Grieving Child in School* (Fastback 460). Bloomington, IN: Phi Delta Kappa Educational Foundation.

Gonzalez, M. L., Huerta-Macias, A., and Tinajero, J. V. (Eds.). (1998). *Educating Latino Students: A Guide to Successful Practice*. Lancaster, PA: Technomic.

Mates, B. (1999). *Adaptive Technology for the Internet: Making Electronic Resources Accessible to All*. Chicago, IL: American Library Association.

Roberts, P. L. (2005). *Family Values through Children's Literature, Grades K–3*. Lanham, MD: Scarecrow Press.

Roberts, P. L. (2005). *Family Values through Children's Books and Activities, Grades 4–6*. Lanham, MD: Scarecrow Press.

Tomlinson, C. A. (1999). *The Differentiated Classroom: Responding to the Needs of All Learners*. Alexandria, VA: Association for Supervision and Curriculum Development.

NOTES

1. As examples, a personalized learning plan for each student is a feature of Celebration School (Celebration, FL)—see the website at *www.cs.osceola.k12.fl.us;* or see Community Learning Center schools (pre–k through adults) and contact Designs for Learning, 1000 Hamline Ave. North Suite 100, St. Paul, MN 55104, (651)645-0200; or see Community for Learning (K–12) and contact *www. temple.edu/LSS/cfl.htm*; or see C. A. Tomlinson, *The Differentiated Classroom: Responding to the Needs of All Learners* (Alexandria, VA: Association for Supervision and Curriculum Development, 1999).

2. J. A. Banks, Multicultural and Citizenship Education in the New Century, *School Administrator, 56*(6), 8–10 (May 1999).

3. L. Baines, Future Schlock, *Phi Delta Kappan, 78*(7), 497 (March 1999).

4. T. L. Good and J. E. Brophy, *Looking in Classrooms,* 9th ed. (New York: Addison Wesley Longman, 2003), p. 127.

5. R. Dunn, *Strategies for Educating Diverse Learners* (Fastback 384). (Bloomington, IN: Phi Delta Kappa Educational Foundation, 1995), p. 9.

6. P. Sone, How We Turned Around a Problem School, *Principal, 72*(2), 34–36. (November 1992). See also B. G. Barron et al., Effects of Time of Day Instruction on Reading Achievement of Below Grade Readers, *Reading Improvement, 31*(1), 59–60 (Spring 1994).

7. D. A. Kolb, *Experiential Learning: Experience as the Source of Learning and Development* (Upper Saddle River, NJ: Prentice Hall, 1984).

8. C. G. Jung, *Psychological Types* (New York: Harcourt Brace, 1923).

9. B. McCarthy, A Tale of Four Learners: 4MAT's Learning Styles, *Educational Leadership, 54*(6), 47–51 (March 1997).

10. R. Karplus, *Science Curriculum Improvement Study, Teacher's Handbook* (Berkeley: University of California, 1974).

11. A. C. Rule, *Using the Learning Cycle to Teach Acronyms, a Language Arts Lesson* (Bloomington, IN: ERIC Clearinghouse on Reading, English and Communication, 1995), ED 383000.

12. The three phases of the learning cycle are comparable to the three levels of thinking, described variously by others. See Elliot Eisner's *The Educational Imagination* (New York: Macmillan, 1979), in which the levels are referred to as "descriptive," "interpretive," and "evaluative."

13. For information about 4MAT, contact About Learning, Inc., 441W. Bonner Rd., Wauconda, IL 60084 or via the Internet at *www.aboutlearning.com/*.

14. B. McCarthy, Using the 4MAT System to Bring Learning Styles to Schools, *Educational Leadership, 48*(2), 33 (October 1990).

15. R. Delay, Forming Knowledge: Constructivist Learning and Experiential Education, *Journal of Experiential Education, 19*(2), 76–81 (August/September 1996). See also the many articles in "The Constructivist Classroom," the November 1999 (Vol. 57, No. 2) theme issue of *Educational Leadership*. For discourse about the question "How does being a constructivist make your teaching different from someone who is not a constructivist?" and other

questions, see Edward G. Rozycki, Preparing Teachers for Public Schools: Just More Cannon Fodder? *Phi Lambda Theta Educational Horizons, 81*(3) (Spring 2003).

16. For Gardner's distinction between *learning style* and *intelligences,* see H. Gardner, Multiple Intelligences: Myths and Messages, *International Schools Journal, 15*(2), 8–22 (April 1996), and the many articles in the "Teaching for Multiple Intelligences" theme issue of *Educational Leadership, 55*(1) (September 1997).

17. See Chapter 2 of L. Campbell and B. Campbell, *Multiple Intelligences and Student Achievement: Success Stories from Six Schools* (Alexandria, VA: Association for Supervision and Curriculum Development, 2000).

18. See L. English, "Uncovering Students' Analytic, Practical, and Creative Intelligences: One School's Application of Sternberg's Triarchic Theory," *School Administrator, 55*(1), 28–29 (January 1998).

19. R. J. Sternberg, Teaching and Assessing for Successful Intelligence, *School Administrator, 55*(1), 26–27, 30–31 (January 1998).

20. R. J. Marzano, 20th Century Advances in Instruction, Chapter 4 (pp. 67–95) in R. S. Brandt (Ed.), *Education in a New Era* (Alexandria, VA: ASCD Yearbook, Association for Supervision and Curriculum Development, 2000), p. 76.

21. P. Guild, The Cultural/Learning Style Connection, *Educational Leadership, 51*(8), 16–21 (May 1994).

22. Dunn, notes, p. 30.

23. B. Mates, *Adaptive Technology for the Internet: Making Elecronic Resources Accessible to All* (Chicago: American Library Association, 1999).

24. For more descriptions of characteristics, see the Companion Website for this text at *www.prenhall.com/roberts* (Credit: *Early Childhood Education,* 3/E by Seefeldt & Barbour © 1994. Adapted by permission of Pearson Education, Inc., Upper Saddle River, NJ); pp. 56–59. Also see L. Berk, *Child Development,* 6th ed. (Needham Heights, MA: Allyn & Bacon, 2003); P. Miller, *Theories of Developmental Psychology,* 3rd ed. (New York: Freeman, 1993); E. Erickson, *Identity and the Life Cycle,* 2nd ed. (New York: Norton, 1980).

25. For more characteristics, see our Companion Website for this text at *www.prenhall.com/roberts.* (Credit: *Early Childhood Education,* 3/E by Seefeldt & Barbour © 1994. Adapted by permission of Pearson Education, Inc., Upper Saddle River, NJ); pp. 59–63; Also see J. Flavell, P. Miller, and S. Miller, *Cognitive Development,* 3rd ed. (Upper Saddle River, NJ: Prentice Hall, 1993) and Berk, *ibid.*

26. For more characteristics, see our Companion Website (*www.prenhall.com/roberts*) and adaptation *Caught in the Middle: Educational Reform for Young Adolescents in California Public Schools* (Sacramento: California State Department of Education, 1987), pp. 144–148. Also see L. Berk, *Development Through the Lifespan,* 2nd ed. (Boston: Allyn & Bacon, 2001).

27. See M. L. Yell, The Legal Basis of Inclusion, *Educational Leadership, 56*(2), 70–73 (October 1998). For information about education law as related to special education students, see *The Law and Special Education* by Mitchell L. Yell (Merrill/Prentice Hall) as found at *www.ed.sc.edu/spedlaw/lawpage.htm.*

28. E. Tiegerman-Farber and C. Radziewicz, *Collaborative Decision Making: The Pathway to Inclusion* (Upper Saddle River, NJ: Merrill/Prentice Hall, 1998), pp. 12–13.

29. For a sample lesson using multilevel instruction and a discussion of other inclusive teaching techniques, see G. M. Johnson, Inclusive Education: Fundamental Instructional Strategies and Considerations, *Preventing School Failure, 43*(2), 72–78 (Winter 1999).

30. See L. Farlow, A Quartet of Success Stories: How to Make Inclusion Work, *Educational Leadership 53*(5), 51–55 (April 1996), and other articles in this theme issue of "Students with Special Needs."

31. See P. Berman et al., *School Reform and Student Diversity, Volume II: Case Studies of Exemplary Practices for LEP Students* (Berkeley, CA: National Center for Research on Cultural Diversity and Second Language Learning, 1995).

32. See, for example, F. Genesee, Teaching Linguistically Diverse Students, *Principal, 79*(5), 24–27 (May 2000).

33. For more information, see J. Echevarria and A. Graves, *Sheltered Content Instruction* (Upper Saddle River, NJ: Merrill/Prentice Hall, 1998); H. Hernandez, *Teaching in Multilingual Classrooms* (Upper Saddle River, NJ: Merrill/Prentice Hall, 1997); C. Ovando, Language Diversity and Education, in J. Banks and C. Banks (Eds.), *Multicultural Education: Issues and Perspectives,* 3rd ed. (Boston: Allyn & Bacon, 1997); and S. Peregoy and O. Boyle, *Reading, Writing, and Learning in ESL,* 3rd ed. (New York: Longman, 2001).

34. See J. Fitzgerald, English as a Second Language Learners' Cognitive Reading Processes: A Review of Research in the United States, *Review of Educational Research, 65*(2), 145–190 (1995); and D. R. Walling, *English as a Second Language: 25 Questions and Answers* (Fastback 347). (Bloomington, IN: Phi Delta Kappa Educational Foundation, 1993).

35. See K. M. Johns and C. Espinoza, *Mainstreaming Language Minority Children in Reading and Writing* (Fastback 340). (Bloomington, IN: Phi Delta Kappa Educational Foundation, 1992).

36. C. Minicucci et al., School Reform and Student Diversity, *Phi Delta Kappan, 77*(1), 77–80 (September 1995).

37. See the discussion in G. Clark and E. Zimmerman, Nurturing the Arts in Programs for Gifted and Talented Students, *Phi Delta Kappan, 79*(10), 747–751 (June 1998).

38. See J. F. Feldhusen, Programs for the Gifted Few or Talent Development for the Many? *Phi Delta Kappan, 79*(10), 735–738 (June 1998).

39. For more information about students who are gifted and talented, see C. Dixon, L. Mains, and M. J. Reeves, *Gifted and At Risk* (Fastback 398). (Bloomington, IN: Phi Delta Kappa Educational Foundation, 1996), p. 7; and P. D. Slocumb and R. K. Payne, Identifying and Nurturing the Gifted Poor, *Principal, 79*(5), 28–32 (May 2000).

40. For more about gifted underachievers, see B. Louis, R. Subotnik, P. Breland, and M. Lewis, Establishing Criteria for High Ability versus Selective Admission to Gifted Programs: Implications for Policy and Practice, *Educational Psychology Review, 12*(3), 295–314 (2000); S. B. Rimm, Underachievement Syndrome: A National Epidemic, in N. Colangelo and G. A. Davis (Eds.), *Handbook of gifted education,* 2nd ed. (Needham Heights, MA: Allyn & Bacon, 1997), p. 416.

41. From S. Schwartz, *Strategies for Identifying the Talents of Diverse Students,* ERIC/CUE Digest, Number 122, (New York: ERIC Clearinghouse on Urban Education, May 1997), ED 410323.

42. Dixon, Mains, and Reeves, note 39, pp. 9–12. By permission of the Phi Delta Kappa Educational Foundation.

43. Dixon, Mains, and Reeves, note 39, p. 21.

44. See J. J. Gallagher, Accountability for Gifted Students, *Phi Delta Kappan, 79*(10), 739–742 (June 1998).

45. D. G. Gil, *Violence Against Children: Physical Child Abuse in the United States* (Cambridge, MA: Rand McNally, 1970).

46. K. Burrett and T. Rusnak, *Integrated Character Education* (Fastback 351). (Bloomington, IN: Phi Delta Kappa Educational Foundation, 1993).

47. Burrett and Rusnak, *Ibid.,* p. 15.

48. See Chapter 11 of D. W. Johnson and R. T. Johnson, *Reducing School Violence through Conflict Resolution* (Alexandria, VA: Association for Supervision and Curriculum Development, 1995).

What Are the Expectations, Responsibilities, and Facilitating Behaviors of a Classroom Teacher?

Visual Chapter Organizer and Overview

The Teacher's Professionalism and Commitment

> Noninstructional Responsibilities
> Instructional Responsibilities

Identifying and Building Your Instructional Competencies

> Characteristics of the Competent Classroom Teacher: An Annotated Teacher Progress Report Card

Teacher Behaviors That Facilitate Student Learning

The Teacher as a Reflective Decision Maker

> Decision-Making Phases of Instruction
> Reflection, Locus of Control, and Teacher Responsibility

Teaching Style

> Multilevel Instruction

The Theoretical Origins of Teaching Styles and Their Relations to Constructivism

Looking at Teachers

In her third-grade classroom, the teacher explained the concept of transplanting. One of her students with learning disabilities got excited when he heard the teacher's explanation about transplanting and he talked about his idea of transplanting flowers—a idea that led him to a service-learning project. The teacher encouraged the student to present his idea to the youth council at school. This council was a group that provided students an opportunity to work through personal problems and make contributions to the school. With the teacher's support, the student and his classmates began planting and transplanting purple pansies to give to different teachers as gifts. The student continued with his interest in transplanting and said he thought the kids needed some shade and looked in a book about trees. He said that the book gave him the idea to plant small trees inside of peat pots first and then transplant them somewhere where people wouldn't step on them.

Eventually, all of the student's classmates were involved in working on a landscaping project for their school. The teacher saw the student's tree-planting idea as the springboard for the class to get involved in scientific research in an interdisciplinary way:

- The students investigated trees, soil conditions, and climate. (science)
- With more research, they learned where to get the seeds. (economics)
- They learned when to start the peat pots, when to set them out, and how to care for the saplings. (botany)

Working on activities outside strict academics on this service-learning project improved the student's confidence and his grades. In addition, the skills and information that he and his classmates acquired surpassed the content of their third-grade science books.

A research agency evaluated the impact of service-learning as an instructional approach and compared classes in the same district and grade level in a western state (Colorado) where service-learning *was* and *was not* provided. The results indicated the following:

- On their state standardized reading test, 79% of students who participated in service-learning scored ratings of *advanced* or *proficient* compared to 42% of nonparticipating students.
- On their state standardized math test, 53% of students who participated in service-learning scored *advanced* or *proficient* ratings compared to 38% of nonparticipating students.
- On their state standardized writing test, 49% of students who participated in service-learning scored ratings of *advanced* or *proficient* compared to 42% of nonparticipating students.
- Students who participated in service-learning reported higher grade-point averages than comparison students. They also increased their GPAs over time while the comparison students' GPAs decreased over time.

It appears that service-learning contributed to higher achievement.[1]

As shown in this teacher vignette, the primary expectation of any teacher is to facilitate student learning. As an elementary school classroom teacher, your professional responsibilities will extend well beyond the ability to work effectively with a group of children in a classroom attending school from approximately 8:30 A.M. until midafternoon. Attending school can be stressful for students. Look at Ronald Morgan in *Today Was a Terrible Day* (New York: Puffin Books/Penguin, reprint, 1987) by Patricia Reilly Giff. In one day, Ronald drops his pencil, accidentally squirts water on Joy's dress, eats Jimmy's sandwich instead of his own, loses his ice cream money, doesn't catch the game-winning ball while playing baseball, and drops the teacher's plant while watering it. He also knows that he is a slow reader. Luckily, Ronald had Miss Tyler for a teacher. Miss Tyler understood that children have different developmental levels and that bad days happen to everyone. She sends a positive note home with Ronald. He discovers that he can read the whole thing including the fact that Miss Tyler's birthday was the next day. He brings her a

plant as a present. Teachers like Miss Tyler show they care about students in many ways.

In this chapter, you will learn about the many responsibilities you will assume, as Miss Tyler did, and the competencies and behaviors necessary for fulfilling them. Four categories of responsibilities and important competencies are identified: (a) your commitment to children as learners and to the teaching profession, (b) your noninstructional responsibilities, (c) your instructional responsibilities and fundamental teaching behaviors, and (d) your responsibility as a reflective decision maker.

CHAPTER OBJECTIVES

Specifically, on the completion of this third chapter, you should be able to:

1. Demonstrate your developing understanding of the concepts of professionalism/commitment and the basic areas of professional responsibilities of a beginning teacher.

2. Demonstrate your understanding of selected instructional competencies such as teacher use of praise, multilevel instruction, and hands-on and minds-on learning.
3. Demonstrate your understanding of the contrast between the facilitating behaviors and instructional strategies that teachers use.
4. Describe the decision-making and thought-processing phases of instruction and one or more of the types of decisions you could make during each phase
5. Develop a profile and a statement about your own emerging teaching style.

THE TEACHER'S PROFESSIONALISM AND COMMITMENT

The classroom teacher is expected to demonstrate commitment to the school's mission and to the personal as well as the intellectual development of the children. Not only do the most accomplished teachers expect, demand, and receive positive results in learning from their students while in the classroom, they are also interested and involved in the activities of the children outside the classroom. They are willing to sacrifice personal time to give their students attention and guidance.

Noninstructional Responsibilities

The daily behaviors of the teacher with professional commitments take on a very real dimension when you consider specific noninstruction-related and instruction-related responsibilities of the classroom teacher. Figure 3.1 categorizes the many noninstructional matters with which you should become familiar. Beginning teachers often underestimate the importance of these tasks and the time they require.

Student Physical Safety: Rules and Guidelines

Teachers are responsible for preventing accidents and ensuring that the classroom is as safe as possible. Nevertheless, accidents and resulting injuries do occur to children at school. For instance, a student is injured by glass from a falling windowpane when the teacher attempts to open a stuck window. A student is injured when she falls and lands on a lawn-sprinkler head on the playground during recess. While doing a science experiment, a student is burned by a candle flame.

As a teacher, you need to understand what you can do to prevent accidents from happening. You also need to know what you should and should not do when an accident does happen. Figure 3.2 lists classroom safety rules and guidelines that you can use as a basis for discussion with your classmates. The school

Figure 3.1
Noninstructional responsibilities of the elementary classroom teacher

---

Related to the Students
1. Be knowledgeable about activities of interest to the students.
2. Become familiar with the backgrounds of the students.
3. Get acquainted with your role in administering standardized assessments of student achievement.

Related to the School and Community
4. Become familiar with the school campus and community.
5. Get acquainted with members of the faculty and the support staff.
6. Be knowledgeable about school and district policies.
7. Become knowledgeable about procedures for such routine matters as arranging for and preparing displays for common areas of the school; class dismissal; collection of money for lunch; daily attendance records; distribution and collection of textbooks and other school materials; fire drills, emergency schedules, and severe weather schedules; planning and scheduling of before- and after-school activities; restroom regulations; school assemblies; and sharing of instructional space with other teachers.
8. Perform duties such as maintaining a cheerful, pleasant, productively efficient, and safe learning environment; obtaining materials/audiovisuals/technology needed for each lesson; keeping supplies orderly; and supervising students who are helpers.
9. Attend the many required conferences, such as those between teacher and teacher; teacher and resource specialist; teacher and student; teacher and parent/guardian; teacher, student, and parent/guardian; teacher and administrator; and teacher and a parent or community representative.
10. Attend professional meetings such as those of the faculty, the teaching team, other school and district committees, parent–teacher and community groups, and local, regional, state, and national professional organizations.
11. Become familiar with your role in the school's advisory or homeroom program.
12. Take time to relax and enjoy friends, family, and hobbies.

in which you ultimately teach will, of course, have its own separate written rules and guidelines that may be more or less extensive than those found in Figure 3.2.

Referring back to Figure 3.1, item 8 includes the responsibility of providing a safe environment, both psychological and physical. The physical safety aspect is highlighted in Figure 3.2 and is basically a set of commonsense reminders that deserves to be mentioned; the psychological aspect of safety is discussed later in this chapter and in Chapter 4.

Instructional Responsibilities

The instructional responsibilities you will have as a classroom teacher are listed in Figure 3.3. These responsibilities, along with the areas of class management, assessment, and professional development, are the primary focus of study in the remainder of this resource guide. After reviewing the lists of instructional and noninstructional responsibilities of the classroom teacher, do Application Exercise 3.1.

Figure 3.2
Safety rules and guidelines for the elementary school teacher and classroom

---

Accidents and First Aid

1. Maintain a well-supplied first aid kit in the classroom.
2. Know exactly what to do in case of emergencies, and have emergency procedures posted in the classroom.
3. Whenever an accident happens, notify the school office immediately by telephoning or sending a pair of students to the office.
4. You should give first aid only when necessary to save a child's life or limb. When that is not at risk, you should follow school policy by referring the student immediately to professional care. When immediate professional care is unavailable and you believe that immediate first aid is necessary, then you can take prudent action, as if you were that child's parent or legal guardian. But you must always be cautious and knowledgeable about what you are doing, so as not to cause further injury. To prepare for this, some teachers take beginning first aid courses offered in their local areas.
5. Unless you are a licensed medical professional, you should never give medication to a child, whether prescription or over the counter. See your school policy on this because some districts require written permission from the parent/guardian for any required medically approved medications to be taken by a child.
6. Avoid allowing children to overheat or overexert themselves.

Place-Based Learning (Field Trips and Virtual Field Trips)

7. When taking children on a field trip, solicit adult help, even when the destination is only a short distance from the school. A recommended guideline is one or more adults for every 10 children. If you are interested in a virtual field trip (a web quest or a field trip on a site on the Internet), there is more about this topic at our Companion Website **(www.prenhall.com/roberts)** in the *Additional Content* module.

Figure 3.3
Instructional responsibilities of the classroom teacher

---

1. Prepare the classroom; identify sources and resources.
2. Become familiar with relevant curriculum standards and assessment tools.
3. Reacquaint yourself with the developmental characteristics of children.
4. Learn the backgrounds of children with special problems who might cause concerns in the classroom.
5. Learn the interests of the children so the lessons and learning activities will reflect those interests.
6. Incorporate the individual learning modalities, learning styles, and capacities of the students into lesson plans.
7. Prepare activities, lessons, and units.
8. Develop techniques and plans for using cross-age tutoring, peer coaching, cooperative learning, project work, and other instructional strategies.
9. Develop an effective classroom management system.
10. Read student papers.
11. Assess and record student progress and achievements.
12. Reflect on and participate in professional growth and development, which may include attending university courses, workshops, and other presentations offered by the school district or professional organizations and reading professional literature.
13. Devote time to team planning and to student and parent conferences.

For Your Notes

APPLICATION EXERCISE 3.1 REVIEWING THE PROFESSIONAL RESPONSIBILITIES OF A FIRST-YEAR TEACHER

Instructions: The purpose of this exercise is to review the responsibilities of a first-year teacher. Have the class of teacher candidates divide into groups of four. Within each group, each member should play one of the following roles: (a) group facilitator, (b) recorder, (c) materials manager, or (d) reporter. The group is to choose one of these six categories of responsibilities:

1. Audiovisual/media
2. Classroom environment
3. Clerical
4. Instructional
5. Professional activities
6. Supervision.

The group should then read the responsibilities for its selected category listed on the following cards and arrange them in prioritized order, beginning with the most important. The group facilitator will lead this discussion. Under the guidance of the materials manager, the group may cut the cards apart so that they can be physically manipulated as priorities are discussed. The recorder should take notes of the group's work, which can then be discussed to develop the report that will be made to the class.

After a prearranged discussion time, recall the entire class and ask each reporter to share the group's (a) prioritized order of responsibilities and (b) estimate of the amount of time that a beginning teacher might devote to these responsibilities each week.

As each group reports, all members of the class should enter its list of priorities and time estimate on the Recap Sheet.

After completion of this exercise, the class may wish to discuss the group dynamics of this model of cooperative learning (see Chapter 10). For discussion in either large or small groups, key questions might be:

1. Would you use this form of discussion in your own teaching?

2. How would you divide a class into groups of four?

Other questions may be generated by the group work. *Example:* Could a group member design a generic template for this activity? In what way would this be helpful?

For Your Notes

CARDS FOR EXERCISE 3.1
AUDIOVISUAL/MEDIA RESPONSIBILITIES

Selecting, ordering, and returning cassettes, films, videodisks, and other materials

Preparing and operating equipment	Reviewing selected materials
Planning class introduction to the audiovisual materials	Other responsibilities as determined

Estimated hours a beginning teacher will devote to audiovisual/media responsibilities each week = _____

CARDS FOR EXERCISE 3.1
CLASSROOM ENVIRONMENT RESPONSIBILITIES

Planning and constructing displays	Preparing bulletin boards
Reading, announcing, and posting class notices	Managing a classroom library

Opening and closing windows, arranging furniture, cleaning the writing board; other responsibilities as determined

Estimated hours a beginning teacher will devote to classroom environment responsibilities each week = _____

CARDS FOR EXERCISE 3.1
CLERICAL RESPONSIBILITIES

Maintaining attendance and tardy records	Entering grades, scores, or marks into a record book or onto the computer
Preparing progress and grade reports	Typing, drawing, and duplicating instructional materials
Locating resource ideas and materials to support lessons	Other responsibilities as determined

Estimated hours a beginning teacher will devote to clerical responsibilities each week = _____

CARDS FOR EXERCISE 3.1
INSTRUCTIONAL RESPONSIBILITIES

Giving additional instruction (e.g., to students who need one-to-one attention, those who have been absent, or small review groups)	Correcting student work
Preparing special learning materials	Preparing, reading, and scoring tests; helping students self-evaluate
Writing information on the board	Preparing long-range and daily lesson plans
Grouping for instruction	Other responsibilities as determined

Estimated hours a beginning teacher will devote to instructional responsibilities each week = _____

CARDS FOR EXERCISE 3.1
PROFESSIONAL ACTIVITIES RESPONSIBILITIES

Researching and writing teacher reports	Attending teachers' and school district meetings
Planning and attending parent–teacher meetings	Attending local teachers' organization meetings
Attending state, regional, and national professional organizations; taking university classes	Other responsibilities as determined

Estimated hours a beginning teacher will devote to professional activities responsibilities each week = _____

CARDS FOR EXERCISE 3.1
SUPERVISION RESPONSIBILITIES

Supervising before- or after-school activities	Supervising hallways, lunchrooms, and bathrooms
Supervising student assemblies	Supervising field trips
Supervising laboratory activities	Helping students settle dispute

Other responsibilities as determined

Estimated hours a beginning teacher will devote to supervision responsibilities each week = _____

✎ APPLICATION EXERCISE 3.1 RECAP SHEET

Audiovisual/Media Responsibilities

1. _____
2. _____
3. _____
4. _____
5. _____

Estimated hours = _____

Classroom Environment Responsibilities

1. _____
2. _____
3. _____
4. _____
5. _____
6. _____

Estimated hours = _____

Clerical Responsibilities

1. _____
2. _____
3. _____
4. _____
5. _____
6. _____

Estimated hours = _____

Instructional Responsibilities

1. _____
2. _____
3. _____
4. _____
5. _____
6. _____
7. _____
8. _____

Estimated hours = _____

APPLICATION EXERCISE 3.1 *(continued)*

Professional Activities Responsibilities

1. _____
2. _____
3. _____
4. _____
5. _____
6. _____

   Estimated hours = _____

Supervision Responsibilities

1. _____
2. _____
3. _____
4. _____
5. _____
6. _____
7. _____

   Estimated hours = _____

IDENTIFYING AND BUILDING YOUR INSTRUCTIONAL COMPETENCIES

The overall purpose of this resource guide is to assist you in building your instructional competencies. To do that, we want to begin with the identification and presentation of 22 specific competencies.[2] You will want to continue to reflect on and build on these competencies through your study of the remaining chapters of this book and, indeed, throughout your professional career.

Characteristics of the Competent Classroom Teacher: An Annotated Teacher Progress Report Card

Before you read further, we want to caution you not to feel overwhelmed by the lists on our simulated Teacher Progress Report Card (Figure 3.4). It may well be that no teacher expertly models all of the characteristics that are listed on the card. The characteristics on the Teacher Progress Report Card do, however, represent an ideal model to strive for in four important professional education areas: management, instruction, assessment, and professional development.

If it would be helpful to your group, we suggest that group members brainstorm characteristics of the competent classroom teacher. Each member then lists on a piece of paper one characteristic about which he or she feels strongly. Members then spend 2 minutes writing examples or further explanations of the characteristic. The members stop, pass their papers clockwise, read what has already been written, and add a paragraph of new ideas. Continue until all members have commented on every characteristic and then discuss the results.

Specific teacher behaviors that facilitate student learning are discussed in the following section, more additional guidelines and resources, such as the accompanying *Technology Tips for the Classroom* feature, that will help in your development of these competencies, permeate this resource guide.

TEACHER BEHAVIORS THAT FACILITATE STUDENT LEARNING

Your ability to perform your instructional responsibilities effectively is directly dependent on your knowledge of children and how they best learn and your knowledge of and the quality of your teaching skills. We believe that development of your strategy repertoire along with your skills in using specific strategies should be ongoing throughout your teaching career. To be most effective, you need a large repertoire from which to select a specific strategy for a particular goal with a distinctive group of children.

Related to specific strategies and behaviors, the top 10 qualities of outstanding educators have been identified by African American students and include the following: (a) explains things well, (b) makes work interesting, (c) gives extra help, (d) has patience, (e) is fair, (f) is friendly, (g) has a sense of humor, (h) challenges students academically, (i) is intelligent, and (j) makes the work relevant.[3] In addition, you need to develop skill in using the strategy that you choose for a particular goal. In support of this, this section of the chapter is designed to help you begin building your repertoire of and to develop your skills in using these strategies.

The basic teacher behaviors create the conditions needed to enable students to think and to learn, whether the learning is a further understanding of concepts from their **prior knowledge,** the internalization of attitudes and values, the development of thinking processes, or the actuating of the most complex behaviors. The basic teacher behaviors are those that produce the following results: (a) The students are physically and mentally engaged in the learning activities, (b) instructional time is efficiently used, and (c) classroom distractions and interruptions are minimal. The effectiveness with which a teacher carries out the basic behaviors can be measured by how well the students learn.

Companion Website
To broaden your knowledge base about teacher behaviors that facilitate student learning, go to our Companion Website at **www.prenhall.com/roberts** and click on the *Additional Content* module for Chapter 3.

THE TEACHER AS A REFLECTIVE DECISION MAKER

During any single school day, you will make hundreds of decisions. Some decisions will have been made prior to meeting your students for instruction, others will be made during the instructional activities, and yet still others will be made later as you reflect on the school day. Let's now consider further the decision-making and thought-processing phases of instruction.

Technology Tips for the Classroom

- Have each student use an electronic handheld device (Palm Pilot™), perhaps purchased by the school's parent support group, for students in the fifth or sixth grades.

(continued)

Figure 3.4
Simulated teacher progress report card: Characteristics of the competent classroom teacher

TEACHER PROGRESS REPORT CARD

CHARACTERISTICS OF THE COMPETENT CLASSROOM TEACHER

NAME _____ SCHOOL YEAR _____

Symbols   S—Satisfactory   N—Needs improvement

MANAGEMENT

1. The teacher is quick to recognize a student who may be in need of special attention. _____

2. The teacher uses effective modeling behavior. _____

3. The teacher is nonprejudiced toward gender, sexual orientation, ethnicity, skin color, religion, special needs/disabilities, socioeconomic status, or national origin. _____

4. The teacher is open to change and willing to take risks and to be held accountable. _____

5. The teacher is a capable communicator. _____

6. The teacher has a healthy sense of humor. _____

INSTRUCTION

7. The teacher understands the processes of learning. _____

8. The teacher is knowledgeable about the subject matter content to be taught. _____

9. The teacher is an educational broker and a technology partner. _____

10. The teacher makes specific and frequent efforts to demonstrate how the subject content may be related to the lives of the students. _____

11. The teacher organizes the classroom and plans lessons carefully. _____

12. The teacher demonstrates concern for the safety and health of the children. _____

13. The teacher can function effectively as a decision maker. _____

ASSESSMENT

14. The teacher demonstrates optimism for the learning of every student, while providing a constructive and positive environment for learning. _____

15. The teacher demonstrates confidence in every student's ability to learn. _____

16. The teacher is skillful and fair in the employment of strategies for the assessment of student learning. _____

PROFESSIONAL DEVELOPMENT

17. The teacher is in a perpetual learning mode, striving to further develop a repertoire of teaching strategies. _____

18. The teacher is reliable. _____

19. The teacher is skillful in working with parents, guardians, colleagues, administrators, and school support staff and at maintaining and nurturing friendly and ethical professional relationships. _____

20. The teacher is an active member of professional organizations, reads professional journals, dialogues with colleagues, and maintains currency both in methodology about the students and the subject content the teacher is expected to teach. _____

21. The teacher demonstrates continuing interest in professional responsibilities and opportunities. _____

22. The teacher exhibits a wide range of interests. _____

Figure 3.4
Simulated teacher progress report card: Characteristics of the competent classroom teacher (*continued*)

COMMENTS/ANNOTATIONS FOR
CHARACTERISTICS OF A COMPETENT CLASSROOM TEACHER

About Management: Progress Report Comments

Characteristic #1. A competent teacher, such as you, is able to recognize any student who demonstrates behaviors indicating a need for special attention. You know how and where to refer the student, doing so with minimal class disruption and without embarrassment to the child. For example, patterns of increasingly poor attendance and of steady negative attention-seeking behaviors are two of the more obvious early signals of a troubled child, one who is potentially at risk of dropping out of school—and you recognize these patterns.

Characteristic #2. As part of your management system, your own behaviors are consistent with those expected of your students. When, for example, you want your students to demonstrate regular and punctual attendance, to have their work done on time, and to have their materials each day for learning, then you do likewise. You model similar behaviors and attitudes for children—cooperative behavior, respect for the rights and possessions of others, an open and inquisitive mind, critical thinking, and proper communication skills. As a teacher, you serve as an important role model for your students. Whether you realize it or not, your behavior sends important messages to students that complement curriculum content. By doing this, you serve the children well when you practice what you teach and when you model inclusive and collaborative approaches to learning.

Characteristic #3. You are cognizant of how teachers, male and female, knowingly or unknowingly, historically have mistreated female students or minority students and you avoid those same errors in your own teaching. Of course, this means no sexual innuendoes, religious or ethnic jokes, or racial slurs. It means that you learn about and attend to the needs of individual students in your classroom. It means having high expectations for every student.

Characteristic #4. You realize that if there were no difference between what is and what can be, than formal schooling would be of little value. As a competent teacher, you know about the historical and traditional values of knowledge, but also about the value of change, and you are willing to carefully plan and experiment, to move between that which is known and that which is not. In the words of Selma Wasserman, "No coward ever got the Great Teacher Award."[4]

Characteristic #5. As a competent teacher, you use thoughtfully selected words, carefully planned questions, expressive voice inflections, useful pauses, meaningful gestures, active listening, and productive and nonconfusing body language. Some of these are carefully and thoughtfully planned before or during instruction and others have, through your practice and reflection, become second-nature skills.

Characteristic #6. You realize that the positive effects of appropriate humor (that is, humor that is not self-deprecating or disrespectful of others) on learning are well established.[5] You understand that humor has been known to have these effects: increase in immune system activity; decrease in stress-producing hormones; drop in the pulse rate; reduction in feelings of anxiety, tension, and stress; activation of T-cells for the immune system; support of antibodies that fight against harmful microorganisms and gamma interferon; support of a hormone that fights viruses and regulates cell growth; and increases in blood oxygen. Because of these effects, you consider humor to be a stimulant not only to healthy living, but also to creativity and higher level thinking. You realize that the students appreciate and learn more from a teacher who shares a healthy sense of humor and laughs with (not at) the children.[6]

About Instruction: Progress Report Comments

Characteristic #7. You ensure that students understand the lesson objectives, your expectations, and the classroom procedures. You make them feel welcome in your classroom, get them involved in the learning activities, and encourage them to have some control over the pacing of their own learning. Furthermore, when preparing lessons, you (a) consider the unique characteristics of each student; (b) see that content is presented in reasonably small doses—and in a logical and coherent sequence; (c) use learning activities that engage all learning modalities, with opportunities for guided practice and reinforcement; and (d) frequently check for student comprehension (we suggest one check every minute or so) to ensure that the students are learning. You accomplish checks for comprehension in different ways, such as by the questions you and the children ask during the lesson, by your awareness and understanding of student facial expressions and body language, and by the use of various kinds of checklists.

Characteristic #8. You have both historical understanding and current knowledge of those subjects you are expected to teach, and you are aware of the facts, principles, concepts, and skills needed to teach those subjects.

Characteristic #9. You learn where and how to discover information about content you are expected to teach. You realize that you cannot know everything there is to know about each subject—indeed, you know that you will not always be able to predict all that will be learned—but you are knowledgeable about where and how to best research it and how to assist your students in developing those same skills. Among other things, this means that you are computer literate; that is, you have the ability to understand and use computers for research, writing, and communicating—as you do for reading and writing in verbal literacy.

Characteristic #10. You make a potentially dry and dull topic significant and bring it alive when you teach it. Regardless of the topic, one of the significant characteristics of your effectiveness is that you make the topic come alive and relevant to yourself and to your students, helping the students to make relevant connections. You realize that educational studies point out what should be obvious: Children don't learn much from dull, meaningless "drill-and-kill" exercises and assignments. Such unmotivated teaching may be one of the principal causes of student loss of interest and motivation and subsequent estrangement from school. Obtaining ideas from professional journals, attending workshops, communicating with colleagues either personally or via electronic bulletin boards and websites, and using project-based and interdisciplinary thematic instruction are ways you have of discovering how to make a potentially dry and boring topic interesting and alive for students (and for yourself).

Characteristic #11. Thoughtfully, you prepare and revise activities, lessons, and long-range plans or units reflectively, and implement them with creative, motivating, and effective strategies and skill.

Characteristic #12. As a competent teacher, you consistently model safety procedures (see, for example, Figure 3.2), ensuring precautions necessary to protect the safety of children. You strive to maintain a comfortable room temperature with adequate ventilation and to prevent safety hazards in the classroom. You encourage students who are ill to recuperate at home and to get well. Rather than bringing germs to school, you model this same expectation. You are aware that the Centers for Disease Control and Prevention has recommended that anyone with a cough or other respiratory symptoms immediately don a surgical mask (at a medical facility, this also means isolation from others) to minimize the threat of passing on infections such as influenza, tuberculosis, and pneumonia. If you suspect that a student may be ill or may be suffering from neglect or abuse at home, you promptly act on that concern.

Characteristic #13. You realize that the elementary school classroom is a complex place, busy with fast-paced activities. As a competent teacher, you are in control of classroom events rather than being controlled by them. You initiate, rather than merely react; you are proactive and in control of your interactions. You have learned how to manage time to analyze and develop effective interpersonal behaviors.

About Assessment: Progress Report Comments

Characteristic #14. As part of your assessment methods, both common sense and research tell you clearly that students enjoy and learn better when you are positive and optimistic, encouraging, nurturing, and happy, rather than when you are negative and pessimistic, discouraging, uninterested, and grumpy.

Characteristic #15. For a student, nothing is more satisfying than when you demonstrate confidence in that student's abilities. Unfortunately for some children, your show of confidence may be the only positive indicator that child ever receives. As a competent teacher, you demonstrate this confidence with each and every student. This doesn't mean that you must personally like every student with whom you will ever come into contact; it does mean that you accept each one as a person of dignity who is worthy of receiving your respect and professional skills. You remember that each child is a work in progress.

Characteristic #16. As a competent teacher, you are knowledgeable about the importance of providing immediate intensive intervention when learning problems become apparent; you implement appropriate learning assessment tools and avoid the abuse of power you have through the assessment process.

About Professional Development: Progress Report Comments

Characteristic #17. As discussed earlier, as a competent teacher, you are a good student, and often continue your own learning by reflecting on and assessing your work, by attending workshops, by studying the work of others, and by talking with students, parents, guardians, and colleagues.

Characteristic #18. As a competent teacher, you can be relied on to fulfill professional responsibilities, promises, and commitments. You realize that a teacher who cannot be relied on is quick to lose credibility with colleagues and administrators (as well as with students, parents, guardians, and community members). You also know that, regardless of the teacher's potential for effectiveness, an unreliable teacher is an incompetent teacher. And for whatever reason, a teacher who is chronically absent from his or her teaching duties is a teacher at risk.

Characteristic #19. You realize that teachers, parents, guardians, administrators, cooks, bus drivers, custodians, secretaries, and other adults of the school community all share one common purpose—to serve the education of the children. It is done best when they do it collaboratively. As a skillful teacher, you work with others to ensure that parents or guardians are involved in their children's learning.

Characteristic #20. As a competent teacher, you are a learner among learners. This learning is supported through workshops, advanced university course work, and coaching and training; through the acquisition of further knowledge by reading and study; and through collaboration with colleagues and role modeling of other educators. Through your precredential work and beyond, you will be in a perpetual learning mode about teaching and learning.

Characteristic #21. Knowing that ultimately each and every school activity has an effect on the classroom, you assume an active interest in the school community. You realize that the purpose of the school is to serve the education of the children, and the classroom is the primary, but not only, place where this occurs. You understand that every committee meeting, school event, team meeting, faculty meeting, school board meeting, program, and any other planned function that is related to school life shares in the ultimate purpose of better serving the education of the children who attend your school.

Characteristic #22. You realize that this includes professional interest in the activities of the students and the many aspects of the school and its surrounding community. As a competent teacher, you are interesting to others because of your interests; and when you have varied interests, you will more often motivate and capture the attention of more students. You realize that a teacher with no interests outside the classroom is likely, for the children, to be an exceedingly dull teacher.

Teacher Progress:

The basic characteristics of a competent classroom teacher have been satisfactorily met in:

Management _____ **Instruction** _____ **Assessment** _____ **Professional Development** _____

Assignment for next year: _____

- Consider asking the older students and their parents to sign a contract agreeing to replace any of the electronic devices that are lost, stolen, or damaged.
- Ask the students to use the address book component of their electronic handheld device to create a dictionary with definitions for a unit of study or for selected terms for studying math, science, and social studies.
- Load a drawing program such as *Sketchy* into the electronic handheld device so the students can create drawings of the water cycle or other processes the students are studying.
- Load a program such as *Classroom Wizard* into the handheld device that students can use to take quizzes and tests.
- Use digital cameras to make digital videos so the parents can see how technology is used in the classroom on Back to School Night, and if the school's home page is available, show some of the videos there.

Companion Website

To find links to resources about documenting and citing electronic sources, go to our Companion Website at **www.prenhall.com/roberts** and click on the *Web Destinations* module for Chapter 3.

Decision-Making Phases of Instruction

Instruction can be divided into four decision-making and thought-processing phases: (a) the planning or preactive phase, (b) the teaching or interactive phase, (c) the analyzing and evaluating or reflective phase, and (d) the application or projective phase.

Here are some clarifying explanations:

- The *preactive phase* consists of all those intellectual functions and decisions you will make prior to actual instruction. This includes decisions about the target goals and objectives, homework assignments, what children already know and can do, appropriate learning activities, questions to be asked (and possible answers), and the selection and preparation of instructional materials and the classroom.

- The *interactive phase* includes all the decisions made spontaneously during the teaching act. This includes maintaining student attention, questions to be asked, types of feedback given to children, and ongoing adjustments to the lesson plan. Decisions made by you during this phase are likely to be more intuitive, unconscious, and routine than those made during the planning phase.

- The *reflective phase* occurs when you reflect on, analyze, and judge the decision and behaviors that occurred during the interactive phase. It is during reflection that you make decisions about student learning, student grades, feedback given to parents and guardians, and adjustments on the content and instruction to follow.

- As a result of this reflection, decisions are made to use what was learned in subsequent teaching actions. At this point, you are in the *projective phase*, abstracting from your reflection and projecting your analysis into subsequent teaching behaviors.

Reflection, Locus of Control, and Teacher Responsibility

During the reflective phase, teachers have a choice of whether to assume full responsibility for the instructional outcomes or whether to assume responsibility for only the positive outcomes of the planned instruction while placing the blame for the negative outcomes on outside forces (e.g., parents and guardians, society in general, peers, other teachers, administrators, textbooks). Where the responsibility for outcomes is placed is referred to as **locus of control.**

Teachers who are intrinsically motivated and professionally accomplished tend to assume full responsibility for the instructional outcomes, regardless of whether or not the outcomes are as intended from the planning phase.[8] Of course, every teacher realizes that some factors cannot be controlled, such as the negative effects on children from alcohol and drug abuse, gangs, and poverty. Therefore, teachers must do what they can within the confines of the classroom and their time with the children to reduce the negative effects of such outside factors. History is full of examples of how a relatively few but positive moments with a truly caring and knowledgeable teacher can drastically change for the better the life of a child who, until then, had a history of mostly negative experiences.

Now, further your understanding of reflective decision making by doing Application Exercise 3.2.

For Your Notes

APPLICATION EXERCISE 3.2 THE TEACHER AS A REFLECTIVE DECISION MAKER

Instructions: The purpose of this exercise is to learn more about the nature of the decisions and the decision-making process used by teachers. To accomplish this, you are to talk with and observe one elementary or middle school teacher for 1 hour. Obtain permission from a cooperating teacher by explaining the purpose of your observations. A follow-up thank-you note would be appropriate.

Using the following format, tabulate the number of decisions the teacher makes during that period. You may first want to make your tabulations on a separate sheet of paper and then organize and transfer them to this page. To tabulate the decisions made before and after instruction, confer with the teacher after class. Share the results with your classmates.

School, teacher, and class observed: _____

1. Decisions made before instruction (examples: objectives of lesson; amount of time to be devoted to particular activities, classroom management procedures)

_____

_____

_____

_____

_____

_____

_____

_____

2. Decisions made during instruction (examples: called on someone to answer a question; remained silent until students in back corner became quiet; talked with a tardy student)

_____

_____

_____

_____

_____

_____

_____

_____

3. Decisions made after instruction (examples: to review a particular concept tomorrow; to arrange a conference to talk with a student about his hostility in class; to make a revision in the next day's homework assignment)

_____

_____

_____

_____

_____

APPLICATION EXERCISE 3.2 *(continued)*

4. What was the total number of decisions made by this teacher before instruction? _____ During instruction? _____ After instruction? _____ Compare your results with those of others in your class.

5. What evidence, if any, did you observe that this teacher assumed full responsibility for the learning outcomes of this class session? Describe the evidence. _____

_____

_____

6. What percentage of all decisions by this teacher were planned? _____ Spontaneous? _____

7. How did you share the results of this exercise with the cooperating teacher? _____

_____

What were his or her reactions?

_____

_____

_____

_____

_____

_____

_____

_____

8. What are your conclusions from this exercise? _____

_____

_____

Table 3.1
Two contrasting teaching styles

Characteristic	Traditional Style	Facilitating Style
Teacher is:	Autocratic	Democratic
	Explicit	Implicit
	Dominative	Interactive
	Formal	Informal
	Informative	Inquiring
	Prescriptive	Reflective
Classroom is:	Curriculum-centered	Student-centered
	Linear	Grouped or circular
	Teacher-centered	Student-centered
Instructional modes are:	Abstract learning	Concrete learning
	Lectures	Peer, cross-age coaching
	Competitive	Cooperative
	Demonstrations	Inquiries by students
	Teacher-centered	Student-centered
	Transmission of information from teacher to students	Dialogue among all with reciprocal teaching, student discussions
	Some problem solving	Problem solving

TEACHING STYLE

The phrase **teaching style** refers to the way teachers teach, which includes their distinctive mannerisms complemented by their choices of teaching behaviors and strategies. A teacher's style affects how the teacher presents information and interacts with students. The manner and pattern of those interactions with students determine a teacher's effectiveness in promoting student learning, positive attitudes about learning, and students' self-esteem.

A teacher's style is determined by the teacher's personal characteristics (especially the teacher's own learning style), experiences, and knowledge of research findings about how children learn. Teaching style can be altered, intentionally or unintentionally, as a result of changes in any of these three areas. Although there are other ways to label and describe teaching styles, we will consider in Table 3.1 two contrasting styles—the traditional and the facilitating styles—to emphasize that, although today's teacher must use aspects from each (that is, be eclectic in style choice), there must be a strong inclination toward the facilitating style.

Multilevel Instruction

As emphasized in Chapter 2, children in your classroom have their own independent ways of knowing and learning. It is important to try to attend to how each student best learns and to where each student is developmentally, that is, to personalize both the content and the methods of learning. In essence, although perhaps not as detailed as the individualized

education programs (IEPs) prepared for special education students, at various times during the school year, you will be developing personalized educational plans for each student, perhaps in collaboration with members of your teaching team. To accomplish that, you can use multilevel instruction (known also as multitasking). Referring back to Chapter 2 and the classroom vignette for that chapter, multilevel instruction is when individual students and groups of students are working at different tasks to accomplish the same or different objectives. For example, while some students may be working independently of the teacher—that is, within the facilitating mode of the teacher—others may be receiving explicit instruction—that is, more within the traditional mode.

When integrating student learning, as reviewed in Part II of this resource guide, multitasking is an important, useful, and perhaps even obligatory strategy. Project-based learning is an instructional method that easily allows for the provision of multilevel instruction.

THE THEORETICAL ORIGINS OF TEACHING STYLES AND THEIR RELATIONS TO CONSTRUCTIVISM

Constructivism (also known as **cognitivism**) teaching and the integration of curriculum are not new to education. The importance of constructivism and curriculum integration approaches are found, for example, in the writings of John Dewey,[9] Arthur W. Combs,[10] Jean Piaget,[11] and Lev Vygotsky.[12]

Instructional styles are deeply rooted in certain theoretical assumptions about learners and their development. Although it is beyond the scope of this resource guide to explore these assumptions in depth, we should mention here three major theoretical positions with research findings, each of which is based on certain philosophical and psychological assumptions that suggest different ways of working with children. The theoretical positions are described briefly in the next three paragraphs.

Central to the theoretical positions of **romanticism-maturationism** is the assumption that the learner's mind is neutral–passive to good–active, and the main focus in teaching should be the addition of new ideas to the subconscious store of old ones. Key proponents of this theory include Jean J. Rousseau and Sigmund Freud; key instructional strategies include classic lecturing with rote memorization.

A major part of the theoretical position of **behaviorism** is the assumption that the learner's mind is neutral–passive with innate reflexes and needs, and the main focus in teaching should be on the successive, systematic changes in the learner's environment to increase the possibilities of desired behavioral responses. Key proponents include John Locke, B. F. Skinner, A. H. Thorndike, Robert Gagné, and John Watson; key instructional strategies include programmed instruction and practice and reinforcement as in workbook drill activities.

Linked to the theoretical position of **cognitive-experimentalism** (including constructivism) is the assumption that the learner is a neutral–interactive, purposeful individual in simultaneous interaction with the physical and biological environments. The main focus in teaching should be on facilitating the learner's gain and construction of new perceptions that lead to desired behavioral changes and ultimately to a more fully functioning individual. Key proponents are John Dewey, Lev Vygotsky, Jerome Bruner, Jean Piaget, and Arthur W. Combs; key instructional strategies include discovery, inquiry, project-centered teaching, cooperative and social-interactive learning, and integrated curriculum.

It is our opinion that to be most effective with a diversity of students, an elementary schoolteacher must be eclectic, but with a strong emphasis on cognitive-experimentalism-constructivism because of this theory's divergence in learning and the importance given to learning as a change in perception(s). An effective approach is to use, at appropriate times, the best of strategies and knowledgeable instructor behaviors, regardless of whether they can be individually classified within any style dichotomy, such as explicit vs. implicit, formal vs. informal, traditional vs. progressive, or didactic vs. facilitative. Now, to further your understanding, do Application Exercise 3.3.

In this chapter, teaching style has been defined as the way teachers teach, their distinctive mannerisms complemented by their choices of teaching behaviors and strategies. Style develops from tradition, from experience, and from research findings. Many variables affect a teacher's style, some of which we know very little about, but what is believed about the reciprocal process of teaching and learning is that to effectively reach the highest percentage of students the competent teacher must utilize a style that is eclectic. Chapter 4 further helps you identify your own teaching skills and weaknesses, an important first step in the development of a teaching style.

APPLICATION EXERCISE 3.3 USING A QUESTIONNAIRE TO DEVELOP A PROFILE AND A STATEMENT ABOUT MY OWN EMERGING TEACHING STYLE

Instructions: The purpose of this questionnaire is to help you clarify and articulate your own assumptions about teaching and learning. You will develop a profile of your emerging teaching style and, from that, a statement representative of your current thinking about teaching and learning.

Step 1. Read each of the statements that follow and rate your feelings about each as follow:

1 = strongly agree; 2 = neutral; 3 = strongly disagree

Instruction

I believe that

_____ 1. learning takes place more effectively when children are working cooperatively with one another. _____

_____ 2. for a child to benefit the most from his/her learning, a child should assume part of the responsibility of what should be learned. _____

_____ 3. a child enjoys discussing his/her ideas about learning with the teacher and other children. _____

_____ 4. learning should be the addition of new ideas to the subconscious store of old ideas of a child. _____

_____ 5. a child learns from the addition of successive, systematic changes in the child's environment to increase the possibilities of a desired behavioral response. _____

_____ 6. a child learns more from the addition of interactions with the child's physical and biological environments. _____

_____ 7. a child learns more by working on his/her own than by working with others, i.e., most of what children learn, they learn on their own. _____

_____ 8. a child should be given opportunities to participate actively in planning and implementing lessons. _____

_____ 9. a child enjoys working in a classroom that has clearly defined objectives and assessment criteria. _____

_____10. most of what a child learns is learned from other children. _____

_____11. learning should help a child become a better thinker. _____

_____12. most of what a child learns is learned from a teacher. _____

_____13. learning is most effective when the children are in competition with one another. _____

_____14. an effective teacher should try to convince a child that certain ideas are valid and exciting. _____

_____15. ideas in children's textbooks are usually accurate. _____

_____16. most of what a child learns is learned from books. _____

_____17. a child can learn more by working with an enthusiastic teacher than by working alone. _____

_____18. the ideas of other children are useful in helping a child understand the content of a lesson. _____

APPLICATION EXERCISE 3.3 *(continued)*

_____19. a child should study what the teacher says is important and not necessarily what the child thinks is important. _____

_____20. a teacher often gives children too many trivial assignments. _____

_____21. ideas contained in a child's textbook should be the primary source of the content sought. _____

_____22. the ideas a child brings to class are useful in helping the child understand the subject content. _____

_____23. learning takes place more effectively when a child is working independently of other children. _____

_____24. a child's ideas about content are often better than the ideas found in a text. _____

I favor

_____25. maximizing a child's independence to learn from his/her own experience and believe a teacher's teaching methods and classroom procedures should reflect this. _____

_____26. maximizing interchanges between the children and the teacher to provide better ideas about content than those ideas found in a text. _____

_____27. maximizing lesson interactions between the teacher and the child. _____

_____28. maximizing the learning of subject matter content with correlated teaching methods and lesson procedures. _____

_____29. discussions in the classroom and see them as beneficial learning experiences. _____

Management

I think that

_____30. an important part of a child's education is learning to work with others. _____

_____31. an important part of teaching and learning should be for a child to learn how to work independently. _____

_____32. a child, to get the most out of his/her learning, must be aware of the primary concerns and biases of a teacher. _____

_____33. a child must be assertive to do well in school. _____

_____34. a child has to be able to work effectively with others to do well in school. _____

_____35. a teacher should clearly explain what it is that he/she expects from the children. _____

_____36. a teacher should encourage a child to disagree with or challenge that teacher in the classroom. _____

_____37. a teacher should not be contradicted or challenged by a child in the classroom. _____

_____38. an ineffective teacher is a teacher who makes the children do learning activities that they do **not** want to do. _____

_____39. a teacher who lets a child do whatever he/she wants is incompetent. _____

_____40. a teacher who does not motivate a child's interest in the subject matter is incompetent. _____

_____41. some teachers often give children too much freedom of choice in selecting content and procedures. _____

_____42. some teachers often are too personal with the children in their classrooms. _____

APPLICATION EXERCISE 3.3 *(continued)*

Assessment

I believe that

_____43. in an effective learning environment, grades are inappropriate. _____

_____44. the child's education should help the child become a successful and contributing member of society. _____

_____45. a child's education should help the child become a sensitive human being. _____

_____46. an important part of a child's education is learning how to perform under testing and evaluating conditions. _____

_____47. a child should be concerned about getting good grades. _____

_____48. a child should not be given high grades unless the grades are clearly earned. _____

_____49. a child should be given high grades as a means of motivating him/her and increasing the child's self-esteem. _____

_____50. a child should be concerned about other children's reactions (feedback) to his/her work in the classroom. _____

Step 2. From the preceding list of items, write the numbers of those items with which you strongly agreed in one column and the numbers of those with which you strongly disagreed in the other column. Ignore those items to which you were neutral.

Strongly Agreed   *Strongly Disagreed*

Step 3. In groups of three or four, discuss the lists you generated in step 2 with others in your group. After the discussion, you may rearrange any items you wish.

APPLICATION EXERCISE 3.3 *(continued)*

Step 4. You now have a finalized list of those items with which you agree and those with which you disagree. On the basis of those two lists, write a paragraph that summarizes your philosophy about teaching and learning. It should be no longer than one-half to one page in length. This statement is the theoretical representation of your present teaching philosophy.

_____

_____

_____

_____

_____

_____

_____

_____

_____

_____

_____

_____

Step 5. Compare your philosophical statement with the three theoretical positions discussed earlier in this chapter. Can you clearly identify your position? Name it.

_____

Explain why you selected the theoretical position you chose.

_____

_____

_____

_____

_____

_____

_____

APPLICATION EXERCISE 3.3 *(continued)*

\

At the completion of this text, you may want to revisit your philosophical statement and perhaps even to revise it. It will be useful for you to have your educational philosophy in mind for your teaching interviews at a later date.

Sources: Earlier versions of this concept for developing a philosophical statement were by William H. Berquist and Steven R. Phillips, *A Handbook for Faculty Development* (Washington, DC: The Council for Independent Colleges, June 1975), pp. 25–27; and Richard D. Kellough and Patricia L. Roberts, *A Resource Guide for Elementary School Teaching: Planning for Competence* (New York: Macmillan, 1985), pp. 83–85.

For Your Notes

About Praxis and Other Teacher Tests

About Praxis Teacher Tests. To continue to support your interest in preparing for Praxis II Principles of Teaching and Learning tests and some of the other teacher tests, all applications in this chapter offer opportunities for you to reflect generally on the content about elementary school teaching and learning and, specifically, on the expectations, responsibilities, and facilitating behaviors of an elementary classroom teacher. For example, in Chapter 3, precredentialed teachers are asked to participate cooperatively and collaboratively and to do the following:

- Review the professional responsibilities of a first-year teacher (Application Exercise 3.1).
- Learn more about the nature of the decisions and the decision-making process used by teachers (Application Exercise 3.2).
- Use a questionnaire to develop a profile and a statement about your own teaching style (Application Exercise 3.3).
- Turn to our Companion Website (**www.prenhall.com/roberts**) and click on the *Additional Application Exercise* module to complete additional application exercises, namely, The Preactive Phase of Instruction and Web Destinations of use to Elementary School Teachers.

If you want to respond to a constructed response-type question similar to those found on the Praxis II Elementary Education tests, turn to the Praxis Warm-Up in the end-of-chapter material. This warm-up takes another look at the classroom vignette found in the Looking at Teachers section at the beginning of this chapter.

 Other Teacher Tests. For those of you who will be teaching in states that do not administer the Praxis II Principles of Learning and Teaching tests, go to our Companion Website at **www.prenhall.com/roberts** and click on the *Other Teacher Tests* module for Chapter 3 to access information about teacher tests other than the Praxis.

SUMMARY

You have reviewed the realities of the responsibilities of today's elementary school classroom teacher. Becoming a competent teacher takes time, commitment, concentrated effort, and just plain hard work. Nobody truly knowledgeable about it ever said that competent teaching was easy.

You have learned that your professional responsibilities as a teacher will extend well beyond the four walls of the classroom, the 6 hours of the school day, the 5 days of the school week, and the many days of the school year. You learned of the many expectations: (a) to be committed to young students, to the school's mission, and to the profession; (b) to develop facilitating behaviors and to provide effective instruction; (c) to fulfill numerous noninstructional responsibilities; and (d) to demonstrate effective decision-making related to the many expectations. As you have read and discussed these responsibilities, you should have begun to fully comprehend the challenge and reality of becoming a competent classroom teacher.

Today, there seems to be much agreement that the essence of the learning process is a combination of self-awareness, self-monitoring, and active reflection. Children learn these skills best when exposed to teachers who themselves effectively model those same behaviors. The most effective teaching and learning is an interactive process and involves not only learning, but also thinking about learning and learning how to learn.

Related to the teaching–learning process, you reviewed the way teachers teach, that is, their teaching style, their distinctive mannerisms complemented by their choices of teaching behaviors and strategies. Style develops from tradition, from one's beliefs and experiences, and from one's knowledge of the best of research findings. You began the development of your philosophy about teaching and learning, a philosophical statement that should be useful to you during later job interviews.

Exciting research findings continue to emerge from several related areas: learning, conceptual development and thinking, and neurophysiology. The findings continue to support the hypothesis that an elementary school classroom teacher's best teaching style choice is eclectic with an emphasis on a facilitating style, at least until the day arrives when students of certain styles of learning can be practically matched to teachers with particular teaching styles. The future may give us additional insight into the relationships among pedagogy, pedagogical styles, and student thinking and learning.

What's to Come. The next, and final, chapter of Part I of this resource guide presents ways of establishing an effective learning environment within which to carry out your professional responsibilities.

EXTENDING MY PROFESSIONAL COMPETENCY

Praxis Warm-Up: A Constructed Response-Type Question

Think back to the chapter's opening teacher vignette to the third-grade teacher who explained the concept of transplanting to her class and who motivated one of the students to initiate a service-learning project. With this motivation, eventually all of the student's classmates were involved in working on a landscape project for their school.

Related to this, describe two different learning activities that you would use to help the children with learning problems in this class who do not fully understand the concept of transplanting. Give examples of what the third-grade students would be doing during the two activities. Explain, how you, the teacher, would assess these two activities and the third graders' understanding of the concept of transplanting after they have completed the activities.

Hints for responding to Praxis Warm-Ups are found in the Appendix.

> **Praxis.** To do another Praxis Warm-Up with a constructed response-type question, go to our Companion Website at **www.prenhall.com/roberts** and click on the *Praxis Warm-Up* module for Chapter 3. Constructed response-type questions are designed to help you prepare for the Praxis II Principles of Learning and Teaching tests.

For Your Discussion

1. **Teacher Roles.** If a colleague asks me about the roles teachers are asked to take, what will I say? What is the contrast between a teacher's facilitating behaviors and instructional strategies? **To do:** About four decades ago, a publication entitled *Six Areas of Teacher Competencies* identified six roles of the classroom teacher: director of learning, counselor and guidance worker, mediator of the culture, link with the community, member of the school staff, and member of the profession. Compare those six areas with ways the roles have changed for today's classroom teacher.

2. **Philosophy of Education.** If a colleague asks me to articulate my philosophy of education, what will I say? **To do:** To prepare for your response, refer back to Application Exercise 3.3 in this chapter. Indicate your understanding of how children learn and your responsibility as a classroom teacher in one handwritten page. Give your written philosophy to someone in your group for feedback and discuss any parts that indicate professionalism and commitment. Discuss how your philosophy will affect your teaching style with someone in your group. You may rewrite your statement from time to time, but save it; you will be revisiting it in Chapter 11.

3. **Prior Concepts.** How would I describe any prior concepts (perhaps related to praise, multilevel instruction, hands-on, minds-on learning, or other concepts) I held that changed as a result of my experiences with this chapter? **To do:** Write a one-page handwritten paper to describe the changes and discuss your paper with a partner in your group.

4. **Educational Practice.** I want to clearly identify one specific example of educational practice (perhaps decision-making or thought-processing phases of instruction) that seems contradictory to exemplary practice or theory as presented in this chapter. How would I do that? **To do:** Write a one-page handwritten paper to present your explanation about this discrepancy. Share with a member of your group.

5. **Chapter Content.** If a colleague asks me about questions I have generated by reading the content of this chapter, how will I respond? **To do:** If you have some questions, list them along with ways answers might be found. Share this information with others in your group.

Online Portfolio Activities

Supporting knowledge of students and teaching behaviors (Praxis II Assessments) and a supportive learning environment (Principles 2, 3, and 5 of INTASC and Standards 2, 3, 5, and 7 of NBPTS): At the Companion Website (**www.prenhall.com/roberts**), click on the *Online Portfolio Activities* module to continue your online portfolio supporting knowledge of students.

>
> **Companion Website**
> Also on the Companion Website at **www.prenhall. com/ roberts,** you can measure your understanding of chapter content in the *Objectives* and *Self-Check* modules and apply concepts in the *For Your Discussion* module.

FOR FURTHER READING

Bellanca, J. (1998). Teaching for Intelligence: In Search of Best Practices. *Phi Delta Kappan, 79*(9), 658–660.

Bondy, E. (2000). Warming Up to Classroom Research in a Professional Development School. *Contemporary Education, 72*(1), 8–13.

Danielson, C. (1996). *Enhancing Professional Practice: A Framework for Teaching.* Alexandria, VA: Association for Supervision and Curriculum Development.

Duffy, G. G. (1998). Teaching and the Balancing of Round Stones. *Phi Delta Kappan, 79*(10), 777–780.

Freiberg, H. J. (Ed.) (1999). *Perceiving, Behaving, Becoming: Lessons Learned.* Alexandria, VA: Association for Supervision and Curriculum Development.

Garcia, E. (1994). *Understanding and Meeting the Challenge of Student Cultural Diversity.* Boston: Houghton Mifflin.

Good, T. L., and Brophy, J. E. (2003). *Looking in Classrooms* (9th ed., Chap. 10). New York: Addison-Wesley-Longman.

Jensen, E. (1998). Emotions and Learning, in E. Jensen (Ed.), *Teaching with the Brain in Mind* (Chap. 8). Alexandria, VA: Association for Supervision and Curriculum Development.

Kazemek, F. E. (1999). Why Was the Elephant Late in Getting on the Ark? Elephant Riddles and Other Jokes in the Classroom. *Reading Teacher, 52*(8), 896–898.

Kounin, J. (1970). *Discipline and Group Management in the Classroom.* New York: Holt, Rinehart and Winston.

Lasley II, T. J. (1998). Paradigm Shifts in the Classroom. *Phi Delta Kappan, 80*(1), 84–86.

Marzano, R. J., Marzano, J. S., and Pickering, D. J. (2003). *Classroom Management That Works: Research-Based Strategies for Every Teacher.* Alexandria, VA: Association for Supervision and Curriculum Development.

Palmer, P. J. (1998). *The Courage to Teach: Exploring the Inner Landscape of a Teacher's Life.* San Francisco: Jossey-Bass.

Reid, R. (2002). *Something Funny Happened at the Library: How to Create Humorous Programs for Children and Young Adults.* Chicago: American Library Association.

Roberts, P. L. (1997). *Taking Humor Seriously in Children's Literature: Literature-Based Mini-Units and Humorous Books for Children Ages 5–12.* Lanham, MD: Scarecrow Press.

Stone, R. (1999). *Best Classroom Practices: What Award-Winning Elementary Teachers Do.* Thousand Oaks, CA: Corwin Press/Sage Publications.

Thompson, G. L. (2002). Elementary Teachers. In *African American Teens Discuss Their Schooling Experiences.* Needham Heights, MA: Greenwood Publishing Group.

Thompson, G. L. (2003). *What African American Parents Want Educators to Know.* Needham Heights, MA: Greenwood Publishing Group.

Thompson, G. L. (2003). *What Teachers Want to Know But Are Afraid to Ask About African American Students.* San Francisco: Jossey-Bass.

Wasserman, S. (1999, February). Shazam! You're a Teacher. *Phi Delta Kappan, 80*(6), 464, 466–468.

Wilson-Saddler, D. (1997). Using Effective Praise to Produce Positive Results in the Classroom. *Teaching and Change, 4*(4), 338–357.

NOTES

1. L. Turner, Service Learning and Student Achievement. *Educational Horizons, 81*(4), 188–189, (2003).

2. You may want to compare these competencies with the standards of the Interstate New Teacher Assessment and Support Consortium (INTASC) and with those of the National Board of Professional Teaching Standards (NBPTS) and with the components of Professional practice in C. Danielson, *Enhancing Professional Practice: A Framework for Teaching* (Alexandria, VA: Association for Supervision and Curriculum Development, 1996).

3. G. L. Thompson, *African American Teens Discuss Their Schooling Experiences* (Needham Heights, MA: Greenwood Publishing Group, 2002).

4. S. Wasserman, Shazam! You're a Teacher, *Phi Delta Kappan, 80*(6), 464, 466–468 (February, 1999).

5. R. Reid, *Something Funny Happened at the Library: How to Create Humorous Programs for Children and Young Adults* (Chicago: American Library Association, 2002).

6. P. L. Roberts, *Taking Humor Seriously in Children's Literature: Literature-Based Mini-Units and Humorous Books for Children Ages 5–12* (Lanham, MD: Scarecrow Press, 1997).

7. A. L. Costa, *The School as a Home for the Mind* (Palatine, IL: SkyLight Publishing, 1991), pp. 97–106.

8. See for example, P. Ashton and R. Webb, *Making a Difference: Teachers' Sense of Efficacy and Student Achievement* (New York: Longman, 1986).

9. J. Dewey, *How We Think* (Boston: Health, 1933).

10. A. W. Combs (Ed.), *Perceiving, Behaving, and Becoming: A New Focus for Education* (1962 ASCD Yearbook) (Arlington, VA: Association for Supervision and Curriculum Development, 1962). You might be interested in revisiting the 1962 yearbook; see H. J. Freiberg (Ed.), *Perceiving, Behaving, Becoming: Lessons Learned* (Alexandria, VA: Association for Supervision and Curriculum Development, 1999).

11. You might be interested in reading the original words of J. Piaget in *Science of Education and the Psychology of the Child* (New York: Orion, 1970).

12. L. Vygotsky, *Minds in Society: The Development of Higher Psychological Processes* (Cambridge, MA: Harvard University Press, 1978).

13. *Six Areas of Teacher Competencies* (Burlingame, CA: California Teachers Association, 1964).

What Do I Need to Know to Manage an Effective, Safe, and Supportive Learning Environment?

4

Visual Chapter Organizer and Overview

The Importance of Perceptions

Classroom Control: Its Meaning—Past and Present

Historical Meaning of Classroom Control
Today's Meaning of Classroom Control and the Concept of Classroom Management
Classroom Management: Contributions of Some Leading Authorities
Developing My Own Effective Approach to Classroom Management

Providing a Supportive Learning Environment

Consider the Physical Layout
Create a Positive Classroom Atmosphere
Get to Know the Children as People and Build Intrinsic Motivation for Learning

Preparation Provides Confidence and Success

Using Positive Rewards

Looking at Teachers

Given the teacher's need to establish an effective and safe environment, what is the role of procedures and rules in the classroom from your point of view? Rules must be designed to equally support and value all members of a community of learners in the classroom. With this in mind, what procedures/rules might be needed in some of the following classroom activities? In what ways could you get the students to accept the rules you suggest, assume responsibility for their actions, and make their classroom a community of learners?

In one second-grade classroom, the teacher guided her students in a thematic unit centered on extinct animals—the dinosaurs. The learning activities integrated math and science, drawing and crafts, music and reading, and publishing original books to support the study. Connecting reading to music, the students listened to a song about each dinosaur being studied. Students read sentence strips with the words of the songs. They added sound effects, sang each song several times, and added a rhythmic beat with their fingers and hands. Additionally, the students prepared their own dinosaur-shaped books, wrote original pages, and created illustrations. To survey favorite dinosaurs, graphing was introduced. The students built their own line graph in the classroom and each drew a favorite dinosaur on a small square of paper and placed it on a line that was labeled with the dinosaur's name on a large graph. Students made individual copies of the graph and recorded what was added to the large graph. They marked X's with their pencils in appropriate places. When the class graph was finished, the students read information from it (guided by the teacher) and talked about the information they had gathered.

The unit encompassed a number of multidisciplinary activities related to the topic. For example,

- **History.** Students developed a graphic timeline showing the long period of time that the dinosaurs were dominant on Earth; they visited a museum that featured dinosaur exhibits.
- **Mathematics.** Students categorized the types of dinosaurs and created graphs that illustrated the variety and proportional sizes of dinosaurs.
- **Reading, writing, and art.** Students created and wrote illustrated stories about a favorite dinosaur.
- **Science.** Students speculated about why the dinosaurs were so successful and about the events that led to their rather quick disappearance from Earth.

The culminating event took place at the school's Spring Open House. Each student's assignment for Open House was to bring an adult and to explain to that person what he or she had been learning at school. Confidently, the students told their visitors about dinosaurs and proudly displayed their dinosaur books, dinosaur mobile, dinosaur body shapes from felt, and dinosaur clay models.[1]

To become and remain an effective teacher, as the second-grade teacher was in the preceding classroom vignette, you must (a) apply your knowledge of the characteristics and developmental needs of children with whom you work, (b) practice the behaviors that facilitate student learning, and (c) do so in an environment conducive to learning. The first two requirements have been the foci of the first three chapters and the third requirement is the main focus of this final chapter of Part I in this resource guide. The establishment and maintenance of a conducive classroom learning environment derive from one's knowledge about children and how they learn and from careful thought and planning. These responsibilities should not be left for the new teacher to learn on the job in a sink-or-swim situation.

Teachers know that classroom management is vital for instruction to occur effectively. Students who appreciate and value each other are more likely to work well in academic settings. Cooperation is a key element in making this happen. Reading aloud a story such as *Zinnia and Dot* (New York: Viking, 1992) by Lisa Campbell Ernst demonstrates to students that cooperation has lasting rewards. In the case of two highly competitive chickens, Zinnia and Dot, who lost all but one egg to a weasel, they decided they had to band together to protect their offspring. But working together had its problems. Who would sit on the egg? Whose chick would it be once it was hatched? Only by working together do the hens save the baby chick, which grows up with its two loving mothers. Putting aside individual differences and working as a team are two factors that help Zinnia and Dot succeed. Transferring this message to students can help promote a workable classroom environment and this chapter will provide you with several ways to establish an effective teaching situation in your classroom.

A classroom environment that is conducive to learning is one that is psychologically safe, that helps the children to perceive the importance of what is being taught, that helps them realize they can achieve, and that is instructive and supportive in the procedures for learning. While it is important that they learn to control impulses and delay their need for gratification, children are more willing to spend time on a learning task when they perceive value or reward in doing so, when they possess some ownership in planning and carrying out the task, and when they feel they can indeed accomplish the task.

Thoughtful and thorough planning of your procedures for classroom management, even the careful placement of the desks and other furniture, is as important a part of your proactive (planning) phase of instruction as is the preparation of units and lessons, discussed later in Part II. Indeed, classroom management is perhaps the single most important factor influencing student learning. This chapter presents guidelines and resources that will help you to establish and manage a classroom environment that is safe for children and favorable to their learning.

CHAPTER OBJECTIVES

Specifically, on completion of this fourth chapter, you should be able to:

1. Explain, as a teacher, what helpful information about managing a safe and effective classroom you have received.
2. Describe the steps you should take in preparing a classroom management system that would be implemented during the first few days of school, and emphasize at least three guidelines for acceptable student behavior.
3. Use knowledge about how other teachers manage their classrooms and begin preparing the management system (including rewards if you decide to use them) that you will explain to your students during the first day or first week of school.
4. Describe the value of class meetings and ways some experienced teachers open their meetings.
5. Develop an awareness of at least three common teaching mistakes to avoid, and determine the first action you would take in determining measure of control in a selected situation of your choice.

THE IMPORTANCE OF PERCEPTIONS

Unless you believe your students can learn, they will not. Unless your students believe they can learn and until they want to learn, they will not.

We all know of, or have heard of, teachers who get the very best from their students, even from those students who many teachers find to be the most challenging to teach. Regardless of individual circumstances, those teachers (a) *know* that, when given adequate support and reinforcement, all children can learn; (b) *accept* the best from each student; (c) *establish* a classroom environment that motivates students to do their best; and (d) *manage* their classrooms to see that class time is efficiently used, that is, with the least amount of distraction to the learning process.

Regardless of how well planned you are for the day's instruction, certain perceptions by students must be in place to support the successful implementation of those plans. Students must perceive that (a) the classroom environment is supportive of their efforts, (b) you care about their learning and they are welcome in your classroom, (c) the expected learning is challenging but not impossible, and (d) the anticipated learning outcomes are worthy of their time and effort to try to achieve.

CLASSROOM CONTROL: ITS MEANING—PAST AND PRESENT

Classroom control frequently is of the greatest concern to beginning teachers—and they have good cause to be concerned. Even experienced teachers sometimes find control difficult, particularly with children who come to school with so much psychological baggage that they have already become alienated due to negative experiences in their lives.

In one respect, being a classroom teacher is much like being a medical response ambulance driver/technician who is always concerned about the patient and who must remain alert in different driving conditions—especially difficult ones, such as going down a steep and winding grade. If the driver is not alert, the ambulance most assuredly will go out of control, veer off the highway, and crash. This chapter has been thoughtfully designed to help you with your concerns about control—and to help you avoid a crash.

Historical Meaning of Classroom Control

To set the stage consider what the term **classroom control** has meant historically and what it means today. In the 1800s, instead of classroom control, educators spoke of classroom **discipline,** and that meant punishment. Such an interpretation was consistent with the then-popular learning theory that assumed children were innately bad and that inappropriate behavior could be prevented by strictness or treated with punishment. Schools of the mid-1800s have been described as "wild and unruly places" and full of "idleness and disorder."[2]

By the early 1900s, educators were asking "Why are the children still misbehaving?" The accepted answer was that the children were misbehaving because of the rigid punitive system. On this point, the era of progressive education began, providing students more freedom to decide what they would learn. The teacher's job, then, became one of providing a rich classroom of resources and materials to stimulate the student's natural curiosity. And because the system no longer would be causing misbehavior, punishment would no longer be necessary. Classes of the 1930s that were highly permissive, however, turned out to cause more anxiety than did the restrictive classes of the 1800s.

Today's Meaning of Classroom Control and the Concept of Classroom Management

Today, rather than classroom discipline, educators talk of classroom control, the process of influencing student behavior in the classroom. Classroom control is an important aspect of the broader concept of **classroom management.** Classroom control is part of a management plan designed to (a) prevent inappropriate student behaviors, (b) help children develop self-control, and (c) suggest procedures for dealing with inappropriate student behaviors.

Effective teaching requires a well-organized and business-like classroom in which motivated students work diligently at their learning tasks, free from distractions and interruptions. Providing such a setting for learning requires careful thought and preparation and is called effective classroom management. Effective classroom management is the process of organizing and conducting a classroom so that it maximizes student learning.

A teacher's procedures for classroom control reflect that teacher's philosophy about how children learn and the teacher's interpretation and commitment to the school's stated mission. In sum, those procedures represent the teacher's concept of classroom management. Although often eclectic in their approaches, today's teachers share a concern for selecting management techniques that enhance student self-esteem and that empower the students; that is, the students learn how to assume control of their behavior and ownership of their learning.

While some schools subscribe heavily to one approach or another, such as Albert's cooperative model, or the Fredric Jones model, or Gordon's teacher effectiveness training (TET) model, still others are more eclectic, having evolved from the historical works of leading authorities. Let's consider what some authorities have said. To assist your understanding, refer to Table 4.1, which illustrates the main ideas of each authority and provides a comparison of their recommended approaches. As mentioned in the preceding paragraph, the guidelines and suggestions that are presented throughout this chapter represent an eclectic approach, borrowing from many of these authorities.

Classroom Management: Contributions of Some Leading Authorities

B. F. Skinner (1904–1990). You are probably familiar with the term *behavior modification,* which describes several high-control techniques for changing

behavior in an observable and predictable way. You may also know about B. F. Skinner's ideas on how students learn, how their behavior can be modified by using reinforcers (rewards), and how his principles of behavior shaping have been extended by others.[3]

Behavior modification begins with four steps: (a) identify the behavior to be modified, (b) record how often and under what conditions that behavior occurs, (c) cause a change by reinforcing a desired behavior with a positive reinforcer (a reward), and (d) choose the type of positive reinforcers to award, such as the following:

- **Activity or privilege reinforcers,** such as choice of playing a game, running the projection equipment for the group, caring for a class pet, free reading, decorating the classroom, free art time, choice at a learning center, freed without penalty from doing an assignment or a test, running an errand for the teacher.
- **Graphic reinforcers,** such as numerals and symbols made by rubber stamps.
- **Social reinforcers,** such as verbal attention or praise, and nonverbal such as proximity of teacher to students, and facial (such as a smile) or bodily expressions (a handshake or part on the back) of approval.
- **Tangible reinforcers,** such as badges, books, certificates, stickers, or candy and other edibles to which students are not allergic.
- **Token reinforcers,** such as points, stars, script, or tickets that can be accumulated and cashed in later for a tangible reinforcer, such as a trip to the local pizza place or ice cream store with the teacher (see Figure 4.1).

Lee Canter, Marlene Canter. Lee Canter, a child guidance specialist, and Marlene Canter, a specialist in teaching people with learning disabilities, developed their *assertive discipline model.* Using an approach that emphasizes both reinforcement for appropriate behavior and consequences or punishment for inappropriate behaviors, their model emphasizes four major points. First, as a teacher, you have professional rights in your classroom and should expect appropriate student behavior. Second, your students have the right to choose how to behave in your classroom, and you should plan limits for inappropriate behavior. Third, an assertive discipline approach means you clearly state your expectations in a firm voice and explain the boundaries for behavior. Fourth, you should plan a system of positive consequences (e.g., awards and rewards, special privileges, and sending positive messages home [see Application Exercise 4.1 later in this chapter]) for appropriate behavior and establish

Table 4.1
Comparing approaches to classroom management

Authority	To Know What Is Going On	To Provide Smooth Transitions
Canter/Jones	Realize that the student has the right to choose how to behave in your class with the understanding of the consequences that will follow his or her choice.	Insist on decent, responsible behavior.
Dreikurs/Albert/Nelsen	Realize that the student wants status, recognition and a feeling of belonging. Misbehavior is associated with mistaken goals of getting attention, seeking power, getting revenge, and wanting to be left alone.	Identify a mistaken student goal; act in ways that do not reinforce these goals.
Ginott	Communicate with the student to find out his/her feelings about a situation and about his/herself.	Invite student cooperation.
Glasser/Rogers/Freiberg/Gordon	Realize that the student is a rational being; he/she can control his or her own behavior.	Help the student make good choices; good choices produce good behavior and bad choices produce bad behavior.
Kounin	Develop *with-itness,* a skill enabling you to see what is happening in all parts of the classroom at all times.	Avoid jerkiness, which consists of thrusts (giving directions before your group is ready), dangles (leaving one activity dangling in the verbal air, starting another one, and then returning to the first activity), and flip-flops (terminating one activity, beginning another one, and then returning to the first activity you terminated).
Skinner	Realize value of nonverbal interaction (i.e., smiles, pats, and handshakes) to communicate to students that you know what is going on.	Realize that smooth transition may be part of your procedures for awarding reinforcers (i.e., points and tokens) to reward appropriate behavior.

negative consequences (e.g., time-out, withdrawal of privileges, parent/guardian conference) for inappropriate student misbehavior. Consistent follow-through is necessary.[4]

Today, primarily because of its heavy reliance on the external control of student behavior with the use of threat and punishment, the assertive discipline model is considered to be "less helpful than more eclectically derived programs" that emphasize rationale explanations, logical or natural consequences, and the development of student self-control.[5]

Rudolf Dreikurs (1897–1972). With a *logical* or *natural consequences approach,* Rudolf Dreikurs, a psychiatrist specializing in child and family counseling, emphasized six points:

To Maintain Group Alertness	To Involve Students	To Attend to Misbehavior
Set clear limits and consequences; follow through consistently; state what you expect, state the consequences and why the limits are needed.	Use firm tone of voice; keep eye contact; use nonverbal gestures and verbal statements; use hints, questions, and direct messages in requesting student behavior; give and receive compliments.	Follow through with your promises and the reasonable, previously stated consequences that have been established in your class.
Provide firm guidance and leadership.	Allow students to have a say in establishing rules and consequences in your class.	Make it clear that unpleasant consequences will follow inappropriate behavior.
Model the behavior you expect to see in your students.	Build student's self-esteem.	Give a message that addresses the situation and does not attack the student's character.
Understand that class rules are essential.	Realize that classroom meetings are effective means for attending to rules, behavior, and discipline.	Accept no excuses for inappropriate behavior; see that reasonable consequences always follow.
Avoid slowdowns (delays and time wasting) that can be caused by overdwelling (too much time spent on explanations) and by fragmentation (breaking down an activity into several unnecessary steps). Develop a group focus (active participation by all students in the group) through accountability (holding all students accountable for the concept of the lesson) and by attention (seeing all the students and using unison and individual responses).	Avoid boredom by providing a feeling of progress for the students, by offering challenges, by varying class activities, by changing the level of intellectual challenge, by varying lesson presentations, and by using many different learning materials and aids.	Understand that teacher correction influences behavior of other nearby students (the ripple effect).
Set rules, rewards, and consequences; emphasize that responsibility for good behavior rests with each student.	Involve students in "token economies," in contracts, and in charting behavior performance.	Provide tangibles to students who follow the class rules; represent tangibles as "points" for the whole class to use to "purchase" a special activity.

1. Be fair, firm, and friendly, and involve your students in developing and implementing class rules.
2. Ensure that students clearly understand the standards of expected behavior and the logical consequences for misbehavior. For example, a logical consequence for a student who has painted graffiti on a school wall would be to clean the wall or pay for a school custodian to do it.
3. Allow the students to be responsible not only for their own actions but also for influencing others to maintain appropriate behavior in your classroom.
4. Encourage students to show respect for themselves and for others, and provide each student with a sense of belonging to the class.
5. Recognize and encourage student goals of belonging, gaining status, and gaining recognition.

Figure 4.1
Token reinforcers

- Some teachers give points, stars, script, or tickets to students who are exhibiting target behavior, i.e., working steadily and quietly. The students exchange the reinforcers for activity time in class to engage in educational games and work independently at learning centers.

- Other teachers give a certain number of points to the students each Monday morning. If a student infringes on a procedure/rule, he or she loses a point. On Friday, a student may trade his or her remaining points for a ticket that can be used to acquire something special for the day or following week, i.e., receiving something from a special box, being in charge of the kick ball, being first in line to leave or enter the classroom, selecting a seat in class, moving his or her desk to a special place in the classroom, or participating in an activity center in the room.

- Still other teachers give points as a bonus for a student's improvement in his or her academic work (calculated in points) in the upper elementary and middle school grades. As an example of this, the teacher can average each student's grades for the weekly spelling tests, and then suggest that the students earn bonus points by scoring higher than their average.

- Some teachers give tokens that can be accumulated over time by the students. Tokens of a certain color (A) are given to students who work quietly; five tokens of color A can be turned in for one token of color B; five tokens of color B can be turned in for one token of color C, which can be turned in for a tangible reinforcer.

- Token reinforcers (points, bonus points, stars, script, tickets) can be turned in later for a tangible reinforcer such as a certificate for edibles at a nearby fast-food place or a trip to a pizza restaurant or ice cream store with the teacher. Arrangements with the school/district administration might be made for a local ice cream vendor/truck to drive to the school on Friday afternoon or for a pizza delivery to be made to the school on a certain day so the students' tokens can be turned in for a treat. Other tangible reinforcers can include candy, favorite edibles, badges, certificates, stickers, and books.

6. Recognize but do not reinforce correlated student goals of getting attention, seeking power, and taking revenge.[6]

Linda Albert. Continuing the work of Dreikurs, Linda Albert, a former student of Dreikurs, has developed *cooperative discipline,* a detailed discipline system that is being used in many schools. The cooperative discipline model makes use of Dreikurs' fundamental concepts, with emphasis added on three C's: capability, connectedness, and contributions.[7]

Jane Nelsen. Also building on the work of Dreikurs, psychotherapist Jane Nelsen provides guidelines for helping children develop positive feelings of self. Key points made by Nelsen that are reflected throughout this resource guide are (a) use natural and logical consequences as a means to inspire a positive classroom atmospheres, (b) understand that children have goals that drive them toward misbehavior (assumed adequacy, attention, power, and revenge), (c) use kindness (student retains dignity) and firmness when administering consequences for a student's misbehavior, (d) establish a climate of mutual respect,

(e) use class meetings to give students ownership in problem solving and goal setting, and (f) offer encouragement as a means of inspiring self-evaluation and focusing on the students' behaviors.[8]

William Glasser. Psychiatrist William Glasser developed his concept of *reality therapy* (i.e., the condition of the present, rather than that of the past, contributes to inappropriate behavior) for the classroom. Glasser emphasizes that students have a responsibility to learn at school and to maintain appropriate behavior while there. He stresses that with the teacher's help, students can make appropriate choices about their behavior in school—that they can, in fact, learn self-control.[9] Glasser suggests holding class meetings that are devoted to establishing class rules and identifying standards for student behavior, matters of misbehavior, and the consequences of misbehavior. Since the publication of his first book in 1965, Glasser has expanded his message to include more student needs of belonging and love, control, freedom, and fun, asserting that if these needs are ignored and unattended at school, children are bound to become unmotivated and fail.[10]

Carl Rogers, H. Jerome Freiberg. Today's commitment to quality education is not only largely derived from the recent work of Glasser but also the corresponding concept of the person-centered classroom as advanced by Carl Rogers and H. Jerome Freiberg in their 1994 book *Freedom to Learn.*[11] In schools committed to quality education and the person-centered classroom, students feel a sense of belonging, enjoy some degree of power of self-discipline, have fun learning, and experience a sense of freedom in the process.[12]

Haim G. Ginott (1922–1973). Psychologist Haim G. Ginott emphasized ways for teachers and students to communicate in his *communication model.* He advised teachers to send a clear message or messages about situations rather than about the children. He stressed that teachers must model the behavior they expect from students.[13] Ginott's suggested messages are those that express feelings appropriately, acknowledge students' feelings, give appropriate direction, and invite cooperation.

Thomas Gordon. In his book *Discipline That Works: Promoting Self-Discipline in Children,*[14] clinical psychologist Thomas Gordon emphasizes influence over control and decries the use of reinforcement (i.e., rewards and punishment) as ineffective tools for achieving a positive influence over a child's behavior. Rather than using reinforcements for appropriate behaviors and punishment for inappropriate behaviors, Gordon advocates encouragement and development of student self-control and self-regulated behavior.

To have a positive influence and to encourage self-control, the teacher and school should provide a rich and positive learning environment, with rich and stimulating learning activities. Specific teacher behaviors include active listening, sending *I*-messages (rather than *you*-messages), shifting from *I*-messages to listening when there is student resistance to an *I*-message, clearly identifying ownership of problems to the student when such is the case (i.e., not assuming ownership if it is a student's problem), and encouraging collaborative problem solving.

Fredric Jones. Psychologist Fredric Jones promotes the idea of helping students support their own self-control by way of a negative reinforcement method in which rewards follow good behavior.[15] Preferred activity time (PAT), for example, is an invention derived from the Jones model. The Jones model makes four recommendations. First you should properly structure your classroom so students understand the **rules** (the expectations standards for classroom behavior) and **procedures** (the means for accomplishing routine tasks). Second, you maintain control by selecting appropriate instructional strategies. Third,

you build patterns of cooperative work. Finally, you develop appropriate backup methods for dealing with inappropriate student behavior.

Jacob Kounin. Well known for his identification of the *ripple effect* (i.e., the effect of a teacher's response to one student's misbehavior on students whose behavior was appropriate), Jacob Kounin also emphasizes the teacher's with-itness (i.e., the teacher's ability to remain alert in the classroom and to spot quickly and redirect potential student misbehavior, which is analogous to having "eyes in the back of your head").[16]

Developing My Own Effective Approach to Classroom Management

As you review these classic contributions to today's approaches to effective classroom management, the educational opinions as well as the research evidence will remind you of the importance of doing the following: (a) concentrating your attention on desirable student behaviors; (b) quickly and appropriately attending to inappropriate behavior; (c) maintaining alertness to all that is happening in your classroom; (d) providing smooth transitions, keeping the entire class on task, preventing dead time; and (e) involving students by providing challenges, class meetings, ways to establish rules and consequences, opportunities to receive and return compliments, and chances to build self-control and self-esteem.

Using the criteria of your own philosophy, feelings, values, knowledge, and perceptions, you are encouraged to construct a classroom environment and management system that is positive and effective for you and your students, and then to apply it consistently. Use the guidelines shown in Figure 4.2 to begin the thinking process for developing your personal plan for classroom management, the process that begins now and continues with Application Exercise 4.1 and throughout your professional career.

PROVIDING A SUPPORTIVE LEARNING ENVIRONMENT

For you it is probably no surprise to hear that teachers whose classrooms are pleasant, positive, and challenging but supportive places to be find that their students learn and behave better than do the students of teachers whose classroom atmospheres are harsh, negative, repressive, and unchallenging. What follows now are specific suggestions for making your classroom a pleasant, positive, and challenging place, that is, an environment that is conducive to the development of meaningful understandings.

Figure 4.2
Developing the personal classroom management system

DEVELOPING THE PERSONAL CLASSROOM MANAGEMENT SYSTEM

MY EMERGING PLAN FOR CLASSROOM MANAGEMENT:
A CHECKLIST

Grade level _____   Name _____

Plans Before the First Day

1. I can describe my classroom with respect to the physical room arrangement and organization, and the positive and caring classroom community that I aim to create.

   yes _____   no _____   somewhat _____

2. I can describe communication I will initiate with my students and their families prior to the first day of school.

   yes _____   no _____   somewhat _____

3. I can describe characteristics of my classroom that will signal to the children that it is a friendly and safe place to be.

   yes _____   no _____   somewhat _____

4. I can describe how I will get to know the children and what I will do to help the children get to know me and each other.

   yes _____   no _____   somewhat _____

The First Day

5. I can describe how I will greet the children when they arrive for the first day.

   yes _____   no _____   somewhat _____

6. I can describe the rules or procedural expectations that I will have already in place and how they will be presented to the children. I have made a sketch of a visual aid I could make with a poster board and markers to create a set of procedures/rules to display in the classroom.

   yes _____   no _____   somewhat _____

7. I can describe how I will have children contribute to these rules/procedures and expectations.

   yes _____   no _____   somewhat _____

8. I can describe my classroom procedures for

   - absences
   - making up missed work and instruction
   - assigning helpers for class responsibilities such as taking care of pets, plants, the calendar, and so forth
   - bringing toys, plants, and pets into the classroom
   - collecting notes, money, and forms
   - distributing and collecting papers and materials
   - eating and drinking in the classroom
   - going to the bathroom
   - late arrival and early dismissal
   - movement in the halls

   - storing personal belongings
   - taking attendance
   - using the class sink
   - using the pencil sharpener
   - using the teacher's desk
   - using the water fountain
   - using other materials and equipment
   - wearing hats and other articles of clothing in the classroom
   - what to do in an emergency situation
   - when a visitor comes into the classroom.

   yes _____   no _____   somewhat _____

9. I can describe the morning opening and afternoon closure; I can tell about a teaching activity (20 minutes) I would use for the class in case of an early release procedure for students, bell changes, or other interruptions. I can tell 1–2 short activities I would use (such as lessons in an e-teaching kit, Chapter 11) during brief periods of time when needed during the first 2–3 weeks.

   yes _____   no _____   somewhat _____

Managing the Curriculum

10. I can describe how I will help the children with their organization and assignments.
    yes _____   no _____   somewhat _____

11. I can describe my homework (responsibility papers) expectations. I've answered these questions: Will there be homework? How much and how often? Will parents and guardians be informed? If so, how? What is their involvement to be? Is there a school homework hotline?
    yes _____   no _____   somewhat _____

12. I can describe my procedure for incomplete, unacceptable, or incorrect student work (and for a recovery option).
    yes _____   no _____   somewhat _____

13. I can describe ways I'll provide comments, feedback, or corrections in student work.
    yes _____   no _____   somewhat _____

14. I can describe ways I'll use marks of some sort—grades, value words, figures, and so forth.
    yes _____   no _____   somewhat _____

15. I can describe ways students will be rewarded for their group work, how I'll assess group learning, and how I'll assess individual learning from group work.
    yes _____   no _____   somewhat _____

16. I can describe the student portfolio expectation and indicate where the portfolios will be stored and when the students will work on them.
    yes _____   no _____   somewhat _____

17. I can describe my plan for communication with parents/guardians.
    yes _____   no _____   somewhat _____

Maintaining Classroom Relations and Personal Behavior

18. I can describe how I will bring an off-task child back on task.
    yes _____   no _____   somewhat _____

19. I can describe to students what is and what is not an appropriate level of classroom noise.
    yes _____   no _____   somewhat _____

20. I can describe to students when I signal a need for hands, and when, if ever, it is okay to call out without raising hands.
    yes _____   no _____   somewhat _____

21. I can describe how I will indicate my support for appropriate student behavior.
    yes _____   no _____   somewhat _____

22. I can describe how I will discourage inappropriate student behavior.
    yes _____   no _____   somewhat _____

23. I can describe my order of explicit and implicit behavior intervention strategies.
    yes _____   no _____   somewhat _____

24. I can describe how I will signal my need for attention from the class.
    yes _____   no _____   somewhat _____

25. I can describe how I will respond when two errant behaviors are happening simultaneously at opposing locations in the classroom.
    yes _____   no _____   somewhat _____

26. I can describe how I will position the desks/furniture to maintain positive classroom relations.
    yes _____   no _____   somewhat _____

When the Going Gets Tough

27. I can describe my pattern of escalating consequences.
    yes _____   no _____   somewhat _____

28. I can describe how I will deal with disrespectful, inappropriate comments from students.
    yes _____   no _____   somewhat _____

29. I can describe how I will respond to remarks that are sexist or racist or that stereotype people in inappropriate and cruel ways.
    yes _____   no _____   somewhat _____

30. I can describe how I will respond to serious and dangerous student behaviors.
    yes _____   no _____   somewhat _____

31. I can identify one person I can go to for support.
    yes _____   no _____   somewhat _____

Consider the Physical Layout

There is much in the arrangement of a classroom that can either contribute to or help prevent classroom management problems. There is no one best way to arrange desks or learning stations in a classroom. Some teachers suggest that you sketch the possible traffic patterns in your room on paper before school begins for the year so that you can avoid placing students' desks in the traffic path to the pencil sharpener or water fountain. The arrangement should be kept flexible so children may be deployed in the ways most suitable for accomplishing specific tasks.

The guideline is simple. Just as is true with adults, when children are seated side by side, it is perfectly natural for them to talk to each other. Therefore, if your purpose is to encourage social interaction, such as when using cooperative learning and small-group project work, seat children close together. If you would rather they work independently, such as when taking independent achievement tests, separate them. It is unreasonable to place children in situations that encourage maximum interaction and then to admonish or berate them for whispering and talking. Sometimes, so as not to disturb the learning going on in neighboring classrooms, you may need to remind the children to whisper, talk softly, or "use their six-inch voices."

You should not be seated in your desk chair much of the time during the school day; therefore, it matters little where your teacher's desk is located except that it be out of the way—perhaps away from traffic patterns near the water fountain or pencil sharpener.

Create a Positive Classroom Atmosphere

You have heard it before and now we say it again: All children should feel welcome in your classroom and accepted by you as individuals of dignity. Though these feelings and behaviors should be reciprocal, that is, expected of the children as well, they may have to begin with your frequent modeling of the behaviors expected of the students. You must help students know that any denial by you of a child's specific behavior is not a denial of that individual child as a worthwhile person who is still welcome to come to your class to learn as long as the student agrees to follow expected procedures. Specific things you can do to create a positive classroom environment, some of which are repeated from preceding chapters and others are addressed in later chapters, are discussed next.

For the Classroom

- Attend to the classroom's physical appearance and comfort—it is your place (and the students' place) of work; show pride in that fact.

For Students

- Admonish behavior, not the person.
- Encourage students to set high yet realistic goals for themselves, and then show them how to work in increments toward meeting their goals—letting each child know that you are confident in that child's ability to achieve.
- Ensure that no prejudice is ever displayed against any person.
- Help students develop their skills in interactive and cooperative learning.
- Involve students in every aspect of their learning, including the planning of classroom expectations, procedures, and learning activities, thereby empowering them, that is, giving them part ownership in and responsibility for their learning.
- Make the learning enjoyable, at least to the extent possible and reasonable.

For Self-Reflection

- Be an interesting person and an optimistic and enthusiastic teacher.
- Model the very expectations that you have for the children.
- Recognize and reward truly positive behaviors and individual successes, no matter how meager they might seem to you to be.
- Use interesting and motivating learning activities.
- Send positive messages (sometimes called Happygrams) home to parents or guardians, even if you have to get help to write the message in the language used in the student's home.

Behaviors to Avoid

Two items in the preceding list are statements about giving encouragement. When using encouragement to motivate student learning, there are certain behaviors that you should avoid because they inhibit learning:

- Avoid encouraging competition and comparing one child with another, or one group of children with another.
- Avoid giving up or appearing to give up on any child.
- Avoid telling a child how much better she or he could be.
- Avoid using names of individuals during class meetings that are called for discussing issues where the individuals were involved.
- Avoid using qualifying statements, such as "It's about time."

Get to Know the Children as People and Build Intrinsic Motivation for Learning

For classes to move forward smoothly and efficiently, they should fit the learners' learning styles, learning capacities, developmental needs, and interests. To make the learning meaningful and longest lasting, build curriculum around student interests, capacities, perceptions, and perspectives (as you will learn to do in Part II). Therefore, you need to know your students well enough to be able to provide learning experiences that they will find interesting, valuable, intrinsically motivating, challenging, and rewarding. Knowing your students is as important as knowing the content of the subjects you are expected to teach. The following paragraphs describe a number of actions you can take to get to know your students as people.

Quickly Learn and Use Student Names

Like everyone else, children appreciate being recognized and addressed by name. Quickly learning and using their names is an important motivating strategy. To learn students' names quickly, one teacher, with parental permission, takes snapshot photographs of each child on the first day of school. Later, the children use the photographs as a portion of the covers of their portfolios.

Another technique for learning names quickly is to use a seating chart. Laminate the seating chart onto a clipboard that you can carry in class. Another teacher we know uses an alliteration name game to learn students' names. For the game, each student introduces his or her name with a term related to the content being studied. For science, Lisa might introduce herself as Lithosphere Lisa. Going clockwise in a circle, each student introduces himself or herself, and then the student to the left repeats that alliterative name and then adds his or her own. The third student would repeat the first name, the second, and then his or her own name. The teacher can be last and repeat all of the alliterative names in order.

Some teachers prefer to assign "homebase" seating (an assigned seat for each child to be in at the start and end of each school day) and then make seating charts from which they can unobtrusively check the roll while the students are doing assignment work. It is usually best to get your students into the lesson before taking roll and before doing other housekeeping chores. Ways of assigning student seating are discussed in the section titled The First Day.

The First Day

Addressing students by name every time you speak to them helps you to quickly learn and remember their names. (Be sure to learn to pronounce their names correctly—that helps in making a good impression.) Another helpful way to learn student names is to have elementary students make individual name cards (use tented poster board, 6 by 12 in.) for their desks, or have primary grade students wear name tags on the first days of school, or return papers yourself by calling student names and then handing the papers to them, paying careful attention to each student and making mental notes that may help you associate names with faces.

Let Students Share During the First Week of School

During the first week of school, some teachers take time each day to have students present information about themselves or about the day's lessons or an assignment. For instance, perhaps five or six students each day are selected to answer questions such as "What name would you like to be called by?" "Where did you attend school last year?" "Tell us about your interests or hobbies." "What interested you about yesterday's lesson in?" You might have your students share information of this sort with each other in dyads or small groups, while you visit each group in turn.

Me-in-a-Bag Activity. Another approach is the "Me-in-a-Bag" activity. For this activity, each student brings to school one large grocery bag that contains inexpensive items brought from home that represent that student. Each student is given time in class to share the items he or she brought. (*Note*: Be sure that parents/guardians are aware of the home assignment so nothing of value from home gets lost in the process.)

Sketches. As an option, instead of a home assignment, the students can sketch the items in class on small squares of art paper and place the squares in the bag for the Me-in-a-Bag activity at school.

Answering Questions. How each student answers questions or participates in beginning activities can be as revealing about the student as the information (or the lack thereof) that the student shares. From what is revealed during sharing activities, you sometimes get clues as to additional information you would like to obtain about the student.

Observe Students in the Classroom: Develop and Practice Your With-Itness

During learning activities, the effective teacher is constantly moving around the classroom and is alert to the individual behavior (nonverbal as well as verbal) of each child in the class, whether the student is on task or gazing off and perhaps thinking about other things (i.e., the teacher is exhibiting **with-itness**). Be cautious, however; just because a child is gazing out the window does not mean that the child is not thinking about the learning task. During group work is a particularly good time to observe children and get to know more about each child's skills and interests. For these observations, a behavior checklist is sometimes useful (see Chapter 11).

Observe Students Outside the Classroom

Another way to learn more about students is by observing them outside class, for example, at recess, during lunch, on the playground, and at other school events. Observations outside the classroom can give information about student friendships, interests, personalities, and potential. For instance, you may find that a student who seems phlegmatic, lackadaisical, or uninterested in your classroom is a real fireball on the soccer field.

Have Conferences and Interviews with Students

Conferences with students, and sometimes with family members as well, afford yet another opportunity to show that you are genuinely interested in each child as a person and as a student. Some teachers and teaching teams plan a series of conferences during the first few weeks in which, individually or in small groups, they interview the students. Such conferences and interviews are managed by using open-ended questions. The teacher indicates by the questions, by listening, and by nonjudgmental and empathic responses (i.e., being able to "step into the shoes" of the students, thereby understanding from where the student is coming) a genuine interest in the students. Keep in mind, however, that children who feel they have been betrayed by prior adult associations may at first be distrustful of your sincerity. In such instances, don't force it. Be patient, but do not hesitate to take advantage of the opportunity afforded by talking with individual students outside of the regular classroom. Investing a few minutes of time in a positive conversation with a student, during which you indicate a genuine interest in that child, can pay real dividends when it comes to that child's learning in your classroom.

When using interviews with children, consider having the children individually write one or two questions that they would like to ask you in the interview. This ensures that the child is an active participant.

Plan Student Writing and Questionnaires

Student Writing. Much can be learned about children from what they write or draw. It is important to encourage writing in your classroom, and (with varying degrees of intensity) to read everything that students write and to ask for clarification when needed. Journals and portfolios are valuable for this approach since writing in particular can help children feel more secure during the first days of school. Here are two writing suggestions:

- **Imaginary classmates for grades K–3.** Invite the children to imagine two imaginary classmates and suggest their physical characteristics, clothing, personalities, and fears. Encourage them to share their thoughts about the imaginary classmates with the whole group. Suggest that when any student has a problem, the student can write anonymously to one of the imaginary classmates and "mail" it in a mailbag (a brown paper bag affixed to a bulletin board). If appropriate, distribute the mail to the students and ask them to take the role of the imaginary classmates by writing the advice they would give the sender. The advice letters can be displayed beneath the writing board, and the students can be invited to browse and read during independent reading time.
- **An invisible student for grades 4–6.** Invite the students to imagine an invisible classmate in the room and contribute to the class a list of 15 questions about problems that they would ask the invisible student. Ask the students to copy the list and take a week to answer the questions as if they were the invisible student. At the end of the week, invite the students to read one of the questions and answers aloud to the class. If appropriate, they can suggest additional problems and concerns they are facing at school. Have each student select one problematic situation or concern and write a brief scenario in which the invisible student handles it in the best way possible. Ask for volunteers to read their scenarios aloud to a small group.

Questionnaires. Some teachers use open-ended interest-discovering and autobiographical questionnaires to learn more about their students. Student responses to questionnaires can provide ideas about how to tailor assignments and learning activities for individual students. However, you must assure students that their answers are optional, that you are not invading their privacy.

- **In an interest-discovering questionnaire,** students are asked to answer questions such as "When you read for fun or pleasure, what do you usually read?" "What are your favorite movies, videos, games, or TV shows?" "Who are your favorite music video performers? Athletes?" "How would you describe your favorite hobby or other nonschool-related activity?" "What are your favorite sport activities to participate in and watch as a spectator?" "What would you like to become?" and "How do you like to spend your leisure time?"
- **In an autobiographical quesionnaire,** the student is asked to answer such questions as "How many siblings do you have?" "Where have you lived?" "Do you have any pets?" "Do you have a favorite hobby or interest?" "What is it?" You might want to model the process and begin it by reading to the children your own autobiographical answers.

Rely on Cumulative Records, Discussions with Colleagues, and Experiential Backgrounds

Stored in the school office is the cumulative record for each student, containing information recorded from year to year by teachers and other school professionals—information about the student's academic background and standardized test scores. However, the Family Educational Rights and Privacy Act (FERPA) of 1974, and its subsequent amendments and local policies, may forbid you from reviewing the record, except perhaps in collaboration with an administrator or counselor and when you have a legitimate educational purpose for doing so.

While you must use discretion before arriving at any conclusion about information contained in the cumulative record, the record may afford information for getting to know a particular student better. Remember, though, a student's past is history and should not be held against that child, but instead used as a means for understanding a child's past experiences as part of the child's present learning experience. One of the advantages of schools that use looping (where the teacher and students stay together for more than one year) or small cohorts (families, pods) of students is that teachers and students get to know each other better.

Another way of getting to know your students is to spend time in the neighborhoods in which they live. Observe and listen, finding and noting things that you can use as examples or as learning activities. Some school districts encourage home visits by teachers and even provide financial incentives to teachers who visit the homes of their students. Of course, teachers must exercise safety precautions when making home visits, perhaps traveling in teams rather than alone.

PREPARATION PROVIDES CONFIDENCE AND SUCCESS

For successful classroom management, beginning the school term well may make all the difference in the world. Remember that you have only one opportunity to make a first and lasting impression. Therefore, you should appear at the first class meeting as well-prepared and confident as possible.

In schools, genuinely respond to students, and demonstrate that the teachers and administrators hold high expectations for themselves and for one another.

Perhaps in the beginning, you will feel nervous and apprehensive, but being ready and well-prepared will help you at least appear to be confident. It is likely that every beginning teacher is to some degree nervous and apprehensive; the secret is not to appear to be nervous and apprehensive. Being well-prepared provides the confidence necessary to abate feelings of apprehension. A good antiperspirant and slow under-the-breath counting to 10 at the start can

help, too. Then, if you proceed in a business-like, matter-of-fact way, you won't have much time to be nervous, because the impetus of your well-prepared beginning will, most likely, cause the day, week, and year to proceed as you desired.

Consider preparing a long-term plan or outline too, because a student might ask "What are we learning this year?" or "What will we be doing?" Be assured that your anxieties will lessen with each new school year. And now, to further your understanding of classroom management and to begin the development of your own management system, do Application Exercise 4.1.

Companion Website

To broaden your knowledge base about what you need to know to manage an effective, safe, and supportive learning environment for your students, go to our Companion Website at **www.prenhall.com/roberts** and click on the *Additional Content* module for Chapter 4.

USING POSITIVE REWARDS

Reinforcement theory contends that the gratification a person derives from receiving a reward strengthens the tendency for that person to continue to act in a certain way, while the lack of a reward (or the promise of a reward) weakens the tendency to act that way. For example, according to the theory, if students are promised a reward of preferred activity time (PAT) on Friday if they work well all week long, then the students are likely to work toward that reward, thus improving their standards of learning. Some educators argue that (a) once the extrinsic reinforcement (i.e., the reward from outside the learner) has been removed, the desired behavior tends to diminish; and that (b) rather than extrinsic sources of reinforcement, focus should be on increasing the student's internal sense of accomplishment, an intrinsic reward. Further, rewarding children for complying with expected/standard behavior sends the wrong message. It reinforces the mentality of "What do I get for doing what I am supposed to do?" If the use of rewards is a common school practice, it can carry over into home situations and eventually to adulthood. A principal does not reward a teacher for showing up on time, attending a faculty meeting, or having report cards prepared on time. Those are expected standard behaviors. Perhaps, for the daily work of a teacher in a classroom of many diverse individuals, the practical reality is somewhere between. After all, the reality of classroom teaching is less than ideal, and all activities cannot be intrinsically rewarding. Further, for many children, intrinsic rewards are often too remote to be effective.

For Your Notes

APPLICATION EXERCISE 4.1 BEGINNING THE DEVELOPMENT OF MY MANAGEMENT SYSTEM

Instructions: The purpose of this application exercise is to help you begin to develop the management system that you will explain to your students during the first day or the first week of school. Answer the questions that follow and share those answers with your peers for their feedback. Then make changes as appropriate. On completion of this chapter and the additional content for this chapter on our Companion Website **(www.prenhall.com/roberts),** you may want to revisit this exercise to make adjustments to your management plan, as you will from time to time throughout your professional career.

1. My anticipated grade level and, if relevant, teaching subject:

2. Attention to procedures. Use a statement to explain your procedural expectation for each of the following:

   a. How are students to signal that they want your attention and help?

   b. How do you call on students during question-and-answer sessions?

   c. How and when are students to enter and exit the classroom?

   d. How are students to obtain the materials for instruction? Will you position the desks/ furniture in any special way?

   e. How are students to store their personal items?

   f. What are the procedures for students' going to the drinking fountain or bathroom?

APPLICATION EXERCISE 4.1 *(continued)*

    g. What are the procedures during class interruptions?

    h. What are the procedures for tardy children and early dismissal?

    i. What are the procedures for turning in homework (responsibility papers)? For passing out and collecting papers?

3. Describe your expectations for classroom behavior and the consequences for misbehavior. How do you intend to promote a supportive learning environment and address cognitive, cultural, and linguistic diversity? How might procedures or consequences vary (if at all) according to the grade level taught or according to other criteria such as team teaching?

4. Give one example of your expectations for an effective transition from one activity or lesson to the next.

In discussion with classmates consider the following:

Many modern teachers advocate the use of a highly structured classroom, and then, as appropriate, over time during the school year, they share more of the responsibility with the students. Did you find this to be the case with any of the teachers you've known. Was it more or less the case in any particular grade level(s)? Was it more or less the case with any particular subject areas?

The promise of extrinsic rewards is not always necessary or beneficial. Students generally will work harder to learn something because they want to learn it (i.e., it is intrinsically motivating) than they will merely to earn PAT, points, grades, candy, or some other form of reward (called an extrinsic motivator). In addition, regarding the promise of PAT on Friday, so many children are so preoccupied with the "here and now" that for them, the promise on Monday of preferred activity time on Friday will probably have little desired effect on their behavior on Monday. To them on Monday, Friday seems a long way off.

Activities that are interesting and intrinsically rewarding are not further served by the addition of extrinsic rewards. This is especially true when working with students who are already highly motivated to learn. Adding extrinsic incentives to learning activities that are already highly motivating tends to reduce student motivation. For most students, the use of extrinsic motivators should be minimal and is probably most useful in skills learning, where there is a lot of repetition and the potential for boredom. While we are fully aware of the resentment students might feel if other teachers give out candy, stickers, and so on, and theirs does not, when students are working diligently on a highly motivating student-initiated project of study, extrinsic rewards are probably not necessary and could even have negative effects.[17] To minimize problems, a teacher can discourage time wasting, avoid some common mistakes, and use interventions such as class meetings, conflict resolution, and judicious consequences.[18-21] Furthermore, the teacher can use nonverbal cues, and be aware of students' impulse control.[22,23] See the *Technology Tips for the Classroom* feature for technologically-related information that can support activities that are interesting and intrinsically rewarding.

Companion Website

To find links to resources about educational software programs, go to our Companion Website at **www.prenhall.com/roberts** and click on the *Web Destinations* module for Chapter 4.

Technology Tips for the Classroom

- To create and save your own custom educational game based on your curriculum (or to use preprogrammed cartridges correlated to grade levels for rainy day activities or an after-school program) or on national curriculum standards, check out the wireless version of *Classroom Jeopardy!* Includes scoreboard, keyboard, wireless controllers, host controller, and a sampler game cartridge; connects to classroom TV (Educational Insights, 18730 S. Wilmington Avenue, Rancho Dominguez, CA 90220). 800–995–4436.

- To provide students, grades 3–5, with an opportunity to develop basic keyboarding skills, use your favorite training software tool or *Bernie's Typing Travels* (www.berniestypingtravels.com) software program, a computer story of Bernie, a rodent in a lab, who sends Professor Keys' experiments back in time. Students help recover the experiments by completing lessons about the keyboard. License fee required.

- To avoid the link-by-link moving until the student or teacher finds a web page with the information that is desired, try a one-click reference look-up capability such as *GuruNet Homework Edition.* (www.gurunet.com) This software offers quick bits of information, including acronyms, biographies, definitions, encyclopedia terms, facts on topics, photos, and translations. License fee required.

- To consider a wireless network capability that can connect the students' handhelds to the teacher's computer for two-way communication and provide instant messages to the teacher for the students' answers, review the *LearnTrac* software (www.elearningdynamics.com). The students' answers can provide teachers with an instant poll/survey to see if the students have comprehended a particular point, process, concept, or lesson. Further, with *LearnTrac,* teachers can wirelessly administer brief quizzes, grade them, and correlate the students' grades with such items as class attendance or prior test results. With this item, teachers ensure that students stay on focus since they cannot use their handhelds to surf the Net or e-mail their friends during class. Access to wireless network required.

About Praxis and Other Teacher Tests

About Praxis Teacher Tests. The Praxis Elementary Education: Content Area Exercises Assessment measures your knowledge of the subject areas you will be required to teach in an elementary classroom as well as your thinking skills regarding solutions to an instructional problem and classroom management issues. For instance, the test could measure your development of an instructional plan for a student or group of students.

A typical content area exercises exam has at least four questions that are subject specific. One question usually will focus on reading/language arts, one on mathematics, and one will center on science or social studies. Another question will refer to interdisciplinary instruction related to the subject areas in your elementary classroom. If your state has selected this exam as part of its professional assessment of beginning teachers, your state wants to determine that you have achieved a certain level of mastery of your area before it grants you a credential/license to teach in an elementary classroom.

To continue to support your interest in preparing for this test, as well as some of the other teacher tests, the application exercise in this chapter offers opportunities for you to reflect generally on the content about establishing and maintaining an effective, safe, and supportive learning environment, including classroom management. In this chapter, precredentialed teachers are asked to participate cooperatively and collaboratively and to do the following:

- Begin preparation of the management system that you can explain to the students during the first day or week of school (Application Exercise 4.1).
- Turn to our Companion Website (**www.prenhall.com/roberts**) and click on the *Additional Application Exercise* module to complete additional application exercises, namely, Sending a Positive Message Home, Teachers' Behavior Management Systems, Observations and Analysis of How Experienced Teachers Open Their Class Meetings or the School Day, and Selecting Measures of Control.

If you want to respond to a constructed response-type question similar to those found on the Praxis II Elementary Education: Content Area Exercises Assessment, turn to the Praxis Warm-Up in the end-of-chapter material. This warm-up takes another look at the classroom vignette found in the Looking at Teachers section at the beginning of this chapter.

Other Teacher Tests. For those of you who will be teaching in states that do not administer the Praxis II Principles of Learning and Teaching tests, go to our Companion Website at **www.prenhall. com/roberts** and click on the *Other Teacher Tests* module for Chapter 4 to access information about teacher tests other than the Praxis.

SUMMARY

In this chapter and on its related chapter of the Companion Website (**www.prenhall.com/roberts**), you learned ways to cope with the daily challenges of classroom teaching and guidelines for effectively managing children in the classroom. Within that framework, your attention was then focused on specific approaches and additional guidelines for effective classroom management and control of the learning environment. You were offered advice for setting up and maintaining a classroom environment that is favorable to student learning and for establishing procedures for positively influencing student behavior and encouraging student learning. To become an accomplished classroom manager takes thoughtful and thorough planning, consistent and confident application, and reflective experience. Be patient with

yourself as you accumulate the prerequisite knowledge and practice and hone the necessary skills.

What's to Come. This is the end of the overview about teaching, learning, and class management. You are now ready for Part II, Planning for Curriculum and Instruction.

EXTENDING MY PROFESSIONAL COMPETENCY

Praxis Warm-Up: A Constructed Response-Type Question

In this chapter's teacher vignette, you'll remember that a second-grade teacher wanted to help the children learn about the need for rules/procedures related to their study during a thematic unit. Considering the need for rules is a worthwhile lesson that can be applied for the rest of an individual's life. Focusing on this, you were asked to consider some behaviors that the teacher could model. Perhaps the teacher pointed out that rules must be designed to equally support and value all members of the learning community, including teachers.

As another example, maybe she planned for her students to use watercolor paints at an activity center in the classroom. To follow through on this on the first or second day of class, perhaps she would have instructed the students about what to do when watercolor paint spills in the activity center during their studies.

When the inevitable spill happened as some students were painting their dinosaur pictures, the teacher would not interrupt her teaching for even one minute. While she continued to teach, she expected the students to know where to find extra paper towels and then clean up the spill. She wanted the students to have previous instructions about how to clean up when necessary, so a spill was not a problem. With this understanding, the students accepted the procedures/rules in their classroom and assumed responsibility for their actions in their community of learners.

Related to this focus on rules and procedures, consider that you are now teaching older students in fifth grade, and you are about to begin a unit on the American Revolution and will focus on some of the laws (rules/procedures) during this time period. You want to plan one or two writing activities that will help your students pass along information that they have about the need for communities to have rules and will also help organize their thinking about the idea that rules must be designed to equally support and value all members of a community, even a community in the time period of the American Revolution.

Describe two writing activities (perhaps one creative and the other realistic) that you might use in your unit on the American Revolution and the study of some of the laws in effect in communities during this time period. Give the purposes of both writing activities and describe your specific examples.

Hints for responding to Praxis Warm-Ups are found in the Appendix.

Praxis. To do another Praxis Warm-Up with a constructed response-type question, go to our Companion Website at **www.prenhall.com/roberts** and click on the *Praxis Warm-Up* module for Chapter 4. Constructed response type questions are designed to help you prepare for the Praxis II Principles of Learning and Teaching tests.

For Your Discussion

1. **Corporal Punishment.** What would I say to give my opinion about using corporal punishment at any level of schooling? **To do:** Organize a group discussion or debate on this issue after reviewing the following information: Some educators are concerned about the increased violence in schools, as evidenced by possession of weapons, harassment, bullying, intimidation, gang or cult activity, arson, and the continued use of corporal punishment of students. They argue that schools are responsible for turning a child's behavior into an opportunity to teach character and self-control. When self-disciplined adults create a problem, they apologize, accept the consequences, make restitution, and learn from their mistakes. They also argue that we have a responsibility to teach children to do the same. Further, an important characteristic of exemplary schooling is that of maintaining respect for a child's dignity even when responding to the child's inappropriate behavior.

2. **Classroom Management System.** How would I explain my response if a parent or colleague asked me if I favored being strict with students at first? **To do:** Discuss with others in your group the idea of being strict with students at first and then relaxing once your classroom control has been established. Then discuss the idea of being relaxed at first and then tightening your rules and regulations later if students misbehave. Does it matter? Explain your answer.

3. **Being Consistent.** How would I explain my response if a parent or colleague asked me to tell about the importance of a teacher being consistent about implementing the expected classroom procedures and the consequences for inappropriate behavior? **To do:** With others, discuss the question "When it comes to procedures and consequences, is there a danger associated with a teacher being too rigid or inflexible?" Explain your answers to one another and then describe a time when, if ever, you might be likely to apply a different consequence for the same infraction but by different students.

4. **School Experiences, Past and Present.** What would I say about my own school experiences and the contrast of those experiences with those recently observed in today's schools, especially those related to the exercises of the four chapters of Part I in this resource guide? **To do:** Discuss some compare-and-contrast conclusions in small groups, then share your group's conclusions with those of the entire class.

5. **Further Questions.** How would I respond to a colleague's additional questions about this chapter? **To do:** List the questions along with ways that answers might be found.

Online Portfolio Activities

Supporting the classroom learning environment (Praxis II Assessments; Principles 2 and 5 of INTASC; and Standards 1 and 3 of NBPTS): At the Companion Website **(www.prenhall.com/roberts),** click on the *Online Portfolio Activities* module to continue your online portfolio supporting knowledge of students.

Companion Website

Also on the Companion Website at **www.prenhall. com/roberts,** you can measure your understanding of chapter content in the *Objectives* and *Self-Check* modules and apply concepts in the *For Your Discussion* module.

FOR FURTHER READING

Bodine, R. J., and Crawford, D. K. (1998). *The Handbook of Conflict Resolution Education: A Guide in Building Quality Programs in Schools.* San Francisco: Jossey-Bass.

Brophy, J., and Alleman, J. (1998). Classroom Management in a Social Studies Learning Community. *Social Education, 62*(1), 56–58.

Charles, C. M., Senter, G. W., and Barr, K. B. (1999). *Building Classroom Discipline* (6th ed.). New York: Longman.

Clarke, J. I. (1999). *Time-In: When Time-Out Doesn't Work.* Seattle, WA: Parenting Press.

Cummings, C. (2000). *Winning Strategies for Classroom Management.* Alexandria, VA: Association for Supervision and Curriculum Development.

Curwin, R. L., and Mendler, A. N. (1999). *Discipline with Dignity.* Alexandria, VA: Association for Supervision and Curriculum Development.

DiGiulio, R. (2000). *Positive Classroom Management: A Step by Step Guide to Successfully Running the Show Without Destroying Student Dignity* (2nd ed.). Thousand Oaks, CA; Corwin Press.

Edwards, C. D. (1999). *How to Handle a Hard-to-Handle Kid: A Parent's Guide to Understanding and Changing Problem Behaviors.* Minneapolis, MN: Free Spirit.

Foster-Harrison, E. S., and Adams-Bullock, A. (1998). *Creating an Inviting Classroom Environment* (Fastback 433). Bloomington, IN: Phi Delta Kappa Educational Foundation.

Freiberg, H. J. (Ed.). (1999). *Beyond Behaviorism: Changing the Classroom Management Paradigm.* Boston: Allyn & Bacon.

Gathercoal, F. (1997). *Judicious Discipline* (4th ed.). San Francisco: Caddo Gap Press.

Gibbs, J. L. (2000). Value-based Discipline in a Fifth Grade Classroom. *Middle School Journal, 31*(5), 46–50.

Good, T. L., and Brophy, J. E. (2003). *Looking in Classrooms* (9th ed., Chaps. 4, 5). New York: Addison Wesley Longman.

Hansen, J. M., and Childs, J. (1998). Creating a School Where People Like to Be. *Educational Leadership, 56*(1), 14–17.

Hardin, C. J., and Harris, E. A. (2000). *Managing Classroom Crises* (Fastback 465). Bloomington, IN: Phi Delta Kappa Educational Foundation.

Heinich, R., Molenda, M., Russell, J. D., and Smaldino, S. E. (1999). *Instructional Media and Technologies for Learning* (6th ed.). (Upper Saddle River, NJ: Merrill/Prentice Hall).

Iverson, A. M. (2003). *Building Competence in Classroom Management and Discipline* (4th ed.). Upper Saddle River, NJ: Prentice-Hall.

Jensen, E. (1998). How Threats and Stress Affect Learning. In E. Jensen (Ed.), *Teaching with the Brain in Mind* (Chap. 6). Alexandria, VA: Association for Supervision and Curriculum Development.

Kelly, K. (1999). Retention vs. Social Promotion: Schools Search for Alternatives. *The Harvard Education Letter, 15*(1), 1–3.

Landau, B. M., and Gathercoal, F. (2000). Creating Peaceful Classrooms: Judicious Discipline and Class Meetings. *Phi Delta Kappan, 81*(6), 450–452, 454.

Manning, M. L., and Bucher, K. T. (2003). *Classroom Management: Models, Applications, and Cases.* Upper Saddle River, NJ: Prentice-Hall.

Marshall, M. (1998). *Fostering Social Responsibility* (Fastback 428). Bloomington, IN: Phi Delta Kappa Educational Foundation.

McEwan, B. (2000). *The Art of Classroom Management: Effective Practices for Building Equitable Learning Communities.* Upper Saddle River, NJ: Merrill/Prentice Hall.

Middlebrooks, S. (1998). *Getting to Know City Kids: Understanding Their Thinking, Imagining, and Socializing.* New York: Teachers College Press.

Morgan, R. R., Ponticell, J. A., and Gordon, E. E. (2000). *Rethinking Creativity* (Fastback 458). Bloomington, IN: Phi Delta Kappa Educational Foundation.

Nissman, B. S. (2000). *Teacher-Tested Classroom Management Strategies.* Upper Saddle River, NJ: Merrill/Prentice Hall.

Wong, H., and Wong, R. (2001). *The First Days of School.* Mountain View, CA: Harry K. Wong Publications.

NOTES

1. For facilitative procedures/rules to establish a community of learners, i.e., problem-solving sessions, see R. Bruning, G. Schraw, and R. Ronning, *Cognitive Psychology and Instruction,* 3rd ed. (Upper Saddle River, NJ: Prentice Hall, 1999); for solving conflicts, see J. Lee, C. Pulvino, and P. Perrone, *Restoring Harmony: A Guide for Managing Conflicts in Schools* (Upper Saddle River, NJ: Merrill/Prentice Hall, 1998); involving parents, see J. Brophy, *Teaching Problem Students* (New York: Guilford Press, 1996); taking another's perspective, see R. Weissberg and M. Greenberg, School and Community

Competence-Enhancement Prevention Prevention Programs. In W. Damon (Ed.), *Handbook of Child Psychology,* Vol. 4 (New York: Wiley, 1998); for an equitable learning environment, see B. McEwan, *The Art of Classroom Management: Effective Practices for Building Equitable Learning Communities* (Upper Saddle River, NJ: Merrill/Prentice Hall, 2000).

2. I. A. Hyman and J. D'Allessandro, Oversimplifying the Discipline Problem, *Education Week, 3*(29), 24 (April 11, 1984).

3. See B. F. Skinner, *Beyond Freedom and Dignity* (New York: Knopf, 1971).

4. See L. Canter and M. Canter, *Assertive Discipline: Positive Behavior Management for Today's Schools,* rev. ed. (Santa Monica, CA: Lee Canter & Associates, 1992).

5. T. L. Good and J. E. Brophy, *Looking in Classrooms,* 8th ed. (New York: Addison-Wesley-Longman, 2000), p. 201.

6. See R. Dreikurs, B. B. Grunwald, and F. C. Pepper, *Maintaining Sanity in the Classroom: Classroom Management Techniques,* 2nd ed. (New York: Harper & Row, 1982).

7. L. Albert, *A Teacher's Guide to Cooperative Discipline: How to Manage Your Classroom and Promote Self-Esteem* (Circle Pines, MN: American Guidance Service, 1989, revised, 1996).

8. J. Nelsen, *Positive Discipline,* 2nd ed. (New York: Ballatine Books, 1987), and J. Nelsen, L. Lott, and H. S. Glenn, *Positive Discipline in the Classroom: How to Effectively Use Class Meetings and Other Positive Discipline Strategies* (Rocklin, CA: Prima Publishing, 1993). About class meetings, see also B. M. Landau and P. Gathercoal, Creating Peaceful Classrooms: Judicious Discipline and Class Meetings, *Phi Delta Kappan, 81*(6), 450–452, 454 (February 2000).

9. See W. Glasser, A New Look at School Failure and School Success, *Phi Delta Kappan, 78*(8), 597–602 (April 1997).

10. See W. Glasser, *Schools without Failure* (New York: Harper & Row, 1969), *Control Theory in the Classroom* (New York: Harper & Row, 1986), *The Quality School* (New York: Harper & Row, 1990), and *The Quality School Teacher* (New York: HarperPerennial, 1993).

11. C. Rogers and H. J. Freiberg, *Freedom to Learn* (Columbus, OH: Merrill/Prentice Hall, 1994).

12. See H. J. Freiberg (Ed.), *Beyond Behaviorism: Changing the Classroom Management Paradigm* (Boston: Allyn & Bacon, 1997). See also H. J. Freiberg (Ed.), *Perceiving, Behaving, Becoming: Lessons Learned* (Alexandria, VA: Association for Supervision and Curriculum Development, 1999).

13. See H. G. Ginott, *Teacher and Child* (New York: Macmillan, 1971).

14. T. Gordon, *Discipline That Works: Promoting Self-Discipline in Children* (New York: Penguin, 1989).

15. See F. Jones, *Positive Classroom Discipline* (New York: McGraw-Hill, 1987).

16. J. S. Kounin, *Discipline and Group Management in Classrooms* (New York: Holt, Rinehart and Winston, 1977). Building on Kounin's concept of with-itness, Wong and Wong give ideas for preparing traffic patterns in the classroom in *The First Days of School* (Mountain View, CA: Wong Publications, 2001).

17. See R. R. Morgan, J. A. Ponticell, and E. E. Gordon, *Rethinking Creativity* (Fastback 458) (Bloomington, IN: Phi Delta Kappa Educational Foundation, 2000).

18. At the beginning of student teaching, you may need to follow the opening procedures already established by your host teacher. If those procedures are largely ineffective, then without hesitation, you should talk with your university supervisor about being reassigned to a different placement.

19. D. W. Johnson and R. T. Johnson, *Reducing School Violence through Conflict Resolution* (Alexandria, VA: Association for Supervision and Curriculum Development, 1995), p. 1.

20. Landau and Gathercoal, note 8, pp. 450–452, 454. See also B. McEwan, P. Gathercoal, V. Nimmo, Applications of Judicious Discipline: A Common Language for Classroom Management, in H. J. Freiberg (Ed.), *Beyond Behaviorism: Changing the Classroom Management Paradigm* (Boston: Allyn & Bacon, 1999).

21. See the Internet, *www.cfchildren.org/program_tat.shtml.*

22. See G. Petrie et al., Nonverbal Cues: The Key to Classroom Management, *Principal, 77*(3), 34–36 (January 1998).

23. For further reading about the relation between impulse control and intelligence, see D. Goleman, *Emotional Intelligence: Why It Can Matter More Than IQ* (New York: Bantam Books, 1995), and D. Harrington-Lueker, Emotional Intelligence, *High Strides, 9*(4), 1, 4–5 (March/April 1997).

PLANNING FOR CURRICULUM AND INSTRUCTION

How Do I Plan and Select Content?

Visual Chapter Organizer and Overview

Planning for Instruction

> Providing Successful Transitions
> Teacher–Student Collaborative Team Planning
> Reasons for Planning
> Scope of the Curriculum

Planning with Curriculum Standards That Provide Guidance

> What the National Standards Are
> National Standards by Content Area
> Curriculum Standards and High-Stakes Testing

Planning with State/District Documents That Provide Guidance for Content Selection

Planning with Student Textbooks That Provide Guidance for Content Selection

> Differentiated Instruction
> Multireading Approach

Planning Sequencing of Content

Preparing for and Dealing with Controversy

Planning for Learning Outcomes: Goals and Objectives

Planning with Instructional Objectives

> Learning Targets and Goal Indicators

Planning with Domains of Learning and Developmental Needs of Children

> Cognitive Domain Hierarchy
> Affective Domain Hierarchy
> Psychomotor Domain Hierarchy

Planning with Taxonomies

Planning with Integrated Curriculum

Looking at Teachers

During a sixth-grade brainstorming session with features of listening as the language arts content, a teacher, as part of her planning, is recording student contributions on a large sheet of butcher paper that has been taped to the classroom wall. She solicits student responses about the content being studied. Some of the responses include these: deciding to listen, reading all stimuli, investing time wisely, verifying what was heard, and expending energy to listen. She acknowledges those responses, holds and manipulates the writing pen, walks to the wall, and writes on the paper. Each of these actions requires decisions and movements that consume precious instructional time and that can distract her from her students.

An effective alternative would be to have a reliable student helper (or classroom aide/parent volunteer) do the writing while the teacher handles the solicitation and acknowledgment of student contributions. With that approach, she has fewer decisions and fewer actions to distract her and does not have to turn her back to the students to write their responses on the paper. She does not lose eye contact and proximity with the classroom of students.

As the previous classroom vignette about the sixth-grade teacher points out, effective teaching does not just happen; it is produced through your thoughtful planning of each phase of the learning process. Most effective teachers begin their planning months before meeting students for the first time. Daily activities form daily lessons, which form parts of a larger scheme that is designed to accomplish the teacher's long-range goals for the semester or year and to correlate with the school's mission statement and expectation standards related to district and state documents.

Like the construction of a very large bridge, the most meaningful learning is usually the result of a gradual and sometimes painstakingly slow process. When compared with traditional instruction, teaching in a constructivist mode is slower and involves more discussion, more debate, and the re-creation of ideas. Rather than following clearly defined and previously established steps, the curriculum evolves. Such a curriculum depends heavily on materials, and to a great extent, it is the students' interests and questions that determine it. Less content is covered, fewer facts are memorized and tested for, and progress is sometimes tediously slow.[1] The rationale for careful planning for instruction, the components of that planning, and the selection of content are the main topics of this chapter.

CHAPTER OBJECTIVES

Specifically, on completion of this fifth chapter, you should be able to:

1. Explain your familiarity with the national curriculum standards for various subjects of the K–6 curriculum that can be resources for planning and selecting content.
2. Explain your familiarity with curriculum documents published by your state department of education as well as local curriculum documents.
3. Explain the value of diagnostic and formative assessment of student learning as related to curriculum and instruction.
4. Demonstrate how you would organize your ideas about subject content and the sequencing of content, and also explain your understanding of controversial topics and issues that may arise while teaching and what you might do when they arise.
5. Demonstrate that you can recognize verbs that are acceptable for overt objectives, that you can recognize parts of criterion-referenced instructional objectives, that you can recognize objectives that are measurable, and that you can prepare instructional objectives for each of the three domains of learning and at various levels of the taxonomies within each domain.

PLANNING FOR INSTRUCTION

As a classroom teacher, planning for instruction is a major part of your job, even if you are using an externally developed and highly scripted program. At some level of complexity, you will be responsible for planning the activities, the lessons, the units, and the school year.

You need not do all your instructional planning from scratch, and you need not do all of your planning alone. As a matter of fact, in many elementary schools today, especially for mathematics and reading, the curricula are purchased by the district and handed to the teachers. The program may be highly scripted and the teacher may be expected to follow the script closely or even exactly. However, it is our opinion that because writers of these programs do not know your students as well as you, to be most effective with a particular group of children, any scripted program will need tweaking by the teacher who is using it.

In many schools, curricula are developed or, in the case of scripted programs, are enhanced by a team of teachers. Teams of teachers collectively plan the curricula for their specific cohorts of students. Team members either plan together or divide the responsibilities and then share their individual plans. A final plan is then developed collaboratively.

The heart of good planning is good decision making and at the heart of good decision making is, as mentioned in Chapter 4, knowledge of the children for whom the instruction is planned. For every plan and at each of the levels, you and your team of colleagues must make decisions about the goals and objectives to be set, the subject to be introduced, the materials and equipment to be used, the methods to be adopted, and the assessments to be made. This decision-making process is complicated because so many options are available at each level. Decisions made at all levels result in a total plan.

Although the planning process continues year after year, the task becomes somewhat easier after the first year as you learn to adapt your plans. The process is also made easier via research and communication by reviewing documents and sharing ideas and plans with other teachers. (See the *Technology Tips for the Classroom* feature.)

Providing Successful Transitions

Within the framework of exemplary school organization are several components that form a comprehensive albeit ever-changing program. Central to the school's purpose and its organizational structure is the concerted effort to see that all children make successful **transitions** from one level to the next, from home to school, from one grade to the next, from elementary to middle school, from middle school to high school, and from high school to postsecondary education or work. Every aspect of the elementary school program is, in some way, designed to help children make those transitions. Combining to form the program that students experience are two terms you will frequently encounter, **curriculum** (we define as all experiences students encounter) and **instruction** (we define as experiences associated with methods facilitating student learning).

Technology Tips for the Classroom

- In the classroom, consider additional educational uses for a digital camera, a photo printer, a transfer device, or a data-storage stick (similar to a computer's small flash drive or jump drive unit). Uses can consist of taking photos of your students during the first week of school and then again during the last week of school. During the last week, have the students match up

their photos, write a paragraph or two about what they learned during the year, and then send the photos and writing home with the students as a special end-of-the-year memento for parents and guardians.

- Consider making a classroom memory book that relates to the students' final presentations at the end of a particular unit of study. Print pictures from the class's presentations. Have students punch holes on the left side of each photo and thread with yarn, dental floss, or twine to make an instant "What We Are Studying" book ready to place on a bookshelf—one available for browsing anytime in the classroom.

- In addition to a digital camera phone, you may need an additional wireless phone that sends and receives your e-mail and text messages; that manages your appointments with students, parents, and colleagues in real time; that will accept applications in a transfer/memory slot; that has a built-in speaker phone; and that surfs the web.

Companion Website

To find links to resources about using technology in the classroom, go to our Companion Website at **www.prenhall.com/roberts** and click on the *Web Destinations* module for Chapter 5.

Teacher–Student Collaborative Team Planning

Many teachers and teaching teams encourage their students to participate in the planning of some phase of their learning. Student input ranges from planning complete interdisciplinary thematic units to planning specific activities within a unit. Such collaborative planning tends to give students a proprietary interest in the activities, thereby increasing their motivation for learning. What students have contributed to the plan often seems more meaningful to them than what others have planned for them. Children like to see their own plans succeed. Thus, teacher–student collaboration in planning is usually an effective motivational tool.

Classrooms today tend to be more project oriented and student and group centered than the traditional teacher-centered classroom of the past, in which the teacher served as the primary provider of information. Today's students more actively participate in their learning, in collaboration with the teacher. The teacher provides some structure and assistance, but the collaborative approach requires that students inquire and interact, generate ideas, seriously listen to and talk with one another, and recognize that their thoughts and experiences are valuable and essential to meaningful learning. In such a collaborative atmosphere, children learn not only the subject matter content of the curriculum but develop important and valuable social skills.

Reasons for Planning

Planning is done for a number of reasons, perhaps foremost of which is to ensure curriculum coherence. Periodic activities and lesson plans are an integral part of a larger plan, represented by grade-level goals and objectives and by the school- and district-wide mission statements and district/state outcome standards. Students' learning experiences are thoughtfully planned in sequence and then orchestrated by teachers who understand the rationale for their respective positions in the curriculum. Of course, such plans do not preclude an occasional diversion from predetermined activities.

Another reason for planning is, as discussed in Chapter 2, to give considerations to students' experiential backgrounds, learning capacities and styles, reading levels, and special needs.

Planning is necessary to ensure efficient and effective teaching with a minimum of classroom management problems. After deciding what to teach, you have the important task of deciding how to teach it. To use precious instructional time efficiently, planning should be accomplished with two goals in mind: (a) show that you value everyone's time during instruction and (b) select strategies that most effectively promote the anticipated student learning, that is, the target learning outcomes.

Planning also helps ensure program continuation. The program must continue even if you are absent and a substitute teacher is needed. Planning provides a criterion for reflective practice and self-assessment. After a learning activity and at the end of a school term, you can reflect on and assess what was done and how it affected student learning. Planning provides a means to evaluate your teaching. Your plans represent a criterion recognized and evaluated by administrators. With those experienced in such matters, it is clear that inadequate planning is usually a precursor to incompetent teaching. Put simply, failing to plan is planning to fail.

Scope of the Curriculum

When planning the scope of the curriculum, you must decide what is to be accomplished in that period of time, such as for a semester or for a school year. To help in setting your goals, you should (a) examine school and other resource documents for mandates and guidelines; (b) communicate with colleagues to learn of common expectations; and (c) probe, analyze, and translate your own convictions, knowledge,

and skills into behaviors that foster the intellectual and psychological development of your students.

PLANNING WITH CURRICULUM STANDARDS THAT PROVIDE GUIDANCE

Curriculum standards are defined as what students should know (content) and be able to do (process and performance). At the national level, curriculum standards did not exist in the United States until 1989, when standards were developed and released for mathematics education. Shortly after the release of the mathematics standards, support for national goals in education was endorsed by the National Governors Association. The National Council on Education Standards and Testing recommended that in addition to those for mathematics, national standards for subject matter content in K–12 education be developed for the arts, civics/social studies, English/language arts/reading, geography, history, and science.

The U.S. Department of Education provided initial funding for the development of national standards. In 1994, the U.S. Congress passed the Goals 2000: Educate America Act (amended in 1996 with an appropriations act), encouraging states to set standards. Long before this, however, national organizations devoted to various disciplines were already defining standards as was done earlier for mathematics by the National Council for Teachers of Mathematics.

What the National Standards Are

The national standards represent the best thinking by expert panels about the essential elements of a basic core of subject knowledge that all students should acquire. They serve not as national mandates but rather as voluntary guidelines to encourage curriculum development to promote higher student achievement. It is at the discretion of state and local curriculum developers to decide the extent to which the standards are used. Strongly influenced by the national standards, nearly all 50 states have completed or are currently developing state standards for the various disciplines.

National Standards by Content Area

The following paragraphs describe national standards development for content areas in the K–12 curriculum. The standards are available on the Internet (see Figure 5.1). Do Application Exercise 5.1 to help you become familiar with the national curriculum standards for various subjects of the K–6 curriculum.[5,6,7,8]

Figure 5.1
Internet resources on national and state curriculum standards and frameworks

Arts, visual and performing. Developed jointly by the American Alliance for Theater and Education, the National Art Education Association, the National Dance Association, and the Music Educators National Conference, The National Standards for Arts Education were completed and released in 1994. (www.artsedge.kennedy-center.org/teach/standards.cfm)

Economics. Developed by the National Council on Economic Education, standards for the study of economics were published in 1997. (www.ncee.net/ea/program.php?pid=19)

English/language arts/reading. Developed jointly by the International Reading Association, the National Council of Teachers of English, and the University of Illinois Center for the Study of Reading, standards for English education were completed and released in 1996. (www.ncte.org)

National and State Curriculum Standards and Frameworks

Foreign languages. "Standards for Foreign Language Learning: Preparing for the 21st Century" was completed and released by the American Council on the Teaching of Foreign Languages (ACTFL) in 1996.[2] (www.actfl.org)

Geography. Developed jointly by the Association of American Geographers, the National Council for Geographic Society, standards for geography education were completed and released in 1994.[3] (http://nationalgeographic.com)

State standards. www. statestandards.com
General and multiple disciplines. www.ncrel.org www.enc.org/reform/fworks/index.html

History/civics/social studies. The Center for Civic Education and the National Center for Social Studies developed standards for civics and government, and the National Center for History in the Schools developed the standards for history, all of which were completed and released in 1994. (www.ncss.org/standards)

Health. Developed by the Joint Committee for National School Health Education Standards, "National Health Education Standards: Achieving Health Literacy" was published in 1995.[4] (www.aahperd.org)

Information literacy/standards-based guidelines for school library media programs. Examples posted on the Ohio Department of Education website and on North Dakota Department of Public Instruction. (www.dpi.state.nd.us/standard/content/tech.pdf)

Mathematics. In 1989, the National Council of Teachers of Mathematics (NCTM) published Curriculum and Evaluation Standards for School Mathematics. A revised edition was released in 2000. (www.nctm.org)

Native American Indian supplements. Supplements to national standards are available from the Bureau of Indian Affairs for civics and government, geography, health, language arts, mathematics, science, social studies, and the visual and the performing arts. For districts serving American Indian children in adapting state standards to be more culturally relevant to their communities.[5] (www.doiu.nbc.gov/orientation/bia2.cfm)

Parent-Teacher Association's National Standards. For a copy, contact the National PTA, 541 N. Fairbanks Ct., Suite 1300, Chicago, IL 60611-3396. (www.pta.org/parentinvolvement/standards/index.asp)

Physical education. In 1995, the National Association of Sport and Physical Education (NAASPE) published "Moving into the Future: National Standards for Physical Education." Revised version. (www.aahperd.orgNACPE/template.cfm?template=national_standards.html

Science. With input from the American Association for the Advancement of Science and the National Science Teachers Association, the National Research Council's National Committee on Science Education Standards and Assessment developed standards for science education, which were published in 1995. (www.nctm.org/standards)

Technology. Prepared by the International Technology Education Association, technology literacy standards were released in 2000. (www.iteawww.org or www.aect.org) new URL if used http://cnets.iste.org

APPLICATION EXERCISE 5.1 EXAMINING NATIONAL CURRICULUM STANDARDS

Instructions: The purpose of this exercise is to help you become familiar with the national curriculum standards for various subjects of the K–6 curriculum. Using the sources provided in Figure 5.1 and other sources, such as professional journals, review the standards for your subject or subjects. Use the following questions as a guideline for small- or large-group class discussions. Following small subject-area group discussions, share the developments in each field with the rest of the class.

Subject area _____

1. Name of the standards document reviewed*

2. Year of document publication

3. Developed by

4. Specific K–6 goals specified by the new standards

5. Are the standards specific as to subject matter content for each grade level? Explain.

6. Do the standards offer specific strategies for instruction? Describe.

7. Do the standards offer suggestions for teaching children with special needs? Describe.

APPLICATION EXERCISE 5.1 *(continued)*

8. Do the standards offer suggestions or guidelines for dealing with controversial topics?

9. Do the standards offer suggestions for specific resources? Describe.

10. Do the standards refer to assessment? Describe.

11. In summary, compared with what has been taught and how it has been taught in this field, what is new with the standards?*

12. Is there anything else about the standards you would like to discuss in your group? From these standards, what are the general purposes that you can determine for students' learning in the subject area you reviewed?

*As a reference, also look at your state's Department of Education website for your state's standards for the subject/grade level you are interested in teaching.

Curriculum Standards and High-Stakes Testing

As mentioned previously, curriculum standards define what students should know and be able to do. The adoption of tougher K–12 standards throughout the United States, along with an increased emphasis on high-stakes testing to assess how schools and teachers are helping their students meet those standards, has provoked considerable debate.

Educators, parents/guardians, politicians, and businesspeople have acted and reacted to the adoption of standards and high-stakes testing. Some argue that this renewed emphasis on testing means too much teaching to the test at the expense of more meaningful learning, and that it also means that the influence of the home, community, and other factors in society is being ignored. Some argue that educators need to find ways to identify what others in the business world are doing to promote education, because schools cannot do all the work alone. Nevertheless, here is what some teachers do to prepare for high-stakes testing:

- Responding to the call for increased accountability, some teachers in some schools put aside the regular curriculum for several weeks before the testing date and concentrate on the direct preparation of their students for the test.
- Preparing for the tests, other teachers address the regular curriculum 2 days a week and prepare for tests 3 days a week during a pretest period.
- Still other teachers use selected materials that are available to help prepare students for state-mandated tests, such as the TAAS Texas Assessment of Academic Skills Master Student Practice Books and standards-based material. Other helpful resources are TestSmart Digital Lessons on CD based on the International Reading Association and National Council of Teachers of English standards.[2] The TAAS Practice Books address the objectives for given subject areas, represent instructional targets, focus on content, familiarize students with the test question format, and contain authentic reading passages. The CD digital lessons relate to areas of reading/ language arts standards such as genres, language expressions, mechanics, listening, reading operations, speaking, spelling, study skills, and writing.
- Two additional teacher resources focus on the standards of reading, language arts, and writing. They are *Greening the Reading and Writing Standards: Integrating Environmental Education with Middle School Language Arts*[3] by Lisa A. Packard and *Language Arts & Environmental Awareness: 100+ Integrated Books & Activities for Children*[4] by P. L. Roberts. Packard's resource lists Arizona's state literacy standards and offers suggested activities and related children's literature to address each standard. Roberts' resource has suggested children's literature to use as springboards for linking national standards in reading, language arts, and writing with activities for the classroom as well as home activities.
- Some teachers put aside other test situations and only turn to multiple-choice tests with fill-in-the-bubble answer sheets to help students get acquainted with the answer-response "bubble" format.

Using such pretest materials, teachers are well aware of the possibility (although it is certainly not an all-inclusive situation) that state and federal funding may be withheld from schools and/or jobs may be on the line for teachers and administrators when students do not score well.

Although the interest in student practice for pretesting has been rekindled in recent years, this often-called "drill-and-kill" approach is certainly not new. When comparing standardized testing of today with that of the past half-century, it is probably reasonable to conclude the following:

- The purpose of statewide standardized testing remains unchanged: It is to determine how well students are learning, at least to the extent determined by the particular test instrument.
- The test design is accomplished today with much greater precision and accuracy.
- The focus of today's testing is taking precious time away from the most creative aspects of teaching and learning.
- The manner in which test results are being used today and the long-term results of that use may have ramifications considerably more serious than at any time in education's history.

To keep up-to-date with information about this issue of high-stakes testing and others, use your national professional associations as sources. For these Internet addresses, turn back to Chapter 1 and see Figure 1.4.

PLANNING WITH STATE/DISTRICT DOCUMENTS THAT PROVIDE GUIDANCE FOR CONTENT SELECTION

In addition to relying on national and state standards for planning and selecting curriculum content, you will rely on state and district documents. With the guidance of Application Exercise 5.1 and the additional application exercises on the Companion

Figure 5.2
Methods for preassessing, identifying, and building on students' prior knowledge, and helping students' develop their higher order thinking skills and their comprehension of expository material[10,11]

- **KWL:** Students recall what they already know (K) about a topic (preassessment), determine what they want to learn (W), and later assess what they have learned (L).

- **KWLQ:** Students record what they already know (K) about a topic (preassessment), formulate questions about what they want to learn about the topic (W), assess their answers to their questions (L), and then ask more questions for further study (Q).

- **PQRST:** Students preview (P) material, ask questions (Q), read (R), and state (S) the main idea; they test (T) themselves by answering the questions asked earlier.

- **RR:** Reciprocal reading: Students take turns asking questions, summarizing, making predictions, and clarifying a story.

- **SQ3R:** Students survey (S) the material, ask questions (Q) about what was surveyed, read (R) the material, recite information (R), and review what was read (R).

- **SQ4R:** Students survey the material (S), ask questions about what was surveyed (Q), read to answer the questions (R), recite the answers (R), record important items from the materials into their journals/notebooks (R), then review what was read and done (R).

- **SRQ2R:** Students survey material (S), read it (R), ask questions about what was read (Q), recite the answers (R), and review what was read (R).

Website **(www.prenhall.com/roberts),** you have now examined major types of documents that help guide you in selecting the content of your curriculum. These consisted of national standards, state department of education standards, curriculum documents, school or district curriculum frameworks, courses of study, and school-adopted printed or nonprinted materials. Sources for any future examination of these documents include Internet sites (listed in Figure 5.1), your college or university library, and collaborating teachers or administrative personnel at local schools or the district office.

PLANNING WITH STUDENT TEXTBOOKS THAT PROVIDE GUIDANCE FOR CONTENT SELECTION

In addition to relying on national and state standards, and state and district documents, you will rely on student textbooks for planning and selecting curriculum content. For several reasons—the recognition of the diversity of learning styles, learning capacities and learning modalities of students, the cost of textbooks, and the availability of nonprinted materials—textbook appearance, content, and use has changed considerably in recent years and with advancing computer technology is likely to continue changing.

School districts periodically adopt new textbooks (usually every 5 to 8 years). If you are a student teacher or a first-year teacher, this will most likely mean that someone will tell you, "Here are the student books you will be using."

> **Companion Website**
> To broaden your knowledge base about curriculum planning, go to our Companion Website at **www.prenhall.com/roberts** and click on the *Additional Content* module for Chapter 5.

Differentiated Instruction

You should personalize the learning (provide tiered instruction or differentiated instruction) for students of various reading abilities. Consider the differentiated reading and workbook assignments in the textbook and several supplementary sources such as the multireading approach discussed in the next section. Except to make life simpler for the teacher, there is no advantage in all students working out of the same book and doing the same exercises.

Some students benefit from the drill, practice, and reinforcement afforded by workbooks and computer programs that accompany textbooks, but this is not true for all students, nor do all benefit from the same activity. You should consider demonstrations, cooperative learning, guided oral and silent work, journals, graphic organizers, and the inquiry method. In addition, adjust instruction to meet the students' needs with corrective and developmental instruction, reteaching, follow-up lessons, and enrichment learning activities.

Figure 5.3
Sample multiple readings guide and children's bibliography to assist students in multiple readings about America's revolutionary times

---

Multitext Guide: America's Revolutionary Times

- *Purpose*

  To engage students in multiple readings and to engage students in their own learning by motivating them to explore ideas further for enrichment; by fostering continued interest through discussions about what the students liked/disliked about a selected story; and by role playing, critical thinking, and problem solving related to America's revolutionary times around 1776. Classroom activities and more children's literature related to this Multitext Guide and America's Revolutionary Times can be found on our Companion Website, in the *Additional Content* module for this chapter.

- *Bibliography*

  Anderson, J. *Spanish Pioneers of the Southwest.* Illustrated by G. Ancona. New York: Dutton, 1989. Portrayal of a pioneer family in a Spanish community in New Mexico in the 1700s. Grades 3–6.

  Banim, L. *A Spy in the King's Colony.* Illustrated by T. Yuditskaya. New York: Silver Moon Press, 1994. In Boston in 1775, 11-year-old Emily Parker suspects Robert Babcock of being a Loyalist spy and helps deliver a coded note to General Washington about the movement of cannon from Fort Ticonderoga to Farmingham. Grades 4–5.

  Borden, L. *Sleds on Boston Common: A Story from the American Revolution.* Illustrated by R. A. Parker. New York: Simon & Schuster, 2000. Based on folklore from 1775, 9-year-old Henry wants to use his new sled on the local sled run but finds that General Gage and other British soldiers have camped on the Common in the middle of the best sledding hill. Henry asks the general to clear the run and Gage complies. Grades 2–4.

  Burgan, Michael. *Colonial and Revolutionary Times: A Watts Guide.* New York: Watts, 2003. Provides an overview of this time period with biographical profiles of Native people and colonists in America and European leaders. Grades 5 and up.

  Davis, B. *Black Heroes of the American Revolution.* San Diego: Harcourt, 1976. Depicts the contributions of African Americans during America's Revolutionary War with drawings, etchings, related reading list, and index. Grades 4–6.

  Gilbin, J. C. *George Washington: A Picture Book Biography.* Illustrated by M. Dooling. New York: Scholastic, 1992. Describes Washington's life from boyhood through adulthood. Grades K–3.

  Gilbin, J. C. *Thomas Jefferson: A Picture Book Biography.* Illustrated by M. Dooling. New York: Scholastic, 1995. Gives an account of Jefferson's life. Grades K–3.

  Gray, G. *How Far, Felipe?* New York: HarperCollins, 1978. Felipe and his family move from Mexico to California with the expedition of Colonel Juan de Anza in 1775. Compares and contrasts their lifestyles with those of the colonists on America's East Coast during this time period. Grades K–3.

  Moore, K. *If I Lived During the American Revolution. . . .* New York: Scholastic, 1997. Interesting depiction of the narrated points of view of both sides of the American Revolution through the eyes of children. Grades 2 and up.

In fact, the traditional workbook may eventually become extinct, as it is replaced by computer technology. Computers and other interactive media provide students with a psychologically safer learning environment in which they have greater control over the pace of the instruction, can repeat instruction if necessary, and can ask for clarification without the fear of having to do so publicly. Several methods have been invented by teachers to help their students develop their higher level thinking skills and better comprehend expository materials. Some of these methods are shown in Figure 5.2 and a sample multitext readings guide is found in Figure 5.3.

Just because something is in print or on the Internet does not mean it is necessarily accurate or even true. However much time we spend teaching students

how to find things on the Internet, we need to expend even more effort teaching them how to interpret what they have found. To do this, encourage students to be alert for errors in the text, both in content and printing. You might even give them some sort of credit reward, such as points, when they bring an error to your attention. This helps students develop the skills of critical reading, critical thinking, and healthy skepticism. As an example, an information book about the Pilgrims is reported to have stated that King Henry VIII ruled England in the 1600s. He died, with witnesses, in 1547. For another example, a history book is reported to have stated that the first person to lead a group through the length of the Grand Canyon was John Wesley Powell. Critically thinking students quickly made the point that perhaps Powell was only the first white person to do this, that Native Americans (the first Americans) had traveled the length of the Grand Canyon for centuries.[9]

Multireading Approach

Rather than a single textbook approach, some teachers use a strategy that incorporates multiple readings that vary in detail and vocabulary but have a common focus.[12] This strategy gives children a choice in what they read. The multiple readings allow for differences in reading ability and interest level, and stimulate sharing of what is read and being learned. The use of multiple sources can be helpful in encouraging children to evaluate written communications and to think critically. By using a teacher's guide, such as the sample given in Figure 5.3, all the children can be directed toward specific information and concepts, but they do not have to all read the same selections.

PLANNING SEQUENCING OF CONTENT

As you have reviewed the rationale and components of instructional planning, and examined state and local curriculum documents, national standards, and student reading materials, you have undoubtedly developed your own opinion regarding content that should be included in a subject at a particular grade level. Now it is time to obtain some practical experience in long-range planning. While some authors believe that the first step in planning to teach is to write the learning objectives, others believe that a more logical starting point is to prepare a sequential topic outline from which you can then prepare the major learning objectives.

The topic outlines and learning objectives and even scripted lessons may be presented to most beginning teachers with the expectation that they will teach from them. For you this may be the case, but someone had to have written those curriculum materials and that someone was one or more classroom teachers. Furthermore, some teachers organize their long-term planning by setting up a large sheet of butcher paper (or charts/plain newsprint paper) on a table or wall. They divide it into time segments (six weeks, semester, year) and fill it in with adhesive notes marked with topics, activities, and lesson ideas. They use this visual planner throughout the instructional block being considered and move, add, remove, and rewrite the adhesive notes. The paper is placed where it can be referred to again and again. This approach to the stretches of time involved in long-term planning makes a

teacher's planning immediate, tactile, tangible, and less abstract.

PREPARING FOR AND DEALING WITH CONTROVERSY

Controversial content and issues abound in teaching, for example, in English/language arts, over certain books; in mathematics, over the extent of the use of calculators in the classroom; in science, over biological evolution; and in social studies, over values and moral issues. As a general rule, trust your intuition: If you have concern that a particular topic or activity might create controversy, it probably will.

During your teaching career, you undoubtedly will have to make decisions about how you will handle controversial matters. Some teachers stage several debates at the beginning of the school year so that the students begin to develop the skills to debate and to approach later unanticipated debates ("teachable moments") during the year. When selecting content or methods that might be controversial, consider as guidelines the information in the paragraphs that follow.

Maintain a perspective with respect to your own goal, which is, at the moment, to obtain your teaching credential, and then a teaching job, and then perhaps tenure. Our point is that student teaching is not a good time to become involved in controversy. If you communicate closely with your host teacher and your college or university supervisor, you should be able to prevent most major problems dealing with controversial issues. Sometimes, during normal discussion in the classroom, a controversial topic will emerge spontaneously, catching the teacher off guard. *If this happens, think before saying anything.* Consider suspending further discussion on the topic until you have had an opportunity to review the issues with colleagues or your supervisors.

Controversial topics can seem to rise from nowhere for any teacher, and this is perfectly normal.[13] Children are works in progress! They need to be allowed to develop their skills in flexible thinking (one of the characteristics of intelligent behavior discussed later in Chapter 9), which they can only do as they learn to consider alternative points of view and to deal with several sources of information simultaneously. They are in the process of developing their moral and value systems, and they need and want to know how adults feel about issues that are important to them, particularly those adults they hold in esteem—their teachers. For some children, unfortunately, their classroom teacher may be the only adult whom they can hold in esteem. Students need to discuss issues that are important to society, and there is absolutely nothing wrong with dealing with those issues as long as certain guidelines are observed.

First, students should learn about all sides of an issue. Controversial issues are open-ended and should be treated as such. They do not have "right" answers or "correct" answers. If they did, there would be no controversy. (As used in this book, an issue differs from a problem in that a problem generally has a solution, whereas an issue has many opinions and several alternative solutions.) Therefore, the focus should be on process as well as on content. A major goal is to help children learn how to deal with controversy and to mediate wise decisions on the basis of carefully considered information. Another goal is to help children learn how to disagree without being disagreeable—how to resolve conflict. To that end, children need to learn the difference between conflicts that are destructive and those that can be constructive; in other words, to see that conflict (disagreement) can be healthy, that it can have value. Another goal, of course, is to help students learn about the content of an issue so, when necessary, they can make decisions based on knowledge, not on ignorance.

Second, as with all lesson plans, one dealing with a topic that could lead to controversy should be well thought out ahead of time—that is, during the preactive/planning phase of instruction. Potential problem areas and resources must be carefully considered and prepared in advance. You might want to send home a letter to parents outlining what you plan to teach and the resources you will use. Be sure they sign and return the letter. Consider inviting the parents to a preview night where they hear about how you will approach the topic and see the materials you will incorporate. Write a rationale for your plans that includes your goals and objectives, the materials you reviewed, and why you decided to use the books, videos, and so on that you plan to share, and your lesson plans. Be sure to include the process that the materials went through according to the district Materials Selection Policy (if the materials did). Sign and date the rationale. This verifies your careful planning, should the need arise. It is a good idea to consult with your site administrator about your rationale. If parents or guardians or paraprofessionals work in your classroom, be sure they understand the curriculum. Often these people are your best community liaisons. As we have said before (see Chapter 3, for example), problems for the teacher are most likely to occur when insufficient attention is given to the preactive phase of instruction and decision making.

Third, no matter how carefully you plan, a challenge may arise to something you plan to teach or have taught. This may come from students, parents/guardians, community representatives, or other faculty. Parents or guardians have the right **sans penalty** to ask that their child receive an alternate activity or be excused from the lesson. However, they do not have the right to censor content for all children. Most school districts have written policies that deal with challenges to instructional content or materials. As a beginning teacher, you should become aware of the policies of your school district (often called the Materials Reconsideration Policy). In addition, professional associations such as NCTE, IRA, NCSS, NBTA, and NSTA each have published guidelines for dealing with controversial content or materials. NCTE offers an online resource about censorship at *www.ncte.org/about/issues/censorship?source=ql.* Here's an "APPLE" to help you remember how to deal with censorship:

A = Awareness/Acceptance
To see that the potential for a challenge does exist for any educator.

P = Prepare
To prepare as mentioned previously.

P = Practice
To promote calm, objective responses to a challenge; reflect about how you would handle different types of objections (i.e., sexism, violence, racism, profanity, etc.). Role play your response to a challenge with your peers.

L = Locate
To know where you can get support. Some national organizations are listed in this resource guide.

E = Evaluate
To be aware of any changes occurring in the selection and reconsideration policies of the school district.

Fourth, there is nothing wrong with children knowing a teacher's opinion about an issue as long as it is clear that the students may disagree without reprisal or academic penalty. However, it is probably best to give your opinion only after the children have had full opportunity to study and report on facts and opinions from other sources. Sometimes it is helpful to assist students in separating facts from opinions on a particular issue being studied by setting up a fact–opinion table on the overhead or on the writing board, with the issue stated at the top followed by two parallel columns, one for facts and one for related opinions. Figure 5.4 provides an example of a fact–opinion table.

A characteristic that has made the United States such a great nation is the freedom for its entire people to speak out on issues. This freedom should not be excluded from public school classrooms. Teachers and students should be encouraged to express

Figure 5.4
Fact–opinion table

The issue:	
Statements of fact:	Statements of opinion:

their opinions about the great issues of today, to study the issues, to suspend judgment while collecting data, and to then form and accept each other's reasoned opinions. As educators, we must understand the difference between teaching truth, values, and morals, and teaching *about* truth, values, and morals.

As a public school teacher, there are limits to your academic freedom, much greater than are the limits on a university professor. You must understand this fact. The primary difference is that the students with whom you will be working are not yet adults. As children, they must be protected from dogma and allowed the freedom to learn and to develop their values and opinions, free from coercion from those who have power and control over their learning.

PLANNING FOR LEARNING OUTCOMES: GOALS AND OBJECTIVES

Now that you have examined content typical of the curriculum (even controversial issues) and, perhaps, have exercised the option of preparing a content outline for a subject at a grade level at which you intend to teach, you are ready to write instructional objectives for content learning. **Instructional objectives** (also called **learning objectives**) are **statements describing what the student will be able to do on completion of the instructional experience.** Whereas some authors distinguish between instructional objectives (objectives that are behavior specific), the terms are used here as if they are synonymous to emphasize the importance of writing instructional objectives in terms that are measurable. The phrase *terminal objective* is sometimes used to distinguish between instructional objectives that are intermediate and those that are final, or terminal, to an area of learning.

Companion Website
For more about planning with objectives and other exercises, go to our Companion Website at **www.prenhall.com/roberts** and return to the *Additional Application Exercises* module for this chapter.

PLANNING WITH INSTRUCTIONAL OBJECTIVES

As implied in the preceding paragraphs, goals guide the instructional methods; objectives drive student performance. Assessment of student achievement in learning should be an assessment of that performance. When the assessment procedure matches the instructional objectives, it is sometimes referred to as assessment that is *aligned* or *authentic*. If the term **authentic assessment** sounds rather silly to you, we agree. After all, if the objectives and assessment don't match, then that particular assessment should be discarded or modified until it does match. In other words, assessment that is not authentic is "poor assessment" and should not be used. When objectives, instruction, and assessment match the stated goals we have what is referred to as an **aligned curriculum.** Again, a curriculum that does not align is nonsensical and should be corrected or discarded.[14]

While instructional goals may not always be quantifiable, that is, readily measurable, instructional goals should be measurable. Furthermore, those objectives then become the essence of what is measured for in instruments designed to assess student learning—they are the learning targets. Consider the examples shown in Figure 5.5.

Learning Targets and Goal Indicators

One purpose for writing objectives in performance terms is to be able to assess with precision whether the instruction has resulted in the desired behavior. In

Goals

1. To acquire knowledge about the physical geography of North America.
2. To develop an appreciation for music.
3. To develop enjoyment for reading.

Objectives

1. On a map, the student will identify at least three specific mountain ranges of North America.
2. The student will identify 5 out of 10 different musical instruments by listening to a tape recording of the Boston Pops Symphony Orchestra and identify which instrument is being played at specified times as determined by the teacher.
3. The student will read two books, three short stories, and five newspaper articles at home, within a 2-month period and will maintain a daily written log of these activities.

Figure 5.5
Examples of goals and objectives

many schools, the educational goals are established as **learning targets,** competencies that the students are expected to achieve. These goals are then divided into performance objectives, sometimes referred to as **goal indicators.** Instruction is designed to teach toward those objectives. When students perform the competencies called for by these objectives, their education is considered successful. During recent years, this has become known variously as **criterion-referenced measurement, competence-based instruction, performance-based instruction, results-driven instruction,** or **outcome-based education.** Expecting students to achieve one set of competencies before moving on to the next set is called mastery learning (see Chapter 10). The success of the student achievement, teacher performance, and the school may each be assessed according to these criteria.

PLANNING WITH DOMAINS OF LEARNING AND DEVELOPMENTAL NEEDS OF CHILDREN

Educators attempt to design learning experiences to meet the five areas of developmental needs of the total child: intellectual, physical, emotional/psychological, social, and moral/ethical.[15] As a teacher, you must include objectives that address learning within each of these categories of needs. While the intellectual needs are primarily within the cognitive domain and the physical are within the psychomotor, the other needs are mostly within the affective domain.

Too frequently, teachers focus on the cognitive domain while assuming that the psychomotor and affective domains will take care of themselves. Many experts argue that teachers should do just the

opposite—that when the affective is directly attended to, the psychomotor and cognitive naturally develop. In any case, you should plan your teaching so that your students are guided from the lowest to the highest levels of operation within each of the domains separately or simultaneously.

The three developmental hierarchies are discussed next to guide your understanding of each of the five areas of needs. Notice the illustrative verbs within each hierarchy. These verbs help you fashion objectives when you are developing activities, lesson plans, and unit plans. (To see how goals and objectives fit into one lesson plan, see Figure 7.7 in Chapter 7.) Caution, however, must be urged, because considerable overlap exists among the levels at which some action verbs may appropriately be used. For example, the verb phrase *will identify* is appropriate in each of the following objectives at different levels (identified in parentheses) within the cognitive domain:

The student will identify the correct definition of the term *magnetism.* (knowledge)

The student will identify examples of the principle of magnetic attraction. (comprehension)

The student will identify the magnetic effect when two materials, one magnetic and one nonmagnetic, are brought together. (application)

The student will identify the effect when iron filings are brought into a magnetic field. (analysis)

Cognitive Domain Hierarchy

In a widely accepted taxonomy of objectives, Bloom and his associates arranged cognitive objectives into classifications according to the complexity of the skills and abilities they embodied.[16] The result was a multitiered arrangement ranging from the simplest to the most complex intellectual processes. Within each domain, prerequisite to a student's ability to function at one particular level of the hierarchy is the ability to function at the preceding level or levels. In other words, when a student is functioning at the third level of the cognitive domain, that student is automatically also functioning at the first and second levels. Rather than an orderly progression from simple to complex mental operations as illustrated by Bloom's taxonomy, other researchers prefer a contrastive organization of cognitive abilities that ranges from simple information storage and retrieval, through a higher level of discrimination and concept attainment, to the highest cognitive ability to recognize and solve problems.[17]

The six major categories (or levels) in Bloom's taxonomy of cognitive objectives are (a) **knowledge**—recognizing and recalling information; (b) **comprehension**—understanding the meaning of information; (c) **application**—using the information; (d) **analysis**—dissecting information into its component parts to comprehend their relationships; (e) **synthesis**—putting components together to generate new ideas; and (f) **evaluation**—judging the worth of an idea, notion, theory, thesis, proposition, information, or opinion. In this taxonomy, the top four categories of levels—application, analysis, synthesis, and evaluation—represent higher order thinking skills.[18] A discussion about these categories continues in the *Additional Content* module for this chapter at our Companion Website **(www. prenhall.com/roberts).** 🖰

Affective Domain Hierarchy

Krathwohl, Bloom, and Masia developed a taxonomy of the affective domain.[19] The following are their major levels (or categories) from least internalized to most internalized: (a) **receiving**—being aware of the affective stimulus and beginning to have favorable feelings toward it; (b) **responding**—taking an interest in the stimulus and viewing it favorably; (c) **valuing**—showing a tentative belief in the value of the effective stimulus and becoming committed to it; (d) **organizing**—placing values into a system of dominant and supporting values; and (e) **internalizing**—demonstrating consistent beliefs and behavior that have become a way of life. While there is considerable overlap from one category to another within the affective domain, these categories do give a basis by which to judge the quality of objectives and the nature of learning within this area. A discussion of each of the five categories continues at our Companion Website **(www. prenhall.com/roberts)** in the *Additional Content* module for this chapter. 🖰

Psychomotor Domain Hierarchy

Whereas identification and classification within the cognitive and affective domains are generally agreed on, there is less agreement in the classification within the psychomotor domain. Originally, the goal of this domain was simply to develop and categorize proficiency in skills, particularly those dealing with gross and fine motor control. The classification of the domain presented here follows this lead, but includes at its highest level the most creative and inventive behaviors, thus coordinating skills and knowledge from all three domains. Consequently, the objectives are in a hierarchy ranging from simple gross locomotor control to the most creative and complex, requiring originality and fine locomotor control—for example, from simply turning on a computer to designing a software program. From Harrow, we offer the following taxonomy of the psychomotor domain: (a) *moving,* (b) *manipulating,* (c) *communicating,* and (d) *creating.*[20]

Although space does not allow elaboration here, the different taxonomies include various subcategories within each of the major categories. It is probably less important that an objective be absolutely classified than it is to be cognizant of the hierarchies and to understand the importance of attending to student behavior from lower to higher levels of operation in all three domains. For a further discussion of each of these taxonomies and some action verbs and objectives for each category, turn to our Companion Website **(www.prenhall.com/roberts)** and the *Additional Content* module for this chapter. 🖰

Now, turn to Application Exercise 5.2 to begin writing your own objectives for use in your teaching. You may want to correlate your work with the additional application exercise titled Preparing a Content Outline, which can be found at our Companion Website **(www.prenhall.com/roberts),** or turn ahead to Chapter 7 and correlate writing your own objectives with some of the application exercises given there. 🖰 Share your results with your classmates and your instructor.

APPLICATION EXERCISE 5.2 PREPARING MY OWN INSTRUCTIONAL OBJECTIVES

Instructions: The purpose of this application exercise is to help you begin writing your own behavioral objectives. For guidance, you can refer to Application Exercise 7.1 (Putting Objectives, Resources, and Learning Activities Together for a Teaching Plan) and Application Exercise 7.2 (Preparing a Lesson Plan). Also refer to the Companion Website **(www.prenhall.com/roberts)** application exercise titled Preparing a Content Outline and Rubric Assessment in the Chapter 5 *Additional Application Exercises* module.

For a subject and a grade level of your choice, prepare 10 specific behavioral objectives. It is not necessary to include audience, conditions, and performance level unless requested by your course instructor.* Exchange completed exercises with your classmates. Then discuss and make changes where necessary.

Subject: _____

Grade level: _____

1. Affective (low level) _____

   _____

2. Affective (highest level) _____

   _____

3. Cognitive knowledge _____

   _____

4. Cognitive comprehension _____

   _____

5. Cognitive application _____

   _____

6. Cognitive analysis _____

   _____

7. Cognitive synthesis _____

   _____

8. Cognitive evaluation _____

   _____

9. Psychomotor (low level) _____

   _____

10. Psychomotor (high level) _____

   _____

*For further review, see the levels of the affective domain, cognitive domain, and psychomotor domain and examples of objectives on the Companion Website **(www.prenhall.com/roberts)** *Additional Content* module supporting this chapter.

For Your Notes

PLANNING WITH TAXONOMIES

Theoretically, the taxonomies are constructed such that students achieve each lower level before being ready to move to the next higher level. But, because categories and behaviors overlap, as they should, this theory does not always hold in practice. Furthermore, as explained by others, feelings and thoughts are inextricably interconnected—they cannot be nearly as separated as the taxonomies imply.[21]

The taxonomies are important in that they emphasize the various levels to which instruction must aspire. For learning to be worthwhile, you must formulate and teach to objectives from the higher levels of the taxonomies as well as from the lower ones. Student thinking and behavior must be moved from the lowest to the highest levels of thinking and doing. When all is said and done, it is, perhaps, the highest level of the psychomotor domain (creating) to which we aspire.

In using the taxonomies, remember that the point is to formulate the best objectives for the job to be done. In schools that use results-driven education models, those models describe levels of mastery standards (rubrics) for each target outcome. The taxonomies provide the mechanism for ensuring that you do not spend a disproportionate amount of time on facts and other low-level learning and can be of tremendous help where teachers are expected to correlate learning activities to one of the school's or district's outcome standards.

Preparing objectives is essential to the preparation of good items for the assessment of student learning. Clearly communicating your performance expectations to students and then specifically assessing student learning against those expectations lead to the most efficient and effective teaching, and they make the assessment of the learning closer to being authentic. This does not mean to imply that you will always write performance objectives for everything taught, nor will you always be able to accurately measure what students have learned. As mentioned earlier, learning that is meaningful to students is not as easily compartmentalized as the taxonomies of educational objectives would imply.

PLANNING WITH INTEGRATED CURRICULUM

When learning about **integrated curriculum (IC),** it is easy to be confused by the plethora of terms that are used. Other terms for IC are **interdisciplinary curriculum,** integrated studies, thematic instruction, multidisciplinary teaching, and interdisciplinary thematic instruction. In essence, regardless of which of these terms is being used, they refer to the same approach to teaching.

Because it is not always easy to tell where the term *curriculum* leaves off and the term *instruction* begins, let's assume for now that, for the sake of better understanding the meaning of integrated curriculum, there is no difference between the two terms. In other words, for the intent of this discussion, whether we use the term *integrated curriculum* or the term *integrated instruction,* we will be referring to the same thing.

Let's now look at reinforcing the "how" of planning and selecting content. If learning is defined only as the accumulation of bits and pieces of information, then we already know everything about how to teach and how children learn. But the accumulation of pieces of information is at the lowest end of a spectrum of types of learning. Discoveries are still being made about the processes involved in higher forms of learning—that is, about meaningful understanding and the reflective application of that understanding. The results of recent research support the use of instructional strategies that help children make connections as they learn. These strategies include the literature-based approach to reading, discovery learning, inquiry learning, cooperative learning, and interdisciplinary thematic instruction, with a total curriculum that is integrated and connected to students' life experiences.

This methodology uses what is referred to as **hands-on** and **minds-on learning.** The learner is learning by doing and is thinking about what she or he is doing and learning. When thoughtfully coupled, these approaches help construct, and often reconstruct, the learner's perceptions. Hands-on learning engages the learner's mind, causing questioning. Then, with the teacher's competent guidance, the children devise ways of investigating satisfactory, though sometimes only tentative, answers to their questions.

As a classroom teacher, your instructional task then is twofold: (a) to plan hands-on experiences, providing the materials and the supportive environment necessary for students' meaningful exploration and discovery learning; and (b) to know how to facilitate the most meaningful and longest lasting learning possible once the learner's mind has been engaged by the hands-on learning. To accomplish this requires your knowledge about, and competence in the use of, varied and developmentally appropriate methods of instruction. Assisting you in the acquisition of that knowledge and competence is the primary purpose of this resource guide. The chapters of this part of the resource guide address the planning aspect. As you proceed through these chapters and begin the development of your instructional plans, from time to time, you will want to refer to the topic of assessment of student learning in Chapter 6 and to particular topics in the chapters of Part III. Instruction and assessment go hand in hand and cannot be as easily separated as might be implied from their placement in the organization of this resource guide. Their

---

About Praxis and Other Teacher Tests

About Praxis Teacher Tests. How will your level of knowledge be indicated on these tests? Your level of knowledge will be reflected in a passing score that is based on recommendations of panels of teachers and teacher educators in each area in each state. Further, your state credentialing/licensing agency determines the passing scores (and the scores have been recommended by the panels of educators). To be at this point in your professional preparation and getting ready to take this test, you probably are familiar with studying for and taking tests because you probably have completed a bachelor's degree program in elementary school education or have prepared through an alternative educational program.

To continue to support your interest in preparing for this test, as well as some of the other teacher tests, all application exercises in this chapter offer opportunities for you to reflect generally on planning and selecting of curriculum content. For instance, in this chapter, precredentialed teachers are asked to participate cooperatively and collaboratively to do the following:

- Begin to become familiar with the national curriculum standards for various subjects of the K–6 curriculum (Application Exercise 5.1) and to begin writing your own behavioral objectives (Application Exercise 5.2).
- Turn to our Companion Website (**www.prenhall.com/roberts**) and click on the *Additional Application Exercise* module to complete additional application exercises, namely, Examining State Standards and Curriculum Documents, Examining Local Curriculum Documents, Examining Student Textbooks and Teacher's Editions, Preparing a Course Outline, and Dealing with Controversial Content and Issues.

You can find a constructed response-type question similar to those found on the Praxis II Principles of Learning and Teaching tests in the Praxis Warm-Up section that follows the Chapter Summary. This warm-up takes another look at the classroom vignette found in the Looking at Teachers section at the beginning of this chapter.

 Other Teacher Tests. For those of you who will be teaching in states that do not administer the Praxis tests, go to our Companion Website at **www.prenhall.com/roberts** and click on the *Other Teacher Tests* module for Chapter 5 to access information about teacher tests other than the Praxis.

---

separation here is done not for your implementation of them, but as explained in the preface of this guide, for your understanding of them.

Companion Website

To read about integrated curriculum and other content related to this chapter, go to our Companion Website at **www.prenhall.com/roberts** and click on the *Additional Content* module for Chapter 5.

SUMMARY

In this chapter and in its Companion Website (**www.prenhall.com/roberts**) material, you learned of the differences among the terms *goals* and *objectives*. Regardless of how these terms are defined, the important point is this: *Teachers must be clear about what it is they want their students to learn, must be clear about the kind of evidence needed to verify their learning, and must communicate those things to the students so they are clearly understood.*

You'll recall that many teachers do not bother to write specific objectives for all the learning activities in their teaching plans. However, when teachers do prepare specific objectives (by writing them themselves or by borrowing them from textbooks and other curriculum documents), teach toward them, and assess students' progress against them, student learning is enhanced. This is called *performance-based teaching* and *criterion-referenced measurement*. It is also known as an *aligned curriculum*. In schools using results-driven education mastery learning models, those models describe levels of mastery standards or rubrics for each outcome or learning target. The taxonomies are of tremendous help in schools where teachers are expected to correlate learning activities to the school's outcome standards.

As a teacher, you will be expected to (a) plan your lessons well, (b) convey specific expectations to your students, and (c) assess their learning against that specificity. However, because it tends toward high objectivity, there is the danger that such performance-based teaching could become too objective, which can have negative consequences. If students are treated as objects, then the relationship between teacher and student becomes impersonal and counterproductive to real learning. Highly specific and impersonal teaching can be discouraging to serendipity, creativity, and the excitement of discovery, to say nothing of its possibly negative impact on the development of students' self-esteem.

To be a most effective teacher, your challenge is to use performance-based criteria together with a teaching style that encourages the development of intrinsic sources of student motivation and that allows for, provides for, and encourages coincidental learning—learning that goes beyond what might be considered as predictable, immediately measurable, and representative of minimal expectations. Your final decisions about what content to teach are guided by (a) discussions with other teachers; (b) review of national, state, and local standards and documents, and articles from the professional journals and websites; (c) your personal convictions, knowledge, and skills; and (d) the unique characteristics of your students.

What's to Come. With knowledge of the content of school curriculum and the value of instructional objectives, you are now ready to consider student assessment and then detailed instructional plans with sequenced lessons, the subjects of the next two chapters.

EXTENDING MY PROFESSIONAL COMPETENCY

Praxis Warm-Up: A Constructed Response-Type Question

In this chapter's teacher vignette, you'll recall that a sixth-grade teacher was involved in a student brainstorming session with selected features of listening carefully related to the language arts curriculum as the content. The teacher, as part of her planning, was recording student contributions on a large sheet of butcher paper that had been taped to the classroom wall. Some of the students' contributions were deciding to listen, reading and hearing all stimuli, investing time wisely, verifying what was heard, and expending energy to listen carefully. She solicited more student responses about the content being studied, acknowledged those responses, held and manipulated the writing pen, walked to the wall, and wrote on the paper.

If you were the teacher, describe two writing activities that you might use after this student brainstorming session about this language arts lesson about listening. You want the writing to help your students communicate information and organize their thinking. Include both a realistic and a fanciful kind of writing for these students. Give examples and explain the purposes of the activities you selected.

Hints for responding to Praxis Warm-Ups are found in the Appendix.

Praxis. To do another Praxis Warm-Up with a constructed response-type question, go to our Companion Website at **www.prenhall.com/roberts** and click on the *Praxis Warm-Up* module for Chapter 5. Constructed response-type questions are designed to help you prepare for the Praxis II Principles of Learning and Teaching tests.

For Your Discussion

1. **Integrated Curriculum.** If an interviewer asked you during a job interview the following question, how would you respond?: Can critical-thinking skills be taught while teaching mathematics? Science? Language arts? Social studies? Visual and performing arts? **To do:** Think of ways in which critical thinking skills can be taught in different content areas and pretend that you are being interviewed for your first teaching job. Be able to describe observable behaviors that would enable you to tell whether a child is learning to think critically and tell them to the interviewer (a colleague role-playing the role of the interviewer).

2. **Documents.** If a teaching colleague believes—and fears—that the national curriculum standards are a first step forward toward national assessment of student learning (and thus a teacher's instruction), what would be your response to your colleague's statement? **To do:** Consider the information you have read about the national curriculum standards and explain your point of view about this.

3. **Assessment.** If a parent asks you about assessment of his or her child in your class, what would you tell the parent? **To do:** Consider what you have read about preassessment, assessment during instruction (formative assessment), and assessment after instruction (summative assessment) and explain your view about this to a colleague who role-plays the part of the parent.

4. **Textbooks and Censorship.** If a parent asks you about a topic in a student text that he or she thinks should be censored, what would you tell the inquiring parent? **To do:** Review the information you have about the censorship of material in the elementary school and formulate a response for the parent.

5. **Instructional Objectives.** If a teaching colleague asks you if you believe that it is easier to write instructional objectives after a lesson has been taught, what would be your response? **To do:** Explain the meaning of that point of view in your response to your teaching colleague.

Online Portfolio Activities

Supporting content of applications of knowledge (Praxis II Assessments), knowledge of curriculum (Principles 1, 4, and 7 of INTASC), and knowledge of students (Standards 2 and 6 of NBPTS): At the Companion Website **(www.prenhall.com/roberts),** click on the *Online Portfolio Activities* module to continue your online portfolio supporting knowledge of curriculum and students.

 Companion Website

Also on the Companion Website at **www.prenhall. com/roberts,** you can measure your understanding of chapter content in the *Objectives* and *Self-Check* modules and apply concepts in the *For Your Discussion* module.

FOR FURTHER READING

Barton, K. C., and Smith, L. A. (2000, September). Themes or Motifs? Aiming for Coherence Through Interdisciplinary Outlines. *The Reading Teacher, 54*(1), 54–63.

Battista, M. T. (1999). The Mathematical Miseducation of America's Youth. *Phi Delta Kappan, 80*(6), 425–433.

Burns, P. C., and Roe, B. D. (1999). *Informal Reading Inventory: Preprimer to Twelfth Grade* (5th ed.). Boston: Houghton Mifflin.

Chaney, A. L., and Burk, T. L. (1998). *Teaching Oral Communication in Grades K–8.* Boston: Allyn & Bacon.

Churma, M. (1999). *A Guide to Integrating Technology Standards into the Curriculum.* Upper Saddle River, NJ: Merrill/Prentice Hall.

Cooper, J. (2003). *Classroom Teaching Skills* (7th ed.). Boston: Houghton Mifflin.

Cornett, C. E. (1999). *The Arts as Meaning Makers: Integrating Literature and the Arts throughout the Curriculum.* Upper Saddle River, NJ: Merrill/Prentice Hall.

Cossey, R. (1999). Are California's Math Standards Up to the Challenge? *Phi Delta Kappan, 80*(6), 441–443.

Davidson, D. M., Miller, K. W., and Metheny, D. L. (1999). *Integrating Science and Mathematics in the Elementary Curriculum* (Fastback 444). Bloomington, IN: Phi Delta Kappa Educational Foundation.

Davidson, M., and Myhre, O. (2000). Measuring Reading at Grade Level. *Educational Leadership, 57*(5), 25–28.

Decker, K. A. (1999). Meeting State Standards through Integration. *Science and Children, 36*(6), 28–32, 69.

Duffy, G. G., and Hoffman, J. V. (1999). In Pursuit of an Illusion: The Flawed Search for a Perfect Method. *The Reading Teacher, 53*(1), 10–16.

Duffy-Hester, A. M. (1999). Teaching Struggling Readers in Elementary School Classrooms: A Review of Classroom Reading Programs and Principles of Instruction. *The Reading Teacher, 52*(5), 480–495.

Glickman, C. (2001–2002). Holding Sacred Ground: The Impact of Standardization. *Educational Leadership, 58*(4), 46–51.

Good, T. L., and Brophy, J. E. (2003). *Looking in Classrooms* (9th ed., Chp. 10). New York: Addison-Wesley-Longman.

Jensen, E. (1998). *Teaching with the Brain in Mind.* Alexandria, VA: Association for Supervision and Curriculum Development.

Lambert, L. T. (2000). The New Physical Education. *Educational Leadership, 57*(6), 34–38.

Roberts, P. L. (1998). *Language Arts & Environmental Awareness: 100+ Integrated Books & Activities for Children.* North Haven, CT: Linnet Professional Publication.

Rubin, D. (2000). *Teaching Elementary Language Arts: A Balanced Approach* (6th ed.). Needham Heights, MA: Allyn & Bacon.

TenBrink, T. D. (2003). Instructional Objectives. In J. Cooper (Ed.), *Classroom Teaching Skills* (7th ed.). Boston: Houghton Mifflin.

NOTES

1. B. Watson and R. Konicek, Teaching for Conceptual Change: Confronting Children's Experience, *Phi Delta Kappan, 71*(9), 680–685 (May 1990).
2. Both are available from ECS Learning Systems, Inc., P.O. Box 440 Bulverde, TX 78163.
3. L. A. Packard, *Greening the Reading and Writing Standards: Integrating Environmental Education with Middle School Language Arts* (Master's thesis) (Prescott: University of Arizona, 2003).
4. P. L. Roberts, *Language Arts & Environmental Awareness: 100+ Integrated Books and Activities for Children* (1998). North Haven, CT: Linnet Professional Publication.
5. Contact ACTFL, 700 S. Washington Street, Suite 210, Alexandria, VA 22314.
6. Contact National Geographic Society, P.O. Box 98199, Washington, DC 20090-8199.
7. Contact the American Alliance for Health, Physical Education, Recreation and Dance (AAHPRD), 1900 Association Drive, Reston, VA 20191.
8. Bureau of Indian Affairs, 1849 C Street, NW, Washington, DC 20240–0001; *www.doiu.nbc.gov/orientation/bia2.cfm.*
9. R. Reinhold, Class Struggle, *The New York Times Magazine,* September 29, 1991, p. 46.
10. Source of KWL: D. M. Ogle, K-W-L: A Teaching Model That Develops Active Reading of Expository Text, *Reading Teacher, 39*(6), 564–570 (February 1986) and J. Bryan, K-W-L: Questioning the Known, *Journal of the International Reading Association: Teaching Reading, 51*(7), 618–620 (1998). Source of PQRST: E. B. Kelly, *Memory Enhancement for Educators* (Fastback 365) (Bloomington, IN: Phi Delta Kappa Educational Foundation, 1994), p. 18. Source of SQ3R: See the early work of F. P. Robinson, *Effective Study* (rev. ed.) (New York: Harper & Brothers, 1961). The original source of SQ3R is unknown. For SRQ2R, see M. L. Walker, Help for the 'Fourth-Grade Slum'—SRQ2R Plus Instruction in Text Structure or Main Idea, *Reading Horizons, 36*(1), 38–58 (1995). Source of KWLQ: P. R. Schmidt, KWLQ: Inquiry and Literacy Learning in Science, *Reading Teacher, 52*(7), 789–792 (April 1999). About reciprocal teaching,

see M. M. Dermody and R. B. Speaker, Jr., Reciprocal Strategy Training in Prediction, Clarification, Question Generating and Summarization to Improve Reading Comprehension, *Reading Improvement, 36*(1), 16–23 (Spring 1999), and K. M. King and L. M. Johnson, Constructing Meaning Via Reciprocal Teaching, *Reading Research and Instruction, 38*(3), 169–186 (Spring 1999); A. November, *The Web—Teaching Zack to Think;* retrieved February 5, 2005, from *www.anovember.com/articles/zack.html.*

11. R. Reinhold, note 9.
12. See, for example, B. A. VanSledright and C. Kelly, Reading American History: The Influence of Multiple Sources on Six Fifth Graders, *Elementary School Journal, 98*(3), 239–265 (January 1998); and D. Camp, It Takes Two: Teaching with Twin Texts of Fact and Fiction, *The Reading Teacher, 53*(5), 400–408 (February 2000). See also The Book Review: Grade 5 and Up, *School Library Journal 49*(7), 136 (July 2003).
13. See H. M. Miller, Teaching and Learning about Cultural Diversity: All of Us Together Have a Story to Tell, *The Reading Teacher, 53*(8), 666–667 (May 2000).
14. See J. C. Baker and F. G. Martin, *A Neural Network Guide to Teaching* (Fastback 431) (Bloomington, IN: Phi Delta Kappa Educational Foundation, 1998); and T. L. Good and J. E. Brophy, *Looking in Classrooms,* 9th ed. (New York: Addison-Wesley-Longman, 2003), pp. 252–253.
15. See the articles in The Constructivist Classroom, the November 1999 (Volume 57, Number 3) theme issue of *Educational Leadership;* D. R. Geelan, Epistemological Anarchy and the Many Forms of Constructivism, *Science and Education, 6*(1–2), 15–28 (January 1997); and R. DeLay, Forming Knowledge: Constructivist Learning and Experiential Education, *Journal of Experiential Education, 19*(2), 76–81 (August/September 1996).
16. B. S. Bloom, (Ed.), *Taxonomy of Educational Objectives, Book 1, Cognitive Domain* (White Plains, NY: Longman, 1984).
17. See R. M. Gagné, L. J. Briggs, and W. W. Wager, *Principles of Instructional Design,* 4th ed. (New York: Holt, Rinehart and Winston, 1994).
18. Compare Bloom's higher order cognitive thinking skills with R. H. Ennis's "A Taxonomy of Critical Thinking Dispositions and Abilities," in J. B. Barron and R. J. Sternberg (Eds.), *Teaching Thinking Skills: Theory and Practice* (New York: W. H. Freeman, 1987), and with R. J. Marzano's *A Different Kind of Classroom: Teaching with Dimensions of Learning* (Alexandria, VA: Association for Supervision and Curriculum Development, 1992).
19. D. R. Krathwohl, B. S. Bloom, and B. B. Masia, *Taxonomy of Educational Goals, Book 2, Affective Domain* (New York: Longman, 1984).
20. See the original view of A. J. Harrow in his book *Taxonomy of the Psychomotor Domain* (New York: Longman, 1977). A similar taxonomy for the psychomotor domain is that of E. J. Simpson, The Classification of Educational Objectives in the Psychomotor Domain, in *The Psychomotor Domain, Volume 3* (Washington, DC: Gryphon House, 1972).
21. R. N. Caine and G. Caine, *Education on the Edge of Possibility* (Alexandria, VA: Association for Supervision and Curriculum Development, 1997), pp. 104–105.

How Do I Assess, Use, and Report Student Achievement?

Visual Chapter Organizer and Overview

Purposes of Assessment

> **Authentic Assessment: Advantages and Limitations**

Three Avenues of Assessment

> **Assessing What a Student Says and Does**
> **Assessing What a Student Writes**

Student Involvement in Assessment

> **Using Student Portfolios**
> **Using Checklists**
> **Using Student Conferences**

Testing for Achievement

> **Standardized and Nonstandardized Tests**
> **How to Explain Standardized Test Scores**
> **When Test Scores Are Printed Publicly**
> **Purposes for Testing**

Preparing Assessment Items

Types of Assessment Items: Descriptions, Examples, and Guidelines for Preparation and Use

> **Essay**
> **Multiple Choice**
> **Performance Assessment: Expensive and Intensive**

Reporting: Maintaining Records of Student Achievement

> **Recording Teacher Observations and Judgments**

Grading and Marking Student Achievement

Looking at Teachers

In a middle school in a southern state, one teacher covered the outside of the classroom door with paper painted to look like stone blocks (student-made) inscribed with hieroglyphs. (Patterned paper that looks like rocks, cobblestones, or flagstones is available from *www.ShindigZ.com*.) Inside, the room was changed to reflect the time of Hammurabi, a ruler during the golden age of Babylon around 2000 B.C.E. The classroom walls were covered with pictures of ancient sites that were located east of the Mediterranean Sea. Illustrations of artifacts were placed at strategic locations in the classroom. There was a copy of Hammurabi's code of laws, with examples of some of its 200+ legal provisions, to reflect his interest in the welfare of his people. The code set up a social order built on the rights of the individual, protected by the authority of law. The code's essence was the idea that the strong should not injure the weak. The code also included laws concerning accusations that were false, debts, family rights, land and business law, loans, military service, tariffs, trades, and wages. In addition to Hammurabi's administrative code, he built irrigation canals to improve agriculture, set up maximum prices and minimum wages, and reorganized taxation on a fair and efficient basis.

To help enrich the environment and extend the study beyond Babylon, a picture of a large black Egyptian obelisk stood in one corner. Beside the obelisk was a poster of the Washington monument. To further develop each student's understanding of the multiple connections among world history, social change, and American laws, the teacher asked the students to take on the personas of famous world leaders across history and societies. Some of the roles chosen were Lincoln, Mandela, and Mother Theresa. A conceptual statement, also used as a debate statement in the classroom, was one that brought together some connections among world history, social change, and American laws. The statement was "All men/women are created equal." Questions were asked: "How was this statement brought to life for the people who lived with Hammurabi? For the people who lived under the shadow of the Egyptian obelisk each day? For the people who see the Washington monument each morning? How did Hammurabi's code of laws portray that all men/women were created equal? How does today's code in our town/city/state portray equality? What social changes related to 'All men/women are created equal' have happened since the time of the building of the obelisk up to the building of the Washington monument? What social changes have happened since the time of Hammurabi that you think are the most significant to you?"

In their roles related to world history, the students campaigned for or against the statement. As part of their campaigns as famous world leaders, they prepared their remarks for a videotaped press conference, a campaign commercial, and a classroom discussion/debate. For a final authentic assessment (sometimes called the right evaluation at the right time for the right purpose), the final product was a portfolio of each student's understanding of these connections. The portfolios included a wide variety of materials: essays, videos, short multiple-choice tests, and final reflections on the project. The multiple-choice exams were coordinated with the state's learning objectives. A colleague who taught English helped with the writing assignments and the school technologist used the students in her classes to help edit the videotapes. This project incorporated multiples of many important features of teaching—multiple learning styles, intelligences, contents, and teaching styles.[1]

Today's interest is (or should be) more on what the student can do (performance testing) as a result of learning than merely on what the student can recall (memory testing) from the experience. As a result of these and other concerns, a variety of systems of assessment and reporting have evolved, are still evolving, and will likely continue to evolve throughout your professional career.[2]

When teachers are aware of alternative systems, they may be able to develop assessment and reporting processes that are fair and effective for particular situations. So, after beginning with assessment, the final focus in this chapter considers today's principles and practices in grading and reporting student achievement.

CHAPTER OBJECTIVES

Specifically, on completion of this sixth chapter, you should be able to:

1. Explain the meaning of assessment as a continuous process, what you do with the assessment (information) results, and ways you interpret data for others.
2. Compare and contrast three avenues for assessing student learning as well as when and how to use such assessment as observations, oral reports, records, portfolios, and performance samples.
3. Demonstrate your skill in preparing different types of assessment items.
4. Explain why criterion-referenced grading is preferred over norm-referenced grading and the difference among standardized tests and publisher-produced tests.
5. Differentiate between summative assessment and formative assessment with examples of when and how each can be used at a particular grade level.

6. Self-assess and evaluate your competencies with a midpoint checklist on our Companion Website **(www.prenhall.com/roberts)** in the *Self-Check* module for this chapter. ✍

PURPOSES OF ASSESSMENT

Assessing student progress is an important part of a teacher's responsibility and, as mentioned in Chapter 1, standardized testing is gaining importance as a measure of educational achievement. However, standardized tests are only one form of measurement and one may argue about their usefulness for the individual child. As Miss Malarkey and her colleagues prepare their students for the Instructional Performance Through Understanding (IPTU) test in the picture book *Testing Miss Malarkey* (New York: Walker & Company, 2003) written by Judy Finchler and illustrated by Kevin O'Malley, she assures her class that "THE TEST" will not affect their grades or being promoted to the next grade. But the students play Multiplication Mambo and Funny Phonics at recess, eat fish for lunch because it is considered "brain food," and practice filling in circles as part of art. The principal even sharpens pencils for everyone. One PTA meeting features Dr. Scorewell, "the Svengali of tests," and soon after that, parents abandon bedtime stories for textbook drills. Later, after the school is named #1 IPTU County Champion because of the high test scores, the test quickly fades in importance as the school gets back to its normal routines. While this story is meant to be humorous and is often read by teachers to students to alleviate the stress of formal testing, it does highlight how high-stakes testing can affect a child's daily education and progress. This is why standardized tests should be viewed as just one means of assessment. Multiple measures, as described in this chapter, are necessary to accurately determine a child's skills and knowledge.

Assessment of achievement in student learning is designed to serve several purposes:

1. **To assist in student learning.** This is the purpose usually first thought of when speaking of assessment, and it is the principal topic of this chapter. For the classroom teacher, it is (or should be) the most important purpose.

2. **To identify students' strengths and weaknesses.** Identification and assessment of children's strengths and weaknesses are necessary for two reasons: to structure and restructure the learning activities and to restructure the curriculum. Concerning the first, for example, data on student strengths and weaknesses in content and process skills are important in planning activities appropriate for both skill development and intellectual development. This is diagnostic assessment (known also as preassessment or assessment of student readiness). For the second, data on student strengths and weaknesses in content and skills are useful for making appropriate modifications to the curriculum. Some teachers use their methods of preassessment as ways to build on students' prior knowledge and to help their students develop their comprehension of expository materials and their higher order thinking skills (see Figure 6.1).

3. **To assess the effectiveness of a particular instructional strategy.** It is important for you to know how well a particular strategy helped accomplish a particular goal or achieve a specific objective. Skilled teachers continually reflect on and evaluate their strategy choices, using a number of sources: student achievement as measured by assessment instruments such as student oral reports, records, portfolios, and performance samples; their own intuition and observations; and informal feedback given by colleagues, such as members of a teaching team or mentor teachers. (The topic of mentor teachers is further presented in Chapter 11.)

4. **To assess and improve the effectiveness of curriculum programs.** Components of the curriculum are continually assessed by committees composed of teachers and administrators and sometimes parents, guardians, and students and other members of the school and community. The assessment is usually done both while students are learning **(formative assessment)** and after the instruction **(summative assessment).**

5. **To assess and improve teaching effectiveness.** To improve student learning, teachers are periodically evaluated on the basis of (a) their commitment to working with students at a particular level; (b) their ability to cope with students at a particular age, developmental level, or grade; or (c) their ability to show mastery of appropriate instructional techniques—techniques that are articulated throughout this resource guide.

6. **To provide data that assist in decision making about a student's future.** Assessment of student achievement is important in guiding decision making about grade level and program placement, promotion, school transfer, and eligibility for special recognition and perhaps career planning.

7. **To provide data to communicate with and involve parents and guardians in their children's learning.** Parents and guardians, communities, and school boards all share accountability for the effectiveness of students' learning. Today's schools are reaching out more than ever before and engaging parents, guardians, and the community in their children's education. All teachers play an important role in the process of communicating with, reaching out to, and involving parents, guardians, and the community.

Figure 6.1
TPS, TWPS, KWL, and KWLQ as methods of preassessment*[3]

- **TPS:** Think–pair–share is a strategy in which students, in pairs, examine a new topic about to be studied. The topic/question/issue/problem can be written on the board and the students are asked in pairs to think about the topic, discuss it between themselves, and then the student-pairs share with the whole class what they know or think they already know about it, while the teacher or student volunteer writes the major thoughts on the board, perhaps in the form of a graphic concept web. As an option, after the students in each dyad discuss the topic, they can record what they already know as a preassessment, then they can present their perceptions to the whole group. At this time, some of the students' perceptions may be revealed as misconceptions (something that the students *think* they know). This is an excellent technique for preassessment and for discovery learning about a topic.

- **TWPS:** The think–pair–share strategy can be extended to include a writing step and is referred to as think–write–pair–share. In this extended TPS strategy, students, again in pairs, examine a new topic to be studied. They discuss and write down what they know (as a preassessment tool), but they also go on and refer to what they have written to write conclusions about what they know before sharing their information with the larger group. Remind the students that to write a conclusion means to write about their reasoning about the topic; it can be a judgment based on their reasons and experience and should be a brief summing up of all of their words.

- **KWL:** In the KWL strategy, the students record what they already know to participate in a preassessment (*K* for know) about a topic being studied. With the teacher leading an ensuing discussion, three columns are formed on a chart, on the board, or on a transparency on an overhead projector (the students can take notes or take the dictation of their peers to make their own three-column facsimiles). In the left-hand column, the teacher, classroom aide, or a volunteer writes what students say they already KNOW or think they know about the topic. Then they generate questions about what they want to learn about the topic (*W* for *want* to know). In the middle column, the writer makes a list of what the students WANT to learn about the topic. The right-hand column is left blank. Next the students participate in the study and then they answer their questions to record what they learned; that is, they fill in the right-hand column at the end of the lesson or study with what has been LEARNED about the topic. They then self-assess (formative assessment) their answers (*L* for *learned* what?).

- **KWLQ:** Students record what they already know for preassessment (K) about a topic, formulate questions about what they want to learn about the topic (W), assess their answers to their questions to see what they have learned (L), and then ask more questions for further study (Q).

---

*These methods are avenues to build on students' prior knowledge and also are ways to help students assess their comprehension of expository materials and their higher order thinking skills.

Companion Website

If you are interested further in assessment—for instance, in learning some related principles and selected terms used in assessment, go to our Companion Website at **www.prenhall.com/roberts** and click on the *Additional Content* module for Chapter 6.

Authentic Assessment: Advantages and Limitations

When assessing student achievement, it is important that you use procedures that are compatible with the instructional objectives. This is referred to as **authentic assessment.** Other terms used for authentic assessment are *accurate, active, aligned, alternative*, and *direct assessment.* Note that performance assessment refers to the type of student response that is being assessed, whereas authentic assessment refers to the assessment situation. Although not all performance assessments are authentic, assessments that are authentic are most assuredly performance assessments. This assessment type asks students to do real tasks rather than repeat their knowledge.

Advantages

Advantages claimed for the use of authentic assessment include (a) the explicit (also known as performance-based, criterion-referenced, outcome-based, or direct) measurement of what students should know and can do, and (b) and its emphasis on higher order thinking.

You'll realize that some tests are limited in measuring language use. In language arts, for example, although it may seem fairly easy to develop a criterion-referenced test, administer it, and grade it, tests often measure language skills rather than language use. It is extremely difficult to measure students' communicative competence with a test. Tests do not measure listening and talking very well, and a test on punctuation marks, for instance, does not indicate the students' ability to add punctuation marks to a set of sentences created by someone else or to proofread and spot punctuation errors in someone else's writing.[4] An alternative and far better approach is to examine how students use punctuation marks in their own writing. To authentically assess students' understanding of that which the students have been learning, you would use a performance-based assessment procedure.

Consider another example. "If students have been actively involved in classifying objects using multiple characteristics, it sends them a confusing message if they are then required to take a paper-and-pencil test that asks them to 'define classification' or recite a memorized list of characteristics of good classification schemes."[5] An authentic assessment technique would be to use a performance item that actually involves the students in classifying objects. In other words, to obtain an accurate assessment of a student's learning, the teacher uses a performance-based assessment procedure, that is, a procedure that requires students to produce rather than to select a response.

Limitations

Some limitations of authentic assessment include (a) higher costs to administer; (b) difficulty in making results consistent and usable; and (c) problems with validity (Does the measuring instrument actually measure that which it is intended to measure?), reliability (Does the assessment technique consistently and accurately measure that which it does measure?), and comparability (How would you compare it with direct measurement and show its value for giving consistent and usable results?). In addition, a teacher, unfortunately, may never see a particular student again after a given school semester or year is over; thus, the teacher may never observe the effects he or she had on a student's values and attitudes. In schools where groups or teams of teachers remain with the same cohort of students for longer than the traditional time—as in looping programs where students and teachers remain together for several years—those teachers often do have better opportunity to observe the positive changes in their students' values and attitudes.

THREE AVENUES OF ASSESSMENT

Three general avenues are open to you for assessing a student's achievement in learning. You can assess:

1. What the student *says*—for example, the quantity and quality of a student's contributions to class discussions

2. What the student *does*—for example, a student's performance (e.g., the amount and quality of a student's participation in the learning activities and performance tests)

3. What the student *writes*—for example, as shown by items in the student's portfolio (e.g., homework assignments [also called responsibility papers], checklists, project work, and written tests).

While your own situations and personal philosophy will dictate the levels of importance and weight you give to each avenue of assessment, you should have a strong rationale if you value and weigh the three avenues for assessment differently than one third each.

Assessing What a Student Says and Does

When evaluating what a student says, you should (a) listen to the student's oral reports, questions, responses, and interactions with others and (b) observe the student's attentiveness, involvement in class activities, creativeness, and responses to challenges including the challenges afforded by performance testing. Notice that we say you should *listen* and *observe*. While listening to what the student is saying, you should also be observing the student's nonverbal behaviors. For this, you can use narrative observation forms (see Figure 6.2) or behavioral **checklists,** and **scoring guides** or **rubrics** (see sample checklists in Figures 6.3 and 6.4, and later in Figure 6.5; also see sample scoring guides/rubrics in Figures 6.3 and 6.4). Periodic conferences with the student are also used for assessment.

With each technique used, you must proceed from your awareness of anticipated learning outcomes (the learning target or instructional objectives), and you must assess a student's progress toward meeting those outcomes. This technique is referred to as explicit/direct or **criterion-referenced assessment.**

Observation Form

Figure 6.2, mentioned earlier, illustrates a sample generic form for recording and evaluating teacher observations of a student's verbal and nonverbal behaviors. With modern technology, such as if afforded, for example, by the software program *Learner Profile*, a teacher can record observations electronically anywhere at any time.[6]

Assessing What a Student Writes

When assessing what a student writes, you can use worksheets, written homework, assignment papers, student journal writing, student writing projects,

Figure 6.2
Sample form for evaluating and recording a student's verbal and nonverbal behaviors

Student _____	Grade/Subject _____	School _____
Observer _____	Date _____	Period/Time _____

Objective	Desired behavior	What the student did, said, or wrote

---

Sample scoring guide/rubric for assessing a student's skill in listening

Score Point 3—Strong listener:
    Responds immediately to oral directions.
    Focuses on speaker.
    Maintains appropriate attention span.
    Listens to what others are saying.
    Is interactive.

Score Point 2—Capable listener:
    Follows oral directions.
    Usually attentive to speaker and to discussions.
    Listens to others without interrupting.

Score Point 1—Developing listener:
    Has difficulty following directions.
    Relies on repetition.
    Often inattentive.
    Has short attention span.
    Often interrupts the speaker.

Sample checklist for assessing a student's skill in map work:

Check each item if the map comes up to standard in this particular category
_____ 1. Accuracy
_____ 2. Neatness
_____ 3. Attention to details

Figure 6.3
Checklist and scoring guide/rubric compared*

---

*The difference between a checklist and a rubric is minimal. The difference is that a rubric shows the degrees for the desired characteristics, whereas a checklist usually shows only the desired characteristics. A checklist can easily be made into a scoring guide/rubric and a rubric can easily be made into a checklist.

Figure 6.4
Sample scoring guide/rubric for assessing student writing

Scoring Guide/Rubric: Assessing Student Writing

Student _____ Date _____

Teacher _____ Time _____

Here is an example of data you can get from a student's writing sample.

Did the student	Yes	No	Comment
—have an understanding of the specific assignment	_____	_____	_____
—stay focused on the task	_____	_____	_____
—stay within the time period	_____	_____	_____
—use his or her time well	_____	_____	_____
—show an ability to use syntax (word order)	_____	_____	_____
—use verbs that agree in subject and tense	_____	_____	_____
—use subjective pronouns (he, she, I)	_____	_____	_____
—use objective pronouns (her, him, me)	_____	_____	_____
—rely on invented spelling	_____	_____	_____
—show a positive attitude toward writing	_____	_____	_____
—demonstrate the level of writing skills for the student's age/grade level and level of development	_____	_____	_____
—show organizational skills in thinking and writing	_____	_____	_____

Assessing student writing*   **Scores**

If the student demonstrates
—correct purpose, mode, audience;
—effective elaboration;
—consistent organization;
—clear sense of order and completeness;
—fluent language   Score 4

If the student demonstrates
—correct purpose, mode, audience
—moderate elaboration
—organized but possible brief digressions
—clear, effective language   Score 3

If the student demonstrates
—correct purpose, mode, audience
—some elaboration
—some specific details
—gaps in organization
—limited language control   Score 2

If the student demonstrates
—an attempt to address audience
—being brief, vague, unelaborated
—wandering off topic
—lack of language control
—little or no organization
—wrong purpose and mode   Score 1

---

*Note: Also in a student's writing, a teacher can see patterns of errors and can tell how best to help the students. Some errors might be about word order, verbs, and spelling. To help a student, a teacher can review the proper use of language related to the errors. For example, if there is an error pattern related to the use of pronouns, the teacher can assist the student and review the proper use of each type of pronoun and word order placement in sentences.

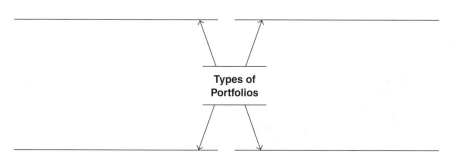

Selected Works Portfolio

Holds samples of work
prompted by teacher

Showcase Portfolio

Holds selections by
students to show best
work

Figure 6.5
Student portfolio categories

**Types of
Portfolios**

Growth Portfolio

Holds student work to show
achievement toward goals
from beginning to end of the
study, semester, or year

Passport Portfolio

Holds work that will
enable student to
transition from one
grade to the next

student portfolios, and tests (all discussed later in this chapter or on our Companion Website for this chapter at **www.prenhall.com/roberts** in the *Additional Content* module). In many schools, portfolios, worksheets, and homework assignments are the tools usually used for the formative evaluation of each student's achievement. Tests, too, should be a part of this evaluation, but tests are also used for summative evaluation at the end of a unit and for diagnostic purposes. Your summative evaluation of a student's achievement and any other final judgment made by you about a student can have an impact on the emotional and intellectual development of that child. Special attention is given to this later in the section titled Recording Teacher Observations and Judgments.

STUDENT INVOLVEMENT IN ASSESSMENT

Students' continuous self-assessment should be planned as an important component of the assessment program. If elementary students are to progress in their intellectual development, then they must receive instruction and guidance in how to become more responsible for their own learning. During that empowerment process, they learn to think in positive ways about themselves and about their individual capabilities. Achieving this self-understanding and improved self-esteem requires the experiences afforded by successes, along with guidance in self-understanding and self-assessment.

To meet these goals, teachers provide opportunities for elementary students to think about what they are learning, about how they are learning it, and about how far they have progressed. One procedure is to ask the students to maintain portfolios of their work, periodically using rating scales or checklists to self-assess their progress.

Using Student Portfolios

Portfolios are used by teachers as a means of instruction and by teachers and students as one means of self-reflection and of assessing student learning. You get, as an initial assessment value, a picture of general development of skills and abilities over time. Though there is little research to support or refute the claim, educators believe that the instructional value comes from the process of the student's assembling and maintaining a personal portfolio. During that creative process, the student is expected to self-reflect and to think critically about what has and is being learned, and the student is assuming some degree of responsibility for her or his own learning.[7]

Student portfolios can be grouped into four general categories, as shown in Figure 6.5. In a given situation, the purpose of portfolios can transcend any combination of the four. Student portfolios should be organized and, depending on the category (which reflects the portfolio's purpose), should contain assignment sheets, worksheets, the results of homework, project binders, forms for student self-assessment and reflection on their work, and other class materials thought important by the students and teacher. Computer software programs are available for assisting students in electronic portfolio development and management.[8]

As a model of a real-life portfolio, you can show the students your own career portfolio (see Chapter 11).

Portfolio Assessment: Dealing with Its Limitations

Although portfolio assessment as an alternative to traditional methods of evaluating student progress has gained momentum in recent years, establishing standards has been difficult. Research on the use of portfolios for assessment indicates that the validity and reliability of teacher evaluation are often quite low.[9] It seems portfolio assessment is not always practical for use by every teacher. For example, if you are the sole art teacher for a school and are responsible for teaching art to all of the 375 children in the school, you are unlikely to have the time or storage capacity for 375 portfolios. In such a case, the use of checklists, scoring guides/rubrics, and student self-assessment may be more practical.[10]

Before using portfolios as an alternative to traditional testing, you are advised to consider carefully and understand clearly the reasons for doing it and its practicality in your situation. Then decide carefully portfolio content, establish scoring guides/rubrics or expectation standards, anticipate grading problems, and consider and prepare for parent and guardian reactions.

Using Checklists

One of the items that can be maintained by students in their portfolios is a series of checklists. A checklist and the included items can be used easily by a student to compare the items with a previous self-assessment. Items on the checklist will vary depending on your purpose and grade level. (See sample forms in Figures 6.6 and 6.7). For example, open-ended questions can be included to allow the student to provide additional information as well as to do some expressive writing. After a student has demonstrated each of the skills satisfactorily, each student receives a check next to the student's name, made either by the teacher alone or in conference with the student.

Using Student Conferences

While emphasizing the criteria for assessment, rating scales and checklists provide children with means of expressing their feelings and give the teacher still another source of input data for use in assessment. To provide students with reinforcement and guidance to improve their learning and development, teachers can meet with individual students to discuss a self-assessment. Such conferences should provide students with understandable and achievable short-term goals as well as help them develop and maintain self-esteem.[11]

Although almost any instrument a teacher uses for assessing student work can be used for student self-assessment, in some cases it might be better to construct specific instruments with the student's understanding of the instrument in mind. Student self-assessment and self-reflection should be done on a regular and continuing basis so students can make comparisons periodically. You will need to help students learn how to analyze these comparisons. Comparisons should provide a student with information previously not recognized about his or her own progress and growth.

TESTING FOR ACHIEVEMENT

One source of information used for determining grades is data obtained from testing for student achievement. Two kinds of tests are used: those that are standardized and those that are not.

Standardized and Nonstandardized Tests

Standardized tests are those constructed and published by commercial testing bureaus and used by states and districts to determine and compare student achievement, principally in the core subjects of reading, mathematics, and science. Usually based on a state or national level, norms for particular age groups of children are established for a test based on its administration to large groups of children. **Norms** are standardized test scores from a representative group of students that are used to construct national norms. Norms can also be the median achievement of a large group; the **median** is the middle score in a distribution of scores achieved by test takers. The **mode** is the most frequent score in a distribution of scores taken by test takers. Standardized **norm-referenced** tests are best for diagnostic purposes and should not be used by a classroom teacher for determining the grades of students.

As mentioned in Chapter 1, the administration of standardized achievement tests and the use of their results have become major concerns to classroom teachers and school principals. In some locales, for example, their salaries and, indeed, their jobs, are contingent on the results of student scores on standardized achievement tests. Now, for the purposes of this resource guide, we will briefly consider standardized achievement testing by explaining test scores and discussing scores related to the Academic Performance Index.

Figure 6.6
Sample checklist: Assessing a student's oral report

Checklist: Oral Report Assessment

Student _____ **Date** _____

Teacher _____ **Time** _____

Did the student:

1. Speak so that everyone could hear?	Yes	No	Comments
2. Finish sentences?	Yes	No	Comments
3. Seem comfortable in front of group?	Yes	No	Comments
4. Give a good introduction?	Yes	No	Comments
5. Seem well informed about the topic?	Yes	No	Comments
6. Explain ideas clearly?	Yes	No	Comments
7. Stay on the topic?	Yes	No	Comments
8. Give a good conclusion?	Yes	No	Comments
9. Use effective visuals to make the presentation interesting?	Yes	No	Comments
10. Give good answers to questions from the audience?	Yes	No	Comments

Figure 6.7
Sample checklist: Student learning assessment for use with interdisciplinary thematic instruction

Checklist: Interdisciplinary Thematic Unit Learning

Student _____ Date _____

Teacher _____ Time _____

Did the student:	Yes	No	Comment
1. Identify theme, topic, main idea of the unit?	____	____	_____
2. Identify contributions of others to the theme?	____	____	_____
3. Identify problems related to the unit study?	____	____	_____
4. Develop skills in the following areas?	____	____	_____
Applying knowledge	____	____	_____
Assuming responsibility	____	____	_____
Categorizing	____	____	_____
Classifying	____	____	_____
Decision making	____	____	_____
Discussing	____	____	_____
Gathering responses	____	____	_____
Impulse control	____	____	_____
Inquiry learning	____	____	_____
Justifying choices	____	____	_____
Listening to others	____	____	_____
Locating information	____	____	_____
Metacognition	____	____	_____
Ordering	____	____	_____
Organizing information	____	____	_____
Problem recognition/identification	____	____	_____
Problem solving	____	____	_____
Reading maps and globes	____	____	_____
Reading text	____	____	_____
Reasoning	____	____	_____
Reflecting	____	____	_____
Reporting to others	____	____	_____
Self-assessing	____	____	_____
Sharing	____	____	_____
Studying	____	____	_____
Summarizing	____	____	_____
Thinking	____	____	_____
Using resources	____	____	_____
Working independently	____	____	_____
Working with others	____	____	_____
(Other unique to the unit)	____	____	_____

Additional teacher and student comments: _____

_____

Figure 6.8
Test scores a teacher can explain

Name of Standardized Test

Teacher _____ Year _____ Grade _____ Student Skills _____

School _____ Semester _____ Form _____ Analysis for Student _____

District _____ Test Date _____ Level _____

Tests	No. of items	Raw Score	Natl. % rank/stanine*	Local % rank/stanine	Grade Equiv
Total Reading	93	48	40–4	41–4	4.1

_____

*According to some test publishers and their way of sending test information, stanines can be indicated to educators by putting stanines after dashes behind a student's percentile rank. It is often published as follows: 40–4. The first numeral tells you the national (or local) percentile rank of the student and the numeral after the dash tells you the stanine the student is in for this particular test.

How to Explain Standardized Test Scores

When explaining standardized tests scores to a parent or guardian, point out that all test scores begin by being raw scores, the number of items that the child answered correctly on a standardized test that had X number of items. (Figure 6.8 provides an example of test scores that teachers can explain.) Point out that we can compare the child's raw score to the scores of other children. To do this, we can use a percentile or a percentile rank (PR or % rank), that is, a ranking that compares a child's score with the scores of all other children who have taken the test. For example, looking at Figure 6.8, the child's raw score of 48 in reading placed her in the 40th percentile nationally and the 41st percentile locally. This means that her score was as high (or higher) than 40 percent of the children who took the test across the nation and 41 percent of the many children who took the test in her district locally.

When talking to parents or guardians, point out that we can compare the child's raw score in still another way, by referring to a stanine. **Stanine** (abbreviation of the term standard nine) refers to a child's standardized test performance based on a scale from 1 to 9 points; also, it is a specific percentage of the normal curve. For instance, in Figure 6.8, the child's total reading score placed her in stanine 4 nationally and stanine 4 locally as you see on the figure. (Sometimes on the test results, you see the stanines placed after the dashes in the National Percentile Rank and Local Percentile Rank columns.) As part of your explanation to a parent or guardian,

you can sketch a normal curve and explain that a normal curve is divided into standard deviations (nine of them—to indicate the term *stanine* or *standard nine*) that are measures of the spread of the scores across the curve (see Figure 6.9). (In your sketch, draw the deviations as straight lines—i.e., horizontal lines drawn down, from north to south, across the curve.) The curve represents the population of the children who took the test. Stanine 5 is at the center of this spread of scores and represents the **mean,** the average score in a distribution of scores achieved by test takers. Stanines 4, 3, and 2 represent a band of scores (shown on the normal curve a half standard deviation in width for each) to the left on the curve. Likewise, stanines 6, 7, and 8 represent another band of scores (shown on the normal curve a half standard deviation in width each) to the right of the normal curve. Stanine 1 is at the far left side of the distribution and stanine 9 is at the far right side.

A child with a score that falls a half standard deviation above the mean will have a stanine score of 6. A child with a score that falls one full standard deviation above the mean will have a stanine score of 7. Note that percentile bands are often shown on the test results that the school receives for a student. These bands show ranges of scores on the areas of the standardized tests that reflect the child's performance; and since the bands/ranges of scores are shown, the schools often consider this a satisfactory indicator of performance for that test. Figure 6.10 shows what the percentile bands look like in relation to the normal curve.

Figure 6.9
Standard deviation curve

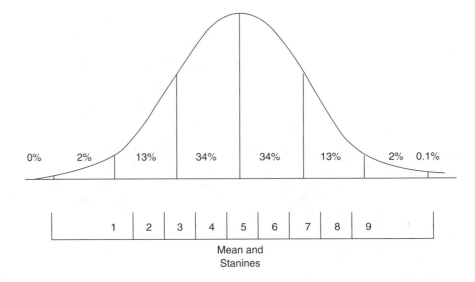

Figure 6.10
Percentile bands in relation to the normal curve

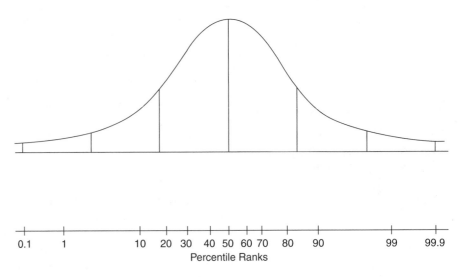

The grade equivalent is another way to report a child's score. The grade equivalent is a numerical value that is determined by comparing a child's score on a standardized test to the scores of students in a particular age group. On the results, the first numeral usually represents the grade and the second, the month of the school year. For instance, if a child has a grade equivalent of 5.5, then this means that she or he scored as well on the test as the average score for those students taking the test who are in the fifth grade and the fifth month based on a 10-month school year.

Talking about grade equivalents with parents and guardians means that you should always talk about grade equivalents *in conjunction with* other measures that reflect the whole child—especially a child's behavior in the classroom, social interaction with others, and his or her performance as shown on teacher-made assessment instruments. To help explain test scores to parents and guardians (and before parent–teacher conferences), you may want to prepare a handout or newsletter, with the assistance and input of your teaching colleagues, so you will have written information to give to parents and to help explain standardized test scores with some clear examples.

Academic Performance Index (API) Scores

Sometimes you need to not only explain the test scores but explain something about the tests themselves. Get acquainted with the tests that your students will encounter during the school year so you can describe how test scores are reported and so you can give an overview of what tests your students will be required to take. For instance, in many states, the Academic Performance Index scores are based on the tests students usually take every spring. The API is used by a state's education officials to measure how individual schools are doing on statewide tests. Sometimes, the core of a school's API score is based on the results of a norm-referenced test, similar to the SAT-9 (Stanford Achievement) or CAT-6 (California

Achievement) tests, which measure the students' performance with their peers across the country. At other times, the core of the API is measured by the results of a state's Standards Tests, which are designed to match up with the state's mandated curriculum and educational standards.

Usually, the API scores (results) can range from 200 to 1,000 and schools that score below 800 must improve each year with their improvement target set by the state. For example, one school may have a six-point improvement target, whereas another school may have a different target. When the index scores improve, teachers and principals usually attribute the improvement to such educational practices as working hard to improve instruction, reading and math intervention programs, structured language arts programs, programs for students testing below grade level, before- and after-school tutoring, and a definite focus on teaching state standards. In some states, the API has caused controversy because state education officials have used the rankings to award money to schools and teachers. Recently, one western state awarded cash bonuses ranging from $5,000 to $25,000 (depending on how much the test scores had improved) to thousands of teachers. Later, these bonuses were suspended when the state experienced budget cuts.

When Test Scores Are Printed Publicly

How do you think that you'll react when your test scores are printed in the local newspaper or put on the Internet? Or when you and other teachers are pressured to improve students' scores? When this happens, it's possible that you and your school faculty or grade-level teaching team will meet and, together, all of you can go over the test scores to identify areas in the curriculum that need greater attention. Your team can organize information about the test scores into a package of assessment information for the students and the parents/guardians. You may want to communicate test results clearly to both the students and their parents/guardians through a handout, newsletter, or a packet of information. When you meet with a student and the parent/guardian during a conference, you can use the assessment information to identify overall areas of strength and areas that need improvement for the school or grade level as well as to serve as a reference for specific information about each individual student's scores.

If a parent/guardian is concerned about test bias, point out that you and your colleagues can use some strategies to eliminate or minimize test bias. For example, first there are other information sources, such as performance assessments, on which parents/guardians can rely. You can assure the parents/guardians that

standardized test results are just one source of information for the child. Second, pre- and post-test examinations can be conducted. You can examine the test content before testing and then analyze the results after testing to help minimize content bias. Third, there are adaptations that could be initiated. Perhaps you can adapt testing procedures to specific student needs (perhaps English language learners need more time) and, before the test, teach students to adapt to testing procedures by giving them opportunities to practice.

At this point in this resource guide, our focus will turn to nonstandardized criterion-referenced tests, ones that you design (or collaboratively design) for your own unique group of students for determination of their level of learning on particular instructional objectives. In no way do we intend to devalue the concern that you will have for more information about standardized norm-referenced achievement testing as a classroom teacher. It simply means that our purpose and space in this guide does not allow for more in-depth attention to that topic; we encourage you to read more about this form of testing by seeing the recommended readings at the end of this chapter.

Purposes for Testing

Tests can be designed for several purposes, and by using a variety of kinds of tests and alternate test items you can keep your testing program interesting, useful, and reliable. As a college student, you are probably experienced with testing for measuring achievement, but you will use tests for other reasons as well. Tests are also used to assess and aid in curriculum development; help determine teaching effectiveness; help students develop positive attitudes, appreciations, and values; help students increase their understanding and retention of facts, principles, skills and concepts; motivate children; provide diagnostic information for planning for personalization of the instruction; provide review and drill to enhance teaching and learning; and serve as informational data for children and their parents or guardians.

PREPARING ASSESSMENT ITEMS

Preparing and writing good assessment items is yet another professional skill, and to become proficient at it takes study, time, practice, and reflection. Because of the importance of an assessment program, you need to assume this professional charge seriously and responsibly. Although poorly prepared items take no time at all to construct, they will cause you more trouble than you can ever imagine.

As a professional, you should take time to study different types of assessment items that can be used and how best to write them, and then practice writing them. Remember, when preparing assessment items, ensure that they match and sufficiently cover the instructional objectives. In addition, you should prepare each item carefully enough to be reasonably confident that each item will be understood by the student in the manner that you anticipate its being understood. With the diversity of children in today's public school classrooms, especially with respect to their proficiency in oral and written English and to students with disabilities, this is an especially important point. Finally, after administering a test you must take time to analyze the results and reflect on the value of each item before using that item again.

TYPES OF ASSESSMENT ITEMS: DESCRIPTIONS, EXAMPLES, AND GUIDELINES FOR PREPARATION AND USE

This section presents descriptions, advantages and disadvantages, and guidelines for preparing and using different types of assessment items. When reading about the advantages and disadvantages of each type, you will notice that some types are appropriate for use in performance assessment, while others are not.

Essay

Description: A question or problem is presented, and the student is to compose a response in the form of sustained prose, using the student's own words, phrases, and ideas, within the limits of the question or problem. The essay item can also be considered a performance test item, perhaps the most familiar example of performance assessment.

Example 1: In the story just read, does the author elaborate the setting in great detail or barely sketch it? Explain your response.

Example 2: A healthy green plant sitting in front of you has been placed in fertile soil and sealed with paraffin in a glass jar. If we place the jar on the windowsill where it will receive strong sunlight and the temperature inside the jar is maintained between 60 and 80 degrees Fahrenheit, how long do you predict the plant will live? Justify your prediction.

Advantages: This type measures conceptual knowledge and higher mental processes, such as the ability to synthesize material and to express ideas in clear and precise written language. It is especially useful in integrated thematic teaching. It provides practice in written expression and can be used in performance assessment, as is the case for Example 2.

Disadvantages: Essay items require a good deal of time to read and to score. They tend to provide an un-

reliable sampling of achievement and are vulnerable to teacher subjectivity and unreliable scoring. Furthermore, they tend to punish the student who writes slowly and laboriously or who has limited proficiency in the written language though the student may have achieved as well as another student who writes faster and is more proficient in the language. Essay items tend to favor students who have fluency with words but whose achievement may not necessarily be better. In addition, unless the students have been given instruction in the meaning of key directive verbs and in how to respond to them, the teacher should not assume that all students understand such verbs (such as *explain* in the first example and *predict* and *justify* in the second).

Guidelines for Using an Essay Item

1. When preparing an essay-only test, many questions, each requiring a relatively short prose response (see the short explanation type later in this discussion), are preferable to a smaller number of questions requiring long prose responses. Briefer answers tend to be more precise, and the use of many items provides a more reliable sampling of student achievement. When preparing a short essay question, be sure to avoid using words verbatim from the student textbook.

2. Allow students adequate time to write a full response.

3. Different qualities of achievement are easier to compare when all students must answer the same questions, as opposed to providing a list of essay items from which students may select a certain number they wish to answer.

4. After preparing essay items, make a tentative scoring guide or key, deciding on the key ideas you expect the students to identify and how many points will be allotted to each.

5. Students should be informed about the relative test value for each item. Point values, if different for each item, can be listed in the margin of the test next to each item.

6. Inform students of the role/importance of spelling, grammar, and sentence structure in your scoring of their essay items.

7. When reading students' essay responses, read all student papers for one item at a time in one sitting. While doing that, make notes to yourself, then repeat and, while reading that item again, score each student's paper for that item. Repeat the process for the next item but alternate the order of the stack of papers so you are not reading them in the same order by student. While scoring essay responses, keep in mind the nature of the objective being measured, which may or may not

include the qualities of handwriting, grammar, spelling, punctuation, and neatness.

8. To nullify the halo effect, an effect that can occur when you know whose paper you are reading, have the students put their name only on the back of the paper, so that while reading each paper, you are unaware of whose paper it is.

9. While having some understanding of a concept, many children are not yet facile with written expression, so you must remember to be patient, tolerant, positive, and prescriptive. Mark papers with positive and constructive comments, showing students how they could have explained or responded more clearly.

10. Prior to administering this type of test item, instruct students in the meaning of selected key directive verbs and help them practice responding to the verbs, such as *compare–contrast, explain–identify*, and *evaluate–summarize*.

Companion Website

To acquire additional information about key verbs for essay item responses and other content related to this chapter, go to our Companion Website at **www.prenhall.com/roberts,** and click on the *Additional Content* module for Chapter 6.

Multiple Choice

Description: This type of test item is similar to the completion item in that statements are presented (the stem), sometimes in incomplete form, but with several options or alternatives, requiring recognition or even higher cognitive processes rather than mere recall.

Example 1: Of four cylinders with the following dimensions, the one that would cause the highest pitched sound would be

(a) 4 inches long and 3 inches in diameter.
(b) 4 inches long and 1 inch in diameter.
(c) 8 inches long and 3 inches in diameter.
(d) 8 inches long and 1 inch in diameter.

Example 2: Which one of the following words is spelled correctly?

(a) trooly
(b) fortey
(c) argament
(d) acquainted

Advantages: Items can be answered and scored quickly. A wide range of content and higher levels of cognition can be tested in a relatively short time. This type is excellent for all testing purposes:motivation, review, and assessment of learning.

Disadvantages: Unfortunately, because multiple-choice items are relatively easy to write, there is a ten-dency to write items measuring only for low levels of cognition. Multiple-choice items are excellent for major testing, but it takes care and time to write quality questions that measure higher levels of thinking and learning.

Guidelines for Using Multiple-Choice Items

1. If the item is in the form of an incomplete statement, it should be meaningful in itself and imply a direct question rather than merely lead into a collection of unrelated true and false statements.

2. Use a level of language that is easy enough for even the poorest readers and those with limited proficiency in English to understand; avoid unnecessary wordiness.

3. If there is much variation in the length of alternatives, arrange the alternatives in order from shortest to longest (i.e., first alternative is the shortest, last alternative is the longest). For single-word alternatives, consistent use of arrangement of alternatives is recommended, such as by length of answer or alphabetically.

4. Arrangement of alternatives should be uniform throughout the test and listed in vertical (column) form rather than in horizontal (paragraph) form.

5. Incorrect responses (distracters) should be plausible and related to the same concept as the correct alternative. Although an occasional humorous distracter may help relieve text anxiety, along with absurd distracters, they should generally be avoided. They offer no measuring value, increase the likelihood of the student guessing the correct response, and increase the time it takes for the student to take the test.

6. It is not necessary to maintain a fixed number of alternatives for every item, but the use of less than three is not recommended. While it is not always possible to come up with four or five plausible responses, the use of four or five reduces chance responses and guessing, thereby increasing reliability for the item. (Three-choice items may be preferable for use with young children and other slower readers.) If you cannot think of enough plausible distracters, include the item on a test the first time as a completion item. As students respond, wrong answers will provide you with a number of plausible distracters that you can use the next time to make the item a multiple-choice type item.

7. Some special needs students may work better when allowed to circle their selected response rather than writing its letters or number in a blank space.

8. Responses such as "all of the above" or "none of the above" should be used only when they will contribute more than another plausible distracter.

Care must be taken that such responses answer or complete the item. "All of the above" is a poorer alternative than "none of the above" because items that use it as a correct response need to have four or five correct answers. Also, if it is the right answer, knowledge of any two of the distracters will cue it.

9. Every item should be grammatically consistent. For example, if the stem is in the form of an incomplete sentence, it should be possible to complete the sentence by attaching any of the alternatives to it.

10. The stem should state a single and specific point.

Companion Website

Now go to our Companion Website (**www.prenhall.com/roberts**) for this chapter and click on the *Additional Content* module to learn more about the use of multiple-choice items and discussion of other assessment types.

Performance Assessment: Expensive and Intensive

Description: Provided with certain conditions or materials, the student solves a problem or accomplishes some other action. For instance, a student is asked to write a retelling of a favorite fable and then create a diorama to go along with the retelling. A performance assessment can also include arrangement (terms or real objects to be arranged in a specified order) and essay types of assessment.

Example 1: A student is given a microscope and asked to carry it properly from one location to another in the room or to hold a jumping rope in place (gross motor skill) or to focus a microscope or to jump rope (fine motor skill).

Example 2: A student or a group of students is given the problem of creating from discarded materials a habitat for an imaginary animal and then instructed to display the habitat, write about it, and orally present their product to the rest of the class.

Advantages: A good program of assessment will use performance testing and other alternate forms of assessment and not rely solely on one form, such as written assessment, or rely on one type of written assessment, such as multiple choice. This type of assessment is a flexible one, because the type of test and items that you use depend on your purpose and objectives. For instance, as a culminating project for a unit on sound, groups of students may be challenged to design and make their own musical instruments. A student's performance assessment can include:

1. Playing the instrument for the group
2. Showing others the part of the instrument that makes the sound
3. Describing the function of the other parts of the instrument
4. Demonstrating how the student can change pitch of the sound
5. Sharing with others how the student made the instrument.

Performance test item types come closer to direct measurement (authentic assessment) of certain expected outcomes than do most other types. As indicated in our Companion Website (**www.prenhall. com/roberts**) discussion of the other assessment types, other types of assessment can actually be prepared as performance-type items, that is, where the student actually does what he or she is being tested for during the performance.

Disadvantages: Performance testing is usually more expensive and time consuming than is verbal testing, which in turn is more time demanding and expensive than is written testing. You need to take the time to attain content validity checks and to account for the individual differences in students, so your performance testing program should include assessment items of different types. This is what writers of articles in professional journals are referring to when they talk about alternative assessment. They are encouraging the use of multiple assessment items (though time consuming), as opposed to the traditional heavy reliance on objective items such as multiple-choice questions. This performance type of assessment can be difficult to administer to a group of students. Adequate supply of materials could be a problem. As with essay-type assessments, scoring of performance items may tend to be subjective. Especially when materials are involved, it could be difficult to give makeup tests to students who were absent.

Guidelines for Using Performance Assessment

Use your creativity to design and use performance tests, since they tend to measure well the important objectives. To reduce subjectivity in scoring, prepare distinct scoring guidelines (rubrics), as discussed earlier.

Now do Application Exercise 6.1 to start the development of your skill in writing assessment items. As you work on Application Exercise 6.1, you may want to correlate it with your work in the *Additional Application Exercises* module from the Companion Website (**www.prenhall.com/roberts**) for Chapter 5.

✎ APPLICATION EXERCISE 6.1 PREPARING ASSESSMENT ITEMS

Instructions: The purpose of this application exercise is to practice your skill in preparing the different types of assessment items discussed in this chapter and in the *Additional Content* module on our Companion Website (**www.prenhall.com/roberts**). ✎ For use in your own teaching, select one specific instructional ob-jective and write assessment items for it. When completed, share this exercise with your colleagues for their feedback.

Objective

_____

Grade and Subject

_____

From the chapter

1. Essay item _____

_____

_____

_____

2. Multiple-choice item _____

_____

_____

_____

3. Performance item _____

_____

_____

_____

From our companion website

4. Arrangement item _____

_____

_____

_____

5. Completion drawing item _____

_____

_____

_____

_____

APPLICATION EXERCISE 6.1 *(continued)*

6. Completion statement item _____

_____

_____

_____

_____

7. Correction item _____

_____

_____

_____

_____

8. Grouping item _____

_____

_____

_____

_____

9. Identification item _____

_____

_____

_____

_____

10. Matching item _____

_____

_____

_____

_____

11. Short-explanation item _____

_____

_____

_____

_____

12. Modified true–false item _____

_____

_____

_____

_____

REPORTING: MAINTAINING RECORDS OF STUDENT ACHIEVEMENT

You must maintain well-organized and complete records of student achievement. You can do this in a written record book or on an electronic record, whichever is furnished by the school. At the very least, the record book should include attendance records and all records of scores on tests, homework, projects, and other assignments. The record book is a legal document that at the end of the school year *may* have to be turned into the school office unless there is a duplicate file of the information in the office computer system.

Daily interactions and events occur in the classroom that may provide informative data about a student's intellectual, emotional, and physical development. Maintaining a dated log of your observations of these interactions and events can provide important information that might otherwise be forgotten. At the end of a unit of study and again at the conclusion of a grading period, you will want to review your records. During the course of the school year, your anecdotal records (and those of other members of your teaching team) will provide important information about the intellectual, psychological, and physical development of each student and ideas for attention to be given to individual students.

Recording Teacher Observations and Judgments

You must think carefully about any written comments that you intend to make about a child. Children can be quite sensitive to what others say about them, and most particularly to comments about them made by their teachers.

Additionally, we have seen anecdotal comments in students' permanent records that said more about the teachers who made the comments than about the recipient students. Comments that have been carelessly, hurriedly, and thoughtlessly made can be detrimental to a child's welfare and progress in school. Teacher comments must be professional; that is, they must be diagnostically useful to the continued intellectual and psychological development of the child. This is true for any comment you make or write, whether on a student's paper, on the child's permanent school record, or on a message sent to the student's home.

For students' continued intellectual and psychological development, your comments should be useful, productive, analytical, diagnostic, and prescriptive. The professional teacher makes diagnoses and prepares descriptions; a professional teacher does *not* label students, with terms such as *lazy, vulgar, slow, stupid, dif-*

ficult, or *dumb*. The professional teacher sees the behavior of a child as being goal directed. The primary professional task of any teacher is not to punish, but to facilitate the learner's understanding (perception) of a goal and help the learner identify acceptable behaviors positively designed to teach that goal.

That which separates the professional teacher from "anyone off the street" is the teacher's ability to go beyond mere description of behavior. Keep that in mind always when you write comments that will be read by the students, by their parents or guardians, and by other teachers.[12] Let us reinforce this concept by now focusing your attention on our Companion Website **(www.prenhall.com/roberts),** especially the additional application exercise titled Evaluating Written Teacher Comments: A Self-Check Exercise.

GRADING AND MARKING STUDENT ACHIEVEMENT

The term *achievement* is used frequently throughout this resource guide. If conditions were ideal (which they are not), and if teachers did their jobs perfectly well (which many of us do not), then all students would receive top marks (the ultimate in mastery or quality learning) and there would be less of a need here to talk about grading and marking. Believing that letter grades do not reflect the nature of the developmental progress of young children, many school districts hold off using letter grades until children are in at least the third grade or even the sixth grade, and instead favor using developmental checklists and narratives.[13] See an example of a progress report for students in Figure 6.11. Mastery learning implies that some end point of learning is attainable (but there probably isn't an end point). In any case, because conditions for teaching are never ideal and we teachers are mere humans, let us continue with this topic of grading and marking that is undoubtedly of interest to you, your students, their parents or guardians; to school counselors, administrators, and members of the school board; and to many others, such as potential employers, providers of scholarships, and college admissions officers.

Companion Website
To broaden your knowledge base about student assessment, go to our Companion Website at **www.prenhall.com/roberts** and click on the *Additional Content* module for Chapter 6.

Figure 6.11
Progress report: subject-specific with student and parent/guardian input

---

PROGRESS REPORT: Arlington Heights School

Student: <u>Anthony von Hauser</u>   Course: <u>Introduction to Algebra grade 6</u>   Date: <u>September 14, 2001</u>

This progress report form incorporates evaluation by student, teacher, and parent. The form will be completed by the student on Wednesday and by the teacher on Thursday and reviewed by the office and returned to the student on Friday. The student will take the form home for parental review, comments, and signature.

Section I: Self-Assessment: The student is asked to evaluate progress in the course in terms of goals and how closely these goals are being achieved. Do you feel you have made progress since the last progress report?

<u>By taking this algebra class I achieved a greater understanding of it. I feel I have made a lot of progress since</u>
<u>I took the class in 6th grade. It is also taught much better which makes it easier.</u>

Section II: Teacher Assessment: The teacher is asked to assess the student's entry, competency, and achievement to date and make recommendations.

<u>Anthony is doing quite well. He has had to make some adjustments from previous work habits (i.e., showing</u>
<u>work), but he has made an excellent transition. Anthony has great skills and strong understanding of concepts.</u>

PRESENT STATUS (Rated A–F)

<u>B+</u> Class work/participation	A = Excellent	
<u>C+</u> Homework	B = Above Average	
<u>A</u> Portfolio	C = Average	
<u>A</u> Quizzes	D = Below Average	
<u>A–</u> Tests	F = Failing	
<u>A–</u> Overall		

WHAT IS NEEDED

<u>✓</u> Emphasis on homework
_____ Improve class participation
_____ More careful preparation for tests
<u>✓</u> Keep up the good work
_____ Contact teacher
_____ Improve portfolio
_____ Other _____
Office Initial <u>CM</u>

Section III: Parent Evaluation and Comments: Parents are asked to respond and sign this progress report.

<u>I thank you for this timely report. I am delighted that Anthony has started off well and is liking the class. He talks at</u>
<u>home a lot about the class and the interesting activities; a tribute to good teaching. I can tell from our</u>
<u>conversations at home that he is feeling much better about his math capability. I thank you.</u>

Eric von Hauser

We have indicated that planning that supports student achievement occurs at three levels: state, district, and local school. You will be responsible for planning school goals for the year, the units of study, and then the lessons/activities. There are seven steps in this process and you'll proceed through these seven steps as you develop your first instructional plan in the following chapter. However, we want you to consider these seven steps now to prepare for this further competency in the next chapter, so we encourage you to turn to our Companion Website **(www.prenhall.com/roberts)** to read Planning for Future Instruction: A Three-Level and Multi-Step

Process in the *Additional Content* module. Also see the *Technology Tips for the Classroom* feature for additional ideas, resources, and suggested technical support for your objectives and lesson planning.

Companion Website
To find links to student achievement and assessment, go to our Companion Website at **www.prenhall.com/roberts** and click on the *Web Destinations* module for Chapter 6.

Technology Tips for the Classroom

- If your school has a website, ask a tech-friendly colleague to help improve the site so that students, parents and teachers can make the most of it related to research. Put on the site some links to encyclopedias, subscription databases, a brief video that shows how to do research, or perhaps a newsletter to parents asking them to help in combating plagiarism. Interactive pages can let students enter information about their science/research projects into teacher-approved website forms.

- Consider using a classroom beaming station if you are working with students who use Palm Pilots in your classroom. The beaming device (by TriBeam Technologies) hangs on the classroom wall and lets you beam quizzes, assignments, e-books, software programs, and other material to your students' Palm Pilots. The students can send messages back to you or to each other, but you stay in control of the process. (www.tribeam.com)

- If there is a growing demand for educational materials in Spanish in your district, ask about *Enciclopedia Universal en Espanol*, an online encyclopedia with an accompanying dictionary and atlas (created by Encyclopedia Britannica). (www.eb.com)

- You can take advantage of two free databases so your students can look up additional information about American history. Let the students know about the databases from the American Indians of the Pacific Northwest Digital Collection (http://content.lib.washington.edu/aipnw) and The Black Oral History Collection. (www.wsulibs.wsu.edu/holland/masc/xblackoral/history.html)

- If you have a color printer and *Adobe Acrobat Reader* software, then download files in the PDF format from the Gale Group website. This site has some free images on bookmarks, reading certificates, flyers/posters, and even thank-you cards. See www.galegroup.com/free_resources/marketing/find_yourself.

About Praxis and Other Teacher Tests

About Praxis Teacher Tests. How will your level of knowledge be indicated on these tests? Your level of knowledge will be reflected in your passing score, which is based on recommendations of panels of teachers and teacher educators in each area in each state. Further, your state credentialing/licensing agency determines the passing scores (and the scores have been recommended by the panels of educators). If you are at this point in your professional preparation and getting ready to take this test, you probably are familiar with studying for tests and taking tests since you likely have completed a bachelor's degree program in elementary school education or have prepared through an alternative educational program.

To continue to support your interest in preparing for this test, as well as some of the other teacher tests, the application exercise in this chapter offers opportunities for you to reflect generally on planning and selecting of curriculum content. In this chapter, precredentialed teachers are asked to participate cooperatively and collaboratively and to do the following:

- Practice your skill in preparing the different types of assessment items discussed in this chapter (Application Exercise 4.1).

- Turn to our Companion Website (**www.prenhall.com/roberts**) and click on the *Additional Application Exercise* module to complete additional application exercises, namely, Evaluating Written Teacher Comments: A Self-Check Exercise and Teacher–Parent Conferences: A Role-Playing Exercise.

You can find a constructed response-type question similar to those found on the Praxis II Principles of Learning and Teaching tests, in the Praxis Warm-Up section that follows the Chapter Summary. This warm-up takes another look at the classroom vignette found in the Looking at Teachers section at the beginning of this chapter.

 Other Teacher Tests. For those of you who will be teaching in states that do not administer the Praxis tests, go to our Companion Website at **www.prenhall.com/roberts** and click on the *Other Teacher Tests* module for Chapter 6 to access information about teacher tests other than the Praxis.

SUMMARY

Whereas the first four chapters of this resource guide addressed the *why* component of teaching and the fifth chapter addressed the *what* component, this chapter has focused your attention on the aspects of assessment and reporting student achievement. Assessment is an integral and ongoing factor in the *what* component as part of the teaching–learning process; consequently, this chapter and the related content on our Companion Website **(www.prenhall.com/roberts)** for this chapter have emphasized the importance of including the following in your teaching performance:

- Consider your assessment and grading procedures carefully, plan them, and explain your policies to the students and their parents and guardians.
- Involve students in the assessment process; keep students informed of their progress. Return papers promptly, review answers to all questions, and respond to inquiries about marks given.
- Maintain accurate and clear records of assessment results so that you will have an adequate supply of data on which to base your judgmental decisions about achievement.
- Make sure to explain any ambiguities that result from the terminology used, and base your assessments on the material that has been taught.
- Strive for objective and impartial assessment as you put your assessment plan into operation.
- Try to minimize arguments about grades, cheating, and teacher subjectivity by involving students in the planning, reinforcing individual student development, and providing an accepting, stimulating learning environment.
- Use a variety of instruments to collect a body of evidence to most reliably assess the learning of students that focus on their individual development.

Because teaching and learning work hand in hand and because they are reciprocal processes where one depends on and affects the other, the focus of this chapter has considered the assessment of the learning of the students as a basis for the *what* component of planning for instruction.

What's to Come. The next chapter of this guide will consider how to prepare for activities, lessons, and units.

EXTENDING MY PROFESSIONAL COMPETENCY

Praxis Warm-Up: A Constructed Response-Type Question

In this chapter's teacher vignette, you'll recall that a middle school teacher wanted to further develop each student's understanding of the multiple connections among world history, social change, and American laws. The students began with a study of Babylon and its laws and then extended the study to other laws in other societies. The students then took on the personas of famous world leaders across history and societies. In their roles related to world history and world societies, the students campaigned for or against the statement "All men/women are created equal." As part of their campaigns as famous world leaders, they prepared their remarks for a videotaped press conference, a campaign commercial, and a classroom discussion/ debate. For an authentic assessment, the final product was a portfolio of each student's understanding of these connections. The portfolios included a wide variety of materials: essays, videos, short multiple-choice tests, and final reflections on the project.

As the teacher, draft two questions for the students to respond to in short-answer essays as part of their assessment to place in their portfolios. Note that you want the questions to give the students an opportunity to demonstrate their higher order thinking and also give them the opportunity to write about what they have learned. The main focus of the questions should be *equality* or the statement "All men/women are created equal." You'll recall that the teacher considered this a conceptual statement and not only used it as a debate statement but a statement of coherence in the classroom. It was also the statement that brought together some connections among world history, social change, and American laws. After you write your questions, tell what kind of higher order thinking each of your questions would require the students to use as they develop their answers and tell how each question would serve to extend the students' knowledge about the topic of equality that they are studying.

Hints for responding to Praxis Warm-Ups are found in the Appendix.

> **Praxis** To do another Praxis Warm-Up with a constructed response-type question, go to our Companion Website at **www.prenhall.com/roberts** and click on the *Praxis Warm-Up* module for Chapter 6. Constructed response-type questions are designed to help you prepare for the Praxis II Principles of Learning and Teaching tests.

For Your Discussion

1. **Grading.** If you told a colleague about a problem in grading that you had personally experienced as a student in school, what would you say was your perceived cause of the problem? **To do:** Explain your thoughts about the following: How

might the problem have been avoided? What was the resolution and how was that resolution arrived at? Was the resolution satisfactory to all concerned? Why or why not?

2. **Alternative Techniques.** If a principal was interviewing you for a teaching job, what would be your response if you were asked, "What three alternative techniques can you identify—other than a paper-and-pencil test—for assessing and reporting student achievement?" **To do:** Think of some alternative techniques for assessing student learning after engaging in activities, during lessons, or at the completion of an instructional unit.

3. **Assessment.** If a colleague asked you to identify one specific example of assessment that seems to be an experimental one, which example would you identify? **To do:** Present your explanation and share what you find with your classmates. Analyze the pros and cons of various systems of assessing and reporting.

4. **Student-Led Parent–Teacher–Student Conferences.** If a principal interviewed you for a teaching job, what would be your response if you were asked, "Do you support student-led parent–teacher–student conferences? Why or why not?" **To do:** Research the topic and report to your class about the practice. Discuss this and your thoughts about it with your classmates.

5. **Instructional Objectives.** If a colleague asked you to describe the roles of objectivity and subjectivity in the assessment of student learning, what would be your reply? **To do:** Review these features and report to your group what you think about the limitations of these two features of assessment. From your point of view, explain the roles of objectivity and subjectivity.

Online Portfolio Activities

Supporting Principle 8 of INTASC and Standards 3, 6, and 8 of NBPTS: At the Companion Website **(www.prenhall.com/roberts),** click on the *Online Portfolio Activities* module to continue your online portfolio supporting assessing student achievement.

Companion Website

Also on the Companion Website at **www.prenhall. com/roberts,** you can measure your understanding of chapter content in the *Objectives* and *Self-Check* modules and apply concepts in the *For Your Discussion* module.

FOR FURTHER READING

Allen, D. (Ed.). (1998). *Assessing Student Learning: From Grading to Understanding.* New York: Teachers College Press.

Allington, R. L., and Guice, S. (1997/1998). Learning to Read. What Research Says Parents Can Do to Help Their Children. *Our Children, 23*(4), 34–35.

Bishop, J. E., and Fransen, S. (1998). Building Community: An Alternative Assessment. *Phi Delta Kappan, 80*(1), 39–40, 57–58.

Black, P., and Cylan, W. (1998). Inside the Black Box: Raising Standards through Classroom Assessment. *Phi Delta Kappan, 80*(2), 139–144, 146–148.

Bracey, G. W. (2000). *A Short Guide to Standardized Testing (Fastback 459).* Bloomington, IN: Phi Delta Kappa Educational Foundation.

Chase, C. I. (1999). *Contemporary Assessment for Educators.* New York: Addison-Wesley-Longman.

Colby, S. A. (1999). Grading in a Standards-Based System. *Educational Leadership, 56*(6), 17–21.

Crockett, T. (1998). *The Portfolio Journey: A Creative Guide to Keeping Student-Managed Portfolios in the Classroom.* Englewood, CO: Teacher Ideas Press.

Danna, S. (2003, February–March). Pursuing National Board Certification. *Educational Horizons,* p. 5.

Doran, R., Chan, F., and Tamir, P. (1998). *Science Educator's Guide to Assessment.* Arlington, VA: National Science Teachers Association.

Ensign, J. (1998). Parents, Portfolios, and Personal Mathematics. *Teaching Children Mathematics, 4*(6), 346–351.

Fiderer, A. (1998). *35 Rubrics and Checklists to Assess Reading and Writing: Time-Saving Reproducible Forms for Meaningful Literacy Assessment (Grades K–2).* New York: Scholastic.

Glazer, S. M. (1998). *Assessment IS Instruction: Reading, Writing, Spelling and Phonics for ALL Learners.* Norwood, MA: Christopher-Gordon.

Kober, N. (2002, June). Teaching to the Test: The Good, the Bad, and Who's Responsible. *Testtalk, 1,* 1–12.

Neumann, F. (1997). Authentic Assessment in Social Studies. Standards and Examples. In G. D. Phye (Ed.), *Handbook of Classroom Assessment: Learning, Achievement, and Adjustment.* San Diego, CA: Academic Press.

Tomlinson, C. A. (1999). *The Differentiated Classroom* (Chap. 5). Alexandria, VA: Association for Supervision and Curriculum Development.

Wiggins, G. (1996–1997). Practicing What We Preach in Designing Authentic Assessment. *Educational Leadership, 54*(4), 18–25.

Wiggins, G., and McTighe, J. (1998). *Understanding by Design.* Alexandria, VA: Association for Supervision and Curriculum Development.

NOTES

1. H. Burley and M. Price, What Works with Authentic Assessment, *Educational Horizons, 81*(4), 2003 193–196.

2. See H. Libit, Report Card Redux, *School Administrator, 56*(10), 6–10 (November 1999).

3. See D. M. Ogle, K-W-L: A Teaching Model That Develops Active Reading of Expository Text, *Reading*

Teacher, 39(6), 564–570 (February 1986); and P. R. Schmidt, KWLQ: Inquiry and Literacy Learning in Science, *Reading Teacher, 52*(7), 789–792 (April 1999).

4. G. E. Thompkins and K. Hoskisson, *Language Arts: Content and Teaching Strategies* (Upper Saddle River, NJ: Prentice Hall, 1991), p. 63.

5. S. J. Rakow, Assessment: A Driving Force, *Science Scope, 15*(6), 3 (March 1992).

6. *Learner Profile* is available from Sunburst Technology, 400 Columbus Ave. Suite 160 E, Valhalla, NY 10595-1349, (914) 747-3310.

7. See the story of the use of portfolios and teacher–student collaboration in a second-grade classroom in A. M. Courtney and T. L. Abodeeb, Diagnostic-Reflective Portfolios, *The Reading Teacher, 52*(7), 708–714 (April 1999).

8. Software packages for the development of student electronic portfolios are available, such as *Classroom Manager* from CTB Macmillan/McGraw-Hill (Monterey, CA), *Electronic Portfolio* from Learning Quest (Corvallis, OR), and *Grady Profile* from Aurbach and Associates (St. Louis, MO).

9. K. S. Shapley and M. J. Bush, Developing a Valid and Reliable Portfolio Assessment in the Primary Grades: Building on Practical Experience, *Applied Measurement in Education, 12*(2), 11–32 (1999).

10. R. J. Stiggins, Student-Involved Classroom Assessment, 3rd ed. (Upper Saddle River, NJ: Prentice Hall, 2001), pp. 443–444.

11. For a discussion of the biological importance and educational benefits of positive feedback, student portfolios, and group learning, see R. Sylwester, The Neurobiology of Self-Esteem and Aggression, *Educational Leadership, 54*(5), 75–79 (February 1997).

12. A. Brualdi, *Teacher Comments on Report Cards* (Washington, DC: ERIC Clearinghouse on Assessment and Evaluation, 1998) ED 42330998.

13. K. Lake and K. Kafka, Reporting Methods in Grades K–8, Chapter 9 (p. 91) in T. R. Guskey (ed.), *Communicating Student Learning* (ASCD Yearbook) (Alexandria, VA: Association for Supervision and Curriculum Development, 1996).

14. See T. R. Guskey (Ed.), *Communicating Student Learning* (ASCD Yearbook) (Alexandria, VA: Association for Supervision and Curriculum Development, 1996), pp. 18–19:

15. For other methods being used to report student achievement, see K. Lake and K. Kafka, note 13.

16. H. G. Andrade, Using Rubrics to Promote Thinking and Learning, *Educational Leadership, 57*(5), 13–18 (February 2000).

17. For suggestions from a school administrator for "delivering powerful presentations to parents" at Back-to-School night, see W. B. Ribas, Tips for Teaching Parents, *Educational Leadership, 56*(1), 83–85 (September 1998).

18. B. J. Ricci, How About Parent–Teacher–Student Conferences? *Principal, 79*(5), 53–54 (May 2000).

19. See J. Taylor, Child-Led Parent School Conferences—In Second Grade?!? *Young Children, 54*(1), 78–82 (January 1999); and J. V. Cleland, We Can Charts: Building Blocks for Student-Led Conferences, *Reading Teacher, 52*(6), 588–595 (March 1999).

20. L. Countryman and M. Schroeder, When Students Lead Parent–Teacher Conferences, *Educational Leadership 53*(7), 64–68 (April 1996).

How Do I Prepare Activities, Lessons, and Units?

7

Visual Chapter Organizer and Overview

Understanding Theoretical Considerations for the Selection of Instructional Strategies

- Decision Making and Strategy Selection
- Principles of Classroom Instruction and Learning: A Synopsis
- Explicit and Implicit Instruction: A Clarification of Terms
- Explicit Versus Implicit Instructional Modes: Strengths and Limitations of Each

Selecting Learning Activities That Are Developmentally Appropriate

- The Learning Experiences Ladder
- Direct, Simulated, and Vicarious Experiences Help Connect Student Learning
- Developing the Learning Activities: The Heart and Spirit of Lessons

Preparing Lesson Plans: Rationale and Assumptions

- Rationale for Preparing Written Lesson Plans
- Assumptions About Lesson Planning

Constructing a Lesson Plan: Format, Components, and Samples

- Basic Elements of a Lesson Plan
- Descriptive Data
- Goals and Objectives
- Rationale
- Procedure
- Assessment, Reflection, and Revision

Preparing Instructional Units

- Planning and Developing Any Unit of Instruction
- Unit Format, Inclusive Elements, and Time Duration

Planning and Developing an Interdisciplinary Thematic Unit

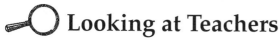
Looking at Teachers

Casey is teaching a sixth-grade humanities block, a 2-hour block course that integrates student learning in social studies, reading, and language arts. On this particular day, while Casey and her students were discussing the topic of Manifest Destiny, one of the students raised his hand and, when acknowledged by Casey, asked the question, "Why aren't we (referring to the United States) still adding states (meaning adding territory to the United States)?" Casey immediately replied with "There aren't any more states to add." By responding too quickly, Casey missed one of those "teachable moments," a time when the teacher has the attention of the students right where she or he wants them, that is, where the students are thinking and asking questions. What could Casey have done? When was Hawaii added as a state? Why hasn't the District of Columbia become a state? Guam? Puerto Rico? Aren't those possibilities? Why *aren't* more states or territories being added? What are the political and social ramifications today of adding states and how do they differ from those of the 1800s?

In this chapter, you will learn how theoretical considerations filter your choices of instructional strategies for activities, lessons, and units. You have learned in past chapters about children in the elementary school, their needs, and the importance of providing an accepting and supportive learning environment, as well as about teacher behaviors that are necessary to facilitate the most meaningful student learning. You also realize that learning modalities and instructional modes affect learning.

In this chapter, we point out that the theoretical considerations you have studied affect the continued building you will do to increase your knowledge base about why planning is important. We give you an opportunity to determine how you can sequence activities into lessons, how you can sequence lessons into units, and how all three—activities, lessons, and units—can be useful pedagogical tools. You'll realize that developing activities, lessons, and units of instruction that integrate student learning and provide a sense of meaning for the students requires coordination throughout the curriculum. Hence, for students, learning is a process of discovering how information, knowledge, and ideas are interrelated so they can make sense out of self, school, and of life. Preparing chunks of information into activities and activities into lessons and lessons into units is one way to help students process and understand knowledge. In this chapter, we help you consider activities and lessons and then develop your first unit of instruction to assist you in becoming a competent planner of instruction.

CHAPTER OBJECTIVES

Specifically, on completion of this seventh chapter, you should be able to:

1. For a specified grade level, give examples of learning experiences/activities from each of these categories: verbal, visual, vicarious, simulated, and direct/explicit.

2. Use a lesson format that is approved by your instructor and prepare a lesson plan for a grade/course of your choice; be able to evaluate your own lesson plan and the plan of one of your peers.

3. Write a specific teaching plan with goals, objectives, resources, and learning activities.

4. Prepare a regular instructional unit or an interdisciplinary thematic unit with sequential lesson plans and a closure, one that you can use in your teaching. If you prepare an interdisciplinary unit, you will demonstrate your knowledge about including activities and lessons that focus on interdisciplinary content.

UNDERSTANDING THEORETICAL CONSIDERATIONS FOR THE SELECTION OF INSTRUCTIONAL STRATEGIES

As you prepare to detail your instructional plan, you will be narrowing in on the selecting and planning of instructional activities. In Chapter 2, you learned about how children differ in learning styles and learning capacities and about the importance of varying the instructional strategies and of using multilevel instruction. In Chapter 3, you learned about specific teacher behaviors that must be in place for students to learn: structuring the learning environment; accepting and sharing instructional accountability; demonstrating with-itness and overlapping; providing a variety of motivating and challenging activities; modeling appropriate behaviors; facilitating students' acquisition of data; creating a psychologically safe environment; clarifying whenever necessary; using periods of silence and teacher talk; and questioning thoughtfully. In the paragraphs that follow, you will learn not only about how to implement some of those fundamental behaviors, but also about the large repertoire of other strategies, aids, media, and resources available to you (see Figure 7.1). You will learn how to select and implement from this repertoire.

Figure 7.1
Selected instructional strategies

Assignment	Group work	Panel discussion
Autotutorial	Guest speaker	Problem solving
Brainstorming	Homework	Project
Coaching	Individualized instruction	Questioning
Collaborative learning	Inquiry learning	Review/practice
Cooperative learning	Interactive media	Role-play
Debate	Journal writing	Self-instructional module
Demonstration	Laboratory investigation	Script writing
Diorama	Laser videodisc	Simulation
Discovery learning	Learning center	Study guide
Drama	Lecture	Symposium
Drill	Library/resource center	Telecommunication
Expository learning	Metacognition	Term paper
Field trip/virtual	Mock-up model	Textbook
Games	Multimedia	Think–pair–share

Decision Making and Strategy Selection

You must make a myriad of decisions to select and implement a particular teaching strategy effectively. The selection of a strategy depends in part on your decision whether to deliver information directly (explicit, expository, or didactic teaching) or to provide students with access to information (implicit or facilitative teaching). Explicit teaching can be seen as teacher centered, whereas implicit teaching can be seen as more student centered. To assist in your selection of strategies, it is important that you understand the basic principles of learning summarized in the following paragraphs.

Explicit and Implicit Instruction: A Clarification of Terms

You are probably well aware that professional education is rampant with its own special jargon, which can be confusing to the neophyte. Indeed, rest assured, it can even be overwhelming to those of us who are well seasoned. The use of the terms **explicit instruction** (or its synonyms, *explicit teaching*, **direct instruction,** *teacher-centered instruction*), and one of its antonyms, **implicit experiences,** provides examples of how confusing the jargon can be. The term *explicit instruction* can also have a variety of definitions, depending on who is doing the defining. (*Note:* In addition to the generic term *explicit* or *direct instruction,* the term *Direct Instruction Model* has evolved from an original curriculum program for beginning reading, language arts, and mathematics developed in 1968 and published by Science Research

Associates (SRA) under the name DISTAR, Direct Instruction System for Teaching and Remediation. This program for grades K–6 is comprised of highly scripted lessons that are designed around a very specific knowledge base and a well-defined set of skills.)[1] For now, you should keep this distinction in mind— do not confuse the term *explicit* or *direct instruction* with the term *explicit* or *direct experiences.* The two terms indicate two separate, though not incompatible, instructional modes. The dichotomy of pedagogical opposites shown in Figure 7.2 provides a useful visual distinction of the opposites. Although terms in one column are similar if not synonymous, they are near or exact opposites (antonyms) of those across from them in the other column.

Degrees of Directness

Rather than having your teaching characterized by thinking and behaving in terms of opposites as may be suggested by Figure 7.2, it is more likely that "degrees of directness (being explicit)" or "degrees of indirectness (being implicit)" will characterize your teaching. For example, for a unit of instruction, the teacher may give directions for a culminating project in an explicit/direct minilesson, followed then by student-designed inquiry learning that leads to the final project.

Rather than focus your attention on the selection of a particular mode of teaching, we emphasize the importance of an eclectic model—selecting the best from various models or approaches. As indicated by the example of the preceding paragraph, there will be times when you want to use an explicit, teacher-centered ap-

Delivery mode of instruction	versus	Access mode
Didactic instruction	versus	Facilitative teaching
Explicit instruction	versus	Implicit instruction
Expository teaching	versus	Discovery learning
Teacher-centered instruction	versus	Student-centered instruction
Direct/explicit teaching	versus	Direct/explicit experiences

Figure 7.2
Pedagogical opposites

proach, perhaps by a minilecture or a demonstration, or both. And then there will be many more times when you will want to use an implicit, student-centered or social-interactive approach, such as the use of cooperative learning and investigative projects. Perhaps there will be even more times when you will be doing both at the same time, for example, working with a teacher-centered approach with one small group of students, perhaps giving them explicit instruction, while another group or several groups of children, in various areas of the classroom, are working on their project studies (a student-centered approach) or at learning stations. The information that follows and specific descriptions that follow in Part III will help you make decisions about when each approach is most appropriate and will provide guidelines for their use.

Principles of Classroom Instruction and Learning: A Synopsis

A child does not learn to write by learning to recognize grammatical constructions of sentences. Neither does a person learn to play soccer solely by listening to a lecture on soccer. Learning is superficial unless the learning activities and instructional methods are developmentally and intellectually appropriate—that is, unless they are (a) developmentally appropriate for the learners and (b) intellectually appropriate for the learners' understanding, skills, and attitudes desired. Memorizing, for instance, is not the same as understanding. Yet far too often, memorization seems to be all that is expected of students in many classrooms. The result is low-level learning, a mere verbalism or mouthing of poorly understood words and sentences. That is not intellectually appropriate and it is not teaching; it is merely the orchestration of short-term memory exercises. An old-fashioned mental model of learning that assumes that a human brain is capable of doing only one thing at a time is invidiously erroneous. When selecting the mode of instruction, bear in mind the basic principles of classroom instruction and learning shown in Figure 7.3.

Procedural and Conceptual Knowledge
Whereas procedural knowledge entails the recording in memory of the meanings of symbols and rules and pro-

cedures needed to accomplish tasks, conceptual knowledge refers to the understanding of relationships. Unless it is connected in meaningful ways for the formation of conceptual knowledge, the accumulation of memorized procedural knowledge is fragmented and will be maintained in the brain for only a brief time.

To help elementary students establish conceptual knowledge, the learning for them must be meaningful. To help make learning meaningful for your students, you should use explicit (direct) and real experiences as often as practical and possible. Vicarious experiences are sometimes necessary to provide students with otherwise unattainable knowledge; however, explicit experiences that engage all of the students' senses and all of their learning modalities are more powerful. Students learn to write by writing and by receiving coaching and feedback about their progress in writing. They learn to play soccer by experiencing playing soccer and by receiving coaching and feedback about their developing skills and knowledge in playing the game. They learn these things best when they are actively (hands-on) and mentally (minds-on) engaged in doing them. This is real learning, learning that is meaningful; it is **authentic learning.**

Explicit Versus Implicit Instructional Modes: Strengths and Limitations of Each

Selecting an instructional strategy entails two distinct choices (modes): Should you deliver information to students directly or should you provide students with access to information? (Refer to the comparison of pedagogical opposites in Figure 7.2.)

The **delivery mode** (known as the **didactic, expository,** or **traditional instructional** style) is to deliver information. Knowledge is passed on from those who know (the teachers, with the aid of textbooks or other media) to those who do not (the students). Within the delivery mode, traditional and time-honored strategies are textbook reading, the lecture, questioning, and teacher-centered or teacher-planned discussions.

With the **access mode,** instead of direct delivery of information and direct control over what is learned, the teacher provides students with access to

Figure 7.3
Basic principles of classroom
instruction

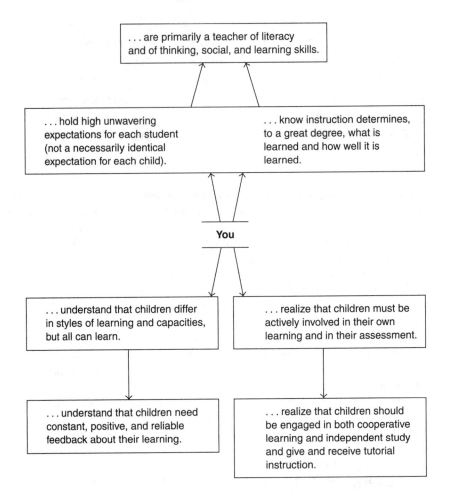

information by working *with* the students. In collaboration with the students, experiences are designed that facilitate their building of their existing schemata and their obtaining new knowledge and skills. Within the access mode, important instructional strategies include cooperative learning, inquiry learning, and student-centered project-based learning, each of which most certainly will use teacher talk and questioning, though the questions more often will come from the students than from you or the textbook or some other source extrinsic to the student. Discussions and lectures on particular topics also may be involved. But when used in the access mode, discussions and lectures occur during or after (rather than before) explicit, hands-on learning by the students. In other words, rather than preceding student inquiry learning, discussions and lectures *result from* student inquiry learning, and then may be followed by further student investigation.

You are probably more experienced with the delivery mode. To be most effective as a classroom teacher, however, you must become knowledgeable and skillful in using access strategies. For young learners, strategies within the access mode clearly facilitate their positive learning and acquisition of conceptual knowledge and help build their self-esteem.

You should appropriately select and effectively use strategies from both modes, but with a strong leaning toward access strategies. Thus, from your study of this chapter and the chapters that follow, you will become knowledgeable about specific techniques so you can make intelligent decisions for choosing the best strategy for particular goals and objectives for subjects you teach and the interests, needs, and maturity level of your own unique group of students.

Figures 7.4 and 7.5 provide an overview of the specific strengths and weaknesses of each mode. By comparing those figures, you can see that the strengths and weaknesses of one mode are nearly mirror opposites of the other. As noted earlier, although as a teacher you should be skillful in the use of strategies from both modes, for the most developmentally appropriate teaching for most groups of elementary school-children, you should concentrate more on using strategies from the access mode. Strategies within that mode are more student centered, hands-on, and concrete.

Figure 7.4
Delivery mode: Its strengths and weaknesses

Delivery Mode

Strengths
- Much content can be covered within a short span of time, usually by formal teacher talk, which then may be followed by an experiential activity.
- The teacher is in control of what content is covered.
- The teacher is in control of time allotted to specific content coverage.
- Strategies within the delivery mode are consistent with competency-based instruction.
- Student achievement of specific content is predictable and manageable.

Potential Weaknesses
- The sources of student motivation are mostly extrinsic.
- Students have little control over the pacing of their learning.
- Students make few important decisions about their learning.
- There may be little opportunity for divergent or creative thinking.
- Student self-esteem may be inadequately served.

Figure 7.5
Access mode: Its strengths and weaknesses

Access Mode

Strengths
- Students learn content in more depth.
- The sources of student motivation are more likely intrinsic.
- Students make important decisions about their own learning.
- Students have more control over the pacing of their learning.
- Students develop a sense of personal self-worth.

Potential Weaknesses
- Content coverage may be more limited.
- Strategies are time consuming.
- The teacher has less control over content and time.
- The specific results of student learning are less predictable.
- The teacher may have less control over class procedures.

Students interact with one another and are actually doing, or are closer to doing what they are learning—that is, the learning is likely more authentic. Learning that occurs from the use of that mode is longer lasting (fixes into long-term memory). And, as the children interact with one another and with their learning, they develop a sense of "can do," which enhances their self-esteem.

SELECTING LEARNING ACTIVITIES THAT ARE DEVELOPMENTALLY APPROPRIATE

Returning to our soccer example, can you imagine a soccer coach teaching students the skills and knowledge needed to play soccer, but without ever letting them play the game? Can you imagine a geography teacher teaching students how to read a map without ever letting them put their eyes and hands on a real map? Can you imagine teaching children the letters of the alphabet without ever letting them put the letters together to form words? Can you imagine teaching a child to play a piano without ever allowing the child to touch a real keyboard? Unfortunately, still today, too many teachers do almost those exact things—they try to teach students to do something without letting the students practice doing it.

In planning and selecting developmentally appropriate learning activities, an important rule to remember is to select activities that are as close to the real thing as possible and sensible. That is learning through direct experiencing. When students are involved in direct experiences, they are using more of their sensory input channels, their learning modalities (see Chapter 2). And when all the senses are engaged, learning is more integrated and is most effective, meaningful, and longest lasting. This "learning by doing" is authentic learning—or hands-on and minds-on learning.

The Learning Experiences Ladder

The learning experiences ladder, a visual depiction of a range of learning experiences from which a teacher can select, is shown in Figure 7.6. Hands-on minds-on learning is at the bottom of the ladder. At the top are abstract experiences, where the learner is exposed only to symbolization (i.e., letters and numbers) and uses only one or two senses (auditory or visual). The teacher lectures while the students sit and watch and hear. Visual and verbal symbolic experiences, while impossible to avoid when teaching, are less effective in ensuring that planned and meaningful learning occurs. This is especially so with young children, learners who have special needs, learners with ethnic and cultural differences, and students who are English learners. Thus, when planning learning experiences and selecting instructional materials, you are advised to select activities that engage the learners in the most explicit/direct experiences possible and that are

Figure 7.6

The learning experiences ladder

(*Sources:* Earlier versions of this concept were from Charles F. Hoban, Sr., et al., *Visualizing the Curriculum* (New York: Dryden, 1937), p. 39; Jerome S. Bruner, *Toward a Theory of Instruction* (Cambridge, MA: Harvard University Press, 1966), p. 49; Edgar Dale, *Audio-Visual Methods in Teaching* (New York: Holt, Rinehart & Winston, 1969), p. 108; and Eugene C. Kim and Richard D. Kellough, *A Resource Guide for Secondary School Teaching*, 2nd ed. (Upper Saddle River, NJ: Merrill/Prentice Hall, 1978), p. 136.)

Verbal Experiences   Teacher talk, written words; engaging only one sense; using the most abstract symbolization; students physically inactive. *Examples*: (a) Listening to the teacher talk about tide pools. (b) Listening to a student report about the Grand Canyon. (c) Listening to a guest speaker talk about how the state legislature functions.

Visual Experiences   Still pictures, diagrams, charts; engaging only one sense; typically symbolic; students physically inactive. *Examples*: (a) Viewing slide photographs of tide pools. (b) Viewing drawings and photographs of the Grand Canyon. (c) Listening to a guest speaker talk about the state legislature and show slides of it in action.

Vicarious Experiences   Laser videodisc programs, computer programs, video programs; engaging more than one sense; learner indirectly "doing"; may be some limited physical activity. *Examples*: (a) Interacting with a computer program about wave action and life in tide pools. (b) Viewing and listening to a video program about the Grand Canyon. (c) Taking a field trip to observe the state legislature in action.

Simulated Experiences   Role playing, experimenting, simulations, mock-ups, working models; all or nearly all senses engaged; activity often integrating disciplines; closest to the real thing. *Examples*: (a) Building a classroom working model of a tide pool. (b) Building a classroom working model of the Grand Canyon. (c) Designing a classroom role-play simulation patterned after the operating procedures of the state legislature.

Direct Experiences   Learner actually doing what is being learned; true inquiry; all senses engaged; usually integrates disciplines; the real thing. *Examples*: (a) Visiting and experiencing a tide pool. (b) Visiting and experiencing the Grand Canyon. (c) Designing an elected representative body to oversee the operation of the school-within-the-school program, and patterned after the state legislative assembly.

ABSTRACT ↑ ↓ CONCRETE

developmentally and intellectually appropriate for your specific group of students.

As can be inferred from the learning experiences ladder, when teaching about tide pools (the first example for each step), the most effective mode is to take the students to a tide pool (explicit/direct experience), where students can see, hear, touch, smell, and perhaps even taste (if not polluted with toxins) the water from the tip of a finger dipped in the tide pool. The least effective mode is for the teacher to merely talk about the tide pool (verbal experience, the most abstract and symbolic experience) engaging only one sense—auditory.

Of course, for various reasons—such as time, matters of safety, lack of resources, and geographic location of your school—you may not be able to take your students to a tide pool. You cannot always use the most explicit/direct experience, so sometimes you must select an experience higher on the ladder. Self-discovery teaching is not always appropriate. Sometimes, it is

more appropriate to build on what others have discovered and learned. While learners do not need to "reinvent the wheel," the most effective and longest lasting learning is that which engages most or all of their senses. On the learning experiences ladder, those are the experiences that fall within the bottom three categories: direct/explicit, simulated, and vicarious. This is as true of adult learners as it is with kindergarten children or students of any age group in between.

Direct, Simulated, and Vicarious Experiences Help Connect Student Learning

Another value of explicit, simulated, and vicarious experiences is that they tend to be interdisciplinary; that is, they blur or bridge subject-content boundaries. That makes those experiences especially useful for teachers who want to help students connect the learning of one discipline with that of others and to bridge what is being learned with their own life experiences. Explicit, simulated, and vicarious experiences are more like real life, which means that the learning resulting from those experiences is authentic.

Developing the Learning Activities: The Heart and Spirit of Lessons

Activities that engage the students in meaningful learning constitute the heart and spirit of the lessons and, thus, the instructional unit. The activities that start with a beginning lesson (or start a unit into motion) are called **initiating activities** or *"launching" activities;* those that comprise the heart of the lessons and the unit are the ongoing **developmental activities;** and those that bring the study to a natural close are **culminating activities** found in the final lessons/end of the unit. Although nearly limitless, the list in Figure 7.1 gives you an idea of the many options from which you can choose activities for any of these three categories, some of which, of course, may overlap and some of which might naturally fit one category better than another.

Initiating Activities

A unit of study can be initiated by a limitless variety of activities and lessons. You must decide which ways are appropriate to incorporate into your lessons for your educational goals and objectives, for your intended time duration, and for your own unique group of students, considering their level of maturity, interests, abilities, and skills. You might start with a current event, a community problem or concern, a student experience, an outdoor adventure, an artifact, a book, or something found on the Internet.

Ongoing Developmental Activities

Once the initiating activities and lessons have been completed, students become occupied with a variety of ongoing activities such as those listed in Figure 7.1. In working with students to select and plan the ongoing learning activities, you will want to keep in mind the concept represented by the Learning Experiences Ladder (Figure 7.6), as well as predetermined goals and target objectives (return to Chapter 5). Now do Application Exercise 7.1.

For Your Notes

APPLICATION EXERCISE 7.1 PUTTING OBJECTIVES, RESOURCES, AND LEARNING ACTIVITIES TOGETHER FOR A TEACHING PLAN

Instructions: The purpose of this application exercise is to write a specific teaching plan for a minimum of one day that incorporates what you have done so far: preparing goals, writing objectives, selecting resources, and selecting and planning learning activities. You may want to reference the learning activities to state frameworks, district documents, and local school curriculum. Ask a peer to read and react to your teaching plan. Does your plan convey what you intended to say? What new questions came to mind as you wrote the plan and as it was reviewed by others?

Teaching Plan

Standard/interdisciplinary unit theme:

Main focus question:

Related subquestions:

Objectives

(What will the students learn?)

(What thinking skills, such as observing, communicating, comparing, contrasting, categorizing, inferring, and applying will the students develop?)

(What attitudes will be fostered?)

Resources

(Media, display visuals, artifacts, computer, and software)

✎ **APPLICATION EXERCISE 7.1** *(continued)*

Specifics of Learning Activities

Preassessment of Student Learning

(How will you determine what students know or think they know about the subject at the start of the unit?)

Example 1: Use a think–pair–share activity where the topic/question is written on the board and the students are asked in pairs to think about the topic, discuss it between themselves, and then the pairs share with the whole class what they know or think they already know about it while the teacher or a selected student writes the major thoughts on the board, perhaps in the form of a visual concept web.

Example 2: Use a KWL reading comprehension activity in which three columns are formed on the board or on a computer projection or overhead projector and the students are asked to make their own three-column format on paper. They write down what they already *KNOW* or think they know about the topic/question in the first left-hand column. They write a list of what they *WANT* to learn about the topic/question in the middle column. They fill in the blank right-hand column at the end or during the study with what is being learned or what has been *LEARNED* about the topic/question.

APPLICATION EXERCISE 7.1 *(continued)*

Formative Assessment

(Techniques used to assess student learning in progress to ensure they are on the right track.)

Check discipline areas selected and give a brief description of how you will assess student learning.

_____ 1. Mathematics

   Description:

_____ 2. Music and dance

   Description:

_____ 3. Painting and sculpture

   Description:

_____ 4. Poetry and prose

   Description:

_____ 5. Physical education/health

   Description:

_____ 6. Reading and language

   Description:

APPLICATION EXERCISE 7.1 *(continued)*

_____ 7. Sciences

Description:

_____ 8. Social sciences/history/geography

Description:

_____ 9. Other

Description:

Feedback:

1. In your opinion, does your plan effectively convey what you originally envisioned?

2. Does it need more detail or revision?

3. Do your selected learning activities appropriately address the varied learning styles of your students?

4. What was the reaction of your peers to your teaching plan?

5. What new questions came to mind as you wrote the plan and as it was reviewed?

Culminating Activities

A culminating activity within a lesson brings a study/unit to a close. Such an activity often includes an exhibition or sharing of the product of the students' study. You could accept the students' suggestions for a culminating activity if it engages them in summarizing and sharing what they have learned with others. A culminating activity that brings closure to the study can give the children an opportunity for synthesis (by assembling, constructing, creating, inventing, producing, or incorporating something) and possibly the opportunity to present that synthesis to an audience, such as by sharing with parents and guardians at a classroom, school, or community event, or by sharing their project on the school's website.

With a culminating activity, you can facilitate the students' move from recording information to reporting on their learning. For example, one activity might be for the students to get involved in place-based learning, that is, to take field trips to study something related to a unit and then synthesize their learning after the trip in a way that culminates the study. During place-based learning, students can carry student-prepared notepads similar to the ones reporters use, take notes, and make sketches of what they see and learn. They can review what questions they have on the ride to the site (See our Companion Website at **www.prenhall.com/roberts** for the *Additional Content* module feature titled Place-Based Learning in Chapter 1). Students can discuss what they liked and did not like on the ride back to school. After the trip, each student can choose something that he or she saw and then build it (or draw it) to scale, so the students can have a scale model of something they saw on the trip that caught their interest.

Teacher and students might devote one full afternoon, or more, to working with rulers, yardsticks, cardboard, clay, and other materials. If drawing something to scale, the teacher might cut up a picture (of something taken with the camera on the trip) into one-inch squares that have been numbered in sequence on the back, one square per student. Giving one square to each student, the teacher asks all to enlarge what they see in their squares in a ratio of 1 to 10 to make a larger picture of their trip. The numbers on the back of the squares help the students keep the sequence of the large mural drawing on the classroom wall. The students can present a narration to tell others what the drawing represents and its importance to their study. The students might also present an art show of drawings about the study with a narration that informs others about their study. You might also schedule a culminating activity that asks students to report on individual projects—the aspect of the study each student formerly reserved for individual study.

Examples of actual culminating activities and products for lessons and units are endless. Culminating activities are opportunities for students to proudly demonstrate and share their learning in different, creative, and individual ways.

PREPARING LESSON PLANS: RATIONALE AND ASSUMPTIONS

As described at the beginning of this chapter, one step in the instructional planning process is the preparation of lessons for class meetings. The process of designing a lesson is important if you are to provide the most efficient use of valuable and limited instructional time and the most effective learning for the students to meet the anticipated learning outcomes.

Notice that the title of this section does not refer to *daily* lesson plans, but rather simply to lesson plans. The focus is on how to prepare a lesson plan, and that plan may, in fact, be a daily plan or it may not. In some instances, a lesson plan may extend for more than one period or block of time or day, perhaps two or three. In other instances, the lesson plan is in fact a daily plan and may run for an entire class period or block of time.

Accomplished elementary schoolteachers are always planning for their teaching. For long-range plans, they plan the scope and sequence and develop content. Within this long-range planning, they develop units and lessons, and within lessons, they design the activities to be used and the assessments of learning to be done. They familiarize themselves with books, materials, media, and innovations in their special fields of interest such as literacy, mathematics, science, or social studies. Some teachers prefer to plan first with activities that fit into lessons that then support a plan for a unit of study. Yet, despite all this planning activity, the lesson plan remains pivotal to the planning process. Regardless of where you begin, consider now the rationale, description, and guidelines for writing detailed lesson plans.

Rationale for Preparing Written Lesson Plans

First, carefully prepared and written lesson plans show everyone—first and foremost your students, then your colleagues, your administrator, and, if you are a student teacher, your host teacher and your college or university supervisor—that you are a committed professional. Sometimes, beginning teachers are concerned about using a written plan in front of their students, thinking it may suggest that the teacher has not mastered the material. On the contrary, a lesson plan is tangible evidence that you are working at your job and demonstrates respect for the students, yourself, and for the profession. A written lesson plan shows that thinking and planning have taken place. There is absolutely no excuse for appearing before a classroom of children without evidence of being prepared.

Written and detailed lesson plans provide an important sense of security, which is especially useful to a beginning teacher. Like a rudder of a ship, a plan helps keep you on course. Without it, you are likely to drift aimlessly. Sometimes a disturbance in the classroom can distract from the lesson, causing the teacher to go off track or to forget an important part of the lesson. Another way to look at its value is that a written and detailed lesson plan provides a road map to guide you and help keep you on the road to your educational destination.

Written lesson plans help you to be or become a reflective decision maker. Without a written plan, it is difficult or impossible to analyze how something might have been planned or implemented differently after the lesson has been taught. Written lesson plans serve as resources for the next time you teach the same or a similar lesson and are useful for teacher self-assessment and for the assessment of student learning and the curriculum.

Written lesson plans help you organize material and search for loopholes, loose ends, or incomplete content. Careful and thorough planning during the preactive phase of instruction includes anticipation of how the lesson activities will develop as the lesson is being taught. During this anticipation you will actually visualize yourself in the classroom teaching the children, using that visualization to anticipate possible problems.

Written plans help other members of the teaching team understand what you are doing and how you are doing it.

Written lesson plans also provide substitute teachers with a guide to follow in your absence from teaching.

These reasons clearly express the need to write detailed lesson plans. The list is not exhaustive, however, and you may discover additional reasons why written lesson plans are crucial to effective teaching. In summary, (a) lesson planning is an important and ongoing process, and (b) teachers must take time to plan, reflect, write, test, evaluate, and rewrite their plans to reach optimal performance. In short, preparing written lesson plans is important professional work.

Assumptions About Lesson Planning

Not all teachers need elaborate written plans for every lesson. Sometimes, accomplished veteran teachers need only a sketchy outline. At other times, they may not need written plans at all. Still other times, accomplished teachers who have taught the topic many times in the past may need only the presence of a classroom of students to stimulate a pattern of presentation that has often been successful (though frequent use of old patterns may lead one into the boring rut of unimaginative and uninspiring teaching). Your skill in being calm and following a train of thought in the presence of distraction will influence the amount of detail necessary when planning activities and writing the lesson plan.

Considering the diversity among elementary schoolteachers, their instructional styles, their students, and what research has shown, certain assumptions can be made about lesson planning, as is done in Figure 7.7.

In summary, well-written lesson plans provide many advantages. They give a teacher an agenda or outline to follow in teaching a lesson; they give a substitute teacher a basis for presenting appropriate lessons to a class, thereby retaining lesson continuity in the regular teacher's absence; they are certainly very useful when a teacher is planning to use the same lesson again in the future; they provide the teacher with something to fall back on in case of a memory lapse, an interruption, or some distraction such as a call from the office or a fire drill; they demonstrate to students that you care and are working for them; and, above all, they provide beginners security because, with a carefully prepared plan, a beginning teacher can walk into a classroom with confidence and professional pride gained from having developed a sensible framework for that day's instruction.

Thus, as a beginning teacher, you should create detailed lesson plans. Naturally, this will require a great deal of work for at least the first year or two, but the reward of knowing that you have prepared and presented effective lessons will compensate for that effort. Now turn to the Companion Website for this resource guide at **www.prenhall.com/roberts** and access the *Additional Content* module for this chapter to read more about the continual process of keeping current with lessons, remaining flexible, making adjustments in future lessons, dealing with time problems, and using the Daily Planning Book.

CONSTRUCTING A LESSON PLAN: FORMAT, COMPONENTS, AND SAMPLES

While it is true that each teacher develops a personal system of lesson planning—the system that works best for that teacher in that teacher's unique situation—a beginning teacher needs a more substantial framework from which to work. For that, this section pro-

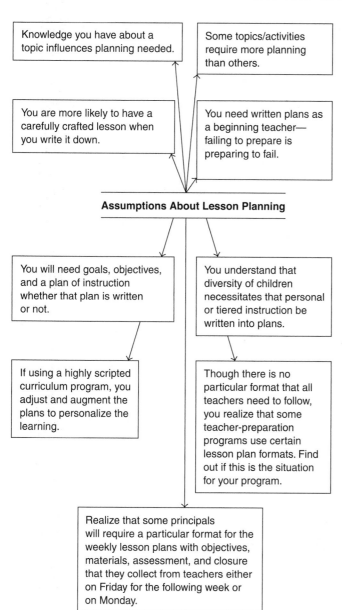

Figure 7.7
Assumptions about lesson planning

vides a preferred lesson plan format (see Figure 7.8.) Nothing is hallowed about this format, however. Review the preferred format and samples, and unless your program of teacher preparation insists otherwise, use it until you find or develop a better model.

Basic Elements of a Lesson Plan

The well-written lesson plan should contain the following basic elements: (a) descriptive data, (b) goals and objectives, (c) rationale, (d) procedure, (e) assignments and assignment reminders, (f) materials and equipment, and (g) a section for assessment of student learning, reflection on the lesson, and ideas for lesson revision.

Note that not all seven elements (as seen in Figure 7.8) and their subsections need to be present in

every written lesson plan, nor must they be presented in any particular order; nor are they inclusive or exclusive. You might choose to include additional components or subsections. Figure 7.9 displays a completed multiple-day lesson plan that incorporates many of the developmentally appropriate learning activities discussed in this resource guide. Following are descriptions of the elements of the preferred format, with examples and explanations of why each is important.

Descriptive Data

A lesson plan's descriptive data are demographic and logistical information that identify details about the group of children. Anyone reading this information should be able to identify when and where the group

Figure 7.8
Preferred lesson plan format with seven components*

---

1. **Descriptive Data**

   Teacher _____ Class _____ Date _____ Grade level _____

   Room number _____ Period _____ Unit _____ Lesson number _____ Topic _____

   Anticipated noise level (high, moderate, low)

2. **Goals and Objectives**

   Instructional goals:

   Specific objectives:

   [*Note:* All three domains not always present in every lesson]

   Cognitive:

   Affective:

   Psychomotor:

3. **Rationale** [*Note:* Rationale not always present in every lesson]

4. **Procedure** [Procedure with modeling examples, planned transitions, and so on; should usually take up most of the space of lesson plan, often a full page]

   _____ minutes. Activity 1: Set (introduction)

   _____ minutes. Activity 2:

Figure 7.8
Preferred lesson plan format with seven components* *(continued)*

_____ minutes. Activity 3: (the exact number of activities in the procedures will vary)

_____ minutes. Final Activity (Lesson Conclusion or Closure):

If time remains:

5. **Assignments and Reminders of Assignments**

Special notes and reminders to myself:

6. **Materials and Equipment Needed**

Audiovisual:

Other:

7. **Assessment, Reflection, and Revision**

Assessment of student learning, how it will be done:

Reflective thoughts about lesson after taught:

Suggestions for revision if used again:

*This blank lesson plan format is placed alone so, if you choose, you may remove it from the book and make copies for use in your teaching.

Figure 7.9
Lesson plan sample: multiple-day, project-centered, interdisciplinary, and transcultural lesson using worldwide communication via the Internet

1. Descriptive Data

Teacher _____ Class/disciplines English/Language Arts/Science

Date _____ Grade level   5–6

Unit   Investigative Research and Generative Writing

Lesson Topic   Writing Response and Peer Assessment via the Internet   Time Duration: several days

2. Goals and Objectives of Unit

Instructional Goals:

2.1 One goal for this lesson is for students to collaborate with and prepare response papers to peers from around the world who have shared the results of their own experimental research findings and research papers about ozone concentrations in the atmosphere.

2.2 The ultimate goal of this unit is for students around the world to prepare and publish for worldwide dissemination a final paper about global ozone levels in the atmosphere.

Objectives:

Cognitive

a. Through cooperative group action, students will conduct experimental research to collect data from at least three different sources about the ozone level of air in their environment. (application)

b. In cooperative groups, students will analyze the results of their experiments. (analyze)

c. Students will compile data from at least three sources as well as their experimental data and make at least two inferences from their sources and experimental data. (synthesis and evaluation)

d. Through collaborative writing groups, the students will prepare at least one final paper that summarizes their research study of local atmospheric ozone levels. (evaluation)

e. Through sharing via the Internet, students will write and share at least three response papers to their peers from other locations in the world. (evaluation)

f. From their own collaborative research and worldwide communications with their peers, the students will draw their conclusions about global atmospheric ozone levels and write at least one conclusion paper. (evaluation)

Affective

a. Students will respond attentively to the response papers of their peers by reading at least one paper and making a comment about the content. (attending)

b. Students will willingly cooperate with others during 9 out of 10 of the group activities. (responding)

c. The students will offer at least one opinion each in writing about the atmospheric levels of ozone. (valuing)

d. The students will form at least one judgment each about the different ozone levels related to local, regional, and world ozone levels. (organizing)

e. The students will communicate accurately their findings in an oral presentation to the group and electronically respond at least once to the work of their worldwide peers. (internalizing)

Psychomotor

a. The students will manipulate the computer so that their e-mail communications are transmitted accurately. (manipulating)

b. In a final summary to the study, students, reading their summaries orally, will describe their thoughts about atmospheric ozone concentrations. (communicating)

c. The students will ultimately create at least one proposal for worldwide dissemination. (creating)

3. Rationale

3.1 Important to improvement in one's writing and communication skills are the processes of selecting a topic, making decisions, arranging, drafting, proofing, reviewing with peers, commenting, revising, editing, rewriting, and publishing the results—processes that are focused on in the writing aspect of this unit.

3.2 Student writers need many readers to respond to their work. Through worldwide communication with peers and dissemination of their final product, this need can be satisfied.

3.3 Students learn best when they are actively pursuing a topic of interest and meaning to them. By brainstorming potential problems and arriving at their own topic, this unit provides that.

3.4 Real-world problems are interdisciplinary and transcultural; involving writing, data collecting, graphing (through English, science, mathematics) and intercultural communication, this unit is an interdisciplinary transcultural unit.

Figure 7.9
Lesson plan sample: multiple-day, project-centered, interdisciplinary, and transcultural lesson using worldwide communication via the Internet *(continued)*
(*Source:* Information about the science experiment is from R. J. Ryder and T. Hughes, *Internet for Educators* (Upper Saddle River, NJ: Prentice Hall, 1997), p. 98.)

4. **Procedure**

   Content:

   At the start of this unit, collaborative groups were established via Intercultural E-mail Classroom Connections (IECC) www.teaching.com/IECC with other classes from schools around the world. These groups of students conducted several scientific research experiments on the ozone levels of their local atmospheric air. To obtain relative measurements of ozone concentrations in the air, students set up experiments that involved stretching rubber bands on a board (no one was allergic to latex to his or her knowledge), then observing the number of days until the bands broke. Students maintained daily journal logs of the temperature, barometric pressure, and the wind speed/direction, and of the number of days that it took for bands to break. After compiling their data and preparing single-page summaries of their results, the students exchanged data with other groups of the Internet. From data collected worldwide, students wrote a one-page summary as to what conditions may account for the difference in levels of ozone. Following the exchange of students' written responses and their subsequent revisions based on feedback from the worldwide peers, students are now preparing a final summary report about the world's atmospheric ozone level. The intention is to disseminate worldwide (to newspaper and contacts via the Internet) this final report.

   Activity 1: Introduction (10 minutes)
   Today, in think–share pairs, you will think about the topic, discuss it between yourselves, and then write your notes about what you know or think you know about the world's ozone level (preassessment, use of prior knowledge). Next, you'll share your notes with the group. We'll write the major thoughts on the board. To begin, consider what you know about the world's ozone level and talk about it with your partner. (Students send e-mail to groups worldwide.)

   Activity 2: Continuation (30 minutes)
   Today, again in think–share pairs, you will prepare initial responses to the e-mail responses we have received from other groups around the world. (Teacher shares the list of places from which e-mail has been received.) Any questions before we get started? As we discussed earlier, here are the instructions: In your think–share-pairs (each pair is given one response received via e-mail), prepare written responses according to the following outline: (a) Note points or information you would like to incorporate in the final paper to be forwarded via the Internet; (b) comment on one aspect of the written response you like best; and (c) provide questions to the sender to seek clarification or elaboration. I think you should be able to finish this in about 30 minutes, so let's try for that.

   Activity 3: (open time)
   Preparation of dyad responses.

   Activity 4: (open time)
   "Let's now hear from each response pair." Dyad responses are shared with the whole group for discussion of inclusion in the response paper to be sent via the Internet.

   Activity 5: (open time)
   Discussion, conclusion, and preparation of final drafts to be sent to each e-mail correspondent to be done by co-operative groups. (The number of groups needed is decided by the number of e-mail correspondents at this time.) Later, as students receive e-mail responses from the groups, the responses will be printed and reviewed. The class then responds to each using the same criteria as before and returns this response to the e-mail sender.

   Closure:
   The process continues until all groups (from around the world) have agreed on and prepared the final report to disseminate.

5. **Assignments and Reminders**

   Remind students of important dates and decisions to be made.

6. **Materials and Equipment Needed**

   School computers with Internet access; printers; copies of e-mail responses.

7. **Assessment, Reflection, and Revision**

   Assessment of student learning for this lesson is preassessment and then formative: journals, daily checklist of student participation in groups, and writing drafts.

   Reflective thoughts about the lesson and suggestions for revision.

meets, who is teaching the class, and what is being taught. Although as the teacher you know this information, someone else may not. Members of the teaching team, administrators, mentors, and substitute teachers (and, if you are the student teacher, your university supervisor and host teacher) appreciate this information, especially when asked to fill in for you, even if only for a few minutes during a class session. Most teachers discover which items of descriptive data are most beneficial in their situation and then develop their own identifiers. Remember this: The mark of a well-prepared, clearly written lesson plan is the ease with which someone else (such as another member of your teaching team or a substitute teacher) could implement it.

As shown in the sample plan of Figure 7.9 the descriptive data include the following:

1. **Name of course or class.** These serve as headings for the plan and facilitate orderly filing of plans.

   English/Language Arts/Science (integrated block course)

2. **Name of the unit** for which the lessons are prepared. Inclusion of this facilitates the orderly control of the hundreds of lesson plans a teacher constructs. For example:

   Unit: Investigative Research and Generative Writing

3. **Topic to be considered within the unit.** This is also useful for control and identification. For example:

   Writing Response and Peer Assessment via the Internet

Anticipated Noise Level

Although not included in the sample lesson plan, you might include in the descriptive data the category of "anticipated classroom noise level" such as "high," "moderate," or "silent or low." Its inclusion, or at least considering the idea, is useful during the planning phase of instruction in that it prompts you to think about how active and noisy the children might become during the lesson, what reminders to give the class before the lesson, how you might prepare for an anticipated noise level (through a class meeting perhaps), and whether you should advise an administrator or the teachers in the neighboring classrooms of the anticipated noise level.

Goals and Objectives

The instructional goals are general statements of intended accomplishments from that lesson. Teachers and students need to know what the lesson is de-

signed to accomplish. In clear, understandable language, the general goal statement provides that information. From the sample, the goals are:

- To collaborate with and prepare response papers to peers from around the world who have shared the results of their own experimental research findings and research papers about ozone concentrations in the atmosphere.
- For students worldwide to prepare and publish for worldwide dissemination a final paper about worldwide ozone levels in the atmosphere.

Because the goals are also included in the unit plan, sometimes a teacher may include only the objectives in the daily lesson plan, but not the goals. As a beginning teacher, it usually is a good idea to include both.

A crucial step in the development of any lesson plan is that of setting the objectives. It is at this point that many lessons go wrong and where many beginning teachers have problems.

Learning Activity versus Learning Objective

Sometimes, teachers confuse the **learning activity** (how the students will learn it) with the **learning objective** (what the students will learn as a result of the learning activity). For example, teachers sometimes mistakenly list what they intend to do—such as "lead a discussion about the Earth's continents"—and fail to focus on just what the learning objectives in these activities truly are—that is, what the students will be able to do (performance) as a result of the instructional activity. Or, rather than specifying what the student will be able to do as a result of the learning activities, the teacher mistakenly writes what the students will do in the class (the learning activity)—such as, "in pairs the students will answer the 10 questions on page 72"—as if that were the learning objective.

When you approach this step in your lesson planning, to avoid error, ask yourself, "What should students learn *as a result* of the activities of this lesson?" Your answer to that question is your objective! Objectives of the lesson are included then as specific statements of performance expectations, detailing precisely what students will be able to do as a result of the instructional activities.

No Need to Include All Domains and Hierarchies in Every Lesson

Not all three domains (cognitive, affective, and psychomotor) are necessarily represented in every lesson. As a matter of fact, any given lesson plan may be directed to only one or two, or a few, specific objectives. Over the course of a unit of instruction, however, all domains, and most, if not all, levels within each should be addressed.

From the sample lesson shown in Figure 7.9, here are some sample objectives with the domain and the level within that domain shown in parentheses:

- Through cooperative group action, students will conduct experimental research to collect data from at least three different sources about the ozone level of air in their environment. (cognitive, application)
- Through sharing via the Internet, students will write and share at least three response papers to their peers from other locations in the world. (cognitive, evaluation)
- The students will form at least one judgment each about the different ozone levels related to local, regional, and world ozone levels. (affective, organizing)
- The students will ultimately create at least one proposal for worldwide dissemination. (psychomotor, creating)

Rationale

The rationale is an explanation of why the lesson is important and why the instructional methods chosen will achieve the objectives. Parents and guardians, students, teachers, administrators, and others have the right to know why specific content is being taught and why the methods employed are being used. Prepare yourself well by always being prepared with intelligent answers to those two questions.

Teachers become reflective decision makers when they challenge themselves to think about *what* (the content) they are teaching, *how* (the learning activities) they are teaching it, and *why* (the rationale) it must be taught. Sometimes, the rationale is included within the unit introduction and goals, but not in every lesson plan of the unit. Some lessons are carryovers or continuations of a lesson; we see no reason to repeat the rationale for a continuing lesson.

Procedure

The procedure consists of the instructional activities for a scheduled period of time. The substance of the lesson (the information to be presented, obtained, and learned) is the content. Appropriate information is selected to meet the learning objectives, the level of competence of the students, and the grade level of course requirements. To be sure your lesson actually covers what it should, you should write down exactly what minimum content you intend to cover. This material may be placed in a separate section or combined with the procedure section. It is most important to be sure that your information is written down so you can refer to it quickly and easily when you need to.

If, for instance, you intend to conduct the lesson using discussion, you should write out the key discussion questions. Or, if you are going to introduce new material using a 10-minute lecture, then you need to outline the content of that lecture. The word *outline* is not used casually—you need not have pages of notes to sift through, nor should you ever read declarative statements to your students. You should be familiar enough with the content so that an outline (in as much detail as you believe necessary) will be sufficient to carry on the lesson.

The procedures to be used, sometimes referred to as the **instructional components,** comprise the **procedure** component of the lesson plan. It is the section that outlines what you and your students will do during the lesson. Appropriate instructional activities are chosen to meet the objectives, to match the students' learning styles and individual needs, and to ensure that all students have an equal opportunity to learn. Ordinarily, you should plan this section of your lesson as an organized entity having a beginning (an introduction or set), a middle, and an end (called the **closure**) to be completed during the lesson. This structure is not always needed, because some lessons are simply parts of units or long-term plans and merely carry on activities spelled out in those long-term plans. Still, most lessons need to include the following in the procedure: (a) an *introduction*, the process used to prepare the students mentally for the lesson, sometimes referred to as the *set* or *initiating activity;* (b) *lesson development,* the detailing of *activities* that occur between the beginning and the end of the lesson, including the transitions that connect activities (see the discussion regarding transitions in Chapter 4); (c) plans for *practice,* sometimes referred to as the *follow-up;* that is, ways that you intend to have students interact in the classroom, such as individual practice, in dyads or small groups, or receive guidance or coaching from each other and from you; (d) the *lesson conclusion* (or closure), the planned process of bringing the lesson to an end, thereby providing students with a sense of completeness and, with effective teaching, accomplishment and comprehension by helping students to synthesize the information learned from the lesson; (e) a *timetable* that serves simply as a planning and implementation guide; (f) a *plan* for what to do if you finish the lesson and time remains; and (g) *assignments,* that is, what students are instructed to do as follow-up to the lesson, either as homework (responsibility papers) or as in-class work, providing students an opportunity to practice and enhance what is being learned. Let's now consider some of those components in detail.

Introduction to the Lesson

Like any good performance, a lesson needs an effective beginning. In many respects, the introduction sets the tone for the rest of the lesson by alerting the students that the business of learning is to begin. The introduction should be an attention-getter. If it is exciting, interesting, or innovative, it can create a favorable mood for the lesson. One teacher we know follows a planned way of introducing the lesson that varies with the subject/discipline being taught. For example, to introduce a science lesson, the teacher sets up specific items for an experiment in the front of the class. As the students walk into the room, they see the items for the lesson and the teacher asks them to write a question/hypothesis that could be reflected in an experiment they can think of that uses those items. Then they read their questions and hypotheses about their experiment ideas in think–pair–share groups. After that, the teacher presents the experiment that involves the items for the lesson. For a language lesson, a teacher can begin a lesson with a sentence on the board with a blank or with a scrambled sentence from the previous lesson that leads into this new lesson.

In any case, a thoughtful introduction serves as a solid indicator that you are well prepared. While it is difficult to develop an exciting introduction to every lesson, many options are available for spicing up the launching of a lesson. You might, for instance, begin the lessons by briefly reviewing the previous lesson, thereby helping students connect the learning. Another possibility is to review vocabulary words from previous lessons and to introduce new ones. Still another possibility is to use the key point of the day's lesson as an introduction and then again as the conclusion. Sometimes, teachers begin a lesson by presenting a strange but true scenario or by demonstrating a discrepant event, that is, an event that is contrary to what one might expect (see Figure 8.3 in Chapter 8) or, as it is sometimes referred to, a "hook."[2] Yet, another possibility is to begin the lesson with a writing activity on some controversial aspect of the ensuing lesson. Consider these examples:

- A sample introduction for history and the study of westward expansion that could lead to writing: The teacher asks, "Who has lived somewhere else other than *(name of your state)?* After students raise hands and answer, the teacher asks individuals why they moved to *(name of your state).* After discussion, the teacher then asks students to recall why the first European settlers came to the United States; then the teacher asks students to write their thoughts about reasons why settlers came to the United States.
- Another sample introduction for science and the study of the science process skill of predicting: The teacher takes a glass filled to the brim with colored water (colored so it is more visible) and asks students to discuss and predict (in dyads) how many pennies can be added to the glass before any water spills over the rim of the glass. The teacher records their predictions on the writing board; then moves to ask the students to record their thoughts about what they learned in their learning journals.

In short, you can use the introduction of the lesson in different ways: to review past learning with the KWL approach; to bridge the new lesson to the previous lesson; to introduce new material; to point out the objectives of the new lesson; to help students connect their learning with other disciplines or with real life; to show what will be learned and why the learning is important; or, to induce in students some motivation and a mind-set favorable to the new lesson.

Lesson Development

The developmental activities comprise the bulk of the plan and are the specifics by which you intend to achieve your lesson objectives. They include activities that present information, demonstrate skills, provide reinforcement of previously learned material, and furnish other opportunities to develop understanding and skill. Furthermore, by actions and words, during lesson development the teacher models the behaviors expected of the children. Children need such modeling. By effective modeling, the teacher can exemplify the anticipated learning outcomes.

Activities in this section of the lesson plan should be described in some detail so (a) you will know exactly what it is you plan to do and so (b) during the interactions of the class meeting, you do not forget important details and content. It is for this reason you should consider, for example, noting answers (if known) to questions you intend to ask and solutions (if known) to problems you intend to have the students solve.

Lesson Conclusion

Having a concise closure to the lesson is as important as having a strong introduction. The concluding activity should summarize and secure what ensued during the developmental stage and should reinforce the principal points of the lesson. As an example, in summarizing a discovery learning activity, the conclusion can reveal the major point of the lesson for the first time. Also, one way to accomplish these ends is to restate the key points of the lesson. Another is to briefly outline the major points. Still another is to review the major concept.

Sometimes the closure is not only a review of what was learned but also the summarizing of a question left unanswered, signaling a change in your plan of activities for the next day. In other words, it becomes a transitional closure. Turn to the Companion Website at **www.prenhall.com/roberts** and the section for this chapter to read more about a timetable and assignments in the *Additional Content* module. ✎

Assessment, Reflection, and Revision

Details of how you will assess students' *prior knowledge* (preassessment), of how well students *are learning* (formative assessment) and how well they *have learned* (summative assessment) should be included in your lesson plan. This does not mean to imply that these types of assessment will be in *every* daily plan, although formative assessment can occur on a daily basis.

Formative assessment of student learning that is taking place should be frequent, perhaps including teacher observations and questions as often as on the average of once every few minutes during direct instruction and during individual or small-group coaching. Checks for comprehension can be in the form of the questions that you ask and that the children ask during the lesson (in the procedural section), as well as in the form of various kinds of checklists.

For summative assessment, teachers typically use review questions at the end of a lesson (as a closure) or at the beginning of the next lesson (as a review or a transfer introduction). They also use student independent practice, quizzes and tests, or summary activities at the completion of a lesson.

In most lesson plan formats, there is a section reserved for the teacher to write reflective comments about the lesson. Some teachers begin their reflective comments with positive comments: They list individual student achievements, the time when they felt the most positive during the lesson, how smooth a transition went between activities, and they write about how well-prepared and organized they thought they were even if part of the lesson was a failure experience. Many student teachers seem to prefer to write their reflections at the end or on the reverse page of their lesson plans. (These comments are easily transferred to the lesson plans on your computer if you are using TaskStream (*www.taskstream.com*) or a similar lesson plan software program; ask your colleagues for their suggestions about additional web-based instructional design/lesson plan material.) One teacher we know has designed a lesson plan template that includes the following: "What went well: _____ ," followed by "How students responded: _____ " and "How the lesson could have been better: _____ ." To feel optimistic and enthusiastic, the teacher reflects on what is *positive* about the lesson *first*.

As well as being useful to yourself, reflections about the lesson are useful for those who are supervising or mentoring you. (See more about this later in the professional development chapter, Chapter 11.) Now, proceed to our Companion Website **(www.prenhall.com/roberts)** and to the *Additional Application Exercises* module for this chapter to gain insight about ways in which activities, lessons, and units can work together. ✎

Writing and later reading your reflections can provide not only ideas that may be useful if you plan to use the lesson again at a later date, but can also offer catharsis, easing any tension caused from teaching. Continuing to work effectively at a challenging task (that is, to prevent intellectual downshifting, which is reverting to earlier learned, lower cognitive level behaviors) requires significant amounts of reflection.

PREPARING INSTRUCTIONAL UNITS

The instructional unit is a major subdivision of a course of study (for one course or a self-contained classroom, there are several to many units of instruction) and is comprised of learning activities that are planned around a central theme, topic, issue, or problem. Organizing the content of the semester or year into units makes the teaching process more manageable than when no plan or only random choices are made by a teacher.

The instructional unit is not unlike a chapter in a book, an act or scene in a play, or a phase of work when undertaking a project such as building a house. Breaking down information or actions into component parts and then grouping the related parts makes sense out of learning and doing. The unit brings a sense of cohesiveness and structure to student learning and avoids the piecemeal approach that might otherwise unfold. You can learn to articulate lessons within, between, and among unit plans and focus on important elements while not ignoring tangential information of importance. Students remember "chunks" of information, especially when those chunks are related to specific units.

While the steps for developing any type of instructional unit are basically the same, units can be organized in a number of ways. For the purpose of this resource guide, we consider two basic types of units: the standard unit and the integrated thematic unit.

A **standard unit** (known also as a conventional, regular, or traditional unit) consists of a series of activities built into lessons centered on a topic, major concept, or block of subject matter. Each lesson builds on the previous lesson by contributing additional subject matter, providing further illustrations, and supplying more practice or other added instruction—all of which are aimed at bringing about mastery of the knowledge and skills on which the unit is centered. See the accompanying *Technology Tips for the Classroom* feature.

When a standard unit is centered on a central theme (as was discussed in Chapter 5), the unit may be referred to as a **thematic unit.** When, by design, the thematic unit integrates disciplines, such as combining the learning of science and mathematics, or combining social studies and English/language arts, or combining all four core or any other disciplines, then it is called an **integrated** or **interdisciplinary thematic unit (ITU)** or, simply, an integrated unit.

Technology Tips for the Classroom

- When your students are out on a field trip, playing an outside activity, exhibiting certain behaviors at recess (or in the classroom), or are on an observation walk, have a digital camera on hand. With the needed permissions to take pictures of your students on file at the school, take all the pictures you want and delete the ones you don't like. You can plug your digital camera into the classroom TV and instantly you will have a "good behavior on the playground" recap or an "outstanding behavior in our classroom" review. If you have a photo printer available in your classroom, connect the photo printer to the class TV, take the transfer device out of the camera, place it into the printer and print some special photos of the good behavior (perhaps to accompany a positive note home to the parents) while the students watch the photos on TV and have a class meeting to talk about what went on. Some digital cameras also have a feature for cropping and resizing the photos if you need to do that.
- If your students are going to take a teacher-conducted walk to observe the neighborhood, its workers, and places of work, use the camera to take photos of buildings and other points of interest. Back in the classroom, plug your digital camera into the classroom TV and you will have an instant replay of the walk for a group discussion. Connect a photo printer to the class TV, take the transfer device out of the camera, place it into the printer, and with the students, review the photos of the neighborhood deleting the ones that are not clear. Print some special photos of areas of interest in the neighborhood while the students watch the photos on TV and discuss what they learned about their neighborhood and the people they met. In addition, have the students simulate the neighborhood with small building blocks or milk cartons and then tape the photos that were taken on the walk to the front of the cartons or blocks to help identify areas in the neighborhood. Repeat the walk another day to collect more photos if needed to complete the simulated neighborhood in the classroom.
- Consider using a wireless digital camera phone on any field trip or observational walk for place-based education. A camera phone, available with different features, permits you to make immediate emergency calls, to call your principal/school and parents, to access news and weather, to take photos of any expected or unexpected events, and to surf the web for backup information needed for place-based education.
- Consider using a set of two-way radios while you are going on your class's field trip or observational walk. This communication arrangement allows you to talk to the adult volunteer who is with the students at the back of the tour group or at the back of the line of students or who is with the last group of students crossing in a safety crosswalk on a busy street.

Companion Website

To find links to resources about education and special education, go to our Companion Website at **www.prenhall.com/roberts** and click on the *Web Destinations* module for Chapter 7.

Planning and Developing Any Unit of Instruction

Whether for a standard unit or an integrated thematic unit, the steps in planning and developing the unit are the same and are described in the following paragraphs:

1. **Select a suitable theme, topic, issue, or problem.** These may already have been identified in your course of study or textbook or have been agreed on by members of your teaching team. Many schools change their themes or add new ones from year to year.
2. **Select the goals of the unit and prepare the overview.** The goals are written as an overview or rationale, covering what the unit is about and what the students are to learn. In selecting the goals, you should (a) become as familiar as possible with the topic and materials used; (b) consult curriculum documents, such as courses of study, state and local frameworks and standards, and resource units for ideas; (c) decide the content and procedures (i.e., what the students should learn about the topic and how); (d) write the rationale or overview, where you summarize what you expect the students will learn about the

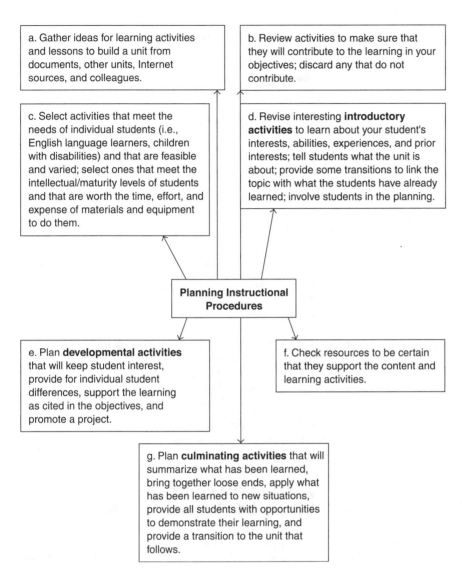

Figure 7.10
Planning instructional procedures

a. Gather ideas for learning activities and lessons to build a unit from documents, other units, Internet sources, and colleagues.

b. Review activities to make sure that they will contribute to the learning in your objectives; discard any that do not contribute.

c. Select activities that meet the needs of individual students (i.e., English language learners, children with disabilities) and that are feasible and varied; select ones that meet the intellectual/maturity levels of students and that are worth the time, effort, and expense of materials and equipment to do them.

d. Revise interesting **introductory activities** to learn about your student's interests, abilities, experiences, and prior interests; tell students what the unit is about; provide some transitions to link the topic with what the students have already learned; involve students in the planning.

Planning Instructional Procedures

e. Plan **developmental activities** that will keep student interest, provide for individual student differences, support the learning as cited in the objectives, and promote a project.

f. Check resources to be certain that they support the content and learning activities.

g. Plan **culminating activities** that will summarize what has been learned, bring together loose ends, apply what has been learned to new situations, provide all students with opportunities to demonstrate their learning, and provide a transition to the unit that follows.

topic; and (e) be sure your goals are congruent with those of the course or grade-level program.

3. **Select suitable instructional objectives.** In doing this, you should (a) include understandings, skills, attitudes, and appreciations; (b) be specific and avoid vagueness and generalizations; (c) write the objectives in performance terms; and (d) be as certain as possible that the objectives will contribute to the major learning and target goals as presented in the overview.

4. **Detail the instructional procedures.** These procedures include the subject content and the learning activities, established as a series of lessons. Proceed with the steps shown in Figure 7.10 during your initial planning of the instructional procedures.

5. **Plan for preassessment and assessment of student learning.** Preassess what students already know or think they know. Assessment of

student progress in achievement of the learning objectives (formative evaluation) should permeate the entire unit; that is, as often as possible, assessment should be a daily component of lessons. Plan to gather information in several ways, including informal observations, checklist observations of student performance and their portfolios, and paper-and-pencil tests. As discussed in Chapters 5 and 6, to be meaningful, assessment must be congruent with the instructional objectives.

6. **Provide for the materials and tools of instruction.** The unit cannot function without materials. Therefore, you must plan long before the unit begins for media equipment and materials, references, reading materials, reproduced materials, and community resources. Librarians and media center personnel are usually quite willing to assist in finding appropriate materials to support a unit of instruction.

Figure 7.11
Elements in a unit plan

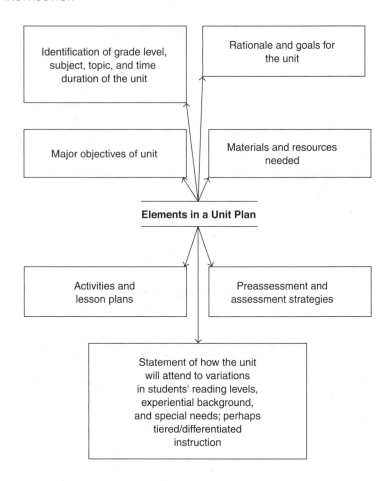

Unit Format, Inclusive Elements, and Time Duration

Follow the previous six steps to develop any type of unit. In addition, two general points should be made. First, while there is no single best format for a teaching unit, there are minimum inclusions. Particular formats may be best for specific disciplines or grade levels, topics, and types of activities. During your student teaching, your college or university program for teacher preparation and/or your host teacher may have a format that you will be expected to follow. Regardless of the format, Figure 7.11 shows seven elements that should be evident in any unit plan.

Second, there is no set time duration for a unit plan, although for specific units, curriculum guides will recommend certain time spans. Units may extend for a minimum of several days or, as in the case of some interdisciplinary thematic units, for several weeks to an entire school year. However, be aware that when standard units last more than 2 or 3 weeks, they tend to lose the character of clearly identifiable units. For the unit of instruction, the exact time duration will be dictated by several factors, including the topic, problem, or theme; the age, interests, and maturity of the students; and the scope of the learning activities.

PLANNING AND DEVELOPING AN INTERDISCIPLINARY THEMATIC UNIT

The six steps mentioned in the preceding section are essential for planning any type of teaching unit, including the interdisciplinary thematic unit (ITU), which may consist of smaller subject-specific conventional units developed according to the immediately foregoing guidelines. Because developing interdisciplinary thematic units is an essential task for many of today's teachers, you should learn this process now.

The primary responsibility for the development of ITUs can depend on a single teacher or on the cooperation of several teachers. A teaching team may develop from one to several interdisciplinary thematic units a year. Over time, then, a team will have several units that are available for implementation. However, the most effective units are often those that are the most current or the most meaningful to students. This means that ever-changing global, national, and local topics provide a virtual smorgasbord from which to choose, and teachers and teaching teams must constantly update old units and develop new and exciting ones. Open lines of communication within, between, and among teams and schools within a school district are critical to the success of interdisciplinary thematic teaching.[3]

Now turn to the Companion Website **(www. prenhall.com/roberts)** and read further in the *Additional Content* module about the common thread of tightly woven components in an ITU, about steps for developing an interdisciplinary thematic unit, and about the checklist for developing an ITU. Then return to this resource guide to review Application Exercise 7.1 and complete Application Exercises 7.2 and 7.3.

For Your Notes

APPLICATION EXERCISE 7.2 PREPARING A LESSON PLAN

Instructions: Use the model lesson format in this resource guide or an alternative format that is approved by your instructor to prepare a _____ -minute lesson (length to be decided in your class) for a grade and subject of your choice. After completing your lesson plan, evaluate it yourself by using the Additional Application Exercise titled Self- and Peer Assessment of My Lesson Plan (see the Companion Website at **www.prenhall.com/roberts**).   Modify the plan and then have your modified version evaluated by at least one other peer before turning it in for your instructor's evaluation. You may use this lesson as one of your lessons for Application Exercise 7.3.

For Your Notes

APPLICATION EXERCISE 7.3 PREPARING AN INSTRUCTIONAL UNIT: BRINGING IT ALL TOGETHER

Instructions: The purpose of this exercise is threefold: (a) to give you experience in preparing an instructional unit and realizing that activities set the sequence for lessons and lessons set the sequence for a unit; (b) to assist you in preparing an instructional unit that you can use in your teaching; and (c) to start your collection of instructional units that you may be able to use later in your teaching.

This is an assignment that will take several hours to complete, and you may need to read ahead in this resource guide or complete additional application exercises for this chapter on our Companion Website (**www.prenhall.com/roberts**). Our advice, therefore, is that the assignment be started early, with a due date much later in the course. Your course instructor may have specific guidelines for your completion of this application exercise; what follows is the essence of what you are to do.

First, your instructor will divide your class into two teams, each with a different assignment pertaining to this exercise. The units completed by these teams are to be shared with all members of the class for feedback and possible use later.

Team 1

Members of this team, individually or in dyads, will develop standard teaching units, perhaps with different grade levels in mind. (You will need to review the content of Chapters 8 through 10). Using a format that is practical, *each member* or *pair* of this team will develop a minimum 2-week (10-day) unit for a particular grade level, subject, and topic. Regardless of the format chosen, each unit plan should include the following elements:

1. Identification of (a) grade level, (b) subject, (c) topic, and (d) time duration.

2. Statement of rationale and general goals.

3. Separate listing of instructional objectives for each daily lesson. Wherever possible, the unit should include objectives from all three domains—cognitive, affective, and psychomotor.

4. List of the materials and resources needed and where they can be obtained (if you have that information). These should be listed for each daily lesson.

5. Ten consecutive daily lesson plans (see Application Exercise 7.2).

6. List of all items, including preassessment (determining students' prior knowledge), that will be used to assess student learning *during* and at *completion* of the unit of study.

7. Statement of how the unit will attend to variations in students' reading levels, socioethnic backgrounds, and special needs.

Team 2

In collaboration, and also following the criteria in the list above, members of this team will develop interdisciplinary thematic units. Depending on the number of students in your class, Team 2 may actually comprise several teams with each team developing an ITU. Each team should be comprised of no less than two members (e.g., a math specialist and a science specialist) and no more than four (e.g., social studies, language arts/reading, mathematics, and science).

For Your Notes

About Praxis and Other Teacher Tests

About Praxis Teacher Tests. Related to the Praxis test that you are interested in taking, find out if there is more than one exam so you can study appropriately. You'll no doubt discover that the test professionals suggest that you prepare for the following:

- Have legible and intelligible handwriting for the constructed response-type questions. You want to make sure that your responses are legible, clearly stated, and that you have attended to all parts of the questions.
- Understand the term *constructed response* to mean that you may construct the response that you think fits best as the response to the question.
- Use your time wisely, so answer questions in your own order (perhaps your strongest areas first). Just keep the answer sheets in order so you write your response on the right sheet for the question you are answering.
- Conserve your time. Be aware of the time that goes by since some questions may take more time to answer than others.
- Again, use your time in the best possible way; this means that you should reread each question to see if you read it correctly and to review all of your answers before you turn in your test to see if you have answered each part of each question.

To continue to support your interest in preparing for the Praxis tests, as well as some of the other teacher tests, all applications exercises in this chapter offer opportunities for you to reflect generally on preparing activities, lessons, and units for instruction. For example, in this chapter, as a precredentialed teacher you were asked to participate cooperatively and collaboratively to do the following:

- Write a specific teaching plan that incorporates the tasks you have done so far: preparing goals, writing objectives, selecting resources, and selecting and planning learning activities (Application Exercise 7.1).
- Prepare a lesson plan using a model lesson format and evaluate it (Application Exercise 7.2).
- Gain experience in preparing an instructional unit; realize that activities help set the sequence of lessons and that lessons help set the sequence of units; prepare an instructional unit that you may be able to use later in your teaching (Application Exercise 7.3).
- Turn to our Companion Website (**www.prenhall.com/roberts**) and click on the *Additional Application Exercise* module to complete additional application exercises, namely, Obtaining Personal Insight Regarding the Connection of Units to Unit Parts, Connecting Questions and Activities for a Unit, Planning Culminating Activities, Self- and Peer-Assessment of My Lesson Plan, Analysis of a Lesson That Failed, Generating Ideas for Interdisciplinary Units, Integrating the Topic, Initiating an ITU with a Question Map, and Connecting Questions and Activities for an ITU.

You can find a constructed response-type question similar to those found on the Praxis II tests in the Praxis Warm-Up section that follows the Chapter Summary. This warm-up takes another look at the classroom vignette found in the Looking at Teachers section at the beginning of this chapter.

About Professional Portfolios and Reflective Assessment. Four Portfolio entries and an assessment are needed for NBPTS certification. The pursuit of certification is a profound form of professional development for a teacher and selection as a National Board Certified Teacher can be one of the highest honors of the teaching profession. Applicants who join a candidates' support group or who work with cognitive coaches or other support programs are generally more successful than applicants who do not.[4]

Other Teacher Tests. For those of you who will be teaching in states that do not administer the Praxis II Principles of Learning and Teaching tests, go to our Companion Website at **www.prenhall.com/roberts** and click on the *Other Teacher Tests* module for Chapter 7 to access information about teacher tests other than the Praxis.

SUMMARY

So far, in this resource guide, you have learned of the importance of learning modalities and instructional modes. You have reviewed information about children, their needs, and the importance of providing an accepting and supportive learning environment, as well as about teacher behaviors that are necessary to facilitate the most meaningful student learning and the value of assessment.

With this chapter in particular, you continued building your knowledge base about why planning is important and developed your understanding of theoretical considerations for the selection of instruction strategies such as explicit and implicit instruction; for the selection of learning activities (initiating, ongoing, culminating) that are developmentally appropriate; and for the preparation of lesson plans that have a rationale, procedures, an introduction, lesson development, and a conclusion. You have considered the importance of assessment, reflection, and revision in planning. Further, you have planned and started to develop your first lesson plan and first unit of instruction and have put objectives, resources, and learning activities together for a teaching plan.

In this chapter, you continued building your knowledge base about why planning is important and how planning activities in lessons and lessons in units are useful pedagogical tools. You found that developing activities, lessons, and units of instruction that integrate student learning and provide a sense of meaning for the students requires coordination throughout the curriculum. Hence, for your students, you realized that learning is a process of discovering how information, knowledge, and ideas are interrelated so they can make sense out of self, school, and life. Indeed, when you turn information into activities, and activities into lessons, and lessons into units you help your students process and understand knowledge. Doing this, you are well on your way to becoming a competent planner of instruction.

What's to Come. To prepare for Part III, you have been guided in Part II (Chapters 5 through 7) through the processes necessary to prepare yourself to teach in a classroom. In the upcoming Part III (Chapters 8–11), your attention will be directed to still more strategies, more effective teaching, and your further professional development. You will find out about the selection and implementation of additional specific strategies, aids, and resources that facilitate student learning of particular skills and content, beginning with teacher talk and the use of questioning. Later, after you have studied Part III, you may choose to revisit this chapter and make revisions to your ideas for activities, lessons, and your completed unit.

EXTENDING MY PROFESSIONAL COMPETENCY

Praxis Warm-Up: A Constructed Response-Type Question

In this chapter's teacher vignette, you'll remember that Casey was teaching a sixth-grade humanities block, a 2-hour block course that integrated student learning in social studies, reading, and language arts. On this particular day, while Casey and her students were discussing the topic of Manifest Destiny, one of the students raised his hand and, when acknowledged by Casey, asked the question, "Why aren't we (referring to the United States) still adding states (meaning adding territory to the United States)?" Casey immediately replied with "There aren't any more states to add." By responding too quickly, Casey missed one of those "teachable moments."

Consider that you are a sixth-grade teacher and, similar to Casey's teaching, you are about to begin a study on Manifest Destiny. You have decided to include several writing activities, including writing a research report, that will help your students organize their thinking about their research (including their thinking about adding territory to the United States) and then communicate information they have acquired. To prepare your sixth graders to write a research report about a topic related to the concept of Manifest Destiny, what steps would you take your students through to guide their writing? Briefly but clearly explain each step. Hints are found in the Appendix at the end of this resource guide.

Hints for responding to Praxis Warm-Ups are found in the Appendix.

Praxis. To do another Praxis Warm-Up with a constructed response-type question, go to our Companion Website at **www.prenhall.com/roberts** and click on the *Praxis Warm-Up* module for Chapter 7. Constructed response-type questions are designed to help you prepare for the Praxis II Principles of Learning and Teaching tests.

For Your Discussion

1. **Effective Schools.** What would I say if a colleague asked me to name some of the characteristics of an effective school that impress me? **To do:** Research B. Taylor's work,[5] The Effective Schools Process: Alive and Well, *Phi Delta Kappan, 83*(5), 375–37 (2002), or another educational researcher's work about the conditions that con-

tribute to a school's effectiveness and identify some of the characteristics (strong administrative leadership, safe environment, basic skills instruction, and high expectations) that impress you.

2. **Lesson Plans.** What would I say if a colleague asked me about the reasons why a student teacher and a first-year teacher needed to prepare detailed lesson plans? **To do:** Discuss with the whole group and describe when, if ever, the teacher can or should divert from the written lesson plan.

3. **Explicit and Implicit Instruction.** What would be my explanation to a parent about these two types of instruction? **To do:** Divide your group into grade-level interest groups. Have each group devise two separate lesson plans to teach the same topic to the same students (identified), but where one plan uses explicit instruction while the other uses implicit. Have groups share the outcomes of this activity with one another.

4. **Access Mode or Delivery Mode.** During a job interview, how will I explain which mode better encourages student thinking? How will I explain that, when taught by access strategies, students learn less content but learn it more effectively? **To do:** Find research evidence to support a point of view related to the effectiveness of either the access or delivery mode. Explain the evidence to others in the group.

5. **Critical Thinking.** How would I explain to parents some of the observable behaviors that enable me to tell the extent to which a child is learning to think critically during an activity? A lesson? A unit? **To do:** Discuss with others: How would I include information about these observable behaviors in an activity, a lesson, or unit? Give some examples.

Companion Website

Also on the Companion Website at **www.prenhall. com/roberts,** you can measure your understanding of chapter content in the *Objectives* and *Self-Check* modules and apply concepts in the *For Your Discussion* module.

Online Portfolio Activities

Supporting Principles 2, 4, 5, and 7 of INTASC and Standards 1 through 6 of NBPTS: At the Companion Website **(www.prenhall.com/roberts),** click on the *Online Portfolio Activities* module to continue your online portfolio supporting knowledge of teaching.

FOR FURTHER READING

Berman, S. (1999). *Performance Based Learning for the Multiple Intelligence Classroom.* Arlington Heights, IL: Skylight Professional Development.

Borich, G. D. (2004). *Effective Teaching Methods* (5th ed.). Upper Saddle River, NJ: Merrill/Prentice Hall.

Boucher, A. C. (1998). Critical Thinking Through Estimation. *Teaching Children Mathematics, 4*(8), 452–455.

Butzow, C. M., and Butzow, J. W. (1998). *More Science through Children's Literature: An Integrated Approach.* Englewood, CO: Teachers Ideas Press.

Costa, A., and Kallick, B. (2000). *Discovering and Exploring Habits of Mind.* Alexandria, VA: Association for Supervision and Curriculum Development.

Fuchs, L. (2000). *Asia and Australia: Language Arts Around the World, Volume III. Cross Curricular Activities for Grades 4–6.* Bloomington, IN: Family Learning Association.

Fuchs, L. (2000). *Europe: Language Arts Around the World, Volume I. Cross Curricular Activities for Grades 4–6.* Bloomington, IN: Family Learning Association.

Gipe, J. P. (1998). *Multiple Paths to Literacy: Corrective Reading Techniques for Classroom Teachers* (4th ed.). Upper Saddle River, NJ: Merrill/Prentice Hall.

Gunning. T. G. (1998). *Assessing and Correcting Reading and Writing Difficulties.* Boston: Allyn & Bacon.

Holt, E. (1998). *Using Primary Sources in the Primary Grades* (ED419773). Bloomington, IN: Clearinghouse for Social Studies/Social Science Education.

Jensen, E. (1998). Getting the Brain's Attention. In E. Jensen (Ed.), *Teaching with the Brain in Mind* (Chap. 5). Alexandria, VA: Association for Supervision and Curriculum Development.

McAllister, E. A., Hildebrand, J. M., and Ericson, J. H. (2000). *People Around Us. Language Arts Theme Units, Volume V. Cross Curricular Activities for Primary Grades.* Bloomington, IN: Family Learning Association.

McAllister, E. A., Hildebrand, J. M., and Ericson, J. H. (2000). *Our Environment. Language Arts Theme Units, Volume I. Cross Curricular Activities for Primary Grades.* Bloomington, IN: Family Learning Association.

Morine-Dershimer, G. (2003). Instructional Planning. In J. Cooper (Ed.), *Classroom Teaching Skills* (7th ed.). Boston: Houghton Mifflin.

Phillips, P., and Bickley-Green, C. (1998). Integrating Art and Mathematics. *Principal, 77*(4), 46–49.

Roberts, P. L., and Kellough, R. D. (2000). *A Guide for Developing an Interdisciplinary Thematic Unit* (3rd ed.). Upper Saddle River, NJ: Merrill/Prentice Hall.

Rogers, L. K. (1999). Spelling Cheerleader. *The Reading Teacher, 53*(2), 110–111.

NOTES

1. For additional information, see the website at *www.adihome.org* or phone (541) 485-1293.
2. C. Ruck *et al.,* Using Discrepant Events to Inspire Writing, *Science Activities, 28*(2), 27–30 (Summer 1991); and R. L. Shrigley, Discrepant Events: Why They Fascinate Students, *Science and Children, 24*(8), 24–25 (May 1987).
3. G. Quinn and L. N. Restine, Interdisciplinary Teams: Concerns, Benefits, and Costs, *Journal of School Leadership, 6*(5), 494–511 (September 1996).
4. See S. Danna, Pursuing National Board Certification, *Phi Lambda Theta Educational Horizons,* February–March 2003, p. 5.

EFFECTIVE INSTRUCTION, TEACHER ASSESSMENT, AND PROFESSIONAL DEVELOPMENT

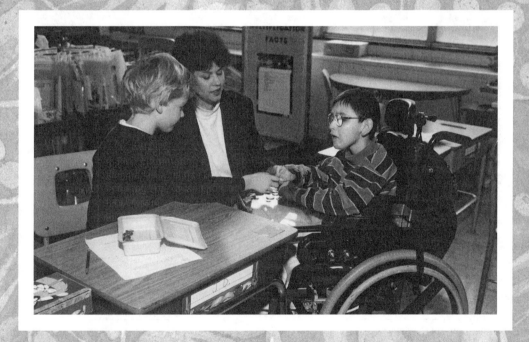

What Do I Need to Know to Use Teacher Talk and Questioning as Effective Instructional Tools?

Visual Chapter Organizer and Overview

Teacher Talk: Formal and Informal

    Teacher Talk: General Guidelines
    Teacher Talk: Specific Guidelines
    Teacher Talk: Cautions

Questioning

Purposes for Using Questioning

    Questions to Avoid Asking

Types of Cognitive Questions

    Clarifying Question
    Convergent-Thinking Question
    Cueing Questions
    Divergent-Thinking Question

Student Thinking and Levels of Cognitive Questions

Guidelines for Using Questioning

    Preparing Questions
    Implementing Questioning

Questions from Students: The Question-Driven Classroom

    Questioning: The Cornerstone of Critical Thinking, Real-World Problem Solving, and Meaningful Learning

Looking at Teachers

Consider what might be done to improve instruction through the use of questions and teacher talk. With this in mind, think about the following classroom anecdote: At the completion of an opening reading lesson, Tara, a kindergarten teacher, asked the children, "Shall we do our math lesson now?" One of the children in the class, Mario, answered, "No, I don't like math." Ignoring Mario's response, Tara began the math lesson.

Could (or should) Tara have done anything differently here? What lesson, if any, did Mario learn from the teacher's lack of response? What do you believe was the intention of Tara's question? What was the lesson intended by Tara when she asked the question? Explain whether you believe the question was planned and written in Tara's lesson plan.

Strategies that are of fundamental importance to any mode of instruction are teacher talk and its related twin, questioning. You will use teacher talk and questioning for so many purposes that you must be skilled in their effective use. Because teacher talk is so important and because it is so frequently used and abused, as is questioning, this chapter is devoted to assisting you in the development of your skills in teacher talk generally and, specifically, in using questioning as an instructional tool.

Teachers need to be able to use teacher talk and ask questions effectively. Questions by a teacher that can be answered "yes" or "no" require very little thinking on the part of the students. In contrast to yes–no questions, open-response questions allow students to reflect on their prior knowledge and generate exploration to find answers. Melvin and Gilda Berger's book *Where Did the Butterfly Get Its Name?* (New York: Scholastic, 2003) allows students to brainstorm possible reasons and then verify their predictions. It gives them a topic to research and allows them to utilize their data for oral or written presentations. In the end, students learn that people used to believe that this winged insect flew into kitchens because it was attracted to butter and milk. They may be surprised to learn that butterflies taste with their feet, that some can make sounds, and that the biggest butterflies can grow to be almost 12 inches across! All of this started with one question.

CHAPTER OBJECTIVES

Specifically, as you construct your understanding of the use of teacher talk and questioning, on completion of this eighth chapter, you should be able to:

1. Describe when and how to use teacher talk for instruction.
2. Describe the value, purpose, and types of advance mental organizers that are available when using teacher talk as an instructional strategy.
3. Recognize various levels/types of questions.

4. Develop your skill in raising questions from one level to the next.
5. Understand the importance of well-worded questions and allowing students time to think.

TEACHER TALK: FORMAL AND INFORMAL

Teacher talk encompasses both lecturing to students and talking with students. For purposes of our presentation in this resource guide, a lecture is considered formal teacher talk, whereas a discussion with students is considered informal teacher talk.

Teacher Talk: General Guidelines

First, you should realize that certain general guidelines are appropriate whether your talk is formal or informal. Related to this, you should begin the talk with an advance mental organizer. Advance organizers are introductions that mentally prepare students for a study by helping them make connections with materials already learned or experienced—a **comparative organizer**—or by providing students with a conceptual arrangement of what is to be learned—an **expository organizer.**[1] The value of using advance organizers is well documented by research.[2]

An advance organizer can be a brief introduction or statement about the main idea you intend to convey and how it is related to other aspects of the students' learning (an expository organizer), or it can be a presentation of a discrepancy to arouse curiosity (a comparative organizer, in this instance, that causes students to compare what they have observed with what they already knew or thought they knew). Preparing an organizer helps you plan and organize the sequence of ideas, and its presentation helps students organize their own learning and become motivated by it. An advance organizer can also make students' learning meaningful by providing important connections between what they already know and what is being learned. Figure 8.1 is a checklist for reviewing some of the other general guidelines for formal and informal teacher talk.

Figure 8.1
Teacher talk general guidelines: A checklist

When considering teacher talk, I will respond to the following:

1. First, when appropriate, I will begin my talk with an advance organizer.
   Done _____ Somewhat done _____ Needs work _____
   My comments:

2. Second, my talk will be planned so that it has a clear beginning and a distinct end, with a logical order in between.
   Done _____ Somewhat done _____ Needs work _____
   My comments:

3. During my talk, I will reinforce my words with visuals. These visuals can include writing unfamiliar terms on the board (to help my students learn new vocabulary), visual organizers, and prepared graphs, charts, photographs, media support, and various other audiovisuals.
   Done _____ Somewhat done _____ Needs work _____
   My comments:

4. Next, I realize that my pacing will be important. My talk will move briskly, but not too fast. My ability to pace the instruction may be difficult to do because some beginning teachers talk too fast and too much; but this is a skill that I want to develop with experience.
   Done _____ Somewhat done _____ Needs work _____
   My comments:

5. I will constantly remind myself during lessons to slow down, provide silent pauses (allowing for think-time), and allow for frequent checks for student comprehension.
   Done _____ Somewhat done _____ Needs work _____
   My comments:

6. Specifically, my talk will:
   • Be energetic, though not so fast that the students cannot understand what I am saying; I'll have occasional slowdowns to change the pace and to check for student comprehension; I will allow students time to think, ask questions, and make notes.
   Done _____ Somewhat done _____ Needs work _____
   My comments:

   • Have a time plan. I realize that a talk planned for 10 minutes (if interesting to students) will probably take longer. If not interesting to them, it will probably take less time.
   Done _____ Somewhat done _____ Needs work _____
   My comments:

Figure 8.1
Teacher talk general guidelines: A checklist (*continued*)

- Be planned with careful consideration paid to the characteristics of the students. For example, if I have a fairly high percentage of English language learners or students with special needs, then my talk may be less brisk, sprinkled with ever more visuals and repeated statements, and with even more frequent checks for student comprehension.
  Done _____   Somewhat done _____   Needs work _____
  My comments:

- Have questions that I want to ask (as comprehension checks) and will include questions that the students might ask during the lesson as well as various kinds of checklists.
  Done _____   Somewhat done _____   Needs work _____
  My comments:

- Have questions that I want to ask that reflect various degrees of difficulty.
  Done _____   Somewhat done _____   Needs work _____
  My comments:

7. Next, I will encourage student participation. I realize that active participation by the children enhances their learning. I can plan this encouragement through the questions that I ask, through the time allowed for students to comment and ask questions, or through a visual or conceptual outline or other activity that children can complete during the talk.
   Done _____   Somewhat done _____   Needs work _____
   My comments:

8. Last, I will plan a distinct ending or closure. I want to be sure that my talk will have a distinct ending, maybe followed by another activity (during the same or next class period) that will help reinforce and secure the learning further. As for all lessons, I want to strive to plan a clear and interesting beginning, an involved lesson, and a firm and meaningful closure. I realize that proper preparation prevents poor performance.
   Done _____   Somewhat done _____   Needs work _____
   My comments:

Teacher Talk: Specific Guidelines

Some specific guidelines for using teacher talk are presented in Figure 8.2 and discussed briefly in the following text.

More on Specific Guidelines
Understand the Various Purposes for Using Teacher Talk. Teacher talk, formal or informal, can be useful to discuss the progress of a unit of study, explain an inquiry learning situation, or introduce a unit of study. Your talk can present a problem, promote student inquiry learning, or critical thinking. It can provide a transition from one unit of study to the next, provide information otherwise unobtainable to students, and, where appropriate, share your experiences. With teacher talk, you can announce your thoughts about steps in an investigation, introduce a problem or process, or summarize a unit of study. And you can teach a thinking skill by thinking "out loud" to model what can be done in a thinking situation to the students.

Figure 8.2
Specific guidelines for effective teacher talk

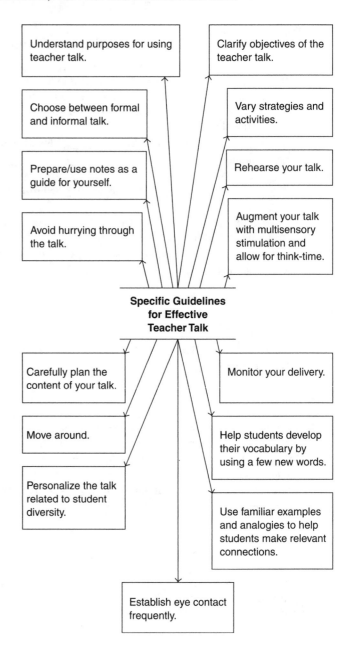

Clarify the Ojectives of the Teacher Talk. Your talk should center around one idea. The learning target objectives, which should not be too numerous for one talk, should be clearly understood by the students.

Choose between Formal and Informal Talk. Long lectures are not appropriate for most, if not all, elementary school teaching; spontaneous interactive informal talks of 5 to 12 minutes are preferred. You should never give long lectures with no teacher— student interaction. If during your student teaching, you have doubts or questions about your selection and use of a particular instructional strategy, discuss your concern with your host teacher or your university supervisor, or both. When you have doubts about the appropriateness of a particular strategy, trust your

instincts: Without some modification, the strategy probably is inappropriate.

Remember also that today's young people are of the media generation; they are accustomed to highly stimulating video interactions and commercial breaks. For some lessons, (especially those that are teacher centered), student attention is likely to begin to stray after about 10 minutes. For that eventuality, you need elements planned to recapture student attention. These planned elements can include a temporary strategy and modality shift, such as more student interaction, that can include a teacher demonstration or a student inquiry. You can:

- Ask students to turn to students on their right and tell them what they learned so far about _____ (topic) in no more than three sentences.

Figure 8.3
Comparison of recapturing student attention by changing the instructional strategy

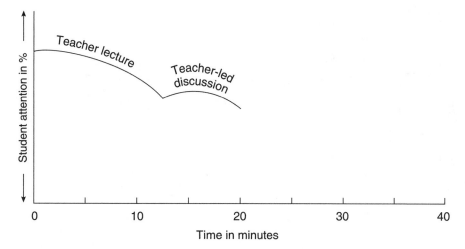

Example 1: Changing from teacher talk (lecture) to more teacher talk (e.g., teacher-led discussion).

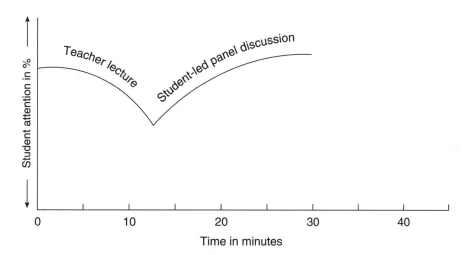

Example 2: Changing from teacher talk (teacher-centered activity) to student-led panel discussion (student-centered activity).

(continued)

- Use analogies to help connect the topic to students' life experiences.
- Use verbal cues such as voice inflections.
- Use pauses to allow reflection about the information.
- Use humor and visual cues such as media presentations, slides, overhead transparencies, charts, board drawings, excerpts from videodiscs, real objects (realia), or body gestures.
- Use sensory cues, such as eye contact and proximity (as in moving around the room, or casually standing close to a student without interrupting your talk).
- Ask students to show their points of view by putting their thumbs up if they agree with _____.

Vary Strategies and Activities Frequently. For the teacher, perhaps the most useful strategy for recapturing student attention is that of changing to an en-

tirely different activity or learning modality. For example, from teacher talk (a teacher-centered strategy) you would change to a student activity (a student-centered strategy). Notice that changing from a lecture (mostly teacher talk) to a teacher-led discussion (mostly more teacher talk) would not be changing to an entirely different modality. Figure 8.3 provides a comparison of different changes.

As a generalization, when using teacher-centered direct instruction, with most groups of children, you will want to change the learning activities about every 10 to 12 minutes. (That is one reason why, in the sample lesson plan format in Chapter 7, you found space for at least four activities, including the introduction and closure.) Although this will vary due to several variables, such as the grade level of the students, the number of students in the class, the subject being

Figure 8.3
Comparison of recapturing student attention by changing the instructional strategy (*continued*)

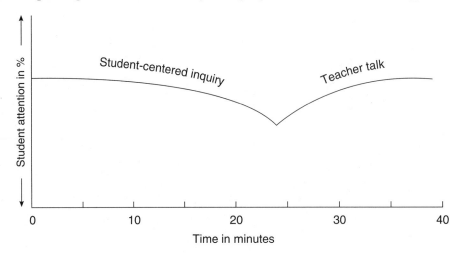

Example 3: Changing from inquiry (student-centered) to teacher-talk fueled by student questions from inquiry.

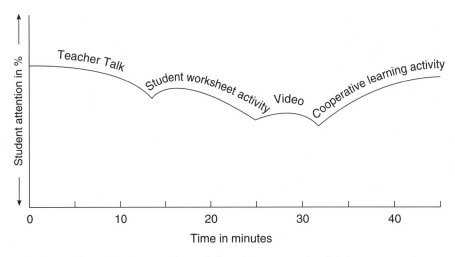

Example 4: Changing from teacher talk (teacher-centered activity) to cooperative learning activity (student-centered activity).

taught (math? art? reading?), generally this means that in a 60-minute time block, you can plan from three to five sequenced learning activities, with one or two activities that are teacher centered and others that are more student centered. In exemplary grade K–6 classrooms, some teachers often have several activities being performed concurrently by children as individuals, in dyads, and in small groups; that is, they are using multilevel (multitasking) instruction. Multitasking is, as we have mentioned in this resource guide, highly recommended as a viable strategy when teaching a classroom of 15 or more students. An example of multitasking is shown in Chapter 2.

Prepare and Use Notes as a Guide for Yourself during Your Talk. Planning your talk and preparing

notes to be used during formal and informal teacher talk is important—just as important as implementing the talk with visuals. There is absolutely nothing wrong with using notes during your teaching. As you move around the room, your notes can be carried on your eye-catching neon-colored clipboard. Your notes for a formal talk can first be prepared in narrative form; whenever appropriate, though, for class use, try to use an outline form. Talks to students should always be from an outline, never read directly from prose. The only time that a teacher's reading from prose aloud to students is appropriate is when reading a story or a poem or when reading a brief published article from a newspaper or a magazine. Also, on rare occasions, a teacher might read aloud carefully formulated questions from his or her lesson plan notes.

In your outline (perhaps a computer-generated outline), consider using coding with abbreviated visual cues to yourself. You will eventually develop your own coding system; whatever coding system you use, keep it simple so that you will always remember what the codes mean. Consider these examples of coding: Where transitions of ideas occur or you want to pause or allow students a silent moment to reflect on the idea, mark *P* for *pause, T* for a *transition,* or *S* for a moment of *silence.* Where a computer presentation, slide projector, or other visual aid will be used, mark *C* for *computer* or *AV* for *audiovisual.* Where you intend to stop and ask a question, mark *TQ* for teacher question, and mark *SQ* or *?* where you want to stop and allow time for student questions. Where you plan to have a discussion, mark *D* or mark *SG* when you plan small-group work and use *I* or *L* where you plan to switch to an investigation or a laboratory-simulated approach; for reviews and comprehension checks, mark *R* and *CC,* respectively.

Share your note organization with the students. Teach them how to take notes and what kinds of things they should write down. If you wish, use colored chalk or marking pens on an overhead transparency, the writing board, or classroom chart to outline and highlight your teacher talk. If it is part of your instructional design, have your students use colored pencils for taking notes so their notes can be color coded to match your writing board notes.

Rehearse Your Talk. Rehearsing your planned talk is the mark of a professional teacher and is important; you want to be good at what you do, especially giving a talk to your students. Using your lesson plan as your guide, rehearse your talk using a camcorder or while talking into a mirror or to a friend or roommate. Is the pacing proper—not too fast and not too slow? Are you speaking clearly? Are your choice of words, voice tone, and body language conveying professionalism and your thorough preparation and confidence? Do you want to include a time plan for each subtopic to allow you to gauge your timing during implementation of the talk?

Avoid Racing Through the Talk Solely to Complete It by a Certain Time. It is more important for students to understand some of what you say than to cover it all and have them understand none of it. If you do not finish, continue it later.

Augment Your Talk with Multisensory Stimulation and Allow for Think-Time. Your presentation should not overly rely on verbal communication. When using visuals, such as photographs, computer screen projections, video excerpts, or overhead transparencies, do not think that you must talk constantly. After clearly explaining the purpose of a visual, give the students sufficient time to look at it, to think about it, and to ask questions about it. If the visual is new to the students, give them time to take it in. Also, be sure you're not blocking their view of the visual. Be sure the visual is large enough for students in the back of the classroom/group to see clearly.

Carefully Plan the Content of Your Talk. The content of your talk should supplement and enhance the material found in the student textbook rather than simply rehash information from the textbook. Students may never read their book if you tell them in an interesting and condensed fashion everything they need to know from it.

Monitor Your Delivery. On one hand, your voice should be pleasant and interesting to listen to rather than a steady, boring monotone or a constantly shrieking, irritating, high pitch. On the other hand, it is a positive teaching attribute to show enthusiasm for what you are talking about during teaching and learning. Occasionally, use dramatic voice inflections to emphasize important points and meaningful body language to give students a visual focus. Practice these skills so they become second nature.

Avoid Standing in the Same Spot for Long Periods of Time. As is always the case when teaching, move around and consider that standing for 10 minutes in the same spot may be too long. You want to monitor student behavior during explicit instruction and use proximity (moving closer to a student) and signal intervention cues (e.g., eye contact, body language, smiles or frowns, have students move response cards up or down to agree or disagree, or use other forms of Every Pupil Response [EPR]) to keep students focused. It is especially during extended periods of explicit instruction that a beginning teacher's skills in with-itness and overlapping behaviors are likely to be put to the test.

View the Vocabulary of Your Talk as an Opportunity to Help Students with New Vocabulary. The children should easily understand the words you use, though you can still model professionalism and help the students develop new vocabulary further. During your lesson planning, predict when you are likely to use a word that is new to most students, and plan to stop to ask a student to help explain its meaning and perhaps demonstrate its derivation. Some teachers first invite students to explain the way the students' textbook (or dictionary, glossary) defines the word and then define the word by demonstrating something about it. Next, students can define the word by describing something about the word and, last, define the word by displaying an illustration that helps show something about the definition of the word or part of it. When you help students with word meaning in these ways, students tend to remember better.

Remember That All Teachers Are Language Arts Teachers. Knowledge of words and their meanings is an important component of skilled reading and includes the ability to generate new words from roots and add prefixes and suffixes. For some students, nearly every subject in the curriculum is like a foreign language. That is certainly true for some English language learners, for whom teacher talk, especially formal teacher talk, should be used sparingly—if at all. Every elementary schoolteacher has the responsibility of helping children learn how to learn, and that includes helping students develop their word comprehension skills, reading skills, thinking and memory skills, and their motivation for learning.

Give Thoughtful and Intelligent Consideration to Student Diversity. During the planning phase, while preparing your talk, consider the children in your classroom who are culturally and linguistically different and those who have special needs. Personalize the talk for them by choosing your vocabulary carefully and appropriately, speaking slowly and methodically, and repeating often, and by planning meaningful analogies, giving examples, and having relevant audio and visual displays.

Use Familiar Examples and Analogies to Help Students Make Relevant Connections (links, bridges). Although this step sometimes takes a great deal of creative thinking as well as action during the planning phase, it is important that you attempt to connect the talk with ideas and events with which the students are already familiar (such as the names of events, places, and people from their neighborhood and community). The most effective teacher talk is talk that makes frequent and meaningful connections between what students already know and what they are learning.

Establish Eye Contact Frequently. Your primary eye contact should be with your students—always! This important point cannot be overemphasized. Only momentarily should you look at your computer screen, your notes, your visuals, the projection screen, the writing board, the bulletin board, and other adults or objects in the classroom. While you will probably raise your eyebrows when you read this, it is true and it is important that with practice, you can learn to scan a classroom of 30 students, establishing eye contact with each student at least once a minute. To establish eye contact means that the student is aware that you are looking at him or her. Frequent eye contact can have two major benefits. First, as you "read" a child's

body posture and facial expressions, you obtain important clues about that student's attentiveness and comprehension. Second, eye contact helps to establish rapport between you and a student. A look with a smile or a headshake from the teacher to a child can say so much! Be alert, though, for children who are from cultures where eye contact is infrequent or even unwanted and could have negative consequences.

Frequent eye contact is easier when using an overhead projector than when bending down to look at the computer screen or using the writing board. When using a computer screen, you have to bend your head down, and when using a writing board, you have to turn at least partially away from your audience, and you may also have to pace back and forth from the board to the students to be able to retain that important proximity to them.

While talking to the children, you must be alert and demonstrate your with-itness; that is, you must stay aware and attentive to everything that is happening in the classroom, such as student behavior as well as the content of your talk. No one ever said that good teaching is easy; if they did, they didn't know what they were talking about. But don't be dismayed: With the knowledge of the preceding guidelines, the cautions that follow, and with practice, experience, and intelligent reflection, you will quickly develop the skills important to an accomplished teacher.

Teacher Talk: Cautions

Whether your talk is formal or informal, you need to be mindful of certain cautions when teaching. Perhaps the most important caution is that of talking too much. If a teacher talks too much, the significance of the teacher's words may be lost because some students will tune the teacher out.

Another caution, we repeat, is to avoid talking too fast. Your students can hear faster than they can comprehend what they hear. It is also important to remember that your one brain is communicating with the brains of your many students, each of whom responds to the sensory input (auditory in this instance) at different rates. Because of this, you will need to (1) pause to let the students reflect on the words, (2) pause to repeat important ideas, and (3) pause during transitions from one point or from one activity to the next to allow each of those students to make the necessary shift in their thinking. It is a good idea to remind yourself to talk slowly and to check frequently for student comprehension of what you are talking about. One student said the following to a teacher after a teacher talk: "You were telling me more than I wanted to know."

A third caution is to be sure you are being heard and understood. Sometimes, teachers talk in too low a pitch, or use words that are not understood by many of the students, or both. You should vary the pitch of your voice, and you should stop and help students with their understanding of vocabulary that may be new to them.

A fourth caution is to remember that just because students have heard something before does not necessarily mean that they understood it or learned it. From our earlier discussions of learning experiences (such as the learning experiences ladder in Chapter 7), remember that, although verbal communication is an important form of communication, because of its reliance on the use of abstract symbolization, it is not always a very reliable form of communication. Teacher talk relies on words and on skill in listening, a skill that is not mastered easily by many children (or for that matter, even many adults). For that and other reasons, to ensure student understanding, it is good to reinforce your teacher talk with either explicit or simulated learning experiences.

A related caution is to resist believing that children have attained a skill or have mastered content that was taught previously by you or by another teacher. During any discussion, rather than assuming that your students know something, you should ensure they know it. For example, if the discussion and a student activity involve a particular thinking skill, you should make sure that students know how to use that skill. (Thinking skills are discussed later in Chapter 9.)

Our last caution is to avoid talking in a humdrum monotone. Children need teachers whose voices exude enthusiasm and excitement (though not to be overdone) about the subject and about teaching and learning. A voice that demonstrates enthusiasm for teaching and learning is more likely to motivate children to learn. Enthusiasm and excitement for learning are contagious.

QUESTIONING

A strategy that is of fundamental importance to any mode of instruction is questioning. You will use questioning for so many purposes that you must be skilled in its use to teach effectively. Because it is so important, and because it is so frequently used and abused, the rest of this chapter is devoted to assisting you in the development of your skills in using questioning as an instructional tool.

PURPOSES FOR USING QUESTIONING

You can adapt the type and form of each question to the purpose for which it is asked. The purposes that questions can serve can be separated into five categories, as shown in Figure 8.4 and discussed, with examples, in the next paragraphs.

Figure 8.4
Purpose of questions

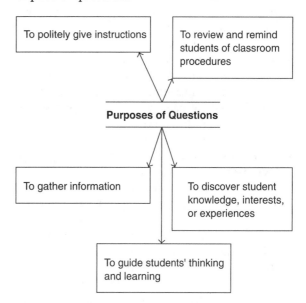

1. **To politely give instructions.** Examples are "Let's move on to the next problem now" or "Lupe, would you please turn out the lights to we can show the slides?" Although they probably should avoid doing so, teachers sometimes use rhetorical questions for the purpose of regaining student attention and maintaining classroom control—for example, "Chris, would you please attend to your work?" Rhetorical questions such as this one can sometimes backfire on the teacher. In this situation, for instance, Chris might say "no." Then the teacher would have a problem that could perhaps have been avoided if the teacher had been more explicit at first and simply told Chris to attend to his work instead of asking him if he would.

Consider the vignette at the beginning of this chapter in the Looking at Teachers section. The kindergarten teacher, Tara, seemed to have a purpose for transitioning from the reading lesson to the mathematics lesson. If Tara was indeed planning to ask the question "Shall we do our math lesson, now?", then she must be prepared to deal with and not ignore the student responses to her question. An improved transition in this instance might be simply to say "It is time for us to do our math lesson" and follow that with a transition statement: "So it's time to put away our reading materials and get out our math papers (books, ruler, etc.)." The teacher can then follow that with a question, such as "Who can review for us one thing that we learned (or did) yesterday in math?"

2. **To review and remind students of classroom procedures.** For example, if students continue to

talk when they shouldn't, you can stop the lesson and say "I think we need to review the procedure for listening when someone else is talking. Who can tell me the procedure for listening that we agreed on at our class meeting?"

3. **To gather information.** Examples are "How many of you are ready to raise your hand to show that you have finished the assignment?" or to find out if a student has knowledge about the topic, "Joe, can you please explain to us the difference between a synonym and antonym?"

4. **To discover student knowledge, interests, or experiences.** Examples include "Where do you think our drinking water comes from?" or "How many of you have visited the local water treatment plant?" or "How many of you (raise your hands or put thumbs up) think you know the process by which water in our city is made drinkable?"

5. **To guide students' thinking and learning.** It is this category of questioning that is the primary focus here. Questions in this category can be used for the following:

   - **To build the curriculum.** It is the students' questions that provide the basis for the learning that occurs in an effective program that is based on inquiry learning and is project centered. More on this subject is given in the next two chapters.

   - **To develop appreciation.** Here's an example: "What do you understand about the water cycle we've been talking about?" or "What is the water cycle?"

   - **To develop student thinking.** For example, "When standing water is sprayed with an insecticide that kills mosquito larvae, what do you suppose the effects to the environment are?"

   - **To diagnose learning difficulty.** For example, "What part of the problem don't you understand, Eric?"

   - **To emphasize major points.** For example, "If no one has ever been to the sun, how do we know what it is made of?"

   - **To encourage students.** Here's an example: "OK, so you didn't remember the whole process. What really impressed me in your writing is what you did understand about photosynthesis. Do you know what part impressed me?"

   - **To establish rapport.** For example, "Do you think we have a conflict here?" "Do you think we can resolve it if we put our heads together?" "What do you think ought to be our first step?"

   - **To evaluate learning.** For example, "Sean, what is the effect when two rough surfaces, such as two slices of toasted bread, are rubbed together?"

   - **To give practice in expression.** Here's an example: "Yvonne, would you please share with us the examples of Impressionism that you found?"

   - **To help students in their metacognition** (that is, their thinking about thinking). For example, "Yes, something did go wrong in the experiment. Do you still think your original hypothesis is correct? If not, then where was the error in your thinking?" or "If you still think your hypothesis is correct, then where might the error have been in the design of your experiment? How might we find out?"

   - **To help students interpret information and materials.** For example, "Something seems to be wrong with this compass. How do you suppose we can find out what is wrong with it? For instance, if the needle is marked N and S in reverse, as suggested by Hannah, how can we find out if that is, in fact, the problem?"

   - **To help students organize information and materials.** Here's an example: "If you really want to carry out your proposed project, then we are going to need certain information and materials. We are going to have to deal with some questions here, such as What information and materials do we think we need? Where can we find those things? Who will be responsible for getting them? and How will we store and arrange them?"

   - **To provide drill and practice.** For example, "Research Team A has prepared some questions that they would like to use as practice questions for our test at the end of the unit; they are suggesting that we use them to play the game of Educational Jeopardy on Friday. Is everyone okay with their suggestion?"

   - **To provide review.** For example, "Today in your groups, you are going to study the unit review questions that I have prepared. After each group has studied and prepared its answers to these written questions, your group will choose another group and ask them your set of review questions. Each group has a different set of questions. Members of Research Team A are going to keep score, and the group that has the highest score from this review session will receive free pizza at tomorrow's lunch. Ready?"

   - **To show agreement or disagreement.** For example, "Some people believe that stricter gun control laws would reduce violence. With evidence that you have collected from recent newspaper articles, magazines, and the Internet, do you agree with this conclusion? Explain why or why not."

Figure 8.5
Questions to avoid in the classroom

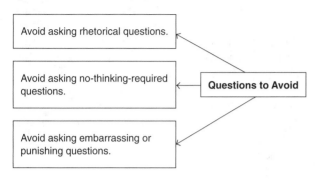

- **To show relationships, such as cause and effect.** Here's an example: "What do you suppose would be the worldwide effect if just one inch of the entire Antarctic ice shelf were to suddenly melt?"

Questions to Avoid Asking

Before reviewing some types of cognitive questions in the next section, take a minute or two to consider the kinds of questions a teacher should avoid asking in the classroom, as shown in Figure 8.5.

Rhetorical and No-Thinking-Required Questions. While it is important to avoid asking rhetorical questions, that is, questions for which you do not intend or even want a response, you should also avoid asking questions that call for little or no student thinking, such as those that can be answered with a simple yes or no or some other sort of alternative answer response. Unless followed up with questions calling for clarification, questions that call for simple yes or no responses have little or no diagnostic value; embarrassing, punishing questions can lead to inappropriate student response that can cause classroom control problems for the teacher.

TYPES OF COGNITIVE QUESTIONS

In this section, we define, describe, and provide examples for each of the different types of cognitive (a process of knowing) questions that you will use in teaching. Although we refer to these types of questions as cognitive questions, we realize that any question type could relate to any of the three domains of learning (cognitive, affective, or psychomotor). In addition, the types of questions are not exclusive or categorically pure. For an example, a question that is classed as a divergent-thinking-type question might also be classed as a focus question, and vice versa. In the discussion that follows, your attention is focused on the levels of cognitive questions. Let's start by looking at Figure 8.6.

Figure 8.6
Types of cognitive questions

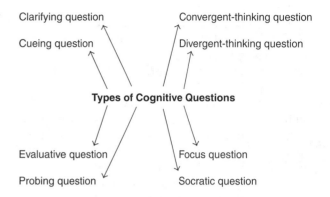

Clarifying Question

The clarifying question is used to gain more information from a student to help the teacher and classmates better understand a student's ideas, feelings, and thought processes. Often, asking a student to elaborate on an initial response will lead the student to think more deeply, restructure his or her thinking, and, while doing so, discover a fallacy in the original response. Examples of clarifying questions are "What I hear you saying, John, is that you would rather work alone than in your group. Is that correct?" "So, Mary, you think the poem is a sad one, is that right?" Research has shown a strong positive correlation between student learning and the development of metacognitive skills and the teacher's use of questions that ask for clarification.[3] In addition, by seeking clarification, you are likely to be demonstrating an interest in the child as a person and in that child's thinking.

Convergent-Thinking Question

Convergent-thinking questions, also called **narrow questions,** are low-order thinking questions that have a single correct answer (such as recall questions, discussed further in the next section). Examples of convergent questions are "How is the Earth classed, as a star or a planet?" "If the radius of a circle is 20 meters, what is its circumference?" "What is the name of the person who was the first president of the United States?" Sometimes, as with the first example, it is good to come back with follow-up questions to move the student's thinking beyond simple recall. With this example, a follow-up question could be "Why is Earth classified as a planet?" or "What characteristics are necessary for a celestial body to be classified as a planet?"

Cueing Question

If you ask a question and wait sufficient wait time (longer than 2 seconds) and no students respond (or their responses indicate they need more information), then you can ask a question that cues the answer or the response you are seeking.[4] In essence, you are going backward in your questioning sequence to cue the students. For instance, in the preceding example, if there were no response then the teacher could ask. "Who can name a characteristic that distinguishes stars and planets?"

As an introduction to a lesson on the study of prefixes, a teacher might ask the students "How many legs each do crayfish, lobsters, and shrimp have?" If there is no accurate response, then the teacher might cue the answer with the following information and question: "The class to which those animals belong is class Decapoda. Does that give you a clue about the number of legs they have?" If that clue is not enough, and after allowing sufficient wait time for students to think (remember, it's longer than 2 seconds), then the teacher might ask "What is a decathlon?" or "What is the Decalogue?" or "In what way does the term *decimal system* give you a clue or hint?" or "What is a decimeter?" or "What is a decibel?" or "What is a decade?"

When questioning students about reading material in particular, consider using the question–answer relationship (QAR) strategy. QAR involves asking a question and, if a student is unable to respond, providing one of three types of cues. The cues are related to the level of thinking required. "Right there" is used for questions for the lowest level, that is, in which the answer can be found explicitly stated in the sentence or paragraph. "Search and think" means the answer is not directly stated and therefore must be inferred. "On your own" is used for highest level critical thinking questions for which the answers are neither explicit nor inferred in the text.[5]

Divergent-Thinking Question

Divergent-thinking questions (also known as **broad,** *reflective, open-ended,* or *thought* questions) usually having no singularly correct answer. These high-order thinking questions require analysis, synthesis, or evaluation. Students must think creatively, leave the comfortable confines of the known, and reach out into the unknown. Examples of questions that require divergent thinking are "What measures could be taken to improve safety in our community?" "What might be done to improve school spirit?" and "Who would like to tell us why they believe there are (or are not) any yet undiscovered planets in our solar system?"

Evaluative Question

Whether convergent or divergent, some questions require students to place a value on something or to take a stance on some issue; these are referred to as **evaluative questions.** If the teacher and the students all agree on certain premises; then the evaluative question would also be a convergent question. If the original assumptions differ, then the response to the evaluative question would be more subjective and, therefore, that evaluative question would be divergent. Examples of evaluative questions are "Should the United States allow clear-cutting in its national forests?" "Should school officials have the right to search student lockers?" and "Is the president of the United States or any other person above the law?"

Focus Question

A focus question is any question that is designed to center and focus student thinking. For example, the first question of the preceding paragraph is a focus question when the teacher asking it is attempting to focus student attention on the economic issues involved in clear-cutting. Deliberately constructed focus questions, such as "Should every citizen have the right to own a gun?," are especially useful for stimulating student interest at the beginning of a unit of instruction such as a unit on the U.S. Constitution.

Probing Question

Similar to a clarifying question, a probing question requires student thinking to go beyond superficial first-answer or single-word responses. Examples of probing questions are "Why, Sean, do you think it to be the case that every citizen has the right to have a gun?" Always be cautious, though, that you do not probe so far that the question embarrasses the student.

Socratic Question

In the fifth century B.C.E., Socrates used the art of questioning so successfully that to this day we still hear of the Socratic method.[6] What, exactly, is the Socratic method? Socrates' method or strategy was to ask his students a series of leading questions that gradually took them up to the point where they had to look carefully at their own ideas and to think rigorously about themselves. The questions focused on challenging assumptions, exposing contradictions, questioning the question, and answering a question with further questions. Today, that strategy is referred to as the Socratic method.

Socratic discussions were informal dialogues that took place in a natural, pleasant environment. Although Socrates sometimes had to go to considerable lengths to ignite his students' intrinsic interest, their response was natural and spontaneous. In his dialogues. Socrates, pretending to know nothing about the subject, tried to aid students in developing ideas.

He did not impose his own notions on the students. Rather, he asked questions to help them find out the truth independently and encouraged them to develop their own conclusions and draw their own inferences. Of course, Socrates may have had preconceived notions about what the final learning should be and carefully aimed his questions so that the students would arrive at the desired conclusions. Still, his questions were open ended, causing divergent rather than convergent thinking. The students were free to go mentally wherever the facts and their thinking led them.

Throughout history, teachers have tried to adapt the methods of Socrates to the classroom. However, we must remember that Socrates used this method in the context of a one-to-one relationship between the student and himself. Some teachers have adapted it for whole-class explicit instruction by asking questions first of one student and then of another, moving slowly about the class. This technique may work, but it is difficult because the underpinning of the Socratic method is to build question upon question in a logical fashion so that each question leads the student a step further toward the understanding sought. When you spread the questions around the classroom, you may find it difficult to build up the desired sequence and to keep all the students involved in the discussion. Sometimes, you may be able to use the Socratic method by directing all of the questions at one student volunteer—at least for several minutes to demonstrate the method—while the other students look on and listen in. That is how Socrates did it. When the topic is interesting enough, this technique can be useful, successful, and even fun, but in the long run, the Socratic method works best when the teacher is working in one-on-one coaching situations or with small groups of children, rather than in whole-class explicit instruction.

STUDENT THINKING AND LEVELS OF COGNITIVE QUESTIONS

Thinking Is the Quintessential Activity. In using Socratic questioning, the focus is on the questions, not answers, and thinking is valued as the quintessential activity.[7] To conduct Socratic questioning, have the student or group identify a student- or teacher-posed question and then ask the students a series of probing questions designed to cause them to examine critically the problem and potential solutions to it. The main thrust of the questioning and the key questions must be planned in advance so that the questioning will proceed logically. To think of quality probing questions on the spur of the moment is too difficult. With guidance from your instructor, you

can decide to use the Socratic method in Application Exercise 8.1 later in this chapter.

Remember, the questions you pose act as cues to your students about the level of thinking expected of them. The levels range from the lowest level of mental operation, requiring simple recall of knowledge (convergent thinking), to the highest, requiring divergent thought and application of that thought. It is important that you be knowledgeable about the levels of thinking, that you understand the importance of attending to student thinking from lower to higher levels of operation, and that you understand that what for one child may be a matter of simple recall of information may for another, require a higher order mental activity, such as figuring something out by deduction.

You should structure and sequence your questions (and assist students in developing their skills in structuring and sequencing questions) in a way that is designed to guide students to higher levels of thinking and to connect their understandings. For example, when children respond to your questions in complete sentences that provide supportive evidence for their ideas, it is fairly safe to assume that their thinking is connected to their knowledge and experiences and is at a higher level than would be the case if the response were an imprecise and nondescriptive single-word answer.

To help your understanding further, three levels of questioning and thinking are described in the following paragraphs.[8] You should recognize the similarity between these three levels of questioning and the six levels of thinking from Bloom's taxonomy of cognitive objectives (Chapter 5). For your daily use of questioning, you will find it just as useful and more practical to think and behave in terms of these three levels, rather than of six:

1. **Lowest level (the data input phase): gathering and recalling information.** At this level, questions are designed to solicit from the students some concepts, information, feelings, or experiences that were gained in the past and stored in memory. This is the level where you focus on the following key words and desired behaviors:

   complete, count, define, describe, identify, list, match, name, observe, recall, recite, select

   Thinking involves receiving data through the sensory receptors (the senses), followed by the processing of those data. Inputting without processing is brain-dysfunctional. Information that has not been processed is stored only in short-term memory.

2. **Intermediate level (the data processing phase): processing information.** At this level, questions are designed to draw relationships

about cause and effect, to synthesize, analyze, summarize, compare, contrast, or classify data. This is the level where you ask the students to respond to the following key words and desired behaviors:

analogy making, analyze, classify, compare, contrast, distinguish, explain, group, infer, organize, plan, synthesize

Thinking and questioning that involve processing of information can be conscious or unconscious. When students observe you, the teacher, modeling your thinking aloud, and when you urge them to think aloud and analyze their thinking as it occurs, you are helping them in the process of developing their intellectual skills.

At the processing level, this internal analysis of new data may challenge a student's preconceptions (and misconceptions—also called **naive theories**) about a phenomenon. The student's brain will naturally resist this challenge to his or her existing beliefs. The greater the mental challenge, the greater the brain's effort to draw on data already in storage. With increasing data, the mind will gradually examine existing concepts and ultimately, as necessary, develop new mental concepts.

If there is a match between new input and existing mental concepts, no problem exists. Piaget called this process **assimilation.**[9] If, however, in processing new data there is no match with existing mental concepts, then the situation is what Piaget called **cognitive disequilibrium.** The brain is "discontent" with this disequilibrium and will drive the search for an explanation for the discrepancy. Piaget called this process **accommodation.**

Although learning is enhanced by challenge, in situations that are threatening, the brain is less flexible in accommodating new ideas. As discussed in Chapter 4, that is why each student must feel welcomed in the classroom and the classroom environment must be perceived by the student as challenging but nonthreatening—what is referred to as an environment of **relaxed alertness.**[10]

Questions and experiences must be designed to elicit more than merely recalled memory responses (see the accompanying *Technology Tips for the Classroom* feature). Many teachers find it useful to use strategies that create cognitive disequilbrium, such as to demonstrate discrepant events in order to introduce lessons and concepts. Hearing about or especially seeing a discrepancy stirs the mind into processing and into higher mental activity, without which, mental development does not occur. (See the examples in Figure 8.7 and in Figure 8.8.)

Figure 8.7
Example of a discrepant event demonstration

Combustible Won't Burn

Practice this first. Wrap a dollar bill (or a $20 if you are confident) around a drinking glass. While holding the bill tightly around the glass, try to ignite the bill with a match or lighter. The paper bill will not ignite because the glass conducts the heat away too rapidly, maintaining the paper below its kindling point. After removing the bill from the glass you may (if you wish and are wealthy) ignite the bill for a moment to prove to the children that it will indeed burn.

Technology Tips for the Classroom

- To serve as a motivator and to use when a student finishes his or her regular assignments and has improved in academic work performance, consider using a portable DVD player in the classroom and giving permission for the student to work on it and give you a report on the information gained from the DVD educational material. You can give the student a teacher-constructed DVD information form for completion while watching the information. Have the student hand the form back to you when finished so you can review the student's notes to determine the educational value of what was learned at the DVD player.

- Consider developing a learning activity to support a study that is going on in the classroom. For example, you and the students can create eye masks that correlate with a topic of study. Use the digital camera to take pictures of each student with and without the mask. Print the photos and ask the students to match up the pairs of photos for each student. At the end of the unit of study, hand a matched pair of photos to each student and ask that they write paragraphs explaining, generally, what they learned from the unit of study and, specifically, what they learned about the person/people whom the mask represents. Send the photos and the paragraphs home with the students. Here are additional suggestions—if the students are:
  - **in kindergarten** and studying workers now and long ago, they might make eye masks that represent workers they know about;
  - **in first grade,** the students might make eye masks that reflect workers in their neighborhood;

Figure 8.8
Examples of questions that use appropriate cognitive terminology

Instead of	Say
"How else might it be done?"	"How could you *apply. . . ?*"
"Are you going to get quiet?"	"If we are going to hear what Joan has to say, what do you need to do?"
"How do you know that is so?"	"What evidence do you have?"
"What do you think might happen?"	"What do you *predict* might happen?"

- **in second grade,** they can create eye masks that represent people who supply a neighborhood's needs, i.e., farmers, orchardists, dairy workers, and people who move the food from the farm to the market;
- **in third grade,** the students can decorate eye masks that represent some of the early people who lived in their geographic region;
- **in fourth grade,** they can make eye masks that represent different people who formed part of an immigration group into their state;
- **in fifth grade,** the students can create eye masks that represent people living in one of the time periods being studied, i.e., America's War for Independence;
- **in sixth grade,** they can decorate eye masks that represent people living in the areas of early civilizations being studied, e.g., Near East, Africa, Mesopotamia, Egypt, Greeks, India, and China.
- Students with access to computers can practice and prepare for the state-mandated standardized tests online. In schools with the required computer technology and with the appropriate number of computers to provide access time to individual students, selected software programs can help students prepare for the tests. Proponents of such online preparation argue that a major advantage is the immediate scoring of practice testing with feedback about each student's areas of weakness, thereby providing the teacher with information necessary for immediate remediation. If their arguments are accurate, then it would seem that students of such technology-rich schools would clearly be at an advantage over students in schools where this technology is not available. It would follow that district and government agencies that mandate the standards and specific assessment practices should provide avenues and tools to ensure equity and success for all students in reaching the expected learning outcomes within the designated learning time. Contact your curriculum resource representative to ask about software programs that are recommended for your district.

Companion Website

To find links to resources about questioning, go to our Companion Website at **www.prenhall.com/ roberts** and click on the *Web Destinations* module for Chapter 8.

3. **Highest level (the data output phase): applying and evaluating in new situations.** At the highest level of thinking, questions are designed to encourage learners to think intuitively, creatively, and hypothetically; to use their imagination; to expose a value system; or to make a judgment. This is the level at which you encourage the students to get involved with the following key words and desired behaviors:

apply a principle, build a model, evaluate, extrapolate, forecast, generalize, hypothesize, imagine, judge, predict, speculate

You must use questions at the level best suited for the purpose, use a variety of questions at different levels, and structure questions in a way intended to move student thinking to higher levels. When teachers use higher level questions, their students tend to score higher on tests of critical thinking and on standardized tests of achievement.[11]

With the use of questions as a strategy to move student thinking to higher levels, the teacher is facilitating the students' intellectual development. Developing your skill in using questions requires attention to detail and practice. The guidelines and exercises that follow in this chapter will provide that detail and some initial practice, but first, to check your comprehension about the various levels of questions, turn to our Companion Website **(www.prenhall.com/ roberts),** click on the *Additional Application Exercises* module for this chapter, and do the application exercise titled Identifying the Cognitive Levels of Questions—A Self-Check Exercise.

GUIDELINES FOR USING QUESTIONING

As emphasized many times in several ways throughout this resource guide, the goals for instruction extend far beyond merely filling students' minds with bits and pieces of information that will likely last only a brief time in their short-term memory. You must help your students learn how to solve problems, to make intelligent decisions and value judgments, to think creatively and critically, and to feel good about themselves, their school community, and their learning. How you construct your questions and how you implement questioning are important to the realization of these goals.

Preparing Questions

When preparing questions, consider these two important tenets:

- Key questions should be planned, thoughtfully worded, and written into your lesson plan.
- Match questions with their target purposes.

Key Questions Should Be Planned, Thoughtfully Worded, and Written into Your Lesson Plan. Thoughtful preparation of questions helps to ensure that they are clear, specific, and not ambiguous; that the vocabulary is appropriate for the children's understanding; and that each question matches its purpose. Incorporate questions into your lessons as instructional devices, welcomed pauses, attention grabbers, and as checks for student comprehension. Thoughtful teachers even plan questions that they intend to ask specific students, targeting questions to the readiness level, interest, or learning profile of a student.

Match Questions with Their Target Purposes. Careful planning of questions allows them to be sequenced and worded to match the levels of cognition expected of students. To help students in developing their thinking skills, you need to demonstrate how to do this. To demonstrate, you must use terminology that is specific and that provides students with examples of experiences consonant with the meanings of the cognitive words. Explicitly using cognitive terms with students—terms such as *apply, interpret,* and *predict*—encourages the construction of new mental concepts.[12] Again, refer to the examples in Figure 8.8.

Implementing Questioning

Careful preparation of questions is one part of the skill of questioning. Implementation is the other part. Figure 8.9 presents a checklist of teaching behaviors that you should reflect on related to effective implementation of questioning.[13]

 Companion Website
Turn to our Companion Website **(www.prenhall.com/roberts)**, click on the *Additional Content* module for this chapter, and find out more about Implementing Questioning.

QUESTIONS FROM STUDENTS: THE QUESTION-DRIVEN CLASSROOM

Student questions can and should be used as springboards for further questioning, discussions, and inquiry learning. Indeed, in a constructivist learning environment, student questions often drive content. Children should be encouraged to ask questions that challenge the textbook, the process, the Internet source, or other persons' statements, and they should be encouraged to seek the supporting evidence behind a statement.

Being able to ask questions may be more important than having the right answers. Knowledge is derived from asking questions. Being able to recognize problems and to formulate questions is a skill and the key to problem solving and critical-thinking skill development. You have a responsibility to encourage children in your classroom to formulate questions and to help them word their questions in such a way that tentative answers can be sought. That is the process necessary to build a base of knowledge that can be drawn on whenever necessary to link, interpret, and explain new information in new situations.

Now, to better understand the art of questioning, the importance of well-worded questions and well-prepared and clear instructions, and the importance of allowing students time to think, go to our Companion Website **(www.prenhall.com/roberts)**, click on the *Additional Application Exercises* module for this chapter, and complete the application exercise titled Wait Time and the Art of Questioning: An In-Class Simulation.

Questioning: The Cornerstone of Critical Thinking, Real-World Problem Solving, and Meaningful Learning

Real-world problem solving usually offers no absolute correct answers. Rather than "correct" answers, some are better than others. The student with a problem needs to learn how to (a) recognize the problem, (b) formulate a question about the problem (e.g., Should I hang out with this person or not? Should I tell what I know or not? Should I join the gang or not?

Figure 8.9
A reflection list after implementing questioning

After implementing questioning in your teaching, respond and reflect on the following:

1. I always ask a well-worded question *before* calling on a student for a response.
   Always _____   Sometimes _____   Forgot _____
   My comments:

2. I avoid bombarding my students with too much teacher talk.
   Always _____   Sometimes _____   Forgot _____
   My comments:

3. Before I ask a question, I provide students with adequate time (wait time) to think.[13]
   Always _____   Sometimes _____   Forgot _____
   My comments:

4. I can give the same minimum amount of wait time (think-time) to all students.
   Always _____   Sometimes _____   Forgot _____
   My comments:

5. I practice gender equality.*
   Always _____   Sometimes _____   Forgot _____
   My comments:

6. I practice calling on all students.
   Always _____   Sometimes _____   Forgot _____
   My comments:

7. I ask that the student raise their hands to be called on.
   Always _____   Sometimes _____   Forgot _____
   My comments:

8. I actively involve as many students as possible in any question–answer discussion session.
   Always _____   Sometimes _____   Forgot _____
   My comments:

9. I can carefully gauge my responses to students' responses to the questions.
   Always _____   Sometimes _____   Forgot _____
   My comments:

10. I use strong praise sparingly.
    Always _____   Sometimes _____   Forgot _____
    My comments:

_____

*Some teachers use the term *gender equality* in the classroom with clear statements such as "I have just called on two boys—so to practice gender equality, I will call on a girl now." When a girl answers a question, the teacher can ask the student to call on a boy to answer the next question and vice versa, thus involving the students in efforts to include girls and boys equally.

Should I use illegal drugs or not?), (c) collect data, and (d) arrive at a temporarily acceptable answer to the problem, while realizing that at some later time, new data may indicate that a review of the former conclusion is required. For instance, if a biochemist believes that she has discovered a new enzyme, there is no textbook or teacher or any other outside authoritative source to which she may refer to find out if she is correct. Rather, on the basis of her self-confidence in problem identification, asking questions, collecting sufficient data, and arriving at a tentative conclusion based on those data, she assumes that, for now, her conclusion is safe.

Can You Encourage Students to Ask Questions About Content and Process? Question asking often indicates that the inquirer is curious, puzzled, and uncertain; it is a sign of being engaged in thinking about a topic. And yet, in too many classrooms, too few students ask questions.[14] Students should be encouraged to ask questions. Actually, children are naturally curious and full of questions. Their natural curiosity should never be stifled. After all, we learn in school that what is called *knowledge* is in reality the answers to other people's prior questions.

From children, there is no such thing as a "dumb" question. Sometimes, though, in a classroom situation, students, like everyone else, ask questions that could just as easily have been looked up or are seemingly irrelevant or show a lack of thought or sensitivity. Those questions can consume precious class time. For a teacher, they can be frustrating (but we remind you of an anonymous saying we've heard: "The fool wonders while the wise person asks"). A teacher's initial reaction may be to quickly and mistakenly brush off that type of question with sarcasm, while assuming that the student is too lazy to look up an answer. In such instances, you are advised to think before responding and to respond kindly and professionally, although in the busy life of a classroom teacher, that may not always be so easy to remember to do.

Some teachers keep blank slips of paper on their desks and when faced with such questions, they (sparingly) hand a blank slip to the student, ask the student to write the question down for their "teacher homework," and say they'll return the paper with their response to the student the next day. (The paper is often returned at the end of the next day as the student leaves the classroom to allow for student reflection in the afternoon and evening.) Other teachers ask the students to monitor themselves and their questions by considering if their questions are on track with the discussion. If it is not, then the students are handed a "Hold That Thought" slip of paper (sometimes, small pieces of art paper) from a container or holder on the wall. The students write their questions on the paper slips, the teacher collects them, reads them, and answers them during the last 5 minutes of the class, or at the end of the school day, or during a pause in the lesson.

Be assured that there is a reason for a student's question, albeit, it may be the student is signaling a need for recognition or simply demanding attention. In a large school, it is sometimes easy for a child to feel alone and insignificant (though this seems less the case with schools where teachers and students work together in teams and, as in looping, where one cadre of teachers remains with the same cohort of children for 2 or more years).[15] When a child makes an effort to interact with you, this can be a positive sign, so gauge carefully your responses to these efforts. If a child's question is really off the topic, off the wall, out of order, and out of the context of the lesson, consider this as a possible response: "This is an involved question (or comment), and I would very much like to talk with you more about it. Could we talk at lunch or recess time?"

Will You Avoid Bluffing an Answer to a Question for Which You Do Not Have an Answer? Nothing will cause you to lose credibility with children any faster than faking an answer. There is nothing wrong with admitting that you do not know. It helps children realize that you are human. It helps them maintain adequate self-esteem, realizing that they are okay. What *is* important is that you know where and how to find possible answers and that you help children develop that same knowledge and those same process skills. There is nothing wrong with walking over to the desk and picking up a dictionary or encyclopedia, or searching web later to model the process of searching for information that one does not readily have available. Now, to reinforce your understanding of questioning, do Application Exercise 8.1.

Companion Website

To continue to reinforce your understanding of how questioning is used in the classroom, go to our Companion Website at **www.prenhall.com/roberts** and click on the *Additional Content* and *Additional Application Exercises* modules for Chapter 8.

APPLICATION EXERCISE 8.1 PRACTICE IN RAISING QUESTIONS TO HIGHER LEVELS

Instructions: The purpose of this exercise is to develop your skill in raising questions from one level to the next higher level. Complete the blank spaces with questions at the appropriate levels, then share and discuss your responses with your classmates.

Recall Level	Processing Level	Application and Evaluation Level
1. How many of you read a newspaper today?	Why did you read a newspaper today?	What do you think would happen if nobody ever read a newspaper again?
2. What was today's newspaper headline?	Why was that topic important enough to be a headline?	Do you think that news item will be in tomorrow's paper?
3. Who is the vice president of the United States?	How does the work he has done compare with that done by the previous vice president?	
4. Has the United States had a woman president?		
5. (Create your own questions.)		

For Your Notes

About Praxis and Other Teacher Tests

About Praxis Teacher Tests. To continue to support your interest in preparing for a Praxis II Principles of Learning and Teaching test, all of the application exercises related to this chapter offer opportunities for you to reflect generally about teacher talk and questioning as important instructional tools. For example, in this chapter, precredentialed teachers are asked to participate cooperatively and collaboratively and to do the following:

- Develop a skill in raising questions from one level to the next higher level (Application Exercise 8.1).
- Turn to our Companion Website (**www.prenhall.com/roberts**) and click on the *Additional Application Exercise* module to complete the additional applications exercises for this chapter to test your understanding and recognition of the three levels of questions; to further your understanding of the art and power of questioning, the importance of well-worded questions, and the value of allowing students time to think; to discover the level of questions found in instructional materials; to receive practice in writing cognitive questions; to practice preparing and asking questions designed to lead student thinking; and to assess your understanding of the use of certain facilitative behaviors, including questioning.

You can find a constructed response-type question similar to those found on the Praxis II tests in the Praxis Warm-Up section that follows the Chapter Summary. This warm-up takes another look at the classroom vignette found in the Looking at Teachers section at the beginning of this chapter.

 Other Teacher Tests. For those of you who will be teaching in states that do not administer the Praxis II Principles of Learning and Teaching tests, go to our Companion Website at **www.prenhall.com/roberts** and click on the *Other Teacher Tests* module for Chapter 8 to access information about teacher tests other than the Praxis.

SUMMARY

This chapter presented guidelines about formal and informal teacher talk and another significant teaching strategy, questioning. Both of these are perhaps the two most important strategies in your repertoire. It's possible that no other strategy is used more by teachers than teacher talk, and questioning is the cornerstone to meaningful learning, thinking, communication, and real-world problem solving. You reviewed the purposes for using questions, questions to avoid asking, and different types of cognitive questions. After the review, you practiced raising questions to higher levels. You realize that the art of using teacher talk and questioning as instructional devices and as learning tools is something you will continue to develop throughout your teaching career.

What's to Come. In the following two chapters, your attention is directed to the selection and implementation of specific instructional strategies to further facilitate students' meaningful learning of skills and content of the curriculum and to see how teachers group children in the classroom.

EXTENDING MY PROFESSIONAL COMPETENCY

Praxis Warm-Up: A Constructed Response-Type Question

Recall in this chapter's opening that at the completion of an opening reading lesson, the kindergarten teacher, Tara, asked the children the question "Shall we do our math lesson now?" and Tara got the answer "no" from one of the students. Tara ignored the student's remark and started the math lesson.

Consider what might be done to improve instruction in Tara's class through the use of questions and/or teacher talk. Draft two questions: one that the students could respond to at the completion of the reading lesson and then, a second question to assist the transition into the math lesson. The questions should not have one-word answers.

Hints for responding to Praxis Warm-Ups are found in the Appendix.

Praxis. To do another Praxis Warm-Up with a constructed response-type question, go to our Companion Website at **www.prenhall.com/roberts** and click on the *Praxis Warm-Up* module for Chapter 8. Constructed response-type questions are designed to help you prepare for the Praxis II Principles of Learning and Teaching tests. ✍

For Your Discussion

1. **Teacher Talk.** How will I respond if a colleague asks me about cautions that teachers need to be aware of when using teacher talk? **To do:** Review some of the cautions listed in this chapter, and describe them as you would to a teaching colleague.

2. **Advance Mental Organizers.** What would I say if a principal asked me, during a job interview, to describe when, if ever, and how I would use an advance mental organizer with a class of my choice? **To do:** Research advance mental organizers and then describe the value, purpose, and types of advance mental organizers that can be used as an instructional strategy.

3. **Levels/Types of Questions.** What would I reply if a teaching colleague said, "Have you ever noticed that some teachers seem to anticipate a lower level response to their questions from particular students? What do you think about that?" **To do:** Research HOTS (higher order thinking skills) by reading Stanley Pogrow's article titled HOTS: Helping Low Achievers in Grades 4–8 in *Principal* (November, 1996), accessed March 21, 2005, at *www.hots.org/article_helping.html.* Discuss your answer with your peers.

4. **Raising Questions from One Level to the Next.** What would I reply to a colleague if he or she asked how I developed my skill in raising questions from one level to the next higher level? **To do:** Review Application Exercise 8.1, Practice in Raising Questions to Higher Levels, and formulate a response for the colleague.

5. **Importance of Well-Worded Questions and Time to Think.** When questioned by a parent, in what way would I support (or not support) a teacher who plans and writes the questions they ask children during a lesson? Support (or not support) a teacher who engages in wait-time? **To do:** With a colleague, discuss a possible explanation of what you would say to the parent.

Online Portfolio Activities

Supporting Principles 3, 4, and 5 of INTASC and Standards 2, 3, and 4 of NBPTS: At the Companion Website

(www.prenhall.com/roberts), click on the *Online Portfolio Activities* module to continue your online portfolio supporting knowledge of students. ✍

 Companion Website
Also on the Companion Website at **www.prenhall.com/roberts**, you can measure your understanding of chapter content in the *Objectives* and *Self-Check* modules and apply concepts in the *For Your Discussion* module.

FOR FURTHER READING

Brualdi, A. C. (1998). *Classroom Questions* (ED422407). Washington, DC: ERIC Clearinghouse on Assessment and Evaluation.

Chappell, M. F., and Thompson, D. R. (1999). Modifying Our Questions to Assess Students' Thinking. *Mathematics Teaching in the Middle School, 4*(7), 470–474.

Costa, A., and Garmston, R. (2001). Five Human Passions: The Source of Critical and Creative Thinking. In A. Costa (Ed.), *Developing Minds, A Resource Book for Teaching Thinking.* Alexandria, VA: Association for Supervision and Curriculum Development.

Cross, C. T., and Rigden, D. W. (2002). Improving teacher quality. *American School Board Journal, 189*(4), 24–27.

Danna, S. (2003, February/March). Pursuing National Board Certification. *Pi Lambda Theta Educational Horizons,* p. 5.

Deal, D., and Sterling, D. (1997). Kids Ask the Best Questions. *Educational Leadership, 54*(6), 61–63.

Gauthier, L. R. (2000). The Role of Questioning: Beyond Comprehension's Front Door. *Reading Horizons, 40*(4), 239–252.

Gibson, J. (1998). Any Questions, Any Answers? *Primary Science Review, 51,* 20–12.

Good, T. L., and Brophy, J. E. (2003). *Looking in Classrooms* (9th ed., Chap. 9). New York: Addison-Wesley-Longman.

Grambo, G. (1997). Questions in Your Classroom. *Gifted Child Today Magazine, 20*(3), 42–43.

Kligman, P. S., and Aihara, K. A. (1997). Observing Student-Based Questions in a Whole Language Second-Grade Classroom. *Indiana Reading Journal, 29*(3), 17–22.

Landers, D. M., Maxwell, W., Butler, J., and Fagen, L. (2001). Developing Thinking Skills through Physical Education. In A. Costa (ED.), *Developing Minds: A Resource Book for Teaching Thinking.* Alexandria, VA: Association for Supervision and Curriculum Development.

Latham, A. (1997). Asking Students the Right Questions, *Educational Leadership, 54*(6), 84–85.

Martinello, M. L. (1998). Learning to Question for Inquiry. *Educational Forum, 62*(2), 164–171.

Mates, B. (1999). *Adaptive Technology for the Internet: Making Electronic Resources Accessible to All.* Chicago: American Library Association.

National Association of State Directors of Teacher Education and Certification (2000). *NASDTEC Manual 2000:*

Manual on the Preparation and Certification of Educational Personnel (5th ed., Table E-2). Dubuque, IA: Kendall/Hunt Publishing.

Pstergard, S. A. (1997). Asking Good Questions in Mathematics Class: How Long Does It Take to Learn How? *Clearing House, 71*(1), 48–50.

Spargo, P. E., and Enderstein, L. G. (1997). What Questions Do They Ask? Ausubel Rephrased. *Science and Children, 34*(6), 43–45.

NOTES

1. See D. P. Ausubel's classic work, *The Psychology of Meaningful Learning* (New York: Grune & Stratton, 1963).

2. T. L. Good and J. E. Brophy, *Looking in Classrooms,* 9th ed. (New York: Addison-Wesley-Longman, 2003), pp. 252–253.

3. A. L. Costa, *The School as a Home for the Mind* (Palatine, IL: Skylight Publishing, 1991), p. 63.

4. Studies in wait-time began with the classic study of M. B. Rowe, Wait Time and Reward as Instructional Variables, Their Influence on Language, Logic and Fate Control: Part I. Wait Time, *Journal of Research in Science Teaching, 11*(2), 81–94 (1974). See also M. R. Rowe, Science, Silence, and Sanctions, *Science and Children, 34*(1), 35–37 (September 1996).

5. M. E. McIntosh and R. J. Draper, Using the Question—Answer Relationship Strategy to Improve Students' Reading of Mathematics Texts, *Clearing House, 69*(3), 154–152; see also the work of G. Maxim, *The Very Young: Guiding Children from Infancy through the Early Years* (Upper Saddle River, NJ: Merrill/Prentice Hall, 1993); and T. C. Barrett's early work about four levels in "Taxonomy of Reading Comprehension," in *Reading 360 Monograph* (Lexington, MA: Ginn, 1972).

6. Socratic questioning, which includes challenging assumptions, exposing contradictions, and responding to all questions with a further question, is a main feature of Paideia schools. For information and a current listing of Paideia schools, contact the National Paideia Center, 400 Silver Cedar Court, Suite 200, Chapel Hill, NC 27514; (919)962-3128; *www.paideia.org*. Also, Socratic seminars are discussed as performance assessment in *The Performance Assessment Handbook, Volume I* by B. Johnson (Larchmont, NY: Eye on Education, 1997).

7. B. R. Brogan and W. A. Brogan, The Socratic Questioner: Teaching and Learning in the Dialogical Classroom, *Educational Forum, 59*(3), 288–296 (Spring 1995).

8. This three-tiered model of thinking has been described in different ways by other authorities. For a comparison of thinking models, see Costa, note 3, p. 44.

9. J. Piaget, *The Development of Thought: Elaboration of Cognitive Structures* (New York: Viking, 1977) and J. Piaget and B. Inhelder, *The Psychology of the Child* (New York: Basic Books, 1969).

10. R. N. Caine and G. Caine, *Education on the Edge of Possibility* (Alexandria, VA: Association for Supervision and Curriculum Development, 1997), p. 107.

11. B. Newton, Theoretical Basis for Higher Cognitive Questioning—An Avenue to Critical Thinking, *Education, 98*(3), 286–290 (March–April 1978); see also D. Redfield and E. Rousseau, A Meta-Analysis of Experimental Research on Teacher Questioning Behavior, *Review of Educational Research, 51*(2), 237–245 (Summer 1981).

12. J. G. Brooks and M. G. Brooks, *In Search of Understanding: The Case for Constructivist Classrooms* (Alexandria, VA: Association for Supervision and Curriculum Development, 1993), p. 105.

13. See Rowe, Wait Time and Rewards, note 4; M. B. Rowe, Wait Time: Slowing Down May Be a Way of Speeding Up, *American Educator, 11*(1), 38–47 (Spring 1987); see also J. Swift, C. Gooding, and P. Swift, Questions and Wait Time. in J. Dillon (Ed.), *Questioning and Discussion: A Multidisciplinary Study* (Norwood, NJ: Ablex, 1988), pp. 192–212.

14. United States Department of Education, *Tried and True: Tested Ideas for Teaching and Learning from the Regional Educational Laboratories* (Washington, DC: Office of Educational Research and Improvement, U.S. Department of Education, 1997), p. 53.

15. Our definition of a "large" elementary school is one with a population of 400 or more children. For research information about school size, see K. Cushman, How Small Schools Increase Student Learning (and What Large Schools Can Do About It), *Principal Online* (Alexandria, VA: National Association of Elementary School Principals, 1999); retrieved February 9, 2005, from *www.naesp.org/ContentLoad.do?contentId-103*. Also see K. Cotton, *School Size, School Climate, and Student Performance* (*Close-Up Number 20*) (Portland, OR: Northwest Regional Educational Laboratory, 1996); retrieved February 9, 2005, from *www.nwrel.org/scpd/sirs/10/c020.html*; and M. A. Raywid, Small Schools: A Reform That Works, *Educational Leadership, 55*(4), 34–39 (December/January 1997–1998).

What Guidelines Assist My Use of Demonstrations, Thinking, Inquiry Learning, and Games?

Visual Chapter Organizer and Overview

Demonstration

> **Purposes of Demonstrations**
> **Guidelines for Using Demonstrations**

Teaching Thinking for Intelligent Behavior

> **Characteristics of Intelligent Behavior**
> **Explicit Teaching for Thinking and Intelligent Behavior**

Inquiry Teaching and Discovery Learning

> **Problem Solving**
> **Inquiry Versus Discovery**
> **True Inquiry**
> **Critical Thinking Skills of Discovery and Inquiry Learning**

Integrated Strategies for Integrated Learning

> **Learning by Educational Games**

> > **Classification of Educational Games**
> > **Purposes of Educational Games**
> > **Sources of Educational Games**

Looking at Teachers

Consider the fact-finding and decision-making approach of public officials in one state when confronted with the task of making decisions about projects proposed for watersheds in their state. While gathering information, the officials consulted with a state hydrologist. The hydrologist led the officials into the field to demonstrate specific ways that efforts had helped control erosion and rehabilitate damaged streams. The officials were taken by the hydrologist to a natural creek, where they donned high waders and were led down the stream to examine various features of that complex natural stream. The hydrologist pointed out evidence of the creek's past meanders, patterns that had been incorporated into rehabilitation projects. In addition to listening to this scientist's point of view, the public officials listened to other experts to consider related economic and political issues before making final decisions about projects that had been proposed for watersheds in that state.

Just as the state public officials did, students can study a topic and its underlying ideas as well as related knowledge from various disciplines on an ongoing basis when the students are involved in activities, lessons, and units—especially an interdisciplinary thematic unit. The teacher, sometimes with the help of students and other teachers and adults, introduces experiences designed to illustrate ideas and skills from various disciplines, just as the hydrologist introduced information from hydrology. For instance, the teacher might introduce communication skills through creative writing and other projects. Through the study, the students are guided in exploring ideas related to different disciplines to integrate their knowledge.

CHAPTER OBJECTIVES

Specifically, on completion of this ninth chapter, you should be able to:

1. Discuss relationships among thinking, problem solving, inquiry learning, and discovery.
2. Describe characteristics of an effective demonstration and effective use of inquiry learning.
3. Analyze an inquiry learning lesson and text information about integrating strategies to form a synthesis of information for use in your own teaching.
4. Create and demonstrate a brief lesson for a specific grade level or subject and ask your peers for narrative evaluations.
5. Compare/contrast several categories of games for learning.
6. Describe at least two ways of integrating strategies for integrated learning.

This chapter begins with a presentation of guidelines for using demonstrations as a vital instructional strategy. Other important strategies, namely, thinking, educational games, and inquiry learning and discovery, have additional guidelines. These instructional strategies can be integrated and combined to establish additional teaching–learning experiences for the students.

A Special Moment in Teaching:
Advice to Beginning Teachers

We share with you this teaching vignette that we find to be both humorous and indicative of creative thinking. A sixth-grade teacher began a social studies lesson with the question "What comes to mind when you hear the words *Caesar* and *Gladiator*?" Without hesitation, a rather quiet student voice from the back of the room answered, "Salad and a movie." To us, that represented one of those rare and precious moments in teaching, reaffirming our belief that every teacher is well-advised to maintain throughout his or her teaching career a journal in which such intrinsically rewarding moments can be recorded so they can be reviewed and enjoyed again years later.

DEMONSTRATION

Children enjoy demonstrations because the demonstrator is actively engaged in a learning activity rather than merely verbalizing about it. Demonstrations can be used in teaching at any grade level for a variety of purposes. For example, during a social studies lesson, the teacher uses role play to demonstrate violation of First Amendment rights, and in a math lesson, a teacher presents the steps in solving a mathematical problem. As part of a language arts lesson, the teacher demonstrates ways to write attention-getting opening lines to students ready for a creative writing assignment, and during a science lesson, the teacher shows the effect of the absence of light on a plant leaf. Further, in a physical education session, the teacher demonstrates the proper way to serve in volleyball.

Purposes of Demonstrations

A demonstration can be designed to serve any of the following purposes that help give students an opportunity for vicarious participation in active

Figure 9.1
Planning checklist for a demonstration

---

1. I can decide on the most effective way to conduct the demonstration. I can consider these variables: Will it be a verbal or a silent demonstration? Will the demonstration be done by a student or by me? Will I have a student assistant helping me?

   Done _____   Somewhat done _____   To do _____

2. I can decide if the demonstration will be shown to a small group or to the whole group. Will the demonstration have some combination of these suggestions, such as, first, I will do the demonstration and, second, it will be followed by a repeat of the demonstration by a student (or several students)?

   Done _____   Somewhat done _____   To do _____

3. I will be sure that the demonstration is visible to all students. I will consider the use of special lighting to highlight the demonstration. Students may need to move their seats to be able to see better.

   Done _____   Somewhat done _____   To do _____

4. I can set up a slide or overhead projector to be used as a spotlight or I can use an overhead projector when the materials of the demonstration are transparent.

   Done _____   Somewhat done _____   To do _____

5. I will practice with the materials and procedure before demonstrating to the students. During my practice, I will try to prepare for anything that could go wrong during the live demonstration; if I don't prepare, then as Murphy's law says, if anything can go wrong, it will. But, if something does go wrong during the live demonstration, I can use that as an opportunity for a teachable moment.

   Done _____   Somewhat done _____   To do _____

6. I can engage the children in working with me to try to figure out what went wrong or, if that isn't feasible, I can go to Plan B, which I have planned with the use of the aids and media resources mentioned in the *Technology Tips for the Classroom* features in each chapter and on our Companion Website **(www.prenhall.com/roberts)** *Additional Content* module.

   Done _____   Somewhat done _____   To do _____

7. I will consider my pacing of the demonstration, and allow for enough student wait–see and thinking time. At the start of the demonstration, I will explain its purpose and the learning objectives. I will remember this adage: "I'll tell them what I am going to do, do it and show them, and then tell them what they saw."

   Done _____   Somewhat done _____   To do _____

8. As with any lesson, I'll plan my closure and allow time for questions and discussion. During the demonstration, I'll use frequent pauses to check for student understanding.

   Done _____   Somewhat done _____   To do _____

9. I'll be sure that the demonstration table and area are free of unnecessary objects that could detract or be in the way.

   Done _____   Somewhat done _____   To do _____

10. If the planned demonstration will pose a safety hazard to the children or to me, or both, then I won't do it. I will select a safe alternate demonstration.

    Done _____   Somewhat done _____   To do _____

---

learning: to introduce a lesson or unit of study in a way that grabs the students' attention; to review; to illustrate a particular point of content; to assist in recognizing a solution to an identified problem or to set up a discrepancy recognition; to demonstrate a skill, that is, thinking skills or conflict resolution skills; to reduce potential safety hazards; to save time and resources (as contrasted to the entire class doing that which is being demonstrated); and to bring an unusual closure to a lesson or unit of study.

Guidelines for Using Demonstrations

When planning a demonstration, you should consider the checklist shown in Figure 9.1.

TEACHING THINKING FOR INTELLIGENT BEHAVIOR

Pulling together what has been learned about learning and brain functioning, teachers are encouraged to integrate explicit thinking instruction into daily les-

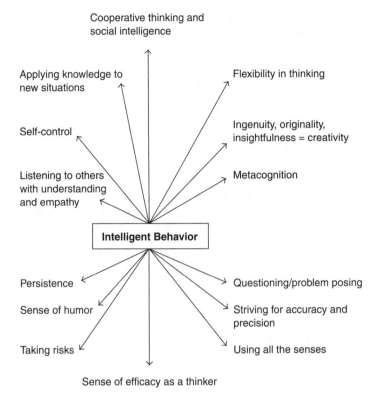

Figure 9.2
Characteristics of intelligent behavior

sons, to teach children the skills necessary for intelligent behavior.

Characteristics of Intelligent Behavior

Characteristics of intelligent behavior that you should model, teach for, and observe developing in your students, as identified by Costa,[1] are shown in Figure 9.2. They are described in the subsequent paragraphs.

Applying Knowledge to New Situations. A major goal of formal education is for students to apply school-learned knowledge to real-life situations. To develop skills in drawing on past knowledge and applying that knowledge to new situations, children must be given an opportunity to practice doing that very thing. Project-based learning (discussed in Chapter 10) and problem recognition and problem solving (discussed next in this chapter) are ways of providing that opportunity.

Cooperative Thinking and Social Intelligence. Humans are social beings. Real-world problem solving in our current social milieu has become so complex that seldom can any person go it alone. Not all students come to school knowing how to work effectively in their classroom societal groups. They may exhibit competitiveness, narrow-mindedness, egocentrism, ethnocentrism, or criticism of others' values, emotions, and beliefs. Altruism, consensus seeking, giving up an idea to work on someone else's, integrating the ideas of others, knowing how to handle

disagreements, knowing how to support group efforts, listening, and sharing—those are behaviors indicative of intelligent human beings, and they can be learned by children at school and in the classroom.

Self-Control. Impulsive behavior can create or worsen conflict and can inhibit effective problem solving.[2] In contrast, students with impulse control think before acting. Students can be taught to think before shouting out an answer, before beginning a task, and before arriving at conclusions with insufficient supporting information. As we have emphasized before in this resource guide (in Chapters 4 and 8 and on our Companion Website), one reason teachers should usually insist on students raising their hands before a student is acknowledged is to help students develop control over any impulsive behavior—including shouting out in class.[3]

Flexibility in Thinking. Sometimes called *lateral thinking,*[4] flexibility in thinking is the ability to approach a problem from a new angle, using a novel approach. With modeling by the teacher, children can develop this behavior as they learn to consider alternative points of view and to deal with several sources of information simultaneously.

Ingenuity, Originality, Insightfulness = Creativity. All children should be encouraged to say "I can" and discouraged from saying "I can't." Students should be taught in such a way as to encourage intrinsic motivation rather than reliance on extrinsic sources. Teachers must be able to offer criticism/feedback so the student understands that the criticism is not a criticism of the student's self. In exemplary elementary school programs, children learn the value of feedback. They learn the value of their own intuition, of guessing, of risking—and as an integral part of this, they learn the value of "I can."

Listening to Others with Understanding and Empathy. Some psychologists believe that the ability to listen to others, to empathize with and to understand their point of view, is one of the highest forms of intelligent behavior. Empathic behavior is an important skill for conflict resolution. Piaget refers to this behavior as *overcoming egocentrism*. If appropriate, point out to students that in class meetings, brainstorming sessions, think tanks, town meetings, advisory councils, board meetings, and legislative bodies, people from various walks of life convene to share their thinking, to explore their ideas, and to broaden their perspectives by listening to and considering the ideas and reactions of others.

Metacognition. Metacognition (learning to plan, monitor, assess, and reflect on one's own thinking) is another characteristic of intelligent behavior. Cooperative learning groups, journals, portfolio conferences, self-assessment, and thinking aloud in dyads are strategies that can be used to help children develop this intelligent behavior.[5] Also, your thinking aloud is good modeling for your students. Modeling helps them develop their own cognitive skills of thinking, learning, and reasoning.[6]

Persistence. Persistence is the act of sticking to an idea or a task until it is completed. Here are some examples:

- **Thomas Edison.** Persistent in his efforts to invent the electric lightbulb, Edison tried approximately 3,000 filaments before finding one that worked.
- **Wilma Rudolf.** Because of childhood diseases, Rudolf, at age 10, could not walk without the aid of leg braces. Only 10 years later, having won three gold medals in the 1960 World Olympics, she was declared to be the fastest running woman in the world.
- **Babe Ruth.** For years, Ruth was recognized for having not only the highest number of home runs in professional baseball, but also the highest number of strikeouts.
- **Margaret Sanger.** Nearly single-handedly and against formidable odds, Sanger founded the birth control movement in the United States, beginning in 1914 with her founding of the National Birth Control League. In 1953, she was named the first president of the International Planned Parenthood Federation.

Questioning/Problem Posing. Children are usually full of questions and, unless discouraged, they do ask them. We want students to be alert to, and recognize, discrepancies and phenomena in their environment and to freely inquire about their causes. In exemplary school programs, students are encouraged to ask questions (see Chapter 8) and then use those questions as a basis from which to develop a problem-solving strategy to investigate their questions.

Sense of Efficacy as a Thinker. Wonderment, inquisitiveness, curiosity, and the enjoyment of problem solving all contribute to a sense of efficacy as a thinker. Young children express wonderment, an expression that should never be stifled. Through effective teaching, all students can recapture that sense of wonderment as a facilitating teacher guides them into a feeling of "I can" and into an expression of "I enjoy."

Sense of Humor. The positive effects of humor on the body's physiological functions are well established: a drop in the pulse rate, an increase of oxygen in the blood, the activation of antibodies that fight against harmful microorganisms, and the release of gamma interferon, a hormone that fights viruses and regulates cell growth. Humor liberates creativity and supports high-level thinking skills, such as anticipation, finding novel relationships, and visual imagery.[7] The acquisition of a sense of humor follows a developmental sequence similar to that described by Piaget[8] and Kohlberg.[9] Initially, young children may find humor in all the wrong things—human frailty, ethnic humor, sacrilegious riddles, ribald profanities. Later, creative children thrive on finding incongruity and will demonstrate a whimsical frame of mind during problem solving. Remember, however, that to be most effective as a tool for teaching and learning, the humor used should not be self-degrading or offensive to anyone.

Striving for Accuracy and Precision. Teachers can observe children growing in this behavior when students take time to check over their work, review the procedures, avoid drawing conclusions prematurely, and use concise and descriptive language.

Taking Risks: Venturing Forth and Exploring Ideas Beyond the Usual Zone of Comfort. Such exploration, of course, must be done with thoughtfulness; it must not be done in ways that could put the child at risk psychologically or physically. Using the analogy of a turtle going nowhere until it sticks its neck out, teachers should model this behavior and provide opportunities for children to develop this intelligent behavior of risk taking by using techniques such as brainstorming strategies, divergent thinking questioning, think–pair–share activity, cooperative learning, inquiry learning, and project-based learning.

Using All the Senses. As discussed previously in this and other chapters (especially Chapters 2 and 7), children should be encouraged to learn to use and develop all of their sensory input channels—verbal, visual, tactile, and kinesthetic—for learning.

We should strive to help our own students develop these characteristics of intelligent behavior. In Chapter 3, you learned about specific teacher behaviors that facilitate this development. Additionally, you probably reviewed some of the specific teacher behaviors found in classroom interaction in the Chapter 8 additional application exercise from the Companion Website **(www.prenhall.com/roberts)** titled Practice in Identifying Teaching Behaviors in Classroom Interaction: A Self-Check Exercise. To continue, we ask you to take a look now at some additional research findings that offer important considerations in the facilitation of student learning and intelligent behavior.

Explicit Teaching for Thinking and Intelligent Behavior

The curriculum of any school includes the development of skills that are used in thinking, skills such as classifying, comparing, concluding, generalizing, and inferring. Because the academic achievement of children increases when they are taught thinking skills directly, many researchers and educators concur that explicit/direct instruction should be given to all children on how to think and behave intelligently.[10]

Several research perspectives have influenced today's interest in the direct/explicit teaching of thinking. One perspective is the cognitive view of intelligence, which asserts that intellectual ability is not fixed but can be developed. A second perspective is the constructivist approach to learning, which maintains that learners actively and independently construct knowledge by creating and coordinating relationships in their mental repertoire. Another perspective is the social psychology view of classroom experience that focuses on the learner as an individual who is a member of various peer groups in our society. Still another perspective that has influenced educators' interest in thinking about thinking relates to information processing and acquiring information, remembering, and problem solving.[11]

Rather than assuming that children have developed thinking skills, teachers should devote classroom time to teaching them explicitly/directly. When teaching a thinking skill directly, the subject content becomes the vehicle for thinking. For example, a teacher involved in a social studies lesson can teach children how to distinguish fact and opinion; a teacher guiding a language arts lesson instructs children on how to compare and analyze; and a teacher leading a science lesson can teach children how to set up a problem for their inquiry.

Inquiry teaching and discovery learning are both useful tools for learning and for teaching thinking skills. For further insight and additional strategies, as well as for the many programs concerned with teaching thinking, see the resources in this chapter's notes and the list of readings at the end of this chapter.[12]

INQUIRY TEACHING AND DISCOVERY LEARNING

Intrinsic to the effectiveness of both inquiry and discovery is the assumption that students would rather actively seek knowledge than receive it through information delivery (i.e., traditional expository) methods such as demonstrations, lectures, and textbook reading. While inquiry teaching and discovery learning are important instructional tools, there is sometimes confusion about exactly what inquiry teaching is and how it differs from discovery learning. The distinction should become clear as you read the following discussion of these two important tools for teaching and learning.

Problem Solving

Perhaps a major reason why inquiry and discovery are sometimes confused is that, in both, students are actively engaged in problem solving. By *problem solving,* we mean the intellectual ability to accomplish the following: (a) recognize and define or describe a problem, (b) specify a desired or preferred outcome, (c) identify possible solutions, (d) select a procedure to resolve the problem, (e) apply the procedure, (f) evaluate outcomes, and (g) revise these steps where necessary.

Inquiry Versus Discovery

Problem solving is *not* a teaching strategy but a high-order intellectual behavior that facilitates learning. What a teacher can do, and should do, is provide opportunities for students to identify and tentatively solve problems. Experiences in inquiry and discovery can provide those opportunities. With the processes involved in inquiry and discovery, teachers can help students develop the skills necessary for effective problem solving. Two major differences between discovery and inquiry are (a) who recognizes and identifies the problem and (b) the percentage of decisions that are made by the students. Table 9.1 shows three levels of inquiry, each level defined according to what the student does and decides.

It should be evident from Table 9.1 that what is called *Level I inquiry* is actually traditional, didactic teaching, where both the problem and the process for resolving it are defined for the student. The student

Table 9.1
Levels of inquiry

Skill	Level I	Level II	Level III
Problem identification	By teacher or textbook	By teacher or textbook	By student
Process of solving the problem	Decided by teacher or textbook	Decided by student	Decided by student
Identification of tentative solution	Resolved by student	Resolved by student	Resolved by student

then works through the process to its inevitable resolution. If the process is well designed, the result is inevitable, because the student *discovers* what was intended by the writers of the program. This level is also called *guided inquiry* or *guided discovery,* because the students are carefully guided through the investigation to (the predictable) discovery.

Level I is, in reality, a strategy within the delivery mode, the advantages of which were described in Chapter 7. Because Level I inquiry learning is highly manageable and the learning outcome is predictable, it is probably best for teaching basic concepts and principles. However, students who never experience learning beyond Level I are missing an opportunity to engage their highest mental operations, and they seldom (or never) get to experience more motivating, real-life problem solving. Furthermore, those students may come away with the false notion that problem solving is a linear process, which it is not. As illustrated in Figures 9.3 and 9.4, the inquiry cycle and its processes, true inquiry is cyclical rather than linear. For that reason, Level I is not true inquiry learning because it is a linear process. Real-world problem solving is a cyclical rather than a linear process. One enters the cycle whenever a discrepancy or problem is observed and recognized, and that can occur at any point in the cycle.

True Inquiry

By the time children are in the upper elementary school grades, they should be provided experiences for true inquiry learning, which begins with *Level II,* where students actually decide and design processes for their inquiry learning. True inquiry emphasizes the tentative nature of conclusions, which makes the activity more like real-life problem solving, in which decisions are always subject to revision if and when new data so prescribe.

At *Level III inquiry,* students recognize and identify the problem, decide the processes, and reach a conclusion. In project-centered learning, students are usually engaged at this level of inquiry learning. By the time students are in the middle grades, Level III inquiry should be a major strategy for instruction,

which is often the case in schools that use cross-age teaching and interdisciplinary thematic instruction, But it is not easy: Like most good teaching practices, it is a lot of work. But also like good teaching in general, the intrinsic rewards make the effort worthwhile. As exclaimed by one teacher using interdisciplinary thematic instruction with student-centered inquiry, "I've never worked harder in my life, but I've never had this much fun, either."

Critical Thinking Skills of Discovery and Inquiry Learning

In true inquiry, students generate ideas and then design ways to test those ideas. The various processes used represent the many critical thinking skills. Some of those skills are concerned with generating and organizing data; others are concerned with building and using ideas. Figure 9.4 provides four categories of thinking processes and illustrates the place of each within the inquiry cycle. You'll notice that some processes in the cycle are discovery processes and others are inquiry processes. Inquiry processes include the more complex mental operations, including all those in the idea-using category. Project-based learning provides an avenue for doing that, as does problem-centered teaching.

Inquiry learning is a higher level mental operation that introduces the concept of the discrepant event, something that establishes cognitive disequilibrium (using the element of surprise to challenge prior notions) to help students develop skills in observing and being alert for discrepancies. Such a strategy provides opportunities for students to investigate their own ideas about explanations. Inquiry, like discovery, depends on skill in problem solving; the difference between the two is in the amount of decision-making responsibility given to students. Experiences afforded by inquiry help students understand the importance of suspending judgment and also the tentativeness of answers and solutions. With those understandings, students eventually can better deal with life's ambiguities. When children are not provided these important educational experiences, their education is incomplete.

Figure 9.3
The inquiry cycle

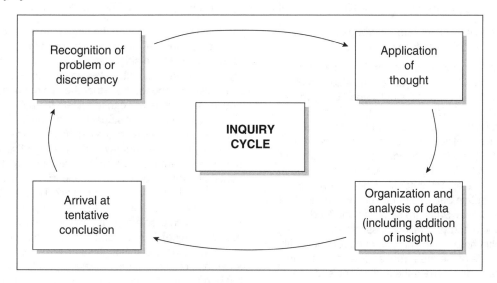

Figure 9.4
Inquiry cycle processes

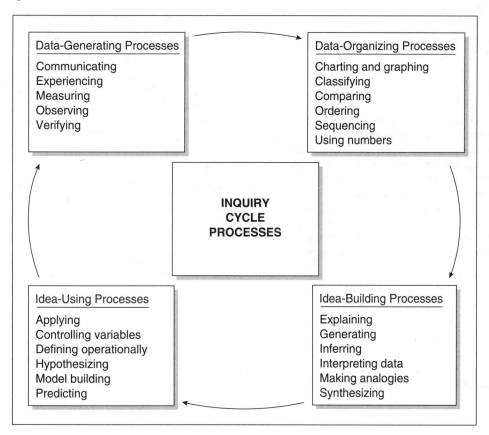

One of the most effective ways of stimulating inquiry learning is to use materials that provoke students' interest. These materials should be presented in a nonthreatening, noncompetitive context, so students can think laterally and hypothesize openly and freely. Your role as the teacher is to encourage the students to form as many hypotheses as possible and then support their hypotheses with reasons. After the students suggest several ideas, your role is to move on to higher order, more abstract questions that involve the development of generalizations and evaluations.

Figure 9.5
Locating a colony: a Level II inquiry
(*Source:* Adapted by permission from unpublished material provided by Jennifer Devine and Dennis Devine.)

Presentation of the Problem. In groups of three or four, students receive the following information.

Background. You (your group is considered as one person) are one of 120 passengers on the ship, the *Prince Charles.* You left England 12 weeks ago. You have experienced many hardships, including a stormy passage, limited rations, sickness, cold and damp weather, and hot, foul air below deck. Ten of your fellow immigrants to the New World, including three children, have died and been buried at sea. You are now anchored at an uncertain place, off the coast of the New World, which your captain believes to be somewhere north of the Virginia Grants. Seas are so rough and food so scarce that you and your fellow passengers have decided to settle here. A landing party has returned with a map they made of the area. You, as one of the elders, must decide at once where the settlement is to be located. The tradesmen want to settle along the river, which is deep, even though this seems to be the season of low water levels. Within ten months they expect deep-water ships from England with more colonists and merchants. Those within your group who are farmers say they must have fertile, workable land. The officer in charge of the landing party reported seeing a group of armed natives who fled when approached. He feels the settlement must be located so that it can be defended from the natives and from the sea.

Directions, step one: You (your group) are to select a site on the attached map which you feel is best suited for a colony. Your site must satisfy the different factions aboard the ship. A number of possible sites are already marked on the map (letters *A–G*). You may select one of these locations or use them as reference points to show the location of your colony. When your group has selected its site, list and explain the reasons for your choice. When each group has arrived at its tentative decision, these will be shared with the whole class.

Directions, step two: After each group has made its presentation and argument, a class debate is held about where the colony should be located.

Notes to teacher: For the debate, have a large map drawn on the writing board or on an overhead transparency, where each group's mark can be made for all to see and discuss. After each group has presented its argument for its location and against the others, we suggest that you then mark on the large map the two, three, or more hypothetical locations (assuming that, as a class, there yet is no single favorite location). Then take a straw vote of the students, allowing each to vote on his or her own, independently rather than as members of groups. At this time you can terminate the activity by saying that if the majority of students favor one location, then that, in fact, is the solution to the problem—that is, the colony is located wherever the majority of class members believe it should be. No sooner will that statement be made by you than someone will ask, "Are we correct?" or "What is the right answer?" They will ask such questions because, as students in school, they are used to solving problems that have right answers (Level I inquiry teaching). In real-world problems, however, there are no "right" answers, though some answers may seem better than others. It is the process of problem solving that is important. You want your students to develop confidence in their ability to solve problems and understand the tentativeness of "answers" to real-life problems.

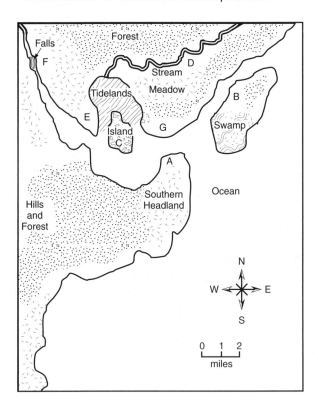

We want to point out that true inquiry problems have a special advantage in that they can be used with almost any group of students. Members of a group can approach the problem as an adventure in thinking and apply it to whatever background they can muster. Background experience may enrich a student's approach to the problem, but it is not crucial to the use or understanding of the evidence presented to the student. As an example, Locating a Colony (Figure 9.5) is a Level II inquiry learning situation. With the members of your group, review the instructions of that inquiry now to see how this inquiry learning was organized for small groups of students. To extend the idea of farmers seeking fertile, workable land as a criterion in the

Figure 9.6
Partially completed thinking process map about farm crops

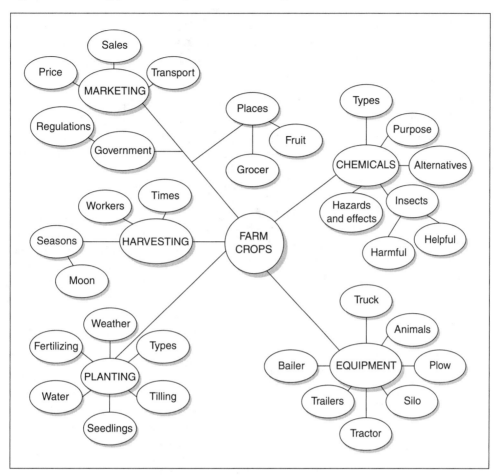

inquiry learning situation, see an example of a thinking process map about farm crops in Figure 9.6.

INTEGRATED STRATEGIES FOR INTEGRATED LEARNING

In today's exemplary elementary school classrooms, instructional strategies are combined to establish the most effective teaching–learning experience. For example, in an integrated language arts program, a teacher is interested in his or her students' speaking, reading, listening, thinking, study, and writing skills. These skills (and not textbooks) form a holistic process that is the primary aspect of integrated language arts. In the area of speaking skills, oral discourse (discussion) in the classroom has a growing research base that promotes methods of teaching and learning through oral language. These methods include cooperative learning, instructional scaffolding, and inquiry teaching.

In cooperative learning groups, students discuss and use language in a way that benefits both their content learning and skills in social interaction. Working in heterogeneous groups, students participate in their own learning and can extend their knowledge base and cultural awareness with students of different backgrounds. When students share information and ideas, they are completing difficult learning tasks, using divergent thinking and decision making, and developing their understanding of concepts—all part of their instructional scaffolding. As issues are presented and responses are challenged, student thinking is clarified. Students assume the responsibility for planning within the group and for carrying out their assignments. When needed, the teacher models an activity with one group in front of the class, and when integrated with student questions, the modeling can become inquiry teaching. Activities can include any from a variety of heuristics (a heuristic is a tool used in solving a problem or understanding an idea), such as those discussed next.

Brainstorming. Members generate ideas related to a key word/concept and record them. Clustering (or chunking), mapping, and a Venn diagram (all discussed later) are variations of brainstorming.

Comparing and Contrasting. Similarities and differences among items are found and recorded.

Chunking or Clustering. Groups of students apply mental organizers by clustering information into chunks for easier manipulation and remembering.

Memory Strategies. The teacher and students model the use of acronyms, mnemonics, rhymes, or the clustering of information into categories to promote learning. Sometimes, such as in memorizing one's Social Security number, one must learn by rote information that is not connected to any prior information. To do that, it is helpful to break the information to be learned into smaller chunks, such as dividing the nine-digit Social Security number into smaller chunks of information (with, in this instance, each chunk separated by a hyphen). Learning by rote is also easier if one can connect that which is to be memorized to some prior knowledge. Strategies such as these are used to bridge the gap between rote learning and meaningful learning and are known as *mnemonics*.[13] Sample mnemonics include the following:

- The ABCDs of writing instructional objectives (see Chapter 5), and CASE for using classroom bulletin boards (see our Companion Website at **www.prenhall.com/roberts**) in *Additional Content* module. ✍

- The notes on a treble staff are FACE for the space notes and EGBDF (Empty Garbage Before Dad Flips or Every Good Boy Deserves Fudge) for the line notes. The notes on the lower staff are All Cows Eat Granola Bars and Grizzly Bears Don't Fly Airplanes).

- The order of the planets from the Sun can be remembered by My Very Educated Mother Just Served Us Nine Pizzas (Mercury, Venue, Earth, Mars, Jupiter, Saturn, Uranus, Neptune, and Pluto). In reality, Pluto and Neptune alternate in this order because of their elliptical orbits.

- The names of the Great Lakes: HOMES for Huron, Ontario, Michigan, Erie, and Superior.

- To recall multiplication tables or grammar rules, consider singing songs as a memory strategy.

- To recall the order of operations when solving algebraic equations, remember **P**lease (parentheses) **E**xcuse (exponents) **M**y (multiply) **D**ear (divide) **A**unt (add) **S**ally (subtract).

Think–Pair–Share. Students, in pairs, examine a new topic or concept about to be studied. They discuss what they already know or think they know about the concept and present their perceptions to the whole group. (Refer back to Chapter 5.)

Visual Tools. A variety of terms for the visual tools useful for learning have been invented—some of which are synonymous—terms such as brainstorming web, mind mapping web, spider map, cluster map or graphic, cognitive map, generalization map, idea map, mental image map, opinion map, semantic map, thought map, Venn diagram, visual scaffold, graphic organizers, and concept map.[14] Hyerle separates these visual tools into three categories according to purpose: (a) brainstorming tools (such as mind mapping, webbing, and clustering) for the purpose of developing one's knowledge and creativity; (b) task-specific organizers, such as life cycle diagrams used in biology, decision trees used in mathematics, and text structures used in reading; and (c) thinking process maps (such as visual mapping) for encouraging cognitive development across disciplines.[15] It is the latter in which we are interested here. Some teachers use *Inspiration,* a computer program that creates graphic organizers.

Based on Ausubel's theory of meaningful learning,[16] thinking process mapping has been found useful for helping learners change their prior notions—their misconceptions, sometimes referred to as naive views. It can help students organize and represent their thoughts and help them connect new knowledge to their past experiences and precepts.[17] Simply put, concepts can be thought of as classifications that attempt to organize the world of objects and events into a smaller number of categories. In everyday usage, the term **concept** means *idea,* as when someone says, "My concept of love is not the same as yours." Concepts embody a meaning that develops in complexity with experience and learning over time. For example, the concept of love that is held by a second grader is unlikely to be as complex as that held by the child's teacher. Thinking process mapping is a graphical way of demonstrating the relationship between and among concepts.

Typically, a thinking process map refers to a visual or graphic representation of concepts with bridges (connections) that show relationships. Figure 9.6 shows a partially completed thinking process map where students have made connections of concepted relationships between fruit orchards, farming, and marketing. The typical procedure for thinking process mapping is to have the students (a) identify important concepts in materials being studied, often by circling those concepts; (b) rank order the concepts from the most general to the most specific; and (c) arrange the concepts on a sheet of paper, connect related ideas with lines, and define the connections between the related ideas. For young children, pictures may be used in each of the circles rather than words.

Meaningful learning can occur in other ways also, as discussed next.

Inferring. For instance, students assume the roles of people (real or fictional) and infer their motives, personalities, and thoughts.

Multiple Sources. Use multiple texts to demonstrate the interpretive nature of historical events.[18] This use is also called using textsets.

Outlining. Each group of children completes an outline that contains some of the main idea but with subtopics omitted.

Paraphrasing. In a brief summary, each student restates a short selection of what was read or heard.

Reciprocal Teaching. In classroom dialogue, students take turns at generating questions, summarizing, clarifying, and predicting.[19]

Study Strategies. Important strategies that should be taught explicitly include vocabulary expansion, reading, and interpreting graphic information, locating resources, using advance organizers, adjusting one's reading rate, and skimming, scanning, and study reading.[20]

Textbook Study Strategies. Students use the SQ4R approach or related study strategies (see Chapter 5).

Vee Mapping. This is a road map completed by the students as they learn to show the route they follow from prior knowledge to new and future knowledge.

Venn Diagramming. This is a technique for comparing two concepts or, for example, two countries, two stories, two personas, to show similarities and differences. Using stories as an example, a student is asked to draw two circles that intersect and to mark the circles *one* and *two,* and the area where they intersect *three*. In circle one, the students lists the characteristics of one story, and in circle two, she or he lists the characteristics of the second story. In the area of the intersection, circle three, the student lists characteristics common to both stories.

Visual Learning Log (VLL). This variation of the road map is completed by the students showing the route they follow from prior knowledge to new and future knowledge, except that the VLL consists of pictograms (free-form drawings) that each student makes and that are maintained in a journal. To further explore inquiry teaching and integrated learning, go to the Companion Website **(www.prenhall.com/roberts)** and do the additional application exercise titled: A Study of Inquiry Learning and Strategy Integration.

LEARNING BY EDUCATIONAL GAMES

Devices classified as educational games include a wide variety of learning activities, such as simulations, role play, sociodrama activities, mind games, board games, and computer games, all of which provide valuable learning experiences for participants. These experiences tend to involve several senses and involve several learning modalities to engage higher order thinking skills and to be quite effective as learning tools.

Of all the arts, drama involves the learner-participant most fully—intellectually, emotionally, physically, verbally, and socially. Interactive drama, which is role playing, is a simplified form of drama, a method by which children can become involved with literature. Studies show that children's comprehension increases and they are highly motivated to read if they are involved in analyzing and actively responding to the characters, plot, and setting of the story being read.[21]

Simulations, a more complex form of drama, serve many of the developmental needs of children. They provide for interaction with peers and allow children of different backgrounds and talents to cooperatively work on a common project. They engage children in physical activity and give them opportunities to try out different roles, which help them to better understand themselves. Simulations also can provide concrete experiences that help children to understand complex concepts and issues, and they provide opportunities for exploring values and developing skill in decision making.[22]

Simulated real-world experiences for use in grades K–8 are available in a program called *MicroSociety*. This program gives children authentic economic experiences and is used in more than 200 schools in at least 40 states. In collaboration with parents and guardians, community members, and teachers, students build a miniature community in the school, establish a center of commerce and governance where they earn wages, pay taxes, resolve issues in court, and operate businesses. At the Johnsontown Road Elementary School (Louisville, Kentucky), for example, students run their own simulated town, from policing the halls of the school to paying rent on their desks with play money.[23]

Classification of Educational Games

What are educational games? Several types of games fall under the general heading of educational games. Table 9.2 shows different types, with characteristics and examples of each. Certain types have greater educational value than do others. Games that do not emphasize the element of competition—that are not contests—are particularly recommended for use in the academic classroom (see types 1, 3, and 5 in Table 9.2).

Purposes of Educational Games

Educational games can play an integral role in interdisciplinary teaching and serve as valuable resources

Table 9.2
Classification of educational games

Type	Characteristics and Examples
1. Pure game*	Fun *Ungame, New Games*
2. Pure content	Stimulates competition; built-in inefficiency[†] *Political contests*
3. Pure simulation*	Models reality *Toddler play*
4. Content/game	Stimulates competition; fun; built-in inefficiency *Golf, Trivial Pursuit*
5. Simulation/game*	Models reality; fun *Our Town's Planning Commission Meeting*[‡]
6. Contest/simulation	Stimulates competition; models reality; built-in inefficiency *Boxcar Derby* (Akron, Ohio)

* These game types do not emphasize competition and thus are particularly recommended for use in the classroom as learning tools.
† Rules for accomplishing the game objective make accomplishment of that objective less than efficient. For example, in golf, the objective is to get the ball into the hole with the least amount of effort, but to do that, one has to take a peculiarly shaped stick (the club) and hit the ball, find it, and hit it again, continuing that sequence until the ball is in the hole. Yet, common sense tells us that the best way to get the ball into the hole with the least amount of effort would be simply to pick up the ball and place it by hand into the hole.
‡ See J. V. Vort, Our Town's Planning Commission Meeting, *Journal of Geography, 96*(4), 183–1900 (July–August, 1997).

for enriching the effectiveness of students' learning. As with any other instructional strategy, the use of games should follow a clear educational purpose, have a careful plan, and be congruent with your school's instructional objectives and the stated mission.

Games can be powerful tools for teaching and learning. A game can serve one or more of the purposes shown in Figure 9.7. Since we trust you are familiar with several games, take a few minutes, recall *one* of your favorites, and write in *one* example for *one* purpose that you select.

Sources of Educational Games

Sources for useful educational games include professional journals (see Figure 9.8 and the readings at the end of this chapter) and your favorite sources on the Internet. Additional sources of commercially available educational games for use in teaching are shown in Figure 9.9 and ways to incorporate technology are given in the *Technology Tips for the Classroom* feature. Now, do Application Exercise 9.1.

Companion Website

To find supportive materials about demonstrations, thinking for intelligent behavior, inquiry learning, and educational games, go to our Companion Website at **www.prenhall.com/roberts** and click on the *Additional Content* module for Chapter 8.

Figure 9.7
Educational games: ABCs of purposes

Purposes
(a) add change of pace   Favorite example:

(b) assess student learning   Favorite example:

(c) teach content   Favorite example:

(d) offer opportunity for deductive thinking   Favorite example:

(e) enhance student self-esteem   Favorite example:

(f) focus on process   Favorite example:

(g) provide experiences   Favorite example:

(h) help reinforce convergent thinking   Favorite example:

(i) introduce skill development and motivation through media usage   Favorite example:

(j) provide skill development in inductive thinking   Favorite example:

(k) use of kinesthetic and tactile modality   Favorite example:

(l) learning through skill development in verbal communication and debate   Favorite example:

(m) motivate students   Favorite example:

(n) encourage learning through peer interaction   Favorite example:

(o) offer a break from the usual rigors of learning   Favorite example:

(p) provide problem-solving situations   Favorite example:

(q) offer questioning opportunity   Favorite example:

(r) reinforce real-life issues through simulation and role playing   Favorite example:

(s) review selected subject matter   Favorite example:

(t) offer divergent and creative thinking   Favorite example:

(u) use of computer   Favorite example:

(v) offer variety   Favorite example:

(w) offer wait time for critical thinking   Favorite example:

(x) can introduce new and (perhaps unfamiliar) vocabulary i.e., *xebec* (Mediterranean vessel with three masts and long bow and stern), *xylem* (a complex tissue in higher plants; woody tissue), and *xylophone* (a percussion instrument)   Favorite example:

(y) yield results of students' time and efforts   Favorite example:

(z) add zip/vigor to gaining information with a brisk, snappy game   Favorite example:

Figure 9.8
Sample professional journals with educational games

- J. Bassett, "The Pullman Strike of 1894," *OAH Magazine of History* 11(2):34–41 (Winter 1997). Role-play simulation.
- D. Bogan and D. Wood, "Simulating Sun, Moon, and Earth Patterns," *Science Scope* 21(2):46, 48 (October 1997). Role-play for middle school.
- C. Collyer, "Winter Secrets: An Instant Lesson Plan," *Pathways: The Ontario Journal of Outdoor Education* 9(2):18–20 (April 1997). Instructions for two games about predator-prey relationships.
- P. Cunningham, "Reading Clinic. Making Decoding Fun with This Cross-Checking Game," *Instructor* 107(2):74–75 (September 1997). For teaching K–3.
- S. A. Farin, "Acting Atoms," *Science Scope* 21(3):46 (November/December 1997). Role-play for middle school.
- J. Gorman, "Strategy Games: Treasures from Ancient Times," *Mathematics Teaching in the Middle School* 3(2):110–116 (October 1997). Presents several games for integrating history and mathematics.
- S. Hightshoe, "Sifting Through the Sands of Time: A Simulated Archaeological Special Feature," *Social Studies and the Young Learner* 9(3):28–30 (January/February, 1997). For elementary and middle school.
- M. J. Howle, "Play-Party Games in the Modern Classroom," *Music Educators Journal* 83(5):24–28 (March 1997). Introduces games that were popular on the 19th-century American frontier.
- T. Levy, "The Amistad Incident: A Classroom Reenactment," *Social Education* 59(5):303–308 (September 1995).
- T. M. McCann, "A Pioneer Simulation for Writing and for the Study of Literature," *English Journal* 85(3):62–67 (March 1996).
- H. Morris, "Universal Games from A to Z," *Mathematics in School* 26(4):35–40 (September 1997). See also F. Tapson, "Mathematical Games," pp. 2–6 of same issue.
- K. D. Owens et al., "Playing to Learn: Science Games in the Classroom," *Science Scope* 20(5):31–33 (February 1997). Games for middle school that encourage abstract thinking.

Figure 9.9
Sources of educational games

Ampersand Press, 750 Lake St., Port Townsend, WA 98368, www.ampersandpress.com

Aristoplay, 901 Lincoln Parkway, Plainwell, MI 49080; (800) 433-GAME, www.aristoplay.com

Carolina Biological Supply Company, 2700 York Road, Burlington, NC 27215; (800) 334-5551; www.carolina.com

Creative Teaching Associates, 5629 E. Westover Ave., Fresno, CA 93727; (800) 767-4282; www.mastercta.com

Dawn Publications, 12402 Bitney Springs Road, Nevada City, CA 95959; (800) 545-7475; www.dawnpub.com

Harcourt Brace School Publishers, 6277 Sea Harbor Dr., Orlando, FL 32887; (800) 225-5425; www.harcourtschool.com

Higher-Order Thinking Company, 1733 N. E. Patterson Dr., Lee's Summit, MO 64063; (816) 524-2701

Latz Chance Games, 1390 Airport Road, Greensboro, GA 30642; (888) 524-4263; www.latzchancegames.com

Optical Data School Media (part of SRA/McGraw Hill, 1221 Ave. of the Americas, New York, NY 10020); (866) 436-8502; www.opticaldata.com

Other Worlds Educational Enterprises, P.O. Box 6193, Woodland Park, CO 80866-6193; (719) 687-3840; www.otherworlds-edu.com

Summit Learning, 755 Rockwell Ave., P.O. Box 755, Fort Atkinson, WI 53538-0755; (800) 777-8817; www.summitlearning.com

Teacher Created Resources, 6421 Industry Way, Westminster, CA 92683; (800) 662-4321; www.teachercreated.com

Young Naturalist Company, 1900 N. Main St., North Newton, KS 67117; (316) 283-4103; http://home.southwind.net/~youngnat/classroomkits.html

APPLICATION EXERCISE 9.1 DEVELOPING A LESSON USING DIFFERENT APPROACHES: INQUIRY LEARNING LEVEL II, THINKING SKILL DEVELOPMENT, A DEMONSTRATION, OR AN INTERACTIVE LECTURE—PEER TEACHING

Instructions: The purpose of this application exercise is to provide an opportunity for you to create a brief lesson (about 20 minutes of instructional time [actual time to be specified by your instructor] designed for a specific grade level and subject). You will try it out on your peers for their feedback in an informal peer teaching demonstration. Join your colleagues in one of four groups. Your task, along with the other members of your group, is to prepare lessons individually that fall into one of four categories: (a) Level II inquiry, (b) thinking level, (c) demonstration, or (d) interactive lecture. To structure your lesson plan, use one of the sample lesson plan formats presented in Chapter 7; however, each lesson should be centered around one major theme or concept and be planned for the specified amount of instruction time.

Group 1: Each develops a Level II inquiry lesson.

Group 2: Each develops a lesson designed to raise the level of student thinking.

Group 3: Each develops a lesson that involves a demonstration.

Group 4: Each develops a lesson that is an interactive lecture.

Other Responsibilities:

1. Help schedule your lessons as class presentations so that each member has the opportunity to present his or her lesson and receive feedback.

2. Review the following scoring rubric with your whole group and, if needed, make modifications to it with the class's input.

3. Be sure that each presenter/teacher obtains *your* feedback on the assessment rubric about the lesson after the lesson (make the number of copies that you will need). For feedback, as part of the audience for the presenter/teacher, you can complete the assessment rubric shown by circling one of the three choices for each of the 10 categories. You should give your completed form to each presenter/teacher for his or her use in self-assessment and analysis.

APPLICATION EXERCISE 9.1 (continued)

Peer and Self-Assessment Rubric for Use with Application Exercise 9.1

For: Group:

	1	0.5	0
1. Lesson beginning	effective	less effective	not effective
Comment:			
2. Sequencing	effective	less effective	rambling
Comment:			
3. Pacing of lesson	effective	less effective	too slow or too fast
Comment:			
4. Audience involvement	effective	less effective	none
Comment:			
5. Motivators (e.g., analogies, verbal cues, humor, visual cues, sensory cues)			
Comment:	effective	less effective	not apparent
6. Content of lesson	well chosen	interesting	boring or inappropriate
Comment:			
7. Voice of teacher	stimulating	minor problem	major problems
Comment:			
8. Vocabulary used	well chosen	appropriate	inappropriate
Comment:			
9. Eye contact	excellent	average	problems
Comment:			
10. Closure	effective	less effective	unclear/none
Comment:			

OTHER COMMENTS:

Technology Tips for the Classroom

- To consider websites in Spanish for students and parents, visit Colorin Colorado! (www.colorincolorado.org), a site that provides literacy information to Spanish-speaking parents. It has suggestions for activities that will teach young children about language and encourages parents to talk, sing, and read to their children every day. Recommends books for parents to share with their children.
- To use a flat-screen monitor to instruct the students or observe them while they work at wireless computers on a math problem as a group, consider a big-ticket item for your district such as Hitachi Software's *StarTablet* system, a flat-screen teaching system that is interactive with a 15-inch LCD monitor. The teacher works at a desktop panel and projects the image on a larger screen. Using a special stylus, the teacher draws on an overlay and the system transmits the image onto a monitor for the class to see. A teacher also can use the system to run educational games for the classes. Also available is Hitachi's *StarBoard* software, which can save a presentation as a series of images similar to a *PowerPoint* presentation. The teacher's important lessons can be saved and made available online for students to study for upcoming tests. Other systems similar to the Hitachi software are Promethean's *ACTIVBoard* system and SMART Technologies' *560* Interactive Whiteboard presentation system.
- To search for children's books by title, subject, author, keyword, publisher, age range, reading level, or awards, use the web version of *Children's Books in Print.* Visit www.childrensbooksinprint.com. District yearly fee required.

Companion Website

To find links to resources about inquiry learning, materials in Spanish, and presentation systems and software, go to our Companion Website at **www.prenhall.com/roberts** and click on the *Web Destinations* module for Chapter 9.

About Praxis and Other Teacher Tests

About Praxis Teacher Tests. Praxis II Principles of Learning and Teaching tests and other tests for beginning educators often take into account the point of view that writing skills are central to the work that educational professionals do. Thus, the tests for credentialing often assess writing tasks that will ask you, the precredentialed teacher, to recognize a particular purpose for writing a short essay or a brief response. The writing tasks often will ask you to organize and develop related ideas and use interesting words, proper mechanics, and appropriate sentence structure in an essay or short response test. To rise to this challenge, you may want to adopt the guidelines about writing essays written in this resource guide's chapter about assessment (Chapter 6) as your *own* guidelines before you write an on-target essay or brief answer. You should also practice to give yourself the opportunity to demonstrate your competence in writing effectively before you are asked to respond through an essay/short response format in a crucial test situation. We suggest you use the topics in the questions at the end of each chapter and the Praxis Warm-Up questions for topics for your practice essays.

About Essay Tests. If you need a particular approach to essay writing to prepare for future tests, consider a three-paragraph approach to coordinate your writing interests and skills in responding to the essay topic. In a three-paragraph approach, you will want to consider a triad of paragraphs i.e., a paragraph to introduce the topic, a paragraph to discuss any transitions, and a paragraph to conclude the essay. You will realize that your introductory paragraph should set your purpose (i.e., One might think there isn't much value in the teaching idea of . . . but as a matter of fact . . . ; or write, "To me, _____ is the best in the world;" Or write, "With a wave of her/his chalk, the teacher . . . ."). You will also realize that your transitional paragraph can summarize one idea and/or introduce another idea about your essay topic (i.e., "As I approached. . . or "Strangely enough. . . " or "Never before . . . " or "As I matured . . . "). Then, your final paragraph should present your concluding statements and then a conclusion ("It, indeed, has value." or "It is still a good _____." or "Maybe I can help change things as that teacher did." or "I realized that teachers . . . ").

To continue to support your interest in preparing for a Praxis II Principles of Learning and Teaching test, as well as some of the other teacher tests, the application exercise for this chapter (and in the *Additional Applications* module on our Companion Website at **www.prenhall.com/roberts**) offer opportunities to consider

(continued)

your use of demonstrations, thinking, and inquiry learning. For instance, in this chapter, prelicensed and pre-credentialed teachers were asked to do the following:

- Develop a lesson using different approaches (Application Exercise 9.1)
- Further explore your knowledge of inquiry by completing the Companion Website's additional application exercise in the *Additional Application Exercises* module titled A Study of Inquiry and Strategy Integration.

You can find a constructed response-type question similar to those found on the Praxis II tests in the Praxis Warm-Up section that follows the Chapter Summary. This warm-up takes another look at the classroom vignette found in the Looking at Teachers section at the beginning of this chapter.

 Other Teacher Tests. For those of you who will be teaching in states that do not administer the Praxis II Principles of Learning and Teaching tests, go to our Companion Website at **www.prenhall. com/roberts** and click on the *Other Teacher Tests* module for Chapter 9 to access information about teacher tests other than the Praxis.

SUMMARY

Central to your selection of instructional strategies should be those strategies that encourage students to become independent thinkers and skilled learners who can help in the planning, structuring, regulating, and assessing of their own learning and learning activities. Important to helping students construct their understanding are the cognitive tools that are available for their use. You have considered the selection and implementation of specific instructional strategies to facilitate student's meaningful learning of skills and content of the curriculum. Additionally, many useful and effective aids, media, and resources from which to draw are on our Companion Website **(www.prenhall.com/roberts)** Use them to plan your instructional experiences.

What's to Come. In the chapter that follows, your attention is directed to how teachers group children in the classroom.

EXTENDING MY PROFESSIONAL COMPETENCY

Praxis Warm-Up: A Constructed Response-Type Question

If you'll recall, this chapter's opening teacher vignette was about real-life problem solving. The emphasis was on integrated learning and about looking at a problem or subject of study from the point of view of many separate disciplines. Such an interdisciplinary approach has been adopted by educators and is the mode of meaningful learning and real-life problem solving. An example of this kind of problem solving related to public officials making decisions about watershed projects in their state was presented and offered as a possible teacher–student discussion.

Just as the state public officials did, students can study a topic and its underlying ideas as well as related knowledge from various disciplines on an ongoing basis when the students are involved in activities; lessons, and units—especially an interdisciplinary thematic unit. The teacher, sometimes with the help of students and other teachers and adults, can introduce experiences designed to illustrate ideas and skills from various disciplines, just as the hydrologist introduced information from hydrology.

Suppose that you use a unit on reading newspaper articles related to a topic of interest to introduce students to the idea of public officials in the real world using related knowledge from various disciplines to help solve one or more of their problems. After a week or two of reading newspaper articles, you discover that some of your students still don't understand some of the key principles of newspaper articles.

Describe two activities might help these students identify main ideas in nonfiction prose. Give specific examples and explain the purpose of the activities.

Hints for responding to Praxis Warm-Ups are found in the Appendix.

Praxis. To do another Praxis Warm-Up with a constructed response-type question, go to our Companion Website at **www.prenhall.com/roberts** and click on the *Praxis Warm-Up* module for Chapter 9. Constructed response-type questions are designed to help you prepare for the Praxis II Principles of Learning and Teaching tests.

For Your Discussion

1. **Demonstration.** What will I say if a parent asks me if I will include a teacher demonstration that is typically done by teachers of a particular grade level and subject at my school? **To do:** Identify a teacher demonstration that you could discuss with a parent, and to a colleague, describe at least one way that you might try to improve on the way that the demonstration is typically done.

2. **Integrating Strategies.** What will I say during a job interview when a principal asks me to give an example of how I would integrate strategies for use in my own teaching? **To do:** Analyze an inquiry learning lesson and text information about integrating strategies to form a synthesis of information for use in your own teaching.

3. **Brief Lesson.** What will I say in response if a teaching colleague asks what I do to teach toward intelligent behavior? **To do:** Select one of the characteristics of intelligent behavior, and (for a grade level of your choice and time limit as decided by your group), write a lesson plan for helping students develop that behavior. If you are interested in one of the first problem-solving models based on classroom experience, read the early writings of G. Polya, *Induction and Analogy in Mathematics* (Princeton, NJ: Princeton University Press, 1954). Give a copy of your plan to others in your group for their analysis and suggestions.

4. **Educational Games for Learning.** What will I say if a parent expresses his or her concern about games and does not approve of the use of educational games for learning in the classroom? **To do:** Research the cautions that teachers need to be aware of when using educational games for teaching and learning. If there are some cautions that you identify, explain to a colleague what you would say to the parent who is concerned about this issue.

5. **Integrating Strategies.** How will I respond if I am asked during a job interview to explain the *meaning* of integrating strategies for integrated learning? **To do:** Talking to a colleague, clearly identify two integrating strategies that support the practice or theory presented in this chapter; and from this discussion, formulate a meaning about integrating strategies for integrated learning from your point of view. Present a brief explanation.

Online Portfolio Activities

Supporting Principles 4 and 5 of INTASC and Standards 1, 3, and 5 of NBPTS: At the Companion Web-site **(www.prenhall.com/roberts),** click on the *Online Portfolio Activities* module to continue your on-line portfolio supporting instruction of students.

 Companion Website
Also on the Companion Website at **www.prenhall. com/roberts,** you can measure your understanding of chapter content in the *Objectives* and *Self-Check* modules and apply concepts in the *Additional Application Exercises, For Your Discussion,* and *Online Portfolio* modules.

FOR FURTHER READING

Bondy, E. (2000). Warming Up to Classroom Research in a Professional Development School. *Contemporary Education, 72*(1), 8–13.

Borich, G. (2003). *Observational Skills for Effective Teaching* (4th ed.). Upper Saddle River, NJ: Merrill/Prentice Hall.

Brisk, M. S., and Harrington, M. M. (2000). *Literacy and Bilingualism: A Handbook for All Teachers.* Mahwah, NJ: Lawrence Erlbaum.

California State Department of Education. (1997). *Descriptions of Practice.* Sacramento: California Standards for the Teaching Profession.

Camp, D. (2000). It Takes Two: Teaching with Twin Texts of Fact and Fiction. *The Reading Teacher, 53*(5), 400–408.

Costa, A., and Garmston, R. (2001). Five Human Passions: The Source of Critical and Creative Thinking. In A. Costa (Ed.), *Developing Minds, A Resource Book for Teaching Thinking.* Alexandria, VA: Association for Supervision and Curriculum Development.

Costa, A., and Garmston, R. (2002). *Cognitive Coaching: A Foundation for Renaissance Schools.* Norwood, MA: Christopher-Gordon.

Eckman, A. 1998. Making Science Popular: Inquiry-Based Instruction Sparks Students' Interest. *Curriculum Update* (Fall 1998), 7.

Hinman, L. A. (2000). What's The Buzz? A Classroom Simulation Teaches Students About Life in the Hive. *Science and Children, 37*(5), 24–27.

Kellough, R. D. (2000). *A Resource Guide for Teaching: K–12* (3rd. ed.). Upper Saddle River, NJ: Merrill/Prentice Hall.

Landers, D., Maxwell, W., Butler, J., and Fagen, L. (2001). Developing Thinking Skills Through Physical Education. In A. Costa (Ed.), *Developing Minds: A Resource Book for Teaching Thinking.* Alexandria, VA: Association for Supervision and Curriculum Development.

Morgan, R. R., Ponticell, J. A., and Gordon, E. E. (2000). *Rethinking Creativity* (Fastback 458). Bloomington, IN: Phi Delta Kappa Educational Foundation.

National Research Council. (2000). *Inquiry and the National Science Education Standards: A Guide for Teaching and Learning.* Washington, DC: National Academy Press.

National Science Foundation. (2000). Foundations, Vol. 2: Inquiry—Thoughts, Views, and Strategies for the K–5 Classroom. Alexandria, VA: Division of Elementary, Secondary and Information Education.

Perkins, D. N. (2000). Schools Need to Pay More Attention to "Intelligence in the Wild." *Harvard Education Letter, 16*(3), 7–8.

Sternberg, R., and Grigorenko, E. (Eds.). (2001). *The Evolution of Intelligence*. Mahwah, NJ: Lawrence Erlbaum.

Tower, C. (2000). Questions That Matter: Preparing Elementary Students for the Inquiry Process. *The Reading Teacher, 53*(7), 550–557.

Wittrock, C. A., and Barrow, L. H. (2000). Blow-by-Blow Inquiry. *Science and Children, 37*(5), 34–38.

NOTES

1. A. L. Costa, *The School as a Home for the Mind* (Palatine, IL: Skylight Publishing, 1991), pp. 20–31. To the 14 characteristics presented here, thinking independently and remaining open to continuous learning have been added. See A. L. Costa and B. Kallick (Eds.), *Habits of Mind* (Alexandria, VA: Association for Supervision and Curriculum Development, 2000). See also 11 qualities of genius noted as creativity, curiosity, flexibility, humor, imagination, joy, playfulness, sensitivity, vitality, wisdom, and wonderment in T. Armstrong, *Awakening Genius in the Classroom* (Alexandria, VA: Association for Supervision and Curriculum Development, 1998), pp. 2–15; and Project Zero's 7 dispositions for good thinking that include (a) being broad and adventurous; (b) wondering, problem-finding, and investigating; (c) building explanations and understandings; (d) plan-making and being strategic; (e) being intellectually careful; (f) seeking and evaluating reasons; and (g) being metacognitive;

2. M. Goos and P. Galbraith, Do It This Way! Metacognitive Strategies in Collaborative Mathematics Problem Solving, *Educational Studies in Mathematics, 30*(3), 229–260 (April 1996).

3. D. Goleman, *Emotional Intelligence: Why It Can Matter More Than IQ* (New York: Bantam Books, 1995), and D. Harrington-Lueker, Emotional Intelligence, *High Strides, 9*(4), 1, 4–5 (March/April 1997).

4. Goleman, *Ibid;* see also E. de Bono, *Lateral Thinking: Creativity Step by Step* (New York: Harper & Row, 1970); B. Brodinsky, Talking Problems Through Lateral Thinking. An Interview with Edward de Bono, *School Administrator, 42*(3), 10–13 (March 1985); or E. de Bono, Lateral Thinking: The Searching Mind, *Today's Education, 58*(8), 20–24 (November 1969).

5. N. Margulies and R. Sylwester, *Discover Your Brain: Emotion and Attention. How Our Brain Determines What's Important* (Tucson, AZ: Zephyr Press, 1998).

6. J. W. Astington, Theory of Mind Goes to School, *Educational Leadership, 56*(3), 46–48 (November 1998).

7. P. L. Roberts, *Taking Humor Seriously in Children's Literature: Literature-based Mini-Units for Children, Ages 5–12* (Lanham, MD: Scarecrow Press/University of America, 1991).

8. J. Piaget, *The Psychology of Intelligence* (Totowa, NJ: Littlefield Adams, 1972).

9. L. Kohlberg, *The Meaning and Measurement of Mind Development* (Worcester, MA: Clark University Press, 1981).

10. S. Haroutunian-Gordon, A Study of Reflective Thinking: Patterns in Interpretive Discussion, *Educational Theory, 48*(1), 33–58 (Winter 1998); and A. C. Boucher, Critical Thinking Through Estimation, *Teaching Children Mathematics, 4*(8), 452–455 (April 1998).

11. M. E. Gredler, *Learning and Instruction: Theory into Practice* (3rd ed.) (Upper Saddle River, NJ: Merrill/Prentice Hall, 1997).

12. For products for teaching thinking, contact Critical Thinking Press & Software, P. O. Box 448, Pacific Grove, CA 93950; (800)458–4849.

13. D. Raschke, S. Alper, and E. Eggers, Recalling alphabet Letter Names: A Mnemonic System to Facilitate Learning, *Preventing School Failure, 43*(2), 80–83 (Winter 1999).

14. J. D. Novak, *Learning, Creating, and Using Knowledge: Concept Maps™ as Facilitative Tools in Schools and Corporations* (Mahwah, NJ: Lawrence Erlbaum, 1998); J. D. Novak, Concept Maps and Vee Diagrams, Two Metacognitive Tools to Facilitate Meaningful Learning, *Instructional Science, 19*(1), 29–52 (1990); J. D. Novak and B. D. Gowin, *Learning How to Learn* (Cambridge, England: Cambridge University Press, 1984); E. Plotnick, *Concept Mapping: A Graphical System for Understanding the Relationship Between Concepts* (Syracuse, NY: ERIC Clearinghouse on Information and Technology, 1997), ED 407938.

15. D. Hyerle, *Visual Tools for Constructing Knowledge* (Alexandria, VA: Association for Supervision and Curriculum Development, 1996).

16. See the early writings of D. P. Ausubel, *The Psychology of Meaningful Learning* (New York: Grune & Stratton, 1963), and The Facilitation of Meaningful Verbal Learning in the Classroom, *Educational Psychologist, 12,* 162–178 (1977).

17. Novak, note 14.

18. R. H. Mayer, Use the Story of Anne Hutchinson to Teach Historical Thinking, *Social Studies, 90*(3), 105–109. (May/June 1999); and R. Mayer and M. Wittrock, Problem-Solving Transfer, in D. Berliner and R. Calfee (Eds.), *Handbook of Educational Psychology* (New York: Macmillan, 1996), pp. 47–62.

19. C. J. Carter, Why Reciprocal Teaching?, *Educational Leadership, 54*(6), 64–68 (March 1997).

20. J. S. Choate and T. A. Rakes, *Inclusive Instruction for Struggling Readers* (Fastback 434) (Bloomington, IN: Phi Delta Kappa Educational Foundation, 1998).

21. R. Coney and S. Kanel, Opening the World of Literature Through Interactive Drama Experiences, Paper presented at the Annual International Conference and Exhibition of the Association for Childhood Education (Portland, OR, April 9–12, 1997).

22. T. Kaldusdal, S. Wood, and J. Truesdale, Virtualville Votes: An Interdisciplinary Project, *MultiMedia Schools, 5*(1), 30–35 (January/February 1998).

23. Johnsontown Road Elementary School (retrieved July 29, 2003, from *www.jefferson.k12.ky.us/Schools/Elementary/Johnstontown.html*). For information about MicroSociety and school sites using the program, contact MicroSociety at 306 Cherry Street, Suite 200, Philadelphia, PA 19106; *www.microsociety.org*.

What Guidelines Assist My Use of Groupings and Assignments to Promote Positive Interaction and Quality Learning?

Visual Chapter Organizer and Overview

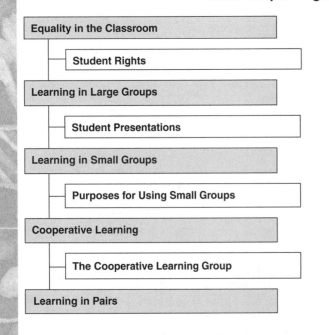

Equality in the Classroom

  | Student Rights |

| Learning in Large Groups |

  | Student Presentations |

| Learning in Small Groups |

  | Purposes for Using Small Groups |

| Cooperative Learning |

  | The Cooperative Learning Group |

| Learning in Pairs |

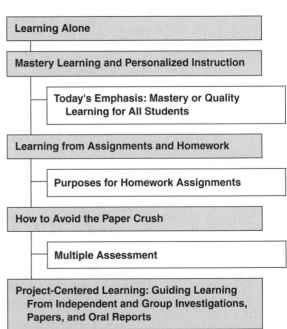

| Learning Alone |

| Mastery Learning and Personalized Instruction |

  | Today's Emphasis: Mastery or Quality Learning for All Students |

| Learning from Assignments and Homework |

  | Purposes for Homework Assignments |

| How to Avoid the Paper Crush |

  | Multiple Assessment |

| Project-Centered Learning: Guiding Learning From Independent and Group Investigations, Papers, and Oral Reports |

Looking at Teachers

Let's suppose that the students from your class have been working nearly all year on an interdisciplinary thematic unit (ITU) entitled *Surviving Natural Disasters* (referring back to the example in Chapter 5 regarding ITU themes). As a culmination to the students' study, they used desktop publishing to publish a document entitled *Natural Disaster Preparation and Survival Guide for* (community name). They proudly distributed the guide to their parents and other members of the community.

Long before preparing the guide, however, the students had to do research. You guided them in this process. To learn about the history of various kinds of natural disasters that had occurred or might occur locally and about the sorts of preparations a community should take for each kind of disaster, students searched sources on the Internet. They found federal documents, scientific articles, and articles from newspapers from around the world where natural disasters had occurred. They also searched in the local library for informational books such as *Dangerous Planet: Natural Disasters That Changed History* (New York: Crown, 2003, ages 8–12) by Bryn Barnard. They read local newspapers' archives to learn about floods, tornadoes, and fires that had occurred during the past 200 years. Much to their surprise, they learned that their community is located very near the New Madrid Fault and did, in fact, experience a serious earthquake in 1811. As a result of that earthquake, two nearby towns completely disappeared; the Mississippi flowed in reverse, and its course changed and even caused the formation of a new lake in Tennessee.

In class meetings, the students decided on different projects to support the publication of their guide and you made a professional effort to ensure equity in your interactions with students. (See Figure 10.1.) Among the student projects were the following:

- **Chat meeting.** The students were encouraged to use their favorite, parent-approved chat source or to use some free chat space available through ParaChat (*www.parachat.com*) to organize a chat session with other students to discuss natural disasters and the consequences, to learn what others did to prepare for disasters, and to learn some survival techniques that were used during and after a disaster. After the chat sessions, the students made recommendations to the class about material they wanted to include in the guide based on the content of their chat discussions.

- **Newsletters through e-mail.** The students were invited to use their favorite bulk e-mail software or, with district permission, to use the software available in the school district. The students gathered e-mail addresses (with parental permission) and advertised their newsletter to other students. They gathered news about their research for the guide, wrote a newsletter about what they were learning, determined their publication schedule, and later, distributed the newsletter through e-mail. (See the accompanying *Technology Tips for the Classroom* feature.)

- **Use of copyrighted sources.** From published and copyrighted sources, including websites, the students also found many useful photographs, graphics, and articles, which they included in whole, or in part, in their natural disaster guide. They cited the sources but did so without obtaining permission from all of the original copyright holders where they used whole materials.

You and the other members of your teaching team and other people were so impressed with the students' work that they were encouraged to offer the document for publication on the school's website. Additionally, the document was received with so much acclaim that the students decided to sell it in local stores. They wanted to help defray the original cost of duplication and be able to continue to supply guides to those who wanted them.

Caution About Copyrighted Sources

Related to the teaching scenario discussed here, there is a positive aspect as well as a negative aspect. The positive aspect is that the students used a valuable technological tool, the Internet, to research a variety of sources, including many primary ones. The negative aspect is that when they published their guidebook on the Internet and when they made copies of their guide to be sold, they did so without the permission from some of the original copyright holders. Unknowingly, they were infringing on copyright law. Students need to be aware that unless there is a clear statement that materials taken from the Internet are in the public domain, it is best for a teacher and students to assume that the materials are copyrighted and should not be used without expressed permission. Figures 10.2, 10.3, and 10.4 provide guidelines for using copyrighted printed materials, computer software, and multimedia programs.

Because educators believe in the learning potential of every student, exemplary schools and accomplished teachers are able to effectively modify the key variables of time, methodology, and grouping to help individual students achieve mastery learning of the planned curriculum rather than dilute standards and expectations. Related to this, in Chapter 1 we discussed ways in which time is modified. Throughout other chapters in this resource guide, we talk of ways of varying the methodology. In this chapter, we focus on ways of grouping students to enhance positive interaction and quality learning.

In the most effective instructional environments, during any given week or day of school, a student will likely experience a succession of group settings. Ways of grouping children for instruction is the

Figure 10.1
Resources on sexual harassment in schools

- L. A. Brown et al., *Student-to-Student Sexual Harassment: A Legal Guide for Schools* (Alexandria, VA: Council of School Attorneys, National School Boards Association, 1998).

- D. L. Siegel, revised by M. Budhos, *Sexual Harassment: Research and Resources,* available from the National Council for Research on Women, 11 Hanover Square, New York, NY 10005, 1995.

- N. Stein and L. Sjostrom, *Flirting or Hurting? A Teacher's Guide on Student-to-Student Sexual Harassment in Schools—Grades 6–12* (Washington, DC: NEA Professional Library, 1994).

- *Title IX at 25: Report Card on Gender Equity,* available from the National Women's Law Center, 11 Dupont Circle, NW, Suite 800, Washington, DC 20036, 1997.

- D. H. Wishnietsky, *Establishing School Policies on Sexual Harassment* (Fastback 370) (Bloomington, IN: Phi Delta Kappa Educational Foundation, 1994).

- E. Yaffe, Expensive, Illegal, and Wrong: Sexual Harassment in Our Schools, *Phi Delta Kappan,* 77(3), K1–K15 (November 1995).

---

initial topic of this chapter, beginning with large-group instruction and moving on to small groups, dyads, and individualized instruction. You also will learn how to ensure equality in the classroom, ways to use assignments and homework, and how to coordinate various forms of independent and small-group project-based study.

CHAPTER OBJECTIVES

Specifically, on completion of this tenth chapter, you should be able to:

1. Describe how to use whole-class discussion as a teaching strategy.
2. Contribute to a list of guidelines for using whole-class discussion as a teaching strategy.
3. Explain how the classroom teacher can personalize the instruction (differentiated/tiered instruction) to ensure success for each student.
4. Present your persuasive argument in favor of or against providing recovery options for students who do not do an assignment or who do not do well on it.

5. Describe your view about how to effectively use one or more of these instructional strategies: assignments, homework/responsibility papers, journal writing, written and oral reports, cooperative learning groups, learning centers, problem-based learning, and student-centered projects.

EQUALITY IN THE CLASSROOM

Especially when using explicit/direct instruction and when conducting whole-group discussions, it is easy for a teacher to develop the habit of interacting with only "the stars," or with only those in the front of the room or on one side, or only the most vocal and assertive. You must exercise caution and avoid falling into that habit. To ensure a psychologically safe and effective environment for learning

---

Technology Tips for the Classroom

- Consider a useful electronic tool for your professional work called Handspring Treo 600, a mobile communication device. It acts like a phone and you can write and read e-mail that comes to the device automatically without having to dial in to access it. You can browse the web or store your contacts or the dates of appointments with faculty or parents. It has a brightly colored screen and the illuminated keyboard is actually big enough to use.

- Another useful tool for your professional use is the HP Compaq Tablet PC TC1100, a laptop computer. This laptop has a screen that can be used like a regular monitor screen or you can fold the monitor down so that it looks like the front of a spiral notebook. In both cases, you can write directly on the screen with a special stylus to take notes in meetings, make handwritten marginalia to your Word documents, or surf the web without the need of the mouse or keyboard. In fact, you can detach the keyboard to make this laptop more mobile.

- Remind your class that if the students need access to the web, most libraries offer free Internet services.

- Still another useful and reusable tool may be the development of an online tutorial for your students by using *Camtasia* (www.techsmith.com) or another tutorial software program. Topics can include how to use a certain word processing program, research skills, and databases.

Figure 10.2
Guidelines for copying printed materials that are copyrighted
(*Source*: Section 107 of the 1976 Federal Omnibus Copyright Revision Act)

Permitted Uses—*You May Make*:

1. Single copies of:
   - A chapter of a book
   - An article from a periodical, magazine, or newspaper
   - A short story, short essay, or short poem even from a collected work
   - A cartoon, chart, diagram, drawing, graph, a character from a reading book to use in a one-time reading lesson
   - An illustration from a book, magazine, or newspaper.

2. Multiple copies for classroom use (not to exceed one copy per student in a course) of:
   - A complete poem if less than 250 words
   - An excerpt from a longer poem, but not to exceed 250 words
   - A complete article, story, or essay of less than 2,500 words
   - An excerpt from a larger printed work not to exceed 10% of the whole or 1,000 words
   - One cartoon, chart, diagram, graph, or picture per book or magazine issue.

Prohibited Uses—*You May Not*:

1. Copy more than one work or two excerpts from a single author during one class term (semester or year).
2. Copy more than three works from a collective work or periodical volume during one class term.
3. Reproduce more than nine sets of multiple copies for distribution to students in one class term.
4. Copy to create, replace, or substitute for anthologies or collective works.
5. Copy "consumable" works, for example, workbooks, standardized tests, answer sheets or game boards, especially those with logos, symbols, or short phrases since these marks are registered trademarks. Be aware that trademark law does not have a fair-use exemption and is much more rigid than copyright law.
6. Copy the same work year after year.

Figure 10.3
Copyright law for use of computer software/videos
(*Source*: December 1980 Congressional Amendment to the 1976 Copyright Act)

Permitted Uses—*You May:*

1. Make a single backup or archival copy of a computer program.
2. Adapt a computer program to another language if the program is unavailable in the target language.
3. Add features to make better use of the computer program.
4. Use videos *directly related to the curriculum in the teaching environment* (that even includes tour buses with TVs and VCRs when students are on the way to a site for real-place education). The term *fair use* allows teachers to show videos directly related to the curriculum (and not for entertainment purposes) to their students in the teaching environment, one time, without the prior permission of the copyright holder.

Prohibited Uses—*You May Not:*

1. Make multiple copies.
2. Make replacement copies from an archival or backup copy.
3. Make copies of copyrighted programs to be sold, leased, loaned, transmitted, or given away.

Figure 10.4
Fair use guidelines for using multimedia programs

You Should:

1. Follow normal copyright guidelines (e.g., the limitations that apply on the amount of material used, whether it be the motion media, text, music, illustrations, photographs, or computer software) for portions of copyrighted works used in your own multimedia production for use in teaching.

2. Obtain permissions from copyright holders before using any copyrighted materials in educational multimedia production for commercial reproduction and distribution or before replicating more than one copy, distributing copies to others, and for use beyond your own classroom.

You May:

1. Display your own multimedia work using copyrighted works to other teachers, such as in workshops.

2. Use your own multimedia production for instruction over an electronic network for education (e.g., distance learning) provided there are limits to access and to the number of students enrolled.

3. The Technology, Education, and Copyright Harmonization (TEACH, 2002) Act now permits accredited, nonprofit, educational institutions that *have copyright policies* available to teachers, students, and staff to make a digital copy of an analog work without prior permission if that single copy is made solely for classroom use and kept only as long as is necessary to meet the teaching objective. Thus, TEACH allows teachers and students to show a DVD and art slides, without prior permission, in the physical classroom and in a virtual classroom that is received by students through digital transmission on a network. TEACH also allows the fair use of parts of a nondramatic work such as articles, books, charts, maps, and poetry. Smaller portions of dramatic works such as videos, films, operas, and dramas can be used in the *digital* classroom. Any work that would be used in the physical classroom and is central to the teaching goals of the class can be used in digital form or on digital networks.

4. You may make one copy of a DVD, to be destroyed later, if a replacement exemption applies, if a teaching exemption applies, or if fair use applies.*

You May Not:

1. Distribute your own multimedia production using copyrighted works over any electronic network (local or wide area) without express permission from copyright holders.

2. Make and distribute copies to colleagues of your own multimedia work using copyrighted works without obtaining permission from copyright holders.

---

*Millennium Copyright Act [DMCA] Sections 110, 108, and 107, and TEACH Act, 2002.

Companion Website

To find links to glossaries and professional electronic tools mentioned in Technology Tips for the Classroom, go to our Companion Website at **www.prenhall.com/roberts** and click on the *Web Destinations* module for Chapter 10.

for every student in your classroom, whatever the grouping arrangement, you must attend to all students and try to involve all students equally in the class activities. Look again at the *Technology Tips for the Classroom* feature for class activities related to technology that can involve the students. You must avoid any biased expectations about certain children, and you must avoid discriminating against students according to their gender, ethnicity, or any other personal characteristic. Discrimination is not only unfair, it is illegal.

Student Rights

You probably already know that as a result of legislation that occurred three decades ago—federal law Title IX of the Educational Amendments of 1972, PL 92-318—a teacher is prohibited from discriminating among students on the basis of their gender. In all aspects of school, male and female students must be treated the same. This means, for example, that a teacher must not put boys against girls in a quiz game or any other activity. Further, no teacher, student, administrator, or other school employee should make sexual advances toward a student (i.e., touching or speaking in a sexual manner). Students should be informed by their schools of their rights under Title IX, and they should be encouraged to report any suspected violations of their rights to the school principal or other designated person. Review Figure 10.1 for additional resources on sexual harassment in schools. Many schools or districts have a clearly delineated statement of steps to follow in the process of protecting students' rights.

Gender Discrimination

Even today, research identifies the unintentional tendency of teachers of *both* sexes to discriminate on the basis of gender. For example, teachers, along with the rest of society, tend to have lower expectations for girls than for boys in mathematics and science. They tend to call on and encourage boys more than girls. They often let boys interrupt girls but praise girls for being polite and waiting their turn. Avoiding such discrimination may take special effort on your part, such as observing National Women's History Month (see *www.nwhm.org/news/press.html* or National Women's History Project *www.nwhp.org*). No matter how aware of the problem you may be, some researchers believe the problem is so insidious that courses about it are needed in teacher education.[1]

Ensuring Equity

To ensure equity in interaction with students, many teachers have found it helpful to ask someone to quietly tally classroom interactions between the teacher and students during a class discussion. After an analysis of the results, the teacher arrives at decisions about his or her own attending and facilitating behaviors. Such an analysis is the purpose of the additional application exercise titled, Teacher Interaction with Students According to Student Gender or Other Personal Characteristics, which can be found on our Companion Website **(www.prenhall.com/roberts).** We encourage you to make blank copies and share them with your teaching colleagues.

In addition to the advice given in Chapter 8 about using teacher talk and questioning, many other strategies can help ensure that children are treated fairly in the classroom, including the following:

- Encourage students to demonstrate an appreciation for one another by applauding all individual and group presentations. Some teachers make a point of shaking hands with a student who has finished a presentation and saying "Thank you."
- Have and maintain high, although not necessarily identical, expectations for all students.
- Insist on politeness in the classroom. For example, a student can be shown appreciation with a sincere remark "I appreciate your contribution," or with a genuine smile for the student's contribution to the learning process.
- Insist on students finishing sentences, without being interrupted by others. Be certain that you model this behavior yourself.
- During whole-class instruction, insist that students raise their hands and be called on by you before they speak.

- Keep a stopwatch handy to unobtrusively control the wait time given to each student. While at first this idea may sound impractical, it works.
- Use a seating chart (perhaps attached to a clipboard) and next to each student's name, make a tally for each interaction you have with a student. This also is a good way to maintain records to reward students for their contributions to class discussion. The seating chart can be laminated and then used day after day by simply erasing the marks of the previous day, which should be made with nonpermanent markers.

Now do the additional application exercise we mentioned earlier by going to our Companion Website **(www.prenhall.com/roberts),** clicking on the *Additional Application Exercises* module for this chapter, and completing the application exercise titled, Teacher Interaction with Students According to Student Gender or Other Personal Characteristics. Also, this application exercise can be modified to include responses and their frequencies according to other teacher–student interactions, such as your calling on all students equally for responses to your questions, your calling on students equally to assist you with classroom helping jobs, or your reminding students about appropriate or inappropriate behavior.

LEARNING IN LARGE GROUPS

Large groups are those that involve eight or more students and very often the entire class. Most often, they are teacher directed. Student presentations and whole-class discussions are two techniques that involve the use of large groups.

Student Presentations

Students should be encouraged to be presenters for discussion of the ideas, opinions, and knowledge obtained from their own independent and small-group study. Several techniques encourage the development of certain skills, such as studying and organizing material, discovery, discussion, rebuttal, listening, analysis, suspending judgment, and critical thinking. Possible forms of discussions involving student presentations include the following:

- **Debate.** The debate is an arrangement in which members of two opposing teams make formal speeches on preassigned and researched topics. The speeches support each team's point of view. The speeches are followed by rebuttals from each team.
- **Jury (mock) trial.** The jury trial is a discussion approach in which the class simulates a courtroom, with class members playing various roles (judge, attorneys, jury members, bailiff, and court recorder).

- **Panel.** The panel is a setting in which from four to six students, with one designated as the chairperson or moderator, discuss a topic they have studied, followed by a question-and-answer period involving the entire class. The panel usually begins with each panel member giving a brief opening statement.
- **Research report.** For research reporting, one or two students, or a small group of students, give a report on a topic that they investigated, followed by questions and discussion by the entire class. Review Figures 10.2, 10.3, and 10.4, for guidelines about copyrighted material.
- **Roundtable.** The roundtable is a small group of three to five students who sit around a table and discuss among themselves (and perhaps with the rest of the class listening and perhaps later asking questions) a problem or issue that they have studied. One member of the panel may serve as moderator.

Similar to when students are involved in cooperative learning groups, students may need coaching from you to develop some of the skills necessary to use the previously mentioned techniques effectively. Individually, in small groups, or in whole-class sessions, the students may need coaching on how and where to gather information; how to listen, take notes, select major points, organize material, present a position succinctly and convincingly, play roles; and how to engage in dialogue and debate with one another without creating conflict.

Whole-Class Discussion

Teacher-directed whole-class discussion is a teaching technique used frequently by most teachers. On this topic, you should consider yourself an expert. Having been a student in formal education for many years, you are undoubtedly knowledgeable about the advantages and disadvantages of whole-class discussions, at least from your personal vantage point. Explore your knowledge further and share your experiences by responding to the additional application exercise titled Whole-Class Discussion as a Teaching Strategy: What Do I Already Know?, which can be found on our Companion Website **(www.prenhall.com/roberts)** for this chapter. Then return to this chapter to do Application Exercise 10.1 to assist in generating guidelines for using whole-class discussions.

APPLICATION EXERCISE 10.1 WHOLE-CLASS DISCUSSION AS A TEACHING STRATEGY: BUILDING ON WHAT I ALREADY KNOW

Instructions: The purpose of this exercise is to generate a list of guidelines for using whole-class discussion as a teaching strategy. If you completed the additional application exercise titled Whole-Class Discussion as a Teaching Strategy: What Do I Already Know?, then share the responses with your colleagues. Next, individually answer the first two questions below. Then, as a group, use all three questions to guide you as you generate a list of five general guidelines for the use of whole-class discussion as a strategy in teaching. Share your group's guidelines with the entire class. Then as a class, derive a final list of general guidelines.

1. How effective was your small-group discussion in sharing the results of the additional application exercise on whole-class discussion?

_____

_____

_____

_____

_____

_____

2. What allowed for or inhibited the effectiveness of that small-group discussion? _____

_____

_____

_____

_____

_____

3. How effective was this small-group discussion? Why?

_____

_____

_____

_____

_____

4. General guidelines generated from small-group discussions:

_____

_____

_____

_____

_____

_____

APPLICATION EXERCISE 10.1 *(continued)*

5. Final list of general guidelines derived from whole group:

_____

_____

_____

_____

_____

_____

_____

_____

_____

_____

_____

_____

_____

_____

_____

LEARNING IN SMALL GROUPS

Small groups are those involving three to eight students, in either a teacher- or student-directed setting. Using small groups for instruction enhances the opportunities for students to assume greater control over their own learning, sometimes referred to as *empowerment.*

Purposes for Using Small Groups

Small groups can be formed to serve a number of purposes that might be useful for a specific learning activity, for example, reciprocal reading groups. Or they might be formed to complete an activity that requires materials that are in short supply or to complete a science experiment or a project, with the groups only lasting as long as the project does. Teachers have various rationales for assigning students to temporary in-class groups. Groups can be formed by grouping children according to (a) personality type (e.g., sometimes a teacher may want to group less-assertive children together to give them an opportunity for greater management of their own learning); (b) social pattern (e.g., sometimes it may be necessary to break up a group of rowdy friends, or it may be desirable to broaden the association among students); (c) common interest; (d) learning styles (e.g., forming groups of either mixed styles or similar styles in common); or (e) their abilities in a particular skill or their knowledge in a particular area.

A teacher we know uses a wheel diagram to randomly select students for groups. To use the categories listed previously as an example, the teacher makes a wheel based on any one of the five categories. Once the teacher assesses where students fit in a category, the teacher places their names on the outside edge of one of three or four wheels stacked on one another and attached in the center with a paper brad/clasp. To randomly create new groups, the teacher spins one of the wheels one space and a second wheel two spaces, et cetera, then records the new groups. Once the groups have been selected, some teachers initiate a specific and well-known type of small-group instruction—the cooperative learning group.

COOPERATIVE LEARNING

Lev Vygotsky (1896–1934) studied the importance of a learner's social interactions in learning situations. Vygotsky argued that learning is most effective when learners cooperate with one another in a supportive learning environment under the careful guidance of a teacher. Cooperative learning, group problem solving, problem-based learning, and cross-age tutoring are instructional strategies used by teachers that have grown in popularity as a result of research evolving from Vygotsky's work.

Although cooperative learning is a genre of instructional strategies for which there are several models, they all share two key components: interdependence among members of the group and individual accountability for learning.[2]

The Cooperative Learning Group

The **cooperative learning group (CLG)** is a heterogeneous group (i.e., mixed according to one or more criteria, such as ability or skill level, ethnicity, learning style, learning capacity, gender, and language proficiency) of two to six students who work together in a teacher- or student-directed setting, emphasizing support for one another. Oftentimes, a CLG consists of three to four students of mixed ability, learning styles, gender and ethnicity, with each member of the group assuming a particular role (see discussion of roles that follows). Teachers usually change the membership of each group several times during the year.

The Theory and Use of Cooperative Learning

The theory of cooperative learning is that when small groups of students of mixed backgrounds and capabilities work together toward a common goal, members of the group increase their friendship and respect for one another. As a consequence, each individual's self-esteem is enhanced, students are more motivated to participate in higher order thinking, and academic achievement is accomplished.[3]

Of special interest to teachers are general methods of cooperative learning, such as these:

- **Student team achievement divisions (STAD).** The teacher presents a lesson, students work together in teams to help each other learn the materials, individuals take quizzes, and team rewards are earned based on the individual scores of the quizzes.
- **Teams–games–tournaments (TGT).** Tournaments (rather than quizzes) are held during which students compete against others of similar academic achievements and then winners contribute toward their team's score.
- **Group investigations.** Students form two- to six-member groups, select subtopics from a broader whole-class unit of study, and produce group reports, followed by each group making a culminating presentation.[4]

The primary purpose of each is for the groups to learn—which means, of course, that individuals within a group must learn. Group achievement in learning, then, depends on the learning of individuals within the group. Rather than competing for rewards for achievement, members of the group cooperate with one another by helping one another learn, so that the group reward will be a good one. This is the interdependence component of cooperative learning.

Normally, the group is rewarded on the basis of group achievement, though individual members within the group can later be rewarded for individual contributions. Because of peer pressure, when using CLGs the teacher must be cautious about using group grading.[5] For example, a student's report card should clearly represent that student's achievement and not be lower than it can be because of who the student works with in groups. For grading purposes, bonus points can be given to all members of a group; individuals can add to their own scores when everyone in the group has reached preset standards. The preset standards must be appropriate for all members of a group. Lower standards or improvement criteria could be set for students with lower ability so everyone feels rewarded and successful. To determine each student's semester or term grades, that is, the grades that go on reports to the child's home, individual student achievement is measured later through individual students' results on tests and a variety of other criteria, including each student's performance in the group work.

Roles within the Cooperative Learning Group

To structure the interdependent nature of cooperative learning, it is helpful to assign roles (specific duties) to each member of the CLG. These roles should be rotated, either during the activity or from one time to the next. Though titles are discretionary, five typical roles are:

- **Group facilitator.** Role is to keep the group on task.
- **Materials manager.** Role is to obtain, maintain, and return materials needed for the group to function.
- **Recorder.** Role is to record all group activities and processes and perhaps to periodically assess how the group is doing.
- **Reporter.** Role is to report group processes and accomplishments to the teacher and/or to the entire class. When using groups of four members, the roles of recorder and reporter can easily be combined.
- **Thinking monitor.** Role is to identify and record the sequence and processes of the group's thinking. This role encourages metacognition and the development of thinking skills.

It is important that students understand and perform their individual roles, and that each member of the CLG performs his or her duties as expected. This is the individual accountability component. No student should be allowed to ride the coattails of the group.

To emphasize the significance of roles in the group, to reinforce the importance of each role, and to be able to readily recognize the role any student is playing during CLG activity, one teacher made a trip to an office supplier and had permanent badges made for the various CLG roles. During CLGs then, each student attaches the appropriate badge to her or his clothing. Some teachers we know use index cards (often laminated) and yarn to create "necklaces" or "slings" for the students to wear to identify their roles. This is useful if funds aren't available to get badges from the office supplier.

What Students and the Teacher Do When Using Cooperative Learning Groups

Actually, for learning by CLGs to work, each member of the CLG must understand and assume two roles or responsibilities: the role he or she is assigned as a member of the group and the role of a facilitator, for example, seeing that all others in the group are performing their roles. Sometimes, to teach children what it means to work cooperatively, some teachers teach cooperation by what it looks and sounds like. For example, cooperation looks like two heads close together and sounds like "What a great idea!" They place charts in their classrooms that reinforce this instruction.

At other times, roles and responsibilities of group work require interpersonal skills that children have yet to learn or to learn well. This is where the teacher must assume additional responsibility. Simply placing children into CLGs and expecting each member and each group to function and to learn the expected outcomes may not work. In other words, skills of cooperation must be taught. These are the skills of altruism, consensus seeking, giving up an idea to work on someone else's, integrating the ideas of others, knowing how to handle disagreements, knowing how to support group efforts, listening, and sharing. If all of your students have not yet learned these skills, and they probably have not, then you will have to teach them. This doesn't mean that if a group is not functioning you immediately break up the group and reassign members to new groups. Part of group learning is learning the process of how to work out any conflicts.

A group may require your assistance to work out a conflict. With your guidance, the group should be able to discover what the problem causing the conflict is, identify some options, and mediate at least a temporary solution. If a particular skill is needed, then with your guidance (and perhaps a class meeting), the students can identify and learn that skill.

When to Use Cooperative Learning Groups

CLGs can be used for experiments, inquiry learning, opinion surveys, problem solving, project work, reviewing, test making, or almost any other instructional purpose. Just as you would organize for small-group work in general, you can use CLGs for most any purpose at any time. As with any other type of instructional strategy, however, it should not be overused. In the early grades, the group work should be highly structured, pleasant, and scheduled for relatively brief periods of time. As students' skills in group processing develop, they can be given gradually longer and more demanding group tasks.[6]

Outcomes of Using Cooperative Learning Groups

When the process is well planned and managed, the outcomes of cooperative learning include (a) improved communication and relationships of acceptance among students, (b) quality learning with fewer off-task behaviors, (c) improved ability to perform four key thinking strategies—problem solving, decision making, critical thinking, and creative thinking—and (d) increased academic achievement. In the words of Good and Brophy,

> Cooperative learning arrangements promote friendships and prosocial interaction among students who differ in achievement, gender, race, or ethnicity, and they promote the acceptance of mainstreamed handicapped students by their nonhandicapped classmates. Cooperative methods also frequently have positive effects, and rarely have negative effects on affective outcomes such as self-esteem, academic self-confidence, liking for the class, liking and feeling liked by classmates, and on various measures of empathy and social cooperation. (p. 291)[7]

Why Some Teachers Have Difficulty Using CLGs

For CLGs to work well, advanced planning and effective management are musts. As emphasized by Tomlinson, "the nest of strategies we call cooperative learning . . . [sometimes] have fallen short of expectations not because of a deficiency in the strategies themselves but because teachers apply them shallowly."[8] Sometimes, when they think they are using CLGs, teachers have difficulty and either give up trying to use the strategy or tell children to divide into groups for an activity and call it cooperative learning when it is simply group work. For the strategy to work, each student must be given *a responsibility of helping others learn* and acquire basic skills in interaction and group processing and must realize that individual achievement rests with that of their group.

Also, as is true for any other strategy, the use of CLGs must not be overused—teachers must vary their strategies.[9] Some teachers monitor cooperative learning groups and look for and note cooperative behaviors that are occurring. These are then shared in a debriefing/class meeting at the end of the work period or the school day (students perhaps writing a self-evaluation: I helped someone learn today when I _____). Students are also encouraged to discuss what worked well and what would help them work better next time.

Children must be instructed in the necessary skills for group learning. Each student must be assigned a responsible role within the group and be held accountable for fulfilling that responsibility. When a CLG activity is in process, groups must be continually monitored by the teacher for possible breakdown of this process within a group. In other words, while children are working in groups, the teacher must exercise with-itness. When a potential breakdown is noticed, the teacher quickly intervenes to reset the group back on track. See Figure 10.5 for additional resources.

LEARNING IN PAIRS

It is sometimes advantageous to pair students (dyads) for learning. Some ways of doing this are described next.

- Center for Research on the Education of Students Placed at Risk, Johns Hopkins University, 3003 N. Charles St., Suite 200, Baltimore, MD 21218; (410) 516-8800; www.csos.jhu.edu/crespar/

- Cooperative Learning Center at the University of Minnesota, 60 Piek Hall, University of Minnesota, Minneapolis, MN 55455; (612) 624-7031; www.co-operation.org/index.html

- Kagan Publishing, P.O. Box 72008, San Clemente, CA 92673-2008; (800) 933-2667; Kagan Professional Development, P.O. Box 72008, San Clemente, CA 92673-2008; (800) 266-7576; www.kaganonline.com

Figure 10.5
Resources on the use of cooperative learning

Peer Tutoring, Mentoring, and Cross-Age Coaching

Peer tutoring, mentoring, or peer-assisted learning is a strategy whereby one student tutors another. It is useful, for example, when one student helps another who has limited proficiency in English or when a student skilled in math helps another who is less skilled. For years, it has been demonstrated repeatedly that peer tutoring is a significant strategy for promoting active learning. Furthermore, peer tutoring increases academic achievement not only for those being tutored but for those students doing the tutoring.[10]

Cross-age coaching is a strategy whereby one student is coached by another from a different, usually higher, grade level. This is similar to peer tutoring, except the coach is from a different age level than the student being coached.[11] As discussed previously in Chapter 1 and in the final section of this chapter, many schools have service learning projects that involve older students mentoring younger children. [12]

Paired Team Learning

Paired team learning is a strategy in which students study and learn in teams of two. Students identified as gifted work and learn especially well when paired. Specific uses for paired team learning include drill partners, reading buddies, book report pairs, summarizing pairs, homework partners/responsibility paper partners, project assignment pairs, and elaborating partners or relating pairs.

Think–Pair–Share

Think–pair–share is a strategy in which students, in pairs, examine a new concept or topic about to be studied. After the students of each dyad discuss what they already know or think they know (misconceptions) about the concept, they present their perceptions to the whole group. This is an excellent technique for discovery learning about a topic. The think–pair–share strategy can be combined in use with the K–W–L strategy. Introducing a writing step, the modification called *think–write–pair–share* is used by a student dyad where the students think and write ideas or conclusions before sharing their work with the larger group.

The Learning Center

Another significantly beneficial way of pairing students for instruction (and for individualizing the instruction and learning or for integrating the learning) is by using a learning center (LC) or learning station. (*Note:* Whereas each learning center can be distinct and unrelated to others, the work at learning stations can be sequenced or in some way linked to one another.) The LC is a special place in the classroom where one student (or two, if student interaction is necessary or preferred at the center) can quietly work, explore, and learn at his or her own pace about a particular topic or improve specific skills. All materials needed are provided at the center, including clear instructions for the operation of the center. Familiar classroom examples of learning centers are the personal computer station and the reading corner.

The value of learning centers as instructional devices undoubtedly lies in the following facts:

- LCs can provide instructional diversity.
- While working at a center, the student can be giving time and quality attention to the learning task (learning toward mastery) and is likely to be engaging the student's preferred learning modality or integrating several or all modalities.
- To adapt instruction to students' individual needs and preferences, it is possible to design a classroom learning environment that includes several **learning resource centers,** each of which incorporates a different medium and modality or focuses on a special aspect of the curriculum.
- Students can work at the various learning centers according to their needs and preferences.

Learning centers are of three types: direct-learning center, open-learning center, and skill center. In the *direct-learning center*, performance expectations for cognitive learning are quite specific and the focus is on mastery of content. In the *open-learning center*, the goal is to provide opportunities for exploration, enrichment, motivation, and creative discovery. In the *skill center*, as in a direct-learning center, performance expectations are quite specific but the focus is on the development of a particular skill or process.

In all instances, the primary reason for using a learning center is to individualize—to provide collections of materials and activities adjusted to the various readiness levels, interests, and learning profiles of students. Other reasons to use an LC are to provide (a) a mechanism for learning that crosses discipline boundaries, (b) a special place for a student with special needs, (c) opportunities for creative work, enrichment experiences, and multisensory experiences, and (d) an opportunity to learn from learning packages that use special equipment or media of which only one or a limited supply may be available for use in your classroom (e.g., science materials, a microscope, a computer, a videodisc player, or some combination of these). Now, if you are interested further in a learning center, turn to our Companion Website **(www.prenhall.com/roberts)** and the *Additional Content* module for this chapter to read further about guidelines for constructing a learning center.

LEARNING ALONE

Some elementary schoolchildren learn well in pairs (dyads); others learn well with their peers in groups—collaboratively, cooperatively, or competitively—or collaboratively with adults; others learn well in combinations of these patterns; and some students learn best alone. Children who best learn alone usually are gifted, nonconforming, able to work at their own pace successfully, and are independently comfortable using media. Or they may be seemingly underachieving but potentially able students for whom unconventional instructional strategies, such as contract learning packages or multisensory instructional packages, encourage academic success.[13] Agreements can be made between you and individual students so they can proceed with certain tasks appropriate to their readiness, interests, or learning profiles in a sequence and at a pace that they select.

MASTERY LEARNING AND PERSONALIZED INSTRUCTION

Learning is an individual or personal experience. Yet, as a classroom teacher, you will be expected to work effectively with children on an individual basis as well as in a group of, perhaps, 30 or more students at a time. Much has been written about the importance of personalizing the instruction for learners. Virtually all the research concerning better instructional practice emphasizes greater individualization, or personalization, of instruction.[14] We know of the individuality of the learning experience and, although some elementary schoolchildren are primarily verbal learners, many more are primarily visual, tactile, or kinesthetic learners. As the teacher, though, you find yourself in the demanding position of simultaneously "treating" many separate and individual learners with individual learning capacities, styles, and preferences.

Common sense tells us that student achievement in learning is related to both the quality of attention and the length of time given to learning tasks. In 1968, Benjamin Bloom, building on a model developed earlier by John Carroll, presented the concept of individualized instruction called **mastery learning,** saying that students need sufficient time on task (i.e., engaged time) to master content before moving on to new content.[15] From that concept, Fred Keller, in the 1970s, developed an instructional plan called the Personalized System of Instruction (PSI) or the Keller plan, which involves a student learning from printed modules of instruction (which today, would likely be presented as computer software programs) that allow the student greater control over the learning pace. The instruction is mastery oriented; that is, the student demonstrates mastery of the content of one module before proceeding to the next.

Today's Emphasis: Mastery or Quality Learning for All Students

Emphasis today is on working toward mastery of content, which is also called *quality* learning, rather than just coverage of content or *quantity* of learning. Mastery of content means that the student demonstrates his or her use of what has been learned. Because of the emphasis and research that indicates that quality learning programs positively affect achievement, the importance of the concept of mastery learning has resurfaced. For example, in today's efforts to restructure schools, two approaches—results-driven education (RDE), also known as outcome-based education (OBE), and the Coalition of Essential Schools (CES)—use a goal-driven curriculum model with instruction that focuses on the construction of individual knowledge through mastery and assessment of student learning against the anticipated outcomes.[16]

In some instances, unfortunately, attention may only be on the mastery of minimum competencies; thus, students are not encouraged to work and learn to the maximum of their talents and abilities.

Assumptions About Mastery or Quality Learning

Today's concept of mastery, or quality, learning is based on six assumptions:

1. Mastery learning can ensure that students experience success at each level of the instructional process. Experiencing success at each level provides incentive and motivation for further learning.
2. Mastery of content, or quality learning, is possible for all students.
3. Although all students can achieve mastery, to master a particular content, some students may require more time than others. The teacher and the school must provide for this difference in time needed to complete a task successfully.
4. For quality learning to occur, *instruction* must be modified and adapted, not the *students*.
5. Most learning is sequential and logical.
6. Most desired learning outcomes can be specified in terms of observable and measurable performance.[17]

Components of Any Mastery Learning Model

Any instructional model designed to teach toward mastery (quality) learning will contain the following five components: (a) clearly defined instructional objectives; (b) a preassessment of the extent of the learner's present knowledge; (c) an instructional component with choices and options for students; (d) practice, reinforcement, frequent comprehension checks (both diagnostic and formative assessment), and corrective instruction at each step of the way to keep the learner on track; and (e) a summative assessment to determine the extent of student mastery of the objectives.

Strategies for Personalizing the Instruction: Working Toward Quality Learning

You can immediately provide personalized instruction by

1. Starting the study of a topic from where the students are in terms of what they know (or think they know) and what they want to know about the topic. The strategies of K–W–L and think–pair–share are examples of doing this.
2. Providing children with choices from a rich variety of learning pathways and hands-on experiences to learn more about the topic.
3. Providing multiple instructional approaches, that is, using multilevel instruction in a variety of settings, from explicit whole-class instruction to learning alone and mastery learning.
4. Empowering students with responsibility and multiple opportunities for decision making, reflection, and self-assessment.

LEARNING FROM ASSIGNMENTS AND HOMEWORK

An assignment is a statement of what the student is to accomplish and reflects one or more instructional objectives. Assignments, whether completed at home or at school, can ease student learning in many ways, but when poorly planned they can discourage the student, dampen ongoing learning, and negatively affect an entire family. *Homework* or *responsibility papers* can be defined as any out-of-class task that a student is assigned as an extension of classroom learning. Like all that you do as a teacher, it is your professional responsibility to think about and plan carefully all homework assignments that you give to students. Before giving students any assignment, consider how you would feel if you were given the assignment and how you would feel if your own child was given the assignment. Think about how much out-of-class time you expect the assignment to take, and to what extent, if any, the parents and guardians should or could be involved in assisting the child in doing the assignment.

The time that a student needs to complete assignments beyond school time will vary according to grade level and school policy. There always seems to be some debate about the value of homework for the elementary grades.[18] Perhaps the issue is, or should be, not with the value of homework per se but with the quality of the homework that is assigned. Having said that, very generally, children in grades K–3 may be expected to spend from none to about 15 minutes each school night on homework, while children in grades 4–6 may spend 40 minutes to an hour or more.

Purposes for Homework Assignments

Purposes for giving homework assignments or assigning responsibility papers can be any one or more of the following, as reflected in the word **PRIDE**:

P To personalize, to practice, and to provide learning opportunities, for example, to personalize the learning for students, to practice and review what has been learned, and to provide a mechanism by which students receive constructive feedback;

R To reinforce, to review, and to reach family members, for example, to reinforce classroom experiences, review content, and to reach parents or guardians and other family members and get them involved in their children's learning;

I To individualize learning, for example, to individualize personal learning;

D To develop skills, for example, to develop students' research skills, study skills, and organization skills; and

E To extend the time that students are engaged in learning.

Parent/Guardian Homework. As a useful strategy to increase home–school communication, we suggest to teachers that one homework assignment each week necessitate adult involvement. This could be an interview, shared reading, and so on. This keeps parents aware of what their children are doing. We know of one teacher who not only gives the students homework, but gives parents brief homework, too. The teacher uses letter writing as a teaching tool that teaches the students to write a weekly letter and increases weekly communication with parents. Each week, the teacher writes brief notes telling what the class has been working on during that week to the parents of her students and then gives her notes to the students to read. To follow up after reading the teacher's note, each student also writes a letter about what was learned each week to his or her parent. The letters are sent home every Friday afternoon. The parents are encouraged to reply in writing to the teacher and to their child, too, in an activity the students call *parent/guardian homework;* this is a term that the students enjoy because they like the idea of their parents/guardians doing homework just as they do. The letters from the parents sent back to school are kept through the year in a binder with covers featuring artwork by the students. In addition to the idea of parent/guardian homework, there are other parent activities that can be done at home with a child to reinforce the child's classroom learning; see Figure 10.6 and refer

Figure 10.6
Activities that can be done at home with a child to reinforce the child's classroom learning
(*Source*: Adapted from a U.S. Department of Education 1977 publication, *Learning Partners: A Guide to Educational Activities for Families* retrieved February 13 2005 from *www.pueblo.gsa.gov/cic_text/family/partner.htm*)

Activities

A child is likely to perform well in school when one or more members of a child's family are involved in and supportive of the child's learning. Here are just a few activity suggestions that a family member can do with a child to reinforce the child's learning.

General

- Ask questions about things the child is learning and doing and encourage lengthy answers.
- Expect the child to succeed in school. Encourage the child with praise for hard work and a job well done.
- Have a special place for studying that is quiet and free of distractions.
- Have paper, pencils, crayons, and washable markers handy. Encourage children to write.
- Keep a variety of reading materials in the home. Use them yourself to show you value reading and learning, too.
- Turn a cardboard box (big enough for notebooks) into a special school box to hold all school things when the child comes home. Have the child decorate the box with pictures, words, and artwork.
- Watch television with the child and talk about the things you like and don't like about the shows. Limit the viewing time.

The Arts

- Keep simple art supplies available around the house; encourage self-expression. Pictures don't have to be something that you recognize.
- Help the child make connections between art and other subjects. Look at and talk about book illustrations when you are reading together.
- Display the child's art and music in the home.
- Encourage the child to sing and to sway and dance to music.
- Encourage the child to learn to play a musical instrument, homemade or otherwise.

Geography

- Where are we? Teach the child your address. Look at maps together to see where you live and where the school is. How close or far are you from the school?
- What makes a place special? List some things about where you live. What is the climate like? What kinds of plants and animals share your environment?
- What impact have people had on where you live?
- What does it mean to live in a global society? Make a chart of the things that are happening in other parts of the world that affect you.
- When you talk with the child, use words that indicate direction: "We are going north to New York to visit Grandma" or "The school is three blocks west of our apartment."

History

- Get to know the history of the town or city or place where you live.
- Read with the child about people and events that have made a difference in the world.
- Select a photo of a person in your family or someone else you admire or respect. Tell the child what the person did. Why do you admire this person? Talk about the results of the person's actions.
- Share family history with the child.
- When you celebrate holidays, explain to the child what is being celebrated and why.

Mathematics

- From the time the child is very young, count everything. When you empty a grocery bag, count the number of apples. Count the number of stairs to your home.
- Help the child do math in his or her head with lots of small numbers, ask questions, "If I have four cups and I need seven, how many more do I need?" or "If I need twelve drinks for the class, how many packages of three drinks will I need?"
- Put objects into groups. When you do laundry, separate items of clothing: all the socks in one pile, shirts in another, and pants in another. Divide the socks by color and count the number of each. Draw pictures and graphs of clothes in the laundry: 4 red socks, 10 blue socks, 12 white socks.
- Show the child that you like numbers. Play number games and think of math problems as puzzles to be solved. Tell the child that anyone can learn math. Point out numbers in the child's life, in terms of weight, measurements involving food preparation, temperature, and time.

Figure 10.6 Activities that can be done at home with a child to reinforce the child's classroom learning (*continued*)

Reading

- Go to the library together and check out books, especially books recommended by the teacher or the librarian.
- If the child has difficulty with a word, you can help in several ways: Have the child skip the word, read the rest of the sentence, and then ask what word would make sense in the sentence; have the child use what is known about letters and the sounds that they make to "sound out" the word; or supply the words and keep reading—enjoyment is the main goal.
- Listen to your child read homework or a responsibility paper to you.
- Point to the words on the page when you read aloud. Move your finger from left to right.
- Read aloud to your child: books, newspaper and magazine articles, words on the cereal box, labels on canned goods, road signs.

Science

- Ask the child questions: How do you suppose a clock works? Why does bird make a nest and what is the nest made of? How does electricity help us every day?
- Ask the child to make predictions about the weather or how fast a plant will grow or how high a piece of paper will fly with the wind. Have the child then test to see if the predictions were correct. Remind the child that it may take several tries before obtaining an answer, and even then it may only be tentative. Keep trying; keep testing.
- Have the child start collections of shells, rocks, or bugs, so that the child can see similarities and patterns.
- Help the child look at what causes things to change. What happens when a plant doesn't have water or sunlight?
- Watch ants in an anthill or around spilled food. Explain that when an ant finds food, it goes back to its "home" to "tell" others. As it goes, it leaves a trail that other ants in the nest can smell. The ants find the food by smelling their way along the trail.

Writing

- Encourage the young child to get ready to write by scribbling, drawing, and making designs with letters.
- Have the child interview a family member or neighbor.
- Play writing and spelling games.
- Show that you write often to make lists, take down messages, send cards, write letters, write e-mail messages.
- Write often to the child. Put a note in the lunch bag/box; make a birthday poster; or send a postcard or brief note from work.

---

back to our Chapter 6 Companion Website **(www. prenhall.com/roberts)** *Additional Content* module to locate Figure, Resources for Developing Home-School Partnerships, and see more resources. If you are interested further in a checklist about guidelines for using assignments and homework, you can find it on our Companion Website for this chapter, in the *Additional Content* module.

Opportunities for Recovery

While it is important to encourage good initial efforts by students, sometimes, for a multitude of reasons, a student's first effort is inadequate or is lacking entirely. Perhaps the student is absent without excuse from school or the student does poorly on as assignment or fails to turn in an assignment on time or at all. While accepting late work from students is extra work for you, many educators report that it is worthwhile to give students opportunity for recovery and a day or so to make corrections and resubmit an assignment for an improved score. We realize that allowing the resubmission of a marked or tentatively graded paper increases the amount of paperwork for you. However, out of regard for the students who do well from the start, you should consider carefully before allowing a resubmitted paper to receive an A grade (unless, of course, it was an A paper originally).

Students sometimes have legitimate reasons for not completing an assignment by the due date. Sometimes, the student may have a perfectly justifiable, although officially unexcused, reason for being absent from school. It is our opinion that you should listen and exercise professional judgment in each instance. As others have said before, there is nothing democratic about treating unequals as equals. The provision of recovery options for students who are educational works in progress seems a sensible, humanly, scholarly, and professionally responsible approach.

HOW TO AVOID THE PAPER CRUSH

A "Waterloo" for some beginning teachers is that of being buried under mounds of student work to be read, marked, and graded, leaving less and less time for effective planning. To keep this from happening to you, consider the following suggestions.

In our opinion, you should read everything that your students write or draw; however, papers can be read with varying degrees of intensity and scrutiny, depending on the purpose of the assignment. For assignments that are designed for learning, understanding, and practice, you can allow students to check papers themselves using either self-checking or peer-checking (but see the caution that follows). During the self- or peer-checking, you can monitor the activity and record the extent to which the student did the assignment or, after the checking, you can collect the papers and do your recording. Besides reducing the amount of paperwork for you, student self- or peer-checking provides other advantages: It allows students to see and understand their errors, it encourages productive peer dialogue, and it helps students develop self-assessment techniques and standards. If the purpose of the assignment is to assess mastery learning and competence, then the papers should be read, marked, and graded only by you, the teacher.

Multiple Assessment

To avoid the paper crush, you can also consider multiple assessment of one piece of writing. To do this, engage your students in writing paragraphs, essays, or responses to open-ended questions. You mention to the students just a few specific skills that you want to target in the written work. For example, you might assign essay writing to students based on an autobiography or biography they have read and mention as part of the specifications that you will grade just on their abilities in the category of mechanical skills—spelling, punctuation, and so on. After evaluating a student's writing on these skills, file the work in the student's portfolio and use it again later for the student's self-editing and mention that this time as part of the specifications, you will grade on a previously unaddressed category of skills. Then select one category—the student's style, use of paragraph structure, including a topic sentence, use of relevant details, logical sequence, or writing a conclusion. Conduct your second evaluation/feedback and again, file the work and use it still another time for self-editing by the student; mention that this time you will assess the student's use of still another category of skills. This time, you announce that you are assessing one of these features—the students' use of content with emphasis on details, good descriptions, or the inclusion and accuracy of cited references. In this multiple assessment approach, a student's written work might be self-edited by the student several times and then examined by you several times and assessed in different categories at different times.

Peer-Checking: Use with Caution

Peer-checking can be a problem. For instance, children might spend more time watching the person checking their paper than accurately checking the one given to them. And the use of peer-checking does not necessarily allow the student to see or understand his or her mistakes.

Of even greater concern is the matter of privacy. When student A becomes knowledgeable about the academic success (or lack thereof) of student B, student A, the "checker," could cause emotional or social embarrassment to student B. Peer-checking of papers should perhaps be done only for the editing of the classmates' drafts of stories or research projects, and for making suggestions about content and grammar, but definitely not assigning a grade or marking answers right or wrong. To protect students' rights to privacy, the use of peers' *grading* each other's papers (along with the public/electronic posting of grades) should be avoided. Harassment and embarrassment have no place in an elementary school classroom; they do not provide for a safe learning environment.

PROJECT-CENTERED LEARNING: GUIDING LEARNING FROM INDEPENDENT AND GROUP INVESTIGATIONS, PAPERS, AND ORAL REPORTS

For the most meaningful student learning to occur, independent study, individual writing, student-centered projects, and oral reports should be major features of your instruction. There will be times when the children will be interested in an in-depth inquiry about a topic and will want to pursue a particular topic for study. This undertaking of a learning project can be flexible—an individual student, a team of two, a small group, or the entire class can do the investigation. The **project** should be a relatively long-term investigative study from which students produce something called the **culminating presentation.** It is a way for students to apply what they are learning. The culminating presentation is a final presentation that usually includes three aspects: (a) an oral report, (b) a hands-on item of some kind (e.g., a display, play or skit, book, song, poem, video, multimedia presentations, website, diorama, poster, maps, charts, computer webquests), and (c) a written report. The latter two are usually given to the teacher for the teacher's review and assessment and sometimes contributed or loaned to a long-term display in the classroom or elsewhere in the school.

Figure 10.7
Values and purposes of project-centered learning

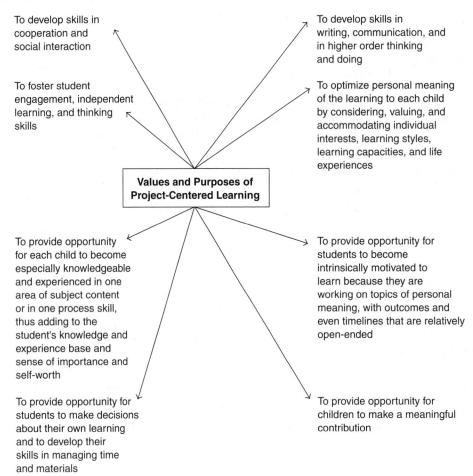

To develop skills in cooperation and social interaction

To foster student engagement, independent learning, and thinking skills

To develop skills in writing, communication, and in higher order thinking and doing

To optimize personal meaning of the learning to each child by considering, valuing, and accommodating individual interests, learning styles, learning capacities, and life experiences

Values and Purposes of Project-Centered Learning

To provide opportunity for each child to become especially knowledgeable and experienced in one area of subject content or in one process skill, thus adding to the student's knowledge and experience base and sense of importance and self-worth

To provide opportunity for students to become intrinsically motivated to learn because they are working on topics of personal meaning, with outcomes and even timelines that are relatively open-ended

To provide opportunity for students to make decisions about their own learning and to develop their skills in managing time and materials

To provide opportunity for children to make a meaningful contribution

Values and Purposes of Project-Centered Learning

The values and purposes of encouraging project-centered learning for students, either individually or in groups, are shown in Figure 10.7.

As has been demonstrated time and again, when students work together on projects, integrating knowledge as the need arises, motivation and learning follow naturally.[19]

Guidelines for Guiding Students in Project-Centered Learning

Choosing the Project

In collaboration with you, your students can select a topic for the project. You can stimulate ideas and provide an opportunity for the students to see the results of other students' projects (sometimes called anchor projects or studies). For example, a group of fourth-grade students from Greenbrook School (South Brunswick, New Jersey) created and produced an animated video about national parks.[20] Such a culminating project as that could be shown year after year

to other groups of students as an anchor study. You can motivate students to share ideas in different ways:

- By providing lists of things students might do
- By mentioning each time an idea comes up in class that this could be a good idea for an independent, small-group, or class project
- By having former students visit your class and tell about their projects
- By showing anchor studies as previously mentioned
- By suggesting Internet resources and readings that are likely to give students ideas
- By holding class discussions to brainstorm ideas.

Collaborating with the Students

Sometimes, you can write the general problem or topic in the center of a graphic web (perhaps designed as the hub of a wheel) and ask the students to brainstorm some questions. The questions (written on spokes that radiate from the hub of the wheel) can be "reserved" by students and lead to ways for them to investigate, draw sketches, construct models, record findings, predict items, compare and contrast, and discuss understandings. In essence, brainstorming such as this is the technique often used by teachers in collaboration with the students for the selection of a theme, topic, or subtopics of an interdisciplinary thematic unit of study.

Establishing Groups

Allow students to individually choose whether they will work in small groups, in pairs, or work alone. If they choose to work in groups, then help them delineate job descriptions for each member of the group. For instance, you can help the students keep the following role descriptions in mind: facilitator, recorder, reporter, materials manager, and thinking monitor. For project work, groups of five or fewer children usually work better than groups of more than five. Even if the project is one the whole class is pursuing, the project should be divided into parts with small groups of students or partners or individuals undertaking independent study of these parts.

Keeping Track of the Students' Progress

You can do this by reviewing periodic (daily or weekly) updates of their work, perhaps as maintained in their journals (see later discussion in this chapter). Set deadlines with the groups. Meet with the groups daily (perhaps a class meeting at the end of the day) to discuss any questions or problems they have. Based on their investigations, the students can prepare to present their findings in culminating presentations.

Providing Coaching and Guidance

You can work with each student or student team in topic selection, as well as in the processes of written and oral reporting. To do this, allow students to develop their own procedures, but guide their preparation of work outlines and preliminary drafts, giving them modeling, constructive feedback, and encouragement along the way. Without frequent progress reporting by the students and guidance and reinforcement from the teacher, a student can get frustrated and quickly lose interest in the project. Guide students in their identification of potential resources and in the techniques of research. Your coordination with the library and resource locations is central to the success of project-centered teaching. Frequent drafts and progress reports from the students are a must. At each of these stages, provide students with constructive feedback and encouragement. Also provide written guidelines for students who legitimately need negotiations. You can negotiate timelines for their outlines, drafts, and the completed projects.

Promoting Sharing

You can plan to have the students share both the progress and the results of their study with the rest of the class. The amount of time allowed for this shar-ing will, of course, depend on any of many variables. The value of this type of instructional strategy comes not only from individual contributions but also from the learning that results from the experience and the communication of that experience with others.

Advising and Guiding Students

Without careful teacher planning, and steady guidance for students, project-based teaching can be a frustrating experience for both the teacher and the students. This is true especially for a beginning teacher who is inexperienced in such a complex instructional undertaking. Students should do projects because they want to and because the project seems meaningful. Therefore, with guidance from you the students should decide *what* project to do and *how* to do it. As part of this guidance, your role is to advise and guide students so they experience success. If you lay out a project in too much detail, that project is a procedure rather than a student-centered project. There must be a balance between structure and opportunities for student empowerment via choices and decision making.

Writing Should Be a Required Component of Project-Centered Learning

You can provide options but insist that writing (or drawing) be a part of each student's work. You realize that research has examined the links among writing, thinking, and learning and this has helped emphasize the importance of writing. Writing is a complex intellectual behavior and process that helps the learner to create and record his or her understanding—that is, to construct meaning. Because of this understanding, insist that writing be a part of the student's work (see the section that follows).

When teachers use project-centered teaching with upper-grade elementary students, a paper and an oral presentation are usually automatically required of all students. It is recommended that you use the **I-search paper** approach rather than the traditional research paper approach. Under your careful guidance, the students (a) list information (queries, phrases, statements) they would like to know and from the list select one that can become the research topic; (b) conduct the study while maintaining a log of their activities and findings, which, in fact, becomes a process journal; (c) prepare a booklet of paragraphs and visual representations that present their findings; (d) prepare a written summary of the findings including the significance of the study and their personal thoughts; and (e) share the project as a final oral report with the teacher and classmates. You may want to make available a book that addresses the needs of young researchers such as *Easy Steps to*

Figure 10.8
Sample scoring rubric for oral presentation of project

Project Presentation Scoring Guide/Rubric

Clear understanding of the project and organized in delivery

Score 5. Excellent presentation
- Made eye contact throughout presentation.
- Spoke loudly enough for all to hear.
- Spoke clearly and distinctly.
- Spoke for time allotted.
- Stood straight and confidently.
- Covered at least five pieces of important information.
- Introduced project.

Well thought out and planned in delivery

Score 4. Well-planned presentation
- Made eye contact throughout most of the presentation.
- Spoke loudly enough and clearly most of the time.
- Spoke for most of time allotted.
- Covered at least four pieces of important information.
- Introduced project.

Mostly organized in delivery

Score 3. Adequate presentation
- Made eye contact at times.
- Some of audience could hear the presentation.
- Audience could understand most of what was said.
- Spoke for about half of allotted time.
- Covered at least three pieces of important information.
- Project was vaguely introduced.

Disorganized and unprepared; incomplete information

Score 2 to 1. Unprepared presentation
- Poor eye contact during presentation.
- Most of audience was unable to hear presentation.
- Information presented was unclear.
- Spoke for only a brief time.
- Covered less than three pieces of information.
- Project not introduced or only vague introduced.

Writing Fantastic Research Reports (New York: Scholastic, 2000) by Jean Dreher.

Assess the Final Product

The final product of the project, including papers, oral reports, and presentations, should be assessed and graded. The method of determining the grade should be clear to students from the beginning, along with the weight of the project grade toward the term grade. You can provide the students with clear descriptions (scoring guides/rubrics) of how assessment and grading will be done. The final grade for the study should be based on four criteria: (a) organization, including meeting draft and progress report deadlines; (b) the quality and quantity of both content and procedural knowledge gained from the experience; (c) the quality of the student's sharing of that learning experience with the rest of the class;

and (d) the quality of the student's final written and/or oral report. A sample scoring rubric for the oral presentation of a project is shown in Figure 10.8. A rubric for a primary grade (see Figure 10.9) often has a visual system attached to it to help young children grasp their achievement. Sometimes this is a series of faces with different expressions. For other grades, the rubric has rating scales, or levels of proficiency with paragraphs describing factors that result in that level, or levels of criteria. More on preparing and using rubrics was discussed in Chapter 6.[21]

WRITING ACROSS THE CURRICULUM

Because writing is a discrete representation of thinking, every teacher should consider himself or herself to be a teacher of writing.

Figure 10.9
Scoring guide/rubric for writing: Completing a sentence frame

Soaring High! (4)
  —I followed directions.
  —I read the example carefully.
  —I added words to the sentence that made sense.
  —I used my best handwriting

Taking Off (3)
  —I followed most directions.
  —I read the example.
  —I added words to the sentence.
  —I need to practice forming my letters.

Getting Ready (2)
  —I followed some directions.
  —I added some words, but I had trouble thinking of them.
  —My letters don't look like the ones on my alphabet strip.
  —I asked for help when I needed it.

Still on the Ground (1)
  —I didn't follow directions.
  —I didn't fill in all the spaces.
  —I need to redo my work.
  —I need to ask for help.

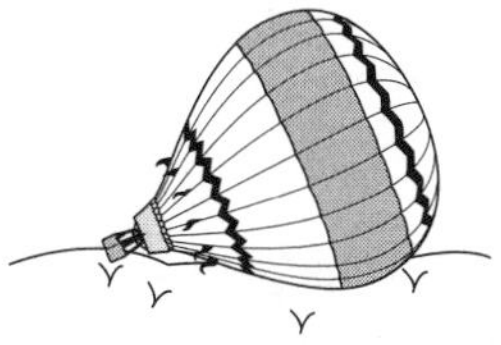

Kinds of Writing

A student should experience a variety of kinds of writing rather than the same form year after year. Perhaps most important is that writing should be emphasized as a process that illustrates one's thinking, rather than solely as a product completed as an assignment. During any school day, writing and thinking develop best when a student experiences various forms of writing to express his or her ideas. Consider the following types of writing.

Analysis and Speculation About Effects. The writer conjectures about the causes and effects of a specific event.

Autobiographical Incident. The writer narrates a special event in his or her life and states or implies the significance of the event.

Character Assumption. The writer writes a story or maintains a diary of his or her reading in the first person, assuming the persona of a character in a book being read or a figure in history being studied.

Evaluation. The writer presents a judgment on the worth of an item—artwork, a book, consumer product, educational film, movie—and supports this with reasons and evidence.

Eyewitness Account. The writer tells about an event, a group, or person that was objectively observed from the outside.

Firsthand Biographical Sketch. Through incidents and descriptions, the writer characterizes a person he or she knows well.

Problem Solving. The writer describes and analyzes a specific problem and then proposes and argues for a solution.

Report of Information. The writer collects data from observation and research and chooses material that best represents a phenomenon or concept.

Story. Using dialogue and description, the writer shows the conflict between characters or between a character and the environment.

Student Journals

Many teachers have their students maintain **student journals** in which they keep a log of their activities, findings, and thoughts (i.e., *process journals*, as discussed previously) and write their thoughts about what it is they are studying (*response journals* are commonly used). Actually, there are two types of response journals: dialogue journals and reading-response journals. *Dialogue journals* are used by students to write anything that is on their minds, usually on the right side of a page, while peers, teachers, and parents or guardians respond on the left side of a page, thereby "talking with" the journal writer. *Response journals* are used by students to write (and perhaps draw a "visual learning log") to present their reactions to what is being studied.

Purpose and Assessment of Student Journal Writing

Normally, academic journals are *not* the personal diaries of the writer's recollection of daily events and the writer's thoughts about the events. Rather, the purpose of journal writing is to encourage students to write, to think about their writing, to record their

creative thoughts *about what they are learning*, and to share their written thoughts with an audience—all of which help in the development of their thinking skills, in their learning, and in their development as writers. Students are encouraged to write about experiences, both in school and out, that are related to the topics being studied. They should be encouraged to record their thoughts about what and how they are learning.

Journal writing provides practice in expression and should not be graded by the teacher. Negative comments and evaluations from the teacher will often discourage creative and spontaneous expression by the students. As the teacher, you should read the journal writing and then offer constructive and positive feedback, but we suggest you avoid negative comments or grading the journals. For grading purposes, you can simply record whether or not a student does, in fact, maintain the required journal and, perhaps, meets due dates. See Figures 10.8 and 10.9 for scoring rubrics.

You'll be interested to know that the National Council of Teachers of English (NCTE) has developed guidelines for journal writing. For a copy, contact NCTE directly or via the Internet. Resources on writing across the curriculum, including NCTE, are shown in Figure 10.10. See also the readings at the end of this chapter.[22,23,24]

Companion Website

To broaden your knowledge base about grouping and assignments, go to our Companion Website at **www.prenhall.com/roberts** and click on the *Additional Content* module for Chapter 10.

Figure 10.10
Resources for writing across the curriculum

- The American Literacy Council, 148 W. 177th Street, New York, NY, 10026; (800) 781-9985; www.americanliteracy.com
- International Reading Association, P.O. Box 8139, 800 Barksdale Road, Newark, DE 19714-8139; 19711; www.reading.org (800) 336-7323
- National Council of Teachers of English, 11111 W. Kenyon Road, Urbana, IL 61801; www.ncte.org
- National Writing Project (NWP), 2105 Bancroft Way, #1042, University of California, Berkeley, Berkeley, CA 94720-1042; www.writingproject.org
- Whole Language Umbrella; affiliated with NCTE; www.ncte.org/groups/wlu/leadership/107155.htm

About Praxis and Other Teacher Tests

About Praxis Teacher Tests. To continue to support your interest in preparing for a Praxis II Principles of Learning and Teaching test, as well as some of the other teacher tests, all application exercises for this chapter offer opportunities for you to reflect generally on grouping and assignments to promote positive interaction and quality learning. For instance, in this chapter, prelicensed and precredentialed teachers were asked to participate cooperatively and collaboratively to do the following:

- Explore your knowledge of whole-class discussion as a teaching strategy (Application Exercise 10.1).
- Turn to our Companion Website (**www.prenhall.com/roberts**) and click on the *Additional Application Exercise* module to examine interactions with students according to selected charactertistics by completing the additional application exercise titled Teacher Interaction with Students According to Student Gender or Other Personal Characteristics.
- Further explore your knowledge of whole-class discussion by completing the Companion Website's additional application exercise titled Whole-Class Discussion as a Teaching Strategy: What Do I Already Know?

You can find a constructed response-type question similar to those found on the Praxis II tests in the Praxis Warm-Up section that follows the Chapter Summary. This warm-up takes another look at the classroom vignette found in the Looking at Teachers section at the beginning of this chapter.

About Future Classroom Performance Assessment. Further considering the Praxis tests, you'll realize that later on in your career your classroom performance will be measured. This measurement takes place in the classroom and is made by a school administrator or by trained assessors who use a set of nationally validated criteria. If you are being observed in the classroom as part of a first-year teaching situation or as part of the pretenure/post-tenure ongoing evaluation process, it is possible that the observation will include a reference to national or state curriculum standards. As an example, the following list serves as an observation guide that is connected to national literacy/English/language arts standards and can provide suggestions for you as you prepare for an observation. You can review other standards related to other areas as appropriate. As you review this list of suggestions related to classroom performance, observation, ask yourself, "Am I involved in any or all of the following?"

- **Grouping/eliciting oral responses.** Are you accepting students' invented spelling while composing writing but later assisting students for correct spellings? Facilitating group discussions? Giving skills instruction to students who need it? Providing time for individual, independent work by students? Promoting discussion, divergent thinking, and multiple responses? Using questioning that promotes dialogue, inquiry learning, and critiques? Using different grouping situations such as cooperative learning groups, flexible small groups, literature circles, dyads/partners, independent activity, and whole-class discussion?
- **Listening/oral response times.** Are you scheduling structured language for listening such as choral reading, debates, discussion time, drama, sharing time, oral reports, students' speaker-bureau, and speeches? Are you modeling listening and encouraging students to keep eye contact when communicating, to expand on the comments they hear from others, to clarify or paraphrase what they hear to demonstrate understanding, and to summarize what was heard? Are you providing listening situations such as Reader's Theater, reports, rehearsed oral reading, and reading aloud daily from a variety of texts? Are you focusing on the listening process, which includes modeling, reading aloud, and sharing your pleasure in reading, writing, and listening related to the topic of study? Providing time for daily, self-selected silent reading and oral and silent reading practice? Modeling the writing process, which includes drafting, sharing, revising, editing, and publishing? Suggesting books that will interest students? Giving daily time to writing?
- **Providing genres/variety of responses.** Are you providing a variety of materials to read, including an atlas, essays, magazines, newspapers? Are you providing genres such as traditional literature, fantasy, poetry, realistic fiction, historical fiction, and nonfiction (biographies and informational books)? Are you encouraging a variety of responses including writing in divergent and creative ways?
- **Scheduling peer conferences/self-assessment/portfolio reviews.** Are you collecting portfolio assessment information that is selected by the student, the parent/guardian, and yourself, the teacher, that helps assess progress? Are you conferring with students? Promoting peer conferences and self-assessment? This observation guide can be a useful resource for supporting your teaching performance.

Other Teacher Tests. For those of you who will be teaching in states that do not administer the Praxis II Principles of Learning and Teaching tests, go to our Companion Website at **www.prenhall.com/ roberts** and click on the *Other Teacher Tests* module for Chapter 10 to access information about teacher tests other than the Praxis.

SUMMARY

This chapter has continued the development of your repertoire of teaching strategies. As you know, young people can be quite peer conscious, can have relatively short attention spans for experiences in which they are uninterested, and prefer active experiences that engage many or all of their senses. Most are intensely curious about things of interest to them. You have found that cooperative learning, student-centered projects, and teaching strategies that emphasize shared discovery learning and inquiry learning within a psychologically safe environment encourage the most positive aspects of thinking and learning for children. Central to your strategy selection should be those strategies that encourage children to become independent thinkers and skilled learners who can help in the planning, structuring, regulating, and assessing of their own learning and learning activities. In addition, a large variety of useful and effective aids, media, and resources are available from which to draw as you plan your instructional experiences; this is the topic of more information in the section on our Companion Website that supports this chapter.

What's to Come. In the next chapter of this resource guide, your attention is directed to techniques designed to help you assess the development of your teaching skills and continue your professional growth, a process that is now only beginning but will continue throughout your teaching career.

EXTENDING MY PROFESSIONAL COMPETENCY

Praxis Warm-Up: A Constructed Response-Type Question

You'll recall that the students from the class discussed at the beginning of this chapter had been working nearly all year on an interdisciplinary thematic unit entitled *Surviving Natural Disasters*. To culminate the students' study, they used desktop publishing to publish a document entitled *Natural Disaster Preparation and Survival Guide for (community name)*. They proudly distributed the guide to their parents and other members of the community.

If you were teaching this class and preparing your students to write the survival guide, what steps would you take to guide them through the writing process? Briefly explain each step. Hints are found in the Appendix of this resource guide.

Hints for responding to Praxis Warm-Ups are found in the Appendix.

Praxis. To do another Praxis Warm-Up with a constructed response-type question, go to our Companion Website at **www.prenhall.com/roberts** and click on the *Praxis Warm-Up* module for Chapter 10. Constructed response-type questions are designed to help you prepare for the Praxis II Principles of Learning and Teaching tests.

For Your Discussion

1. **Grouping.** What would I say to a parent who inquires about the values of cooperative learning groups? **To do:** Describe, to a colleague, any research that you can find on the use of cooperation versus competition in teaching in the elementary classroom.

2. **Recovery.** What would I say to a teaching colleague who asked me if I was for or against providing recovery options for students? **To do:** Present your persuasive argument in favor of or against providing recovery options for students who don't do an assignment or who don't do well on it.

3. **Strategies.** What would I say to a principal during a job interview if I am asked about my use of whole-class discussion as a teaching strategy? **To do:** Think back to your own schooling and what you really remember. Do you remember projects, presentations, the research you did, or do you remember a compliment by a teacher or a pat on the back by peers? Most likely you do not remember the massive amount of content that was covered. Discuss your thoughts about this with your classmates. Share common experiences and common concerns about whole-class discussions.

4. **Effective Use.** How would I respond if a teaching colleague asked me to tell him or her how I plan to effectively use my favorite instructional strategy? **To do:** Consider when and where you plan to use your favorite strategy from the following choices: assignments, homework, journal writing, written and oral reports, cooperative learning groups, learning centers, problem-based learning, and student-centered projects.

5. **Mastery or Personalize.** What would I say to a parent who asks me how I intend to personalize/differentiate/tier the instruction to ensure success for her child and other students? **To do:** Identify and describe at least two ways that will personalize the instruction for students in your classroom. Describe your plans to a colleague (who can take the persona of a parent) in your group.

Online Portfolio Activities

Supporting categories of instructional content, teaching–learning strategies, and diversity (Praxis II Assessments); Principles 1, 3, 4, and 9 of INTASC; and Standards 2, 3, 4, 6, and 7 of NBPTS): At the Companion Website **(www.prenhall.com/roberts),** click on the *Online Portfolio Activities* module to continue your online portfolio supporting knowledge and instruction of students.

Companion Website

Also on the Companion Website at **www.prenhall.com/roberts,** you can measure your understanding of chapter content in the *Objectives* and *Self-Check* modules and apply concepts in the *For Your Discussion* module.

FOR FURTHER READING

Brisk, M. E., and Harrington, M. M. (2000). *Literacy and Bilingualism: A Handbook for All Teachers.* Mahwah, NJ: Lawrence Erlbaum.

Childers-Burpo, D. M. (2002, Spring). Mirrors and Microscopes: The Promise of National Board Certification in the Era of Accountability. *Contemporary Education, 72*(1), 14–17.

Cooper, J. (2003). *Classroom Teaching Skills* (7th ed.). New York: Houghton Mifflin.

Danna, S. (2003, February/March). Pursuing National Board Certification. *Pi Lambda Theta Educational Horizons,* p. 5.

Duncan, D., and Lockhart, L. (2000). *I-Search, You Search, WE All Learn to Research: A How-To-Do-It Manual for Teaching Elementary School Students to Solve Information Problems.* Norwich, CT: Neal-Schuman.

Dunn, M. A. (2000). Staying the Course of Open Education. *Educational Leadership, 57*(7), 20–24.

Hofstadter, D. R. (2000). Analogy as the Core of Cognition. In J. Gleick (Ed.), *The Best American Science Writing 2000.* New York: Ecco Press.

Kagan, S. (1995, May). Group Grades Miss the Mark. *Educational Leadership, 52*(8), 68–71.

Marzano, R. J., Pickering, D. J., and Pollock, J. E. (2001). *Classroom Instruction That Works.* In *Cooperative Learning* (Chap. 7, pp. 84–91). Alexandria, VA: Association for Supervision and Curriculum Development.

Smith, J. A. (2000). Singing and Songwriting Support Early Literacy Instruction. *The Reading Teacher, 53*(8), 646–649.

Solley, B. (2000). *Writers' Workshop: Reflections of Elementary and Middle School Teachers.* Needham Heights, MA: Allyn and Bacon.

Thomason, T., and York, C. (2000). *Write on Target: Preparing Young Writers to Succeed on State Writing Achievement Tests.* Norwood, Ma: Christopher-Gordon.

Tomlinson, C. A. (1999). *The Differentiated Classroom.* Alexandria, VA: Association for Supervision and Curriculum Development.

NOTES

1. S. Zaher, Gender and Curriculum in the School Room, *Education Canada, 36*(1), 26–29 (Spring 1996); and S. M. Bailey, Shortchanging Girls and Boys, *Educational Leadership, 53*(8), 75–79 (May 1996). For information about how to identify equity problems and develop programs to help schools achieve academic excellence for all students, contact EQUITY 2000, 1233 20th St. NW Washington, DC 20036-2304; (202)822–5930.

2. L. S. Walters, Putting Cooperative Learning to the Test, *Harvard Education Letter, 16*(3), 1–6 (May/June 2000); see also M. S. Leighton in J. Cooper's *Classroom Teaching Skills,* 7th ed. (Boston: Houghton Mifflin, 2003); and J. M. Carroll, The Copernican Plan Evaluated, *Phi Delta Kappan, 76*(2), 105–113 (October 1994).

3. J. D. Laney et al., The Effect of Cooperative and Mastery Learning Methods on Primary Grade Students' Learning and Retention of Economic Concepts, *Early Education and Development, 7*(3), 253–274 (July 1996); also see L. Cross and D. Walker-Knight, Inclusion: Developing Collaborative and Cooperative School Communities, *Educational Forum, 61*(3), 269–277 (Spring 1997).

4. For more details about these CLG strategies and others such as Student Teams Achievement Divisions, see R. E. Slavin, *Cooperative Learning: Theory, Research and Practice,* 2nd ed. (Needham Heights, MA: Allyn & Bacon, 1995); for CLG support of student thinking, see M. Keefer, C. Zeitz, and L. Resnick, Judging the Quality of Peer-Led Student Dialogues, *Cognition and Instruction, 18*(1), 53–61 (2000); see also P. Meter and R. Stevens, The Role of Theory in the Study of Peer Collaboration, *Journal of Experimental Education, 69*(1), 113–227 (2000).

5. S. Kagan, Group Grades Miss the Mark, *Educational Leadership, 52*(8), 68–71 (May 1995); D. W. Johnson and R. T. Johnson, The 3 C's of School and Classroom Management, in R. Freiberg (Ed.), *Beyond Behaviorism* (Boston: Allyn & Bacon, 1999), pp. 119–145; and The Role of Cooperative Learning in Assessing and Communicating Student Learning, Chapter 4 in T. R. Guskey, *Communicating Student Learning,* 1996 ASCD Yearbook (Alexandria, VA: Association for Supervision and Curriculum Development, 1996).

6. T. L. Good and J. E. Brophy, *Looking in Classrooms,* 9th ed. (New York: Addison Wesley/Longman, 2003).

7. Good and Brophy, *ibid.* p. 291.

8. For more about tiered instruction, see C. A. Tomlinson, Differentiating Instruction for Academic Diversity, in J. Cooper, *Classroom Teaching Skills* (Boston: Houghton Mifflin, 2003; C. A. Tomlinson, *The Differentiated Classroom* (Alexandria, VA: Association for Supervision and Curriculum Development, 1999), p. 61.

9. V. Randall, Cooperative Learning: Abused and Overused? *Gifted Child Today Magazine, 22*(2), 14–16 (March/April 1999).

10. R. Ryan and E. Deci, Intrinsic and Extrinsic Motivations: Classic Definitions and New Directions, *Contemporary Educational Psychology, 25,* 54–67 (2000); E. S. Foster-Harrison, *Peer Tutoring for K–12 Success* (Fastback 415) (Bloomington, IN: Phi Delta Kappa Educational

Foundation, 1997); E. Kreuger and B. Braun, Books and Buddies: Peers Tutoring Peers, *The Reading Teacher, 52*(4), 410–414 (December/January 1998–1999); P. G. Mathes, M. L. Grek, J. K. Howard, A. E. Babyak, and S. H. Allen, Peer-Assisted Learning Strategies for First-Grade Readers: A Tool for Preventing Early Reading Failure, *Learning Disabilities Research and Practice, 14*(1), 50–60 (Winter 1999); and O. G. Mathes, J. K. Howard, S. H. Allen, and D. Fuchs, Peer-Assisted Learning Strategies for First-Grade Readers: Responding to the Needs of Diverse Learners, *Reading Research Quarterly, 33*(1), 62–94 (January/March 1998). Also see T. Loveless, *The Brown Center Report on American Education* (Washington, DC: Brookings Institute and Brown Center on Education Policy, 2003), which found that, overall, the numbers in surveys from 1984 to 1999 from the National Assessment of Educational Progress did *not* support the popular misconception about excessive homework.

11. For strategies for one-to-one sessions, see R. Barr, Research on the Teaching of Reading, in J. Richardson (Ed.), *Handbook of Research on Teaching*, 4th ed. (Washington, DC: American Educational Research Association, 2001), pp. 390–415; and for ways to adapt assignments, see S. Vaughn, C. Bos, and J. Schumm, *Teaching Exceptional, Diverse, and At-Risk Students in the General Education Classroom* (Boston: Allyn and Bacon, 2000); see also P. F. Vadasy et al., The Effectiveness of One-to-One Tutoring by Community Tutors for At-Risk Beginning Readers, *Learning Disability Quarterly, 20*(2), 126–139 (Spring 1997); and R. B. Schneider and D. Barone, Cross-Age Tutoring, *Childhood Education, 73*(3), 136–143 (Spring 1997).

12. See the story of a project that involved middle school students helping kindergarten children learn Spanish in R. A. Oleksak, Chalkboard: Teaching Spanish as a Community Service, *Our Children, 23*(2), 38 (October 1997).

13. R. Dunn, *Strategies for Diverse Learners* (Fastback 384) (Bloomington, IN: Phi Delta Kappa Educational Foundation, 1995), p. 15.

14. J. M. Carroll, The Copernican Plan Evaluated, *Phi Delta Kappan, 76*(2), 105–113 (October 1994).

15. See B. Bloom, *Human Characteristics and School Learning* (New York: McGraw-Hill, 1987); and J. Carroll, A Model of School Learning, *Teachers College Record, 64*(8)1, 723–733 (May 1963).

16. T. R. Guskey, Defining the Differences Between Outcome-Based Education and Mastery Learning, *School Administrator, 51*(8), 34–37 (September 1994). Information about CES, such as a directory of participating schools, can be obtained from *www.essentialschools.*

org. See also W. Malloy, Essential Schools and Inclusion: A Responsive Partnership, *Educational Forum, 60*(3), 228–236 (Spring 1996).

17. See J. Battistini, *From Theory to Practice: Classroom Application of Outcome-Based Education* (Bloomington, IN: ERIC Clearinghouse on Reading, English and Communication, 1995); and L. Horton, *Mastery Learning* (Fastback 154) (Bloomington, IN: Phi Delta Kappa Educational Foundation, 1981).

18. S. Black, How Are You Smart? *American School Board Journal*, pp. 26–29 (October 1998); and The Truth About Homework, *American School Board Journal*, pp. 48–51 (October 1996).

19. M. Tassinari, Hands-On Projects Take Students Beyond the Book, *Social Studies Review, 34*(3), 16–20 (Spring 1996); D. K. Meyer et al., Challenge in a Mathematics Classroom: Students' Motivation and Strategies in Project-Based Learning, *Elementary School Journal, 97*(5), 501–521 (May 1997); and L. G. Katz and S. C. Chard, *Issues in Selecting Topics for Projects* (Champaign, IL: ERIC Clearinghouse on Elementary and Early Childhood Education, 1998), ED 42403198.

20. A. Algava, Animated Learning, *Educational Leadership, 56*(5), 58–60 (February 1999).

21. H. G. Andrade, Using Rubrics to Promote Thinking and Learning, *Educational Leadership, 57*(5), 13–18 (February 2000). For ways to describe the criteria for grading and the example Oregon Six Traits of Writing Rubric, see R. Stiggins, *Student-Centered Classroom Assessment*, 3rd ed. (Upper Saddle River, NJ: Merrill/Prentice Hall, 2001). For suggestions about format/writing criteria words for the left-hand column in a rubric matrix, see M. Huba and J. Freed, *Learner-Centered Assessment on College Campuses* (Boston: Allyn and Bacon, 2000).

22. Adapted from P. L. Tiedt and I. M. Tiedt, *Multicultural Teaching: A Handbook of Activities, Information, and Resources*, 4th ed. (Boston: Allyn and Bacon, 1995) p. 208; see also related activities in P. L. Roberts, Part I, Stories and Activities for Children, Ages 5–8, and Part II, Stories and Activities for Children, Ages 9–14, in *Multicultural Friendship Stories and Activities for Children, Ages 5–14* (Lanham, MD: Scarecrow Press, 1998).

23. M. H. Sullivan and P. V. Sequeira, The Impact of Purposeful Homework on Learning, *Clearing House, 69*(6), 346–348 (July/August 1996).

24. H. J. Wahlberg, Productive Teaching and Instruction: Assessing the Knowledge Base, *Phi Delta Kappan, 71*(6), 472 (February 1990); see also T. Palardy, The Rank Book: Forum on Education and Academics, *National Forum: Phi Kappa Phi Journal*, pp. 3–9 (Summer 2001).

How Can I Assess My Teaching Effectiveness and Continue My Professional Development?

Visual Chapter Organizer and Overview

Teaching Effectiveness

> Through Student Teaching and Interning
> Student Teaching *IS* the Real Thing
> Getting Ready for Student Teaching
> First Impressions
> Comments from the University Supervisor

Teaching Effectiveness Through E-Teaching: An Emergency E-Teaching Kit

> Purposes of E-Teaching with an Emergency E-Teaching Kit
> Developing an E-Teaching Kit with a Multidisciplinary Emphasis

Finding a Teaching Position

> Guidelines for Locating a Teaching Position
> Through a Professional Career Portfolio
> Resources for Locating Teaching Jobs
> The Professional Résumé
> The In-Person Interview

Professional Development

> Through Reflection
> Through Self-Assessment
> Through Journals or Logbooks
> A Teachalogue for Reflection and Self-Assessment

Professional Development Through Mentoring

Professional Development Through In-Service and Study

Professional Development Through Professional Organizations

Professional Development Through Communications with Other Teachers

Professional Development Through Peer Teaching

🔍 Looking at Teachers

At times, as an elementary schoolteacher, you'll realize that some of the teachers of students in middle school or high school can provide insight into teaching that reflects on your teaching of elementary school students. To illustrate this, we want to point out one teacher's reflection on his classroom research with high school students and how the use of technology in the teacher's classroom focuses on several ideas that can affect you, your elementary school teaching, and your pedagogical interest. Here's a recap of the teacher's reflections (Perry, 2003):

- First, the teacher considered that most of his students could *use technology all they wanted at home* (or at their friend's home) with their computers, the Internet, television, VCRs, DVD players, compact discs, CD-ROMs, electronic games, cell phones, handheld personal digital assistants, and their family's assortment of other high-tech items. So it seemed to the teacher that what his students needed most in his classroom was interaction with a caring, concerned adult (all too often unavailable outside of school from this teacher's point of view).
- Secondly, no technique seemed to be quite as effective as the teacher himself when he made the lectures/discussion interesting and when he drew his students into what was being learned with an occasional joke, question, or allusion to their own lives.
- Third, the most important piece of classroom equipment seemed to be the professional teacher's attitude—his sense of humor, patience, and caring for young people.
- Fourth, the students' *PowerPoint* presentations as a finale to their unit of study were a success and led this teacher to include this as an assignment in all of the rest of his classes, but the teacher *did not* let it replace human caring, or what could be labeled the concerned touch, in his teaching in the classroom. It seemed that, indeed, teacher "affect" was an effective teaching technique when compared with teaching with technology only.

CHAPTER OBJECTIVES

Specifically, on completion of this eleventh chapter, you should be able to:

1. Assess your teaching effectiveness, record self-assessments in student teaching/interning, and assess with standards.
2. Organize your teaching, for example, develop and use an emergency E-teaching kit.
3. Prepare for a job interview.
4. Write a résumé.
5. Develop a portfolio for professional growth and development.
6. Self-assess and evaluate your developing competencies with a final checklist from our Companion Website in the *Self-Check* module.

TEACHING EFFECTIVENESS

Through Student Teaching and Interning

You are excited about the prospect of being assigned as a student teacher or intern to your first classroom, but you are also concerned. Questions linger in your mind. Will your cooperating (host) teacher(s) like you? Will you get along? Will the children accept you? Will you be assigned to the school and grade level that you prefer? What curriculum programs will you be expected to use? What will the children be like? Will there be many classroom management problems? How many full-inclusion students and students with only limited proficiency in English will be in the class? Your questions will be unending.

Indeed, you *should* be excited and concerned, for this experience of student teaching/interning/mentoring is one of the most significant facets of your program of teacher preparation. In some programs, this practical field experience is planned as a co-experience with the college or university theory and methods classes. In other programs, this practical field experience is the culminating experience. Different sequences are represented in different programs. For example, at some colleges, field teaching extends over two or three semesters. In other programs, teacher candidates experience a theory-class-first arrangement, which includes a full second semester of student teaching. Regardless of when and how your student teaching occurs, the experience is a bright and shining opportunity to hone your teaching skills in a real classroom environment. During this experience, you will probably be supported by an experienced college or university supervisor and by one or more carefully selected cooperating teachers, who will share with you their expertise.

Everyone concerned in the teacher preparation program—your cooperating teacher, university instructors, school administrators, and university supervisors—realizes that this is your practicum in learning how to teach. As you practice your teaching, you will no doubt make errors, and with the understanding, wisdom, and guidance of those supervising your work, you will benefit and learn from those errors. Sometimes your fresh approach to motivation, your novel ideas for learning activities, and your energy and enthusiasm make it possible for the cooperating teacher to learn from you. After all, teaching and learning are always reciprocal processes. What is most important is that the children who are involved with you in the teaching–learning process will benefit from your role as the precredentialed teacher in the classroom. The following guidelines are offered to help make this practical experience beneficial to everyone involved.

Student Teaching *IS* the Real Thing

On one hand, because you have a classroom setting for practicing and honing your teaching skills with active, responsive children, your student teaching *is* the real thing. On the other hand, student teaching is *not* real in the sense that your cooperating teacher, not you, has the ultimate responsibility and authority for the classroom and the students' learning.

Getting Ready for Student Teaching

To prepare yourself for student teaching or interning, you must study, plan, practice, and reflect. You should become knowledgeable about your students and their developmental backgrounds. In your theory and methods classes, you learned a great deal about children and how to teach them. Review your class notes and textbooks from those courses or select some readings from the chapters in Part I of this resource guide. Perhaps some of the topics will have more meaning for you now.

In addition to the aforementioned preparation, you will need to be knowledgeable about your assigned school and the community from which its students come. Review the subject areas you will be teaching and the curriculum content and standards in those areas. Carefully discuss with your cooperating teacher (or teachers, as you may have more than one) and your university supervisor all of the responsibilities that you will be expected to assume. Because it is unlikely that you will assume all of the responsibilities at once, there should be a discussion of and agreement on an approximate timeline or schedule showing dates by which you should be prepared to assume various responsibilities.

As a student teacher/intern, you may want to run through each lesson verbally, perhaps in front of a mirror or a camcorder, the night before teaching your lesson. Some student teachers read through each lesson, record the lesson, play it back, and evaluate the extent to which the directions are clear, the instruction is interesting, the sequence is logical, and the lesson closure is concise. Rehearsing a lesson will enable you to ask yourself some of the questions shown in the brief pre-lesson rehearsal checklist of Figure 11.1.

First Impressions

First impressions are often lasting impressions. You have heard that statement before, and now, as you get ready for this important phase of your professional preparation, you hear it again. Heed it—for it is crucial to your success. Remember it as you prepare to meet your school principal and cooperating/collaborating teacher for the first time; remember it as you prepare to meet your students for the first time; remember it as you prepare to meet parents and guardians for the first time; and remember it as you prepare your university supervisor's first observation of your teaching. Remember it again as you prepare for your first teaching job interview. In each case, you have only one opportunity to make a favorable first impression.

For your consideration, information about your student teaching/interning from the viewpoint of a cooperating or mentoring teacher is presented on our Companion Website **(www.prenhall.com/roberts)** in the *Additional Content* module for this chapter. It is in a question-and-answer format and you may want to share it with your cooperating teacher. ✍

Comments from the University Supervisor

When is the supervisor coming? Is the supervisor going to be here today? Do you see a supervisor's observation of your student teaching as a helpful experience or a painful one? Do you realize that classroom observations of your teaching continue during your beginning years of teaching? Being observed and evaluated does not have to be a painful, nerve-racking experience for you. You don't have to become a bundle of raw nerve endings when you realize the supervisor is coming to see you. Whether you are a student teacher being observed by your university/college supervisor or an intern or probationary (untenured) teacher being evaluated by your principal (or by a committee of peers as is the case in some schools), some of the professional suggestions on our Companion Website may help you turn an evaluating observation into a useful, professionally gratifying experience. Turn to our Companion Website **(www.prenhall.com/roberts)** in the *Additional Content* module for this chapter for suggestions for what to do *before* an observation, *during* an observation, and *after* an observation. ✍

As your successful student teaching experience draws to a close, you may be asked to respond to a culminating student teaching experience evaluation. For example, you may be asked to use identified performance evaluation criteria and make comments following each performance section related to your state's teaching performance expecta-

- In what ways are my voice and body language conveying thorough preparation?
  Comments:

- In what ways am I conveying confidence (or uncertainty and confusion)?
  Comments:

- Are my directions clear?
  Comments:

- Is the instruction interesting?
  Comments:

- Are the materials/resources ready?
  Comments:

- Is the sequence logical?
  Comments:

- Is the lesson closure concise?
  Comments:

- In what way am I ready for a Plan B if Plan A turns out to be inappropriate?
  Comments:

Figure 11.1
Brief pre-lesson rehearsal check

tions/standards. Identified criteria could include points such as

3: Evidence of competency met, performance competent, and skills observed during performance.

2: Evidence of satisfactory progress toward competency, performance satisfactory, and skills observed frequently.

1: Performance needs improvement; skills observed infrequently or not demonstrated.

N/A: Not applicable; setting does not apply to demonstration of skill set, knowledge, and/or developmental level.

See the example in Figure 11.2.

Figure 11.2
Sample culminating student teaching evaluation
(*Source:* Reprinted by permission from Dr. Michael Lewis, Dean, developed by College of Education, California State University, Sacramento.)

CALIFORNIA STATE UNIVERSITY, SACRAMENTO
College of Education, Teacher Preparation Programs

Culminating Student Teaching Experience Evaluation

Evaluator

☐ Midterm Evaluation   ☐ University Evaluator
                            ☐ Public School Evaluator
☐ Final Evaluation   ☐ Student Teacher/Intern (final evaluation only)

Student Teacher/Intern _____ Date _____

University Evaluator _____ School/District _____
(Liaison or Supervisor)

School Evaluator _____ Center/Grade _____/_____
(Cooperating or Collaborating Teacher)

Cooperating/Collaborating Teacher, University Liaison or Supervisor, Student Teacher/Intern:
Please respond to each of the competencies by using the performance evaluation criteria provided and comments portion following each section. Each rating should apply to the student teacher's/intern's *"common and typical behavior in the classroom."* All *observed* competencies on the **culminating** evaluation form require a rating of "3" in order for candidates to earn a "credit" grade in the final/culminating student teaching experience.

Performance Evaluation Criteria:

Evidence of competency met	**3**
Evidence of satisfactory progress toward competency	**2**
Performance needs improvement; skills observed infrequently or not demonstrated	**1**
Not applicable; setting not conducive to demonstration of skill, knowledge, disposition and/or developmental level	**NA**

*Note: Criteria ratings N/A, 1, and 2 are listed as options on the Phase II midterm and final. The **culminating** midterm and final evaluation forms include the additional criterion rating of "3" or "Evidence of Competency Met."*

Making Subject Matter Comprehensible to Students
Engaging and Supporting Students in Learning
Planning Instruction and Designing Learning Experiences for Students
Teaching Performance Expectations 1, 4, 5, 6, 7, 8, and 9

---

1. Supports the development and maintenance of a positive learning environment that values cognitive, cultural, and linguistic diversity

    NA _____   1 _____   2 _____   3 _____

2. Effectively delivers large group directions

    NA _____   1 _____   2 _____   3 _____

3. Uses students' responses and involvement to make sound decisions about pacing and the delivery of instruction

    NA _____   1 _____   2 _____   3 _____

4. Demonstrates efficient, smooth, and effective transitions

    NA _____   1 _____   2 _____   3 _____

5. Employs strategies that encourage critical thinking, including various levels of questioning

    NA _____   1 _____   2 _____   3 _____

Figure 11.2
Sample culminating student teaching evaluation (*continued*)

6. Generates a variety of responses from students in order to check for understanding of presented content before moving on to new content

    NA _____   1 _____   2 _____   3 _____

7. Moves around the room to monitor student work and behavior

    NA _____   1 _____   2 _____   3 _____

8. Creates developmentally appropriate lesson plans that include clearly stated objectives (social/collaborative and academic), purpose, anticipatory set, procedures, materials, closure/reflection, and assessment that support achievement of the objectives

    NA _____   1 _____   2 _____   3 _____

9. Plans units of instruction with clearly stated goals and lessons that are sequenced effectively for exploring fully a concept, theme or topic, integrating different content areas, and incorporating multicultural content

    NA _____   1 _____   2 _____   3 _____

10. Demonstrates sound knowledge of academic content standards and English Language Development standards (when applicable) to plan and teach lessons

    NA _____   1 _____   2 _____   3 _____

11. Effectively delivers large group instruction that provides opportunities for active participation of all students

    NA _____   1 _____   2 _____   3 _____

12. Demonstrates instructional strategies, activities, and materials that assess and build upon students' prior knowledge

    NA _____   1 _____   2 _____   3 _____

13. Plans and uses strategies that promote language and academic development of students from non-English backgrounds

    NA _____   1 _____   2 _____   3 _____

14. Utilizes instructional strategies, activities, and materials that encourage student choice and participation and promote students' self-esteem

    NA _____   1 _____   2 _____   3 _____

15. Demonstrates instructional strategies, activities, and materials that appeal to and challenge the diverse interests and abilities of the students (e.g., multiple intelligences, higher level thinking, multiple modalities)

    NA _____   1 _____   2 _____   3 _____

16. Motivates students of diverse backgrounds, interests, abilities, and learning styles to excel using strategies and approaches that are equitable as well as linguistically and culturally inclusive

    NA _____   1 _____   2 _____   3 _____

17. Communicates effectively by adjusting the complexity of his/her language (i.e., oral, written, and nonverbal) to accommodate for the linguistic abilities of both native English and English language learners

    NA _____   1 _____   2 _____   3 _____

18. Incorporates approaches and strategies in the planning of differentiated instruction to provide equal access to the core curriculum and opportunities for all students to participate actively in the learning process (i.e., ELL, special education, gifted)

    NA _____   1 _____   2 _____   3 _____

Comments to clarify or supplement questions 1–18 _____

_____

_____

_____

_____

_____

_____

Student Teacher/Intern _____ (Page 2 of 5, **Culminating** Evaluation Form)

Figure 11.2
Sample culminating student teaching evaluation (*continued*)

Creating and Maintaining Effective Learning Environments
Teaching Performance Expectations 10 and 11

19. (Helps to) establish a productive learning environment that includes clearly stated behavioral and academic expectations for students and provides regular feedback to students about those expectations

    NA _____   1 _____   2 _____   3 _____

20. Establishes and maintains a positive rapport with students in a variety of ways

    NA _____   1 _____   2 _____   3 _____

21. Communicates and interacts respectfully with all students

    NA _____   1 _____   2 _____   3 _____

22. Teaches and reinforces respectful interaction among students by providing opportunities for the students to develop and use social and interpersonal skills

    NA _____   1 _____   2 _____   3 _____

23. Teaches and encourages students to develop self-management skills

    NA _____   1 _____   2 _____   3 _____

24. Utilizes a variety of effective classroom management strategies (e.g., clearly stated expectations, specific constructive feedback, nonverbal cues, proximity, planned ignoring, self-monitoring, positive reinforcement, class meetings, conflict resolution, contingency contracting) to promote productive student behavior and learning

    NA _____   1 _____   2 _____   3 _____

25. Effectively manages student behavior in a variety of situations (i.e., one-to-one, small group, multiple small groups, large group with teacher, large group without teacher)

    NA _____   1 _____   2 _____   3 _____

Comments to clarify or supplement questions 19–25 _____

_____

_____

_____

_____

Assessing Student Learning
Teaching Performance Expectations 2 and 3

26. Together with the teacher, establishes achievement criteria and communicates them clearly to students

    NA _____   1 _____   2 _____   3 _____

27. Applies formal and informal methods to assess students' achievements

    NA _____   1 _____   2 _____   3 _____

28. Uses formative student assessment data to guide changes in teaching content, methods, and/or materials

    NA _____   1 _____   2 _____   3 _____

29. Uses a variety of appropriate assessment tools to determine and document student learning and growth

    NA _____   1 _____   2 _____   3 _____

Student Teacher/Intern _____ (Page 3 of 5, **Culminating** Evaluation Form)

Figure 11.2
Sample culminating student teaching evaluation (*continued*)

30. Uses educational policy resources in planning a curriculum and assessing student progress (e.g., California Subject Matter Frameworks, content standards, district standards, etc.)

    NA _____   1 _____   2 _____   3 _____

Comments to clarify or supplement questions 26–30 _____

_____

_____

_____

Developing as a Professional Educator
Teaching Performance Expectations 12 and 13

---

31. Demonstrates professionalism in personal appearance, presentation and behavior, and good judgment

    NA _____   1 _____   2 _____   3 _____

32. Works effectively as a team member at the school site and with university personnel

    NA _____   1 _____   2 _____   3 _____

33. Accepts responsibilities related to student teaching

    NA _____   1 _____   2 _____   3 _____

34. Participates in school-based activities (e.g., parent conferences, school/staff meetings, back-to-school night)

    NA _____   1 _____   2 _____   3 _____

35. Demonstrates the ability to work collegially with the cooperating/collaborating teacher, other school personnel (e.g., school secretary, classroom aides, etc.), and university faculty

    NA _____   1 _____   2 _____   3 _____

36. Exhibits respect, understanding, and sensitivity toward the cultural heritage, community values, and individual aspirations of diverse students, families, colleagues

    NA _____   1 _____   2 _____   3 _____

37. Interacts with students honestly and equitably by protecting their privacy, respecting their work, and being receptive to their ideas

    NA _____   1 _____   2 _____   3 _____

38. Is willing to self-assess his/her own performance in terms of strengths and weaknesses through a variety of reflection practices

    NA _____   1 _____   2 _____   3 _____

39. Assesses one's strategies for overcoming possible bias toward students from different backgrounds and academic abilities

    NA _____   1 _____   2 _____   3 _____

40. Seeks, accepts, and utilizes constructive feedback for professional growth

    NA _____   1 _____   2 _____   3 _____

41. Demonstrates initiative, self-direction, dedication, and dependability

    NA _____   1 _____   2 _____   3 _____

42. Demonstrates appropriate professional and interpersonal communication skills with students, parents, and school and university personnel

    NA _____   1 _____   2 _____   3 _____

43. Demonstrates positive, active listening skills

    NA _____   1 _____   2 _____   3 _____

Student Teacher/Intern _____ (Page 4 of 5, **Culminating** Evaluation Form)

Figure 11.2
Sample culminating student teaching evaluation (*continued*)

Comments to clarify or supplement questions 31–43 _____

_____

_____

_____

_____

_____

Overall Commendations:

Specific Recommendations to Address Areas Needing Improvement:

Sources of Evidence (check all items that apply)   ☐ Portfolio   ☐ Observations

☐ Written reflections   ☐ Interview/Discussions   ☐ Other (please identify)

Evaluator: Please check the appropriate recommendation

☐ Recommend, based on overall satisfactory performance, for Multiple Subject Credential

☐ Recommend extending or repeating culminating MS student teaching experience

☐ Do not recommend extending or repeating culminating MS student teaching experience

_____   _____   _____

Public School Evaluator   University Evaluator   Student Teacher/Intern

_____   _____   _____

Date   Date   Date

TEACHING EFFECTIVENESS THROUGH E-TEACHING: AN EMERGENCY E-TEACHING KIT

One way to continue your teaching effectiveness is to always be prepared. One way of being prepared, whether you are a precredentialed teacher who is interning or a credentialed teacher who is a substitute teacher, is to consider E-teaching, that is, efficient teaching with preplanned lessons focused on a theme related to selected content or standards. In E-teaching, you also use electronic resources and other support materials to back up your teaching and build a personal emergency E-teaching kit (ETK). Thus, E-teaching is an efficient, ready-for-an-emergency teaching kit backed up with electronic and other resources. An E-teaching kit can include a wide variety of teaching materials that usually cross discipline boundaries; these are materials that you collect, organize into teaching activities, and prepare to support a topic or a theme (such as the topic of friendships or the theme of survival) in ongoing lessons or a unit.

Purposes of E-Teaching with an Emergency E-Teaching Kit

An emergency E-teaching kit can be a useful strategy for teaching and learning that can complement your state's teaching performance expectations and standards. An E-teaching kit can serve any of several purposes and will enable you, as a regular classroom teacher, a substitute teacher, or a student teacher or intern, to do the following:

- Demonstrate instructional strategies, activities, and materials that assess and build on students' prior knowledge with an anticipation guide or another activity/task of your choice.
- Use student choice and participation and promote students' self-esteem and/or cooperative teamwork.
- Incorporate differentiated/tiered instruction, which provide opportunities for all students to participate actively in the learning process; assist students who need to participate more in the learning process.
- Demonstrate instructional strategies, activities, and materials that appeal to and challenge the diverse interests and abilities of all students.
- Establish a positive rapport with students in a variety of ways; motivate learners to show their knowledge of a topic.
- Provide opportunities for the students to develop and use social and interpersonal skills; offer a supportive learning environment through nonthreatening educational activities.
- Use informal methods (such as K–W–L) to assess students' achievements.
- Provide feedback to the learner and to the teacher, through observation, as the students interact with

the topic of the educational activity or lesson; provide opportunities for discussions/debriefings after the educational game to develop insights about content, interaction with others, and, when appropriate, the implications of the topic in a real-life experience.
- Plan a unit of instruction (congruent with the state's content frameworks or state/district/school standards) with clearly stated goals and lessons that are sequenced effectively for exploring a concept, theme or topic; the unit should also integrate content areas, incorporate multicultural content, and have some relevance to real life.

Developing an E-Teaching Kit with a Multidisciplinary Emphasis

As a regular teacher, substitute teacher, precredentialed teacher, or intern, you may want to develop an E-teaching kit that has a multidisciplinary and web emphasis, since this approach is often included in a state's published teaching performance expectations. In the requirements, you may discover that your state's standards also ask you to provide learning that values cognitive diversity, that integrates different content areas into lessons and units, and that incorporates multicultural content into the teaching–learning environment. You can provide for these standards in an E-teaching kit.

By having an E-teaching kit and other E-teaching ideas readily available, you will be prepared for an E-teaching emergency, whether it is for one day or several days. See additional ideas in More Suggestions for E-Teaching: Emergency E-Teaching Kit About Multicultural Friendships on our Companion Website **(www. prenhall.com/roberts)** in the *Additional Content* module for this chapter. Then return to this resource guide and do Application Exercise 11.1.

For Your Notes

✎ **APPLICATION EXERCISE 11.1 DEVELOPING AN EMERGENCY E-TEACHING KIT**

Instructions: The purpose of this exercise is threefold: (a) to give you experience in preparing for E-teaching, (b) to help you collect materials, including websites, for an emergency E-teaching kit, and (c) to start your collection of emergency E-teaching plans that you may be able to use later in your teaching. If appropriate for your group, we suggest that you distribute copies of your plans to one another in the class to begin your collection of E-teaching ideas. This is an assignment that will take several hours to complete. Your emergency E-teaching kit can include the following components:

1. Emergency E-teaching kit topic or theme:

2. Statement of rationale/general goals/justification from a professional teaching expectation document, national or state standards, a state/district/school document, or content framework:

3. Main focus question (optional):

4. Related subquestions (optional):

5. Identification of objective(s) for each of 10 activities; that is, what will the students learn?
   Activity #1:

   Activity #2:

   Activity #3:

APPLICATION EXERCISE 11.1 *(continued)*

Activity #4:

Activity #5:

Activity #6:

Activity #7:

Activity #8:

Activity #9:

Activity #10:

✎ APPLICATION EXERCISE 11.1 *(continued)*

6. A list of the e-resources and other materials needed and where they can be obtained if you have that information.

7. A sequence for the 10 activities (or brief lesson plans):

8. List the approaches that will be used to preassess (consider using the think–pair–share or K–W–L methods) and also assess student learning *during* (formative) and at the *completion* (summative) of the material in the emergency E-teaching plans:

9. Indicate the discipline areas drawn on if you are planning an interdisciplinary thematic approach:

_____ a. Health and physical education

_____ b. Mathematics

_____ c. Music and dance

_____ d. Poetry and prose

_____ e. Painting and sculpture

_____ f. Reading and language

_____ g. Sciences

_____ h. Social sciences/history

_____ i. Other

10. If appropriate for your group, distribute copies of this plan to one another to begin your collection of E-teaching ideas. Other comments:

For Your Notes

FINDING A TEACHING POSITION

As your successful student teaching/interning experience draws to a close, you will embark on the process of finding your first paid teaching job or your first substitute teaching job. The guidelines that follow are provided to help you accomplish your goal.

Guidelines for Locating a Teaching Position

To prepare for finding the position you want or locating a substitute position or internship, focus on

1. Obtaining strong letters of recommendation from your cooperating teacher(s), your college or university supervisor, and, in some instances, the school principal;
2. Your professional preparation as evidenced by your letters of recommendation and other items in your professional portfolio including your résumé; and
3. Your job interviewing skills. First, consider the recommendations about your teaching. Some colleges and universities have a career placement center where there is probably a counselor who can advise you about how to open the job placement file that will hold your professional recommendations. This enables prospective personnel directors or district personnel who are expecting to employ new teachers to review your recommendations. It is your responsibility to request letters of recommendation and, when appropriate, to supply the person writing the recommendation with the required form and an appropriately addresssed, stamped envelope. Sometimes, the job placement files are confidential, so the recommendations will be mailed directly to the placement office. The confidentiality of recommendations may be optional, and, when possible, you may want to maintain your own copies of letters of recommendation and include them in your professional portfolio.

Letters of Recommendation

The letters of recommendation from educators at the school(s) where you did your interning or student teaching should include the information mentioned in the brief checklist that we have placed on our Companion Website (**www.prenhall.com/roberts**) for this chapter. ✎ Review the checklist and then return to this resource guide.

Your Preparation

Next, consider your preparation as a teacher. Teachers, as you have learned, represent a myriad of specialties. Hiring personnel will want to know how you see yourself—for example, as a primary-grade teacher, as a specialist in sixth-grade core, or as an elementary school physical education or music teacher. Perhaps your interest is in teaching children at any level of elementary school or only science in grades 4 through 6. You may indicate a special interest or skill, such as competency in sign language or in teaching English to English language learners. Or, perhaps, in addition to being prepared to teach elementary school core subjects, you also are musically talented or are bi- or multilingual and have had rich and varied cross-cultural experiences. The hiring personnel who consider your application will be interested in your sincerity and will want to see that you are academically and socially impressive.

Your In-Person Interview

Last, consider your in-person interview with a district official. Sometimes, you will have several interviews or you will be interviewed simultaneously with a small group of candidates. There may be an initial screening interview by a panel of administrators and teachers from the district, followed by an interview with a school principal or by a school team composed of one or more teachers and administrators from the interested school or district.

In all interviews, your verbal and nonverbal behaviors will be observed as you respond to various questions, including (a) factual questions about your interning or student teaching or about particular curriculum programs with which you would be expected to work, and (b) hypothetical questions, such as "What would you do if . . . ?" Often these are questions that relate to your philosophy of education (that you began writing in an earlier chapter), your reasons for wanting to be a teacher, your approach to handling a particular classroom situation, and perhaps specifically your reasons for wanting to teach in this district at this particular school. Interview guidelines follow later in this chapter.

Through a Professional Career Portfolio

A way to be proactive in your teaching effectiveness, professional growth, and in your job search is to create a personal professional portfolio (computer-based or hardcopy) to be shared with persons who are considering your application for employment. This is the objective of Application Exercise 11.2, Development of a Professional Portfolio.

For Your Notes

APPLICATION EXERCISE 11.2 DEVELOPMENT OF A PROFESSIONAL PORTFOLIO

Instructions: The purpose of this application exercise is to guide you in the creation of a personal professional portfolio (electronic or hardcopy) that will be shared with persons who are considering your application for employment as a credentialed teacher.

Because it would be impractical to send a complete portfolio with every application you submit, you should consider developing a minimum portfolio (Portfolio B) that could be sent with each application, in addition to a complete portfolio (Portfolio A) that you could make available on request or take with you to an interview. However it is done, the actual contents of the portfolio will vary depending on the specific job being sought; you will continually add to and delete materials from your portfolio based on the particulars of a given job. Suggested categories and subcategories, listed in the order that they may be best presented in Portfolios A and B, are as follows:

1. Table of contents of portfolio (brief)—Portfolio A only.

2. Your professional resume—both portfolios.

3. Evidence of your language and communication skills (evidence of your use of English and other languages including American Sign Language)—Portfolio A. You may state this information briefly in your letter of application. See the résumé section in this chapter and sample of the professional résumé on our Companion Website **(www.prenhall.com/roberts)** in the *Additional Content* module. ✎

   a. Your teaching philosophy written in your own handwriting to demonstrate your handwriting (see Chapter 3).

   b. Other evidence to support this category of communication skills/language skills.

4. Evidence of teaching skills—Portfolio A.

   a. For planning skills, include instructional objectives and a unit plan (see Chapters 5 and 7).

   b. For teaching skills, include a sample plan and a video of your actual teaching (see Chapter 7 and this chapter).

   c. For assessment skills, include a sample personal assessment and samples of student assessment (see Chapters 6 and 11).

APPLICATION EXERCISE 11.2 *(continued)*

5. Letters of recommendation and other documentation to support your teaching skills—both portfolios.

6. Other. For example, list personal interests related to the position for which you are applying—Portfolio A.

The professional career portfolio should be organized to provide clear evidence of your teaching skills and to make you professionally desirable to hiring personnel. A professional portfolio is not just a random collection of your accomplishments that have been placed into an electronic file or a hardcopy folder. Your portfolio should be a deliberate, current, and organized collection of your experiences, attributes, skills, and accomplishments.

Perhaps it would be impractical to send a complete portfolio with every application you submit (electronically or hardcopy), so it might be advisable to have a minimum portfolio (labeled Portfolio B) that could be sent with each application. This would be in addition to your complete portfolio (labeled Portfolio A) that you could make available through e-mail (or regular mail) on request or that you would take with you as hardcopy to an interview. However it is done, the actual contents of the portfolio will vary depending on the specific job being sought; you will continually add (and delete) materials from your portfolio. Application Exercise 11.2 suggests categories and subcategories, listed in the order that they may be best presented in Portfolios A and B.[1]

Resources for Locating Teaching Jobs

Various resources are available for locating teaching and subbing possibilities. To help you make these contacts, we have placed a checklist related to locating teaching or substitute teaching jobs on our Companion Website **(www.prenhall.com/roberts).**[2] This will help you track the resources that you have contacted. Review the checklist in the *Additional Content* module and then return to this resource guide.

State and Territorial Sources for Information About Credential and License Requirements

If you are interested in the credential and licensing requirements for other states and U.S. territories, check the appropriate office of your own college or university teacher preparation program to see what information is available for locations of interest to you, and whether the credential or license that you are about to receive has reciprocity with the other states. Addresses and contact numbers for information about state credentials are available at *www.ed.gov/Programs/bastmp/statelist.html.*

The Professional Résumé

Résumé preparation is the subject of how-to books, computer programs, and commercial services, but a teacher's résumé is specific. While no one can tell you exactly what type of résumé will work best for you, a few basic guidelines are especially helpful for the preparation of hardcopy for a teacher's résumé.

- **Keep it short.** The résumé should be no longer than two pages in length. If it is any longer, it becomes a life history rather than a professional résumé.
- **Neatness counts.** The presentation should be neat and uncluttered.
- **Standard size.** The hardcopy page size should be standard 8 1/2 × 11 inches. Oversized and undersized pages can get lost.
- **Neutral paper color.** Stationery color should be white or off-white.
- **Minimum personal data.** Do not give information such as your age, height, weight, marital status, the number or names of your children, or a photograph of yourself, because including personal data may make it appear that you are trying to influence members of the hiring committee, which is simply unprofessional.
- **Clear, concise writing.** Sentences should be clear and concise; avoid educational jargon, awkward phrases, abbreviations, or words seldom used in daily conversations (e.g., counterintuitive, analog).
- **Organization.** Organize the information carefully. We suggest this order: your name, postal or e-mail addresses, your phone number (give your cell phone number if you do not want your phone number to be part of an online map-to-your-house database in the future), followed by your education, professional experience, credential status, location of file, if applicable, professional affiliations, and honors.
- **Reverse chronological order.** When identifying your experiences—academic, teaching, and life—do so in reverse chronological order, listing your *most recent* degree or your current position first.
- **Honesty.** Be absolutely truthful; avoid any distortions of facts about your degrees, experiences, or any other information that you provide on your résumé.
- **Take your time.** Take time to develop your résumé, and then keep it current. Do not duplicate hundreds of copies; produce a new copy each time you apply for a job. If you maintain your résumé on a computer disk or have an electronic portfolio, then it is easy to make modifications and print a current copy each time one is needed.
- **Cover letter needed.** Prepare a cover letter to accompany your résumé written specifically for the position for which you are applying. Address the letter personally but formally to the personnel director. Limit the cover letter to one page, and emphasize yourself, your teaching experiences and interests, and reasons that you are best qualified for the position. Show a familiarity with the particular school or district. Again, if you maintain a generic application letter in an electronic portfolio on a computer, you can easily modify it to make it specific for each position.

- **Editing needed.** Have your cover letter and résumé edited by someone familiar with résumé writing and editing, perhaps an English-teaching friend. A poorly written, poorly typed, or poorly copied résumé filled with spelling and grammar errors will guarantee that you will not be considered for the job.
- **Meet the deadline.** Be sure that your application reaches the personnel director by the announced deadline. If for some reasons it will be late, then call the director, explain the circumstances, and request permission to submit your application late.

The In-Person Interview

If your application and résumé are attractive to the personnel director, you will be notified and scheduled for a personal or small-group interview, although in some instances, the hiring interview may precede the request for your personal papers. Whichever the case, during the interview you should be honest, and you should be yourself. Practice an interview, perhaps with the aid of a video camera. Ask someone to role-play an interview with you and to ask you some tough questions (for examples of questions, see the questions listed at the end of the chapters in this resource guide). As you view the video, observe how you respond to questions. What is your body language conveying? Do you appear confident?

Plan your interview wardrobe and get it ready the night before. Dress for success. Regardless of what else you may currently be doing for a living, take the time necessary to make a professional and proud appearance.

If possible, long before your scheduled interview, locate someone who works in the school district and discuss curriculum, classroom management policies, popular programs, and district demographics with that person. If you anticipate a professionally embarrassing question during the interview, think of diplomatic ways to respond. This means that you should think of ways to turn your weaknesses into strengths. For instance, if your cooperating teacher has mentioned that you need to continue to develop your room environment skills (meaning that you were sloppy and left your desk and the room cluttered), admit that you realize that you need to be more conscientious about keeping supplies and materials neat and tidy, but mention your concern about the students and the learning and that you realize you have a tendency to interact with students more than with objects. Assure someone that you will work on this skill, and then do it.

The paragraphs that follow offer additional specific guidelines for preparing for and handling the in-person interview. As you peruse these guidelines, please realize that what may seem trite and obvious to one reader is not necessarily the same to another.

You will be given a specific time, date, and place for the interview. Regardless of your other activities, accept the time, date, and location suggested, rather than trying to manipulate the interviewer around a schedule more convenient to you.

Avoid coming to the interview with small children. If necessary, arrange to have them taken care of by someone.

Leave early for your interview so that you arrive in plenty of time. Shake hands firmly with members of the committee, and initiate conversation with a friendly comment, based on your personal knowledge about the school or district.

Be prepared to answer standard interview questions. Sometimes, school districts will send candidates the questions that will be asked during the interview; at other times, these questions are handed to the candidate on arrival at the interview. Some of the questions that are likely to be asked will cover the topics listed in Figure 11.3.

As part of the interview, you may be expected to do a formal but abbreviated (10 to 15 minutes) teaching demonstration (or present a video of one of your lessons). You may or may not be told in advance of this demonstration. If hiring personnel are interested in seeing a video of your teaching, they will inform you. So, it is a good idea to thoughtfully develop and rehearse a model of your teaching, one that you could perform on immediate request. Just in case it might be useful, some candidates carry to the interview a video (or make electronic arrangements to show a teaching episode) of one of their best teaching episodes made during student teaching.

When the interview has obviously been brought to a close by the interviewer, that is your signal to leave. Do not hang around; this might be interpreted as nervousness or a sign of lacking confidence. Follow the interview with a thank-you letter addressed to the personnel director or the one in charge of interview. Even if you do not get the job, you will be remembered for future reference.[3]

Once you are employed as a teacher, your professional development continues. The sections that follow demonstrate ways in which that can happen.

PROFESSIONAL DEVELOPMENT

Through Reflection

Beginning now and continuing throughout your career, you will reflect on your teaching (reflection is inevitable), and you will want to continue to grow as a professional as a result of those reflections (growth is not as inevitable unless it is self-initiated and systematically planned). The most competent

Figure 11.3
Preparing for interview questions: A self-check

Possible questions about:

1. *Your experiences with students of the relevant age.*
   The hiring committee wants to be reasonably certain that I can effectively manage and teach at this level. I can answer questions about this by sharing specific successes that demonstrate that I am a decisive and competent teacher.

   _____ I am prepared   _____ I am working on this

2. *Hobbies and travels.* The committee wants to know more about me as a person to ensure that I will be an interesting and energetic teacher to the students, as well as a congenial member of the faculty.

   _____ I am prepared   _____ I am working on this

3. *Extracurricular interests and experiences.* The committee wants to know about all the ways in which I might be helpful in the school and to know that I will promote the interests and cocurricular activities of students and the school community.

   _____ I am prepared   _____ I am working on this

4. *Classroom management techniques.* I want to convince the committee that I can effectively manage a classroom of diverse learners in a manner that will help the students develop self-control and self-esteem.

   _____ I am prepared   _____ I am working on this

5. *Knowledge of content and standards.* I want to show that I have knowledge of the curriculum standards and the subject taught at the grade for which I am being considered. The committee needs to be reasonably certain that I have command of the subject and its place within the developmental stages of children at this level. This is where I can show my knowledge of national standards and of state and local curriculum standards and documents.

   _____ I am prepared   _____ I am working on this

6. *Knowledge about the teaching of reading.* I want to show the committee my views about teaching reading, and that I am knowledgeable about specific strategies for teaching reading, at any grade level.

   _____ I am prepared   _____ I am working on this

7. *Knowledge of assessment strategies relevant for use in teaching at this level.* I realize that this is my place to shine with my professional knowledge about using scoring guides/rubrics and performance assessment.

   _____ I am prepared   _____ I am working on this

8. *Commitment to teaching at this level.* I want to assure the committee that I am knowledgeable about teaching and learning at this level and committed to the profession (as contrasted with just seeking this job until something better comes along).

   _____ I am prepared   _____ I am working on this

9. *My ability to reflect on experience and to grow from that reflection.* I want to demonstrate that I am a reflective decision maker and a lifelong learner.

   _____ I am prepared   _____ I am working on this

10. *My strengths as a teacher.* I realize that the hiring committee may want to ask me what I perceive as my major strengths as an elementary schoolteacher. I will consider my answer carefully so I can be impressive without taking an inordinate amount of time answering the question.

    _____ I am prepared   _____ I am working on this

11. *My perceived weaknesses.* If I am asked about my weaknesses, I have an opportunity to show that I can effectively reflect and self-assess, that I can think reflectively and critically, and that I know the value of learning from my own errors and how to do it. I will be prepared for this question by identifying a specific error that I have made, perhaps while student teaching, and explaining how I was able to turn that error into a profitable learning experience.

    _____ I am prepared   _____ I am working on this

12. *Interacting with the committee.* Throughout the interview, I will maintain eye contact with the person talking to me while demonstrating interest, enthusiasm, and self-confidence. When an opportunity arises, I will ask one or two planned questions that demonstrate my knowledge of and interest in this position and this community and school or district.

    _____ I am prepared   _____ I am working on this

professional is one who is proactive, that is, one who takes charge and initiates continuing personal, professional development.

Through Self-Assessment

One useful way of continuing to reflect, self-assess, and to grow professionally is by maintaining a professional journal, much as your students do when they maintain journals reflecting on what they are learning. Another is by continuing to maintain the professional career portfolio that you began assembling early in your preservice program (perhaps electronically as mentioned on our Companion Website) and finalized for your job search (as discussed in this chapter).

Through Journals or Logbooks

You may want to maintain a **professional logbook,** which will serve not only as documentation of your specific professional contributions and activities, but also as documentation of the breadth of your professional involvement. You can maintain a research logbook to record the questions that come up during your busy teaching day and then establish a plan for finding some answers.[4] The research logbook strategy can be of tremendous benefit to you in actively researching and improving your classroom work, but also can be of interest to colleagues. Working in teams and sharing your work with team members is still another way of continuing to reflect, self-assess, and grow as a teacher.

A Teachalogue for Reflection and Self-Assessment

To assist you in immediate reflection and self-assessment, consider looking at the "teachalogue" shown in Figure 11.4. This figure offers you a summary of teaching suggestions to consider before a lesson, during a lesson, and after a lesson. Also, this teachalogue can be used as is, or you can personalize it now or at any time during your career.

PROFESSIONAL DEVELOPMENT THROUGH MENTORING

Mentoring, one teacher facilitating the learning of another teacher, can aid in professional development.[5] In what is sometimes called peer coaching, a *mentor teacher* (sometimes called a *consulting teacher*) volunteers or is selected by the teacher who wishes to improve or is selected by a school administrator, formally or informally. The mentor observes and coaches the teacher to help the teacher improve.

Sometimes the teacher simply wants to learn a new skill. In other instances, the teacher being coached remains with the mentor teacher for an entire school year, developing and improving new and old skills or learning how to teach with a new program. In some districts, new teachers are automatically assigned to mentor teachers for their first year, and sometimes a second year, as a program of induction. Induction is often part of the mentoring process in which formalized assistance is given to beginning teachers by district or university supporters.

PROFESSIONAL DEVELOPMENT THROUGH IN-SERVICE AND STUDY

In-service workshops, seminars, and programs are offered for teachers by the school, by the district, and by other agencies such as a country office of education or a nearby college or university. In-service seminars and workshops and programs are usually designed for specific purposes, such as to train teachers in new teaching skills, to update their knowledge in content, and to introduce them to new teaching materials or programs.[6]

University graduate study is yet another way of continuing your professional development. Some teachers pursue master's degrees in academic teaching fields, while many others pursue their degrees in curriculum and methods of instruction or in educational administration or counseling. Some universities offer a master of arts in teaching (MAT), a program of courses in specific academic fields that are especially designed for teachers.

PROFESSIONAL DEVELOPMENT THROUGH PROFESSIONAL ORGANIZATIONS

Many professional organizations—local, statewide, national, and international—are available to teachers. Some organizations are discipline specific, for example, the International Reading Association, the National Council of Teachers of Mathematics, the National Council for the Social Studies, and the National Science Teachers Association (see Chapter 5). Become familiar with the national teachers' organizations such as the National Education Association (NEA),[7] which is the oldest, and more recent ones such as the Association of American Educators (AAE) and the National Association of Professional Educators (NAPE).

Local, district, state, and national organizations sponsor meetings that include guest speakers, workshops, and publishers' displays. Professional meetings

Figure 11.4
My teachalogue

Before the lesson:

1. Did you write specific objectives, and will you share them with your students?
2. Have you prepared tentative assessment strategies and items to be used to determine if objectives are being achieved?
3. Did you refer to the established course of study for your grade level and review your state and local frameworks, the teacher's manuals, scope and sequence charts, and standards?
4. Are your motivational techniques relevant to the lesson, helping children connect their learning to real-world experiences?
5. Are you taking students' interest in a topic for granted, or does your motivational component of the lesson meet their developmental needs and interests?
6. Did you order media materials and equipment pertinent to your lesson, and did you preview these materials?
7. Did you prepare large-size demonstration materials, and will you display them so that all of the children can see them?
8. Have you planned your lesson transitions from one activity to the next or from one lesson to the next?
9. Do you have the necessary supplies and materials ready for the lesson so time is not wasted looking for them once the lesson has begun?
10. Have you mastered manuscript writing so as to provide a model for the primary grades and mastered cursive writing so as to provide a model for the intermediate and upper grades?
11. Have you established efficient, orderly routines and procedures for your class management tasks, such as collecting homework, taking roll, collecting money, sharpening pencils, distributing and collecting books, obtaining attention, moving around in the classroom, and dismissing students for recess, for lunch, and at the end of the school day?
12. Have you planned your preassessment strategy, perhaps as an advance organizer for the lesson, to discover what the students already know, or think they know, about the concept of the lesson?
13. Have you built into your lesson plans strategies for student reflection, metacognition, and self-assessment of their learning?
14. Have you planned your postassessment strategies to find out whether the children have, in fact, learned that which you intend them to learn?
15. To the best of your knowledge, do your assessment strategies authentically assess the learning objectives?
16. Have you planned for frequent checks for student understanding of the material?
17. Have you considered the needs of individual children in your class, such as children who have disabilities or who have limited proficiency in the English language?
18. Do you have a contingency plan in case something goes wrong with the lesson or there is a major disruption of the learning?
19. Are you planning variation in your instructional strategies so that students not only learn subject content but also develop their thinking skills, study skills, social skills, and sense of self-worth?
20. Have you incorporated multitasking in your instruction?
21. Have you intelligently planned the physical layout of your classroom to match the nature of the instruction and learning needs of the children?

During the lesson:

22. Are you clearing the writing board before you begin a new lesson?
23. Are you remembering that sometimes material is clearer to students if they can read it as well as hear it?
24. Are you remembering to write legibly and boldly, with large letters and in an orderly manner, so all can read your writing on the writing board?
25. Are you being gracious and sympathetic to every student, showing that you have confidence in each child's abilities?
26. Are you allowing your students to participate in discussion (to talk) and be heard, and are you giving each student the individual, private, and specific reinforcement that the student deserves?
27. Are you setting the mental stage for the learning of each new idea?
28. Are you varying your class activities sufficiently to best reach each child's learning capacities and modalities?
29. Are you attempting to build on each student's ideas, questions, and contributions during the lesson?
30. Are you making clear all relationships between main ideas and details for your students, and presenting examples of abstract concepts in simple and concrete ways?
31. Are you explaining, discussing, and commenting on any media materials you use in your lesson?

Figure 11.4
My teachalogue (*continued*)

32. When asking questions of students, are you remembering to give them time to review the topic, to hear the frame of reference for your questions, to recognize that your questions are on their level of understanding, and to use "think time" before they respond?
33. Are you remembering to avoid answering your own questions?
34. Are you remembering to interact with and to call on the children and to give them tasks equally according to their gender and other personal characteristics?
35. Are you introducing materials (e.g., rulers, protractors, scissors, magnets, media, art supplies, felt boards) to the children *before* they are needed in your lesson?
36. Are you evincing enthusiasm in your speech and mannerisms, maintaining a moderate pace in your classroom, and insisting that all children give you their attention when you begin a lesson?
37. Are you maintaining proximity and eye contact with all the children?
38. Are you checking frequently during the lesson to see whether the children are "getting it"; that is, that they understand the content and processes being taught?

After the lesson:

39. Are you taking time to reflect on how the lesson went and on what might have been "muddy" and what was "clear," and then reteaching all or portions of it if necessary?
40. Are you making notes to yourself as follow-up to today's lesson, perhaps special attention to be given tomorrow regarding specific content or skills for particular students?

of teachers are educational, enriching, and usually fulfilling for those who attend. In addition, many other professional associations, such as those for reading teachers, supply speakers and publish articles in their journals that are often of interest to teachers, including those beyond the targeted audience.

Professional organizations publish newsletters and journals for their members, and these will likely be found in your college or university library. Sample periodicals are listed in the *Additional Content* module of the Companion Website **(www.prenhall. com/roberts)** for this chapter. Many professional organizations have special membership prices for teachers who are still college or university students, a courtesy that allows for inexpensive initial affiliation with a professional organization.

PROFESSIONAL DEVELOPMENT THROUGH COMMUNICATIONS WITH OTHER TEACHERS

Related to your professional development through communications with other teachers, here are some of the valuable experiences available to you: visiting teachers at other schools; attending in-service workshops, graduate seminars, and programs; participating in teacher study groups[8] and meetings of professional organizations; participation in teacher networks,[9] in video clubs,[10] and in teacher book clubs;[11] and sharing with teachers by analyzing one another's teaching

videos, or communicating by means of electronic bulletin boards. These are all valuable experiences, if for no other reason than to talk and to share with teachers from across the nation and around the world. For examples of topics to include in your sharing, see the *Technology Tips for the Classroom* feature. Your discussions can be a sharing of "front-line" stories and also a sharing of ideas and descriptions of programs, books, materials, and techniques that work.

As in the other process skills, the teacher practices and models skill in communication, in and out of the classroom. This includes communicating with other teachers to improve one's own repertoire of strategies and knowledge about teaching as well as sharing one's experiences with others. Teaching other teachers about your own special skills and sharing your experiences are important components of the communication and professional development processes.

PROFESSIONAL DEVELOPMENT THROUGH THE INTERNET, ADDITIONAL TRAINING, AND WORKSHOPS

In many areas of the United States, workshop retreats and special programs are available to interested teachers. Often these are available especially, though not exclusively, to teachers with special interests in reading and literacy, physical education, mathematics, science, and social studies and are offered by public agencies, private industry, foundations, and research institutes. These organizations are interested in disseminating information and providing opportunities for teachers to update their skills and knowledge, with the ultimate hope that the teachers will stimulate in more students a desire to develop their physical fitness, to understand civic responsibilities, and to consider careers in science and technology.

Participating industries, foundations, governments, and institutes provide on-the-job training with salaries or stipends to teachers who are selected to participate. During the program of short-term employment and depending on the nature of that work, a variety of people (e.g., businesspersons, politicians, scientists, social workers, technicians, and sometimes university educators) meet with teachers to share experiences and discuss what is being learned and its implications for teaching and curriculum development.

Some of the programs for teachers are government sponsored, field centered, and content specific. For example, a program may concentrate on geology, anthropology, mathematics, or reading. At another location, a program may concentrate on teaching methods, using a specific new or experimental curriculum. At still another location, a program may be a part of a distance learning program shown on a television station in your area with e-mail backup to the instructor's computer. These programs, located around the country, may have university affiliation, which means that university credit may be available. Registration fees, room and board, travel, and a stipend are sometimes granted to participating teachers.

Sources of information about the availability of programs include professional journals, a neighboring university or college, the local chamber of commerce, and meetings of the local or regional teacher's organization. In areas where there are no organized retreat or work experience programs for teachers, some teachers have had success in initiating their own by grant writing[12] or establishing contact with management personnel at local businesses or companies.

PROFESSIONAL DEVELOPMENT THROUGH PEER TEACHING

Peer teaching (PT) is a skill-development strategy used for professional development by both precredentialed (preservice, prelicensed) and credentialed (in-service, licensed) teachers. Peer teaching (to which you were introduced previously in this resource guide) is a scaled-down teaching experience involving a

- Limited objective(s),
- Brief interval for teaching a lesson,

- Lesson taught to 8 to 10 peers who take the roles of your students, and
- Lesson that focuses on the use of one or several instructional strategies.

Peer teaching can be a predictor of later teaching effectiveness in a regular classroom. More importantly, it can provide an opportunity to develop and improve specific teaching behaviors. A videotaped PT lesson allows you to see yourself in action for self-evaluation and diagnosis. Evaluation of a PT session is based on

- The quality of the teacher's preparation and lesson implementation,
- The quality of the planned and implemented student involvement,
- The extent to which the target objective(s) was reached, and
- The appropriateness of the cognitive level of the lesson.

Whether you are a precredentialed teacher or a credentialed teacher, you are urged to participate in one or more PT experiences. The PT experience we provide here is formatted differently from previous application exercises in this resource guide. Application Exercise 11.3, Pulling It All Together: Peer Teaching, can represent a summative performance assessment for the course for which this book is being used.

 Companion Website

To continue your interest in professional development, go to our Companion Website at **www.prenhall.com/roberts** and click on the *Additional Content* module for Chapter 11.

Technology Tips for the Classroom

- Note that students can waste valuable time sifting through the information on the Internet and that just because information is found on the Internet doesn't necessarily mean that the students should consider the information accurate or current. Students can be encouraged to use a checklist for evaluating materials found on the Internet. Perhaps you can introduce some of the criteria from the checklist available at www.infopeople.org/bkmk/select.html.
- Be prepared to respond to the critics (perhaps some will be your students' parents and community members) of slide software, such as *PowerPoint*, who have concerns about its use for

(continued)

educational purposes.[13] From critics, you may hear comments similar to "Its emphasis on format over content commercializes and trivializes subjects"; "It's very loud, very slow, and very simple"; "...has a subtle set of biases that indoctrinate users to speak—and think—simply"; and "Its entertainment lulls people into accepting pablum over ideas."

- Help yourself and other educators meet the technology literacy requirements of the National Education Technology Plan within the No Child Left Behind (NCLB) initiative. This plan requires that students become technologically literate by the eighth grade and that each state define a technologically qualified teacher. Consider a new online teacher's aid, the National Leadership Toolkit, developed by the State Educational Technology Directors Association (SETDA), a national professional organization, and the U.S. Department of Education.[14] The toolkit includes

  - Ways to assess teacher skills and advice on assessing students' technological readiness;
  - Some effective professional development sessions for teachers;
  - Some best practices for teaching tech skills;
  - Information on the role of equal access to technology across socioeconomic groups of students; and
  - Some recommendations for designing state research studies that meet the requirements of the NCLB.

  To see the toolkit or download some future information related to recommendations for complying with U.S. Department of Education requirements, the National Education Technology Plan, and the technology literacy requirements of the NCLB, go to www.setda.org.

- Some researchers have found that students who read selections on interactive CD-ROMs scored higher on longer and more difficult comprehension passages on tests than did their peers who read the same selections in print.[15] It seems that the CD-ROMS provide instant help for students confronting new vocabulary because students can click on a word and hear it pronounced, defined, and used in context. Further, the attention

and interest of the students is held by the music, special effects, and the interactive approach.

- Regarding laser pointers, we *do not* recommend these pointers being around children at all (in fact, in some states, laser pointers are prohibited in the schools) since all laser pointers can cause eye damage if someone looks into the beam. If you are interested in using a laser pointer for your own professional presentations for adults, use caution when around any reflective surface or when using any optics to modify the laser beam. You may want to use a laser pointer for these reasons: to highlight text, to include optic features, and to demonstrate certain optics principles. The laser light (green shines the brightest) will highlight text in your presentations and lectures; a laser pointer also adapts to the features of focus, line generation, blinking, projected shapes, and moving beams.

- Check out any recent classroom performance system that can be used as an electronic assessment tool. As an example, Einstruction's performance system (www.einstruction.com) for the PC or the Mac gives each student a wireless remote pad and a connection to the teacher's computer. To work it, the teacher asks a question and students respond by pressing one of eight buttons on their pads. The students' responses are tallied and summarized, making it efficient for monitoring the understanding of the students and for test giving because responses are automatically scored and recorded.

- Note that some teachers are suggesting that picture phones be banned during test taking since some students are taking pictures of test pages and sending them to absent or ill friends who plan to take the test later.

Companion Website

To find resources to support your teaching effectiveness and professional development, go to our Companion Website at **www.prenhall. com/roberts** and click on the *Web Destinations* module for Chapter 11.

APPLICATION EXERCISE 11.3 PULLING IT ALL TOGETHER: PEER TEACHING

Instructions: The purpose of this exercise is to learn how to develop your own PT experiences. You will prepare and teach a lesson that is prepared as a lesson presentation for your peers, at their level of intellectual maturity and understanding (i.e., opposed to teaching the lesson to peers pretending that they are public school students).

This experience has two components:

1. Your preparation and implementation of a demonstration lesson
2. Your completion of an analysis of the summative peer assessment and the self-assessment, with statements of how you would change the lesson and your teaching of it were you to repeat the lesson.

You should prepare and carry out a 15- to 20-minute lesson to a group of peers. The exact time limit for the lesson should be set by your group, based on the size of the group and the amount of time available. When the time limit has been set, complete the time-allowed entry (item 1) of Form A of this exercise. Some of your peers will serve as your students; others will be evaluating your teaching. (The process works best when "students" do not evaluate while being students.) Your teaching should be videotaped for self-evaluation.

For your lesson, identify one concept and develop your lesson to teach toward an understanding of that concept. Within the time allowed, your lesson should include both teacher talk and a hands-on activity for the students. Use Form A for the initial planning of your lesson. Then complete a lesson plan, selecting a lesson plan format as discussed in Chapter 7. Then present the lesson to the "students." The peers who are evaluating your presentation should use Form B of this exercise.

After your presentation, collect your peer evaluations (the Form B copies that you gave to the evaluators). Then review your presentation by viewing the videotape. After viewing the tape, prepare:

- A tabulation and statistical analysis of peer evaluations of your lesson
- A self-evaluation based on your analysis of the peer evaluations, your feelings having taught the lesson, and your thoughts after viewing the videotape
- A summary analysis that includes your selection and description of your teaching strengths and weaknesses, as indicated by this peer-teaching experience, and how you would improve were you to repeat the lesson.

Tabulation of Peer Evaluations

The procedure for tabulating the completed evaluations received from peers is as follows:

1. *Use a blank copy of Form B for tabulating.* In the left margin of that copy, place the letters N (number) and σ (total) to prepare for two columns of numbers that will fall below each of those letters. In the far right margin, place the word *Score*.

2. *For each item (A through Y) on the peer evaluation form, count the number of evaluators who gave a rating (from 1 to 5) on the item.* Sometimes an evaluator may not rate a particular item, so although there may have been 10 peers evaluating your micro peer teaching, the number of evaluators giving you a rating on any one particular item could be less than 10. For each item, the number of evaluators rating that item we call N. Place this number in the N column at the far left margin on your blank copy of Form B, next to the relevant item.

3. *Using a calculator, obtain the sum of the peer ratings for each item.* For example, for item A, Lesson Preparation, you add the numbers given by each evaluator for that item. If there were 10 evaluators who gave you a number rating on that item, then your sum on that item will not be more than 50 (5×10). Because individual evaluators will make their X marks differently, you sometimes must estimate an individual evaluator's number rating; that is, rather than a clear rating of 3 or 3.5 on an item, you may have to estimate it as being a 3.2 or a 3.9. In the left-hand margin of your blank copy of Form B, in the σ column, place the sum for each item.

APPLICATION EXERCISE 11.3 *(continued)*

4. *Now obtain a score for each item, A through Y.* The score for each item is obtained by dividing σ by *N*. Your score for each item will range from 1 to 5. Write this dividend in the column in the right-hand margin under the word *Score* on a line parallel to the relevant item. This is the number your will use in the analysis phase.

Procedure for Analyzing the Tabulations

Having completed the tabulation of the peer evaluations of your teaching, you are ready to proceed with your analysis of those tabulations.

1. To proceed, you need a blank copy of Form C of this exercise, your self-analysis form.

2. On the blank copy of Form C are five items: Implementation, Personal, Voice, Materials, and Strategies.

3. In the far left margin of Form C, place the letter σ for the sum. To its right, and parallel with it, place the word *Average*. You now have arranged for two columns of five numbers each—a σ column and an *Average* column.

4. For each of the five items, get the total score for that item, as follows:

   a. *Implementation.* Add all scores (from the right-hand margin of blank Form B) for the four items a, c, x, and y. The total should be 20 or less (4×5). Place this total in the left-hand margin under σ (to the left of "1. Implementation").

   b. *Personal.* Add all scores (from the right-hand margin of blank Form B) for the nine items f, g, m, n, o, p, q, s, and t. The total should be 45 or less (9×5). Place this total in the left-hand margin under σ (to the left of "2. Personal").

   c. *Voice.* Add all scores (from the right-hand margin of blank Form B) for the three items h, i, and j. The total should be 15 or less (3×5). Place this total in the left-hand margin under σ (to the left of "3. Voice").

   d. *Materials.* Add all scores (from the right-hand margin of blank Form B) for the item k. The total should be 5 or less (1×5). Place this total in the left-hand margin under σ (to the left of "4. Materials").

   e. *Strategies.* Add all scores (from the right-hand margin of blank Form B) for the eight items b, d, e, l, r, u, v, and w. The total should be 40 or less (8×5). Place this total in the left-hand margin under σ (to the left of "5. Strategies").

APPLICATION EXERCISE 11.3 *(continued)*

5. Now for each of the five categories, divide the sum by the number of items in the category to get your peer evaluation average score for that category. For item 1 you will divide by 4; for item 2, by 9; for item 3, by 3; for item 4, by 1; and for item 5, by 8. For each category you should then have a final average peer evaluation score of a number between 1 and 5. If correctly done, you now have average scores for each of the five categories: Implementation, Personal, Voice, Materials, and Strategies. With those scores and evaluator's comments, you can prepare your final summary analysis.

The following table includes three sample analyses of PT lessons based *only* on the scores—that is, without reference to comments made by individual evaluators, although peer evaluator's comments are important considerations for actual analyses.

Sample Analyses of PTs based Only on Peer Evaluation Scores

	Category/Rating					
Teacher	**1**	**2**	**3**	**4**	**5**	**Possible Strengths and Weaknesses**
A	4.2	2.5	2.8	4.5	4.5	Good lesson, weakened by personal items and voice.
B	4.5	4.6	5.0	5.0	5.0	Excellent teaching, perhaps needing a stronger start.
C	2.5	3.0	3.5	1.0	1.5	Poor strategy choice, lack of student involvement.

FORM A: PT PREPARATION

Instructions: Form A is to be used for initial preparation of your PT lesson. (For preparation of your lesson, study Form B.) After completing Form A, proceed with the preparation of your PT lesson using a lesson plan format as discussed in Chapter 7. A copy of the final lesson plan should be presented to the evaluators at the start of your PT presentation.

1. Time allowed _____

2. Title or topic of lesson I will teach _____

3. Concept _____

4. Specific instructional objectives for the lesson:

   Cognitive _____

   _____

   Affective _____

   _____

   Psychomotor _____

   _____

5. Strategies to be used, including approximate time plan:

   Set introduction _____

   _____

   Transitions _____

   _____

   Closure _____

   _____

   Others _____

   _____

6. Student experiences to be provided (i.e., specify for each—visual, verbal, kinesthetic, and tactile experiences): _____

   _____

7. Materials, equipment, and resources needed:

   _____

   _____

FORM B: PEER EVALUATION

Instructions: Evaluators use Form B, making an *X* on the continuum from 5 to 1. Far left (5) is the highest rating; far right (1) is the lowest. Completed forms are collected and given to the teacher upon completion of the teacher's PT and reviewed by the teacher prior to reviewing his or her videotaped lesson.

To evaluators: Comments as well as marks are useful to the teacher.

To teacher: Give one copy of your lesson plan to the evaluators at the start of your PT. (*Note:* It is best if evaluators can be together at a table at the rear of the room.)

Teacher _____   Date _____

Topic _____

Concept _____

1. Organization of lesson	5	4	3	2	1
a. Lesson preparation evident	very		somewhat		no
b. Lesson beginning effective	yes		somewhat		poor
c. Subject-matter knowledge apparent	yes		somewhat		no
d. Strategies selection effective	yes		somewhat		poor
e. Closure effective	yes		somewhat		poor

Comments

_____
_____
_____
_____
_____
_____
_____
_____
_____
_____
_____
_____
_____
_____

2. Lesson Implementation	5	4	3	2	1
f. Eye contact excellent	yes		somewhat		poor
g. Enthusiasm evident	yes		somewhat		no
h. Speech delivery	articulate		minor problems		poor
i. Voice inflection; cueing	effective		minor problems		poor
j. Vocabulary use	well-chosen		minor problems		poor
k. Aids, props, and materials	effective		okay		none

FORM B: PEER EVALUATION *(continued)*

l. Use of example and analogies	effective	need improvement	none
m. Student involvement	effective	okay	none
n. Use of overlapping skills	good	okay	poor
o. Nonverbal communication	effective	a bit confusing	distracting
p. Use of active listening	effective	okay	poor
q. Responses to students	personal and accepting	passive or indifferent	impersonal and antagonistic
r. Use of questions	effective	okay	poor
s. Use of student names	effective	okay	no
t. Use of humor	effective	okay	poor
u. Directions and refocusing	succinct	a bit vague	confusing
v. Teacher mobility	effective	okay	none
w. Use of transitions	smooth	a bit rough	unclear
x. Motivating presentation	very	somethat	not at all
y. Momentum (pacing) of lesson	smooth and brisk	okay	too slow or too fast

Comments

_____
_____
_____
_____
_____
_____
_____
_____
_____
_____
_____
_____

FORM C: TEACHER'S SUMMATIVE PEER EVALUATION

See instructions within Application Exercise 11.3 for completing this form.

1. Implementation (items a, c, x, y)   5   4   3   2   1

2. Personal (items f, g, m, n, o, p, q, s, t)   5   4   3   2   1

3. Voice (items h, i, j)   5   4   3   2   1

4. Materials (item k)   5   4   3   2   1

5. Strategies (items b, d, e, l, r, u, v, w)   5   4   3   2   1

Total = _____

Comments

_____

_____

_____

_____

_____

_____

_____

_____

_____

_____

_____

_____

_____

_____

_____

_____

_____

_____

_____

_____

_____

_____

_____

_____

_____

_____

For Your Notes

About Praxis and Other Teacher Tests

About Praxis Teacher Tests. To continue to support you as you prepare for teaching, all application exercises in this chapter and the related Companion Website offer opportunities for you to reflect generally on your teaching effectiveness and ongoing professional development. For instance, in this chapter, as a prelicensed and precredentialed teacher, you are asked to participate cooperatively and collaboratively and to do the following:

- Demonstrate your planning and teaching skills by developing an E-teaching kit (Application Exercise 11.1).
- Create a personal professional portfolio that will be shared by persons who are considering your application for employment as a licensed/credentialed teacher by doing Application Exercise 11.2.
- Participate in your own peer teaching experience by preparing and teaching a brief lesson (Application Exercise 11.3).
- Turn to our Companion Website (**www.prenhall.com/roberts**) and click on the *Additional Application Exercise* module to complete the additional application exercise titled A Professional Résumé.

You can find a constructed response-type question similar to those found on the Praxis II tests in the Praxis Warm-Up section that follows the Chapter Summary. This warm-up takes another look at the classroom vignette found in the Looking at Teachers section at the beginning of this chapter.

 Other Teacher Tests. For those of you who will be teaching in states that do not administer the Praxis II Principles of Learning and Teaching tests, go to our Companion Website at **www.prenhall.com/roberts** and click on the *Other Teacher Tests* module for Chapter 11 to access information about teacher tests other than the Praxis.

SUMMARY

Because teaching and learning go hand in hand and the effectiveness of one affects that of the other, the sixth chapter and the last chapter of this resource guide have dealt with both aspects of the *how well* component of teacher preparations—how well the students are learning and how well the teacher is teaching. In addition, in this chapter, you have been presented with guidelines about how to obtain your first teaching job and how to continue your professional development. Throughout your teaching career, you will continue improving your knowledge and skills in the many aspects of teaching and learning.

We wish you the very best in your new career. If you are interested in a children's book to read on the last day of school, we suggest that you read one of your favorites or read aloud *Oh, the Places You'll Go!* (New York: Random House, 1990, all ages) by Dr. Seuss. As with his other books, Dr. Seuss has lively cartoons to accent his cadenced advice about moving on and going forward in one's life. Beginning with "Congratulations! Today is your day," and ending with "Your mountain is waiting. So . . . get on your way!" the words offer advice about overcoming a time you are in a slump (start "un-slumping yourself"), about facing loneliness ("face up to your problems"), and about other challenges in one's life. Regardless of what book you read aloud to the stu-

dents to end the year or regardless of the way you close the last day of school, be the very best teacher that you can be every teaching day and for as long as you can. Our nation and our children need you.

P. L. R.

R. D. K.

K. M.

EXTENDING MY PROFESSIONAL COMPETENCY

Praxis Warm-Up: A Constructed Response-Type Question

In this chapter's teacher vignette, we pointed out the value of learning something useful for elementary school teaching from another teacher, this one from a high school teacher. You'll recall that as a finale for his students' unit of study, the teacher assigned *PowerPoint* presentations. The success of the presentations led this teacher to include a *PowerPoint* presentation as an assignment in all of the rest of his ongoing high school classes, but the most important message to you as an elementary schoolteacher is that this teacher did not let the technology replace the human feature in his teaching in the classroom. Indeed, this teacher believed that teacher "affect" was more effective than just teaching with high tech.

For a unit of study of your choice and grade level, describe an end-of-a-unit activity (not a *PowerPoint* presentation) that would be an extension of the study. The activity you describe should be focused on the unit and detailed, and it should demonstrate an understanding of how children at your choice of age and grade level learn.

Hints for responding to Praxis Warm-Ups are found in the Appendix.

Praxis. To do another Praxis Warm-Up with a constructed response-type question, go to our Companion Website at **www.prenhall.com/roberts** and click on the *Praxis Warm-Up* module for Chapter 11. Constructed response-type questions are designed to help you prepare for the Praxis II Principles of Learning and Teaching tests.

For Your Discussion

1. **My Teaching Philosophy.** If a principal interviews me for a teaching job and asks me about my philosophy of teaching students, how will I respond? **To do:** You will recall that, in Chapter 3, you participated in an exercise during which you developed your first draft of your teaching philosophy. It was mentioned that at the completion of this text, you might want to revisit your philosophical statement and perhaps even to revise it. Do this now. It will be useful for you to have your educational philosophy in mind for your future teaching interviews.

2. **Educational Concepts.** If a colleague asks me about prior concepts I held that changed as a result of my experiences with this resource guide, what will I say? **To do:** Describe the changes with others in your group.

3. **Contradictory Educational Practice.** What would I say if a parent or a colleague mentioned an example of an educational practice that seems contradictory to exemplary practice or theory presented in this resource guide? **To do:** Present your explanation for the discrepancy to others in your group.

4. **Professional Teacher Organizations.** What would I pass along for information if a colleague asked me about teacher organizations to join in my geographical area? **To do:** Share what you find with others in your group and attend a local, regional, or national meeting of a professional teachers' association. Report to your group what it was like and what you learned. Tell others

about any free or inexpensive teaching materials you obtained.

5. **Positive or Negative: High Tech's Offer.** If a parent asks me if I thought too many students were wasting time on the web, just clicking around without any focus from location to location, what would be my response? **To do:** Research information about the point of view of educators and others related to students spending too much time looking for glossy media and driving the cyber road to find barely linked facts on the web. When do you think that students have time to *think* about what they have found? When do students give the teacher some evidence that they understand the content or that they have given the subject some individual thought? Consider reading your instructor's recommended source on the topic or read *The Flickering Mind: The False Promise of Technology in the Classroom and How Learning Can Be Saved* (New York: Random House, 2003) by Todd Oppenheimer. Formulate Your response.

6. **Further Questions.** What would be my response if a colleague asked me if I have any lingering questions in my mind about elementary school teaching? **To do:** List them and try to find answers.

Congratulations! You have reached the end of this resource guide and the supporting resources on our Companion Web.

Online Portfolio Activities

Supporting categories of content of professional growth and development (Praxis II Assessment); Principles 9 and 10 of INTASC; and Standards 9, 10 and 11 of NBPTS: At the Companion Website **(www.prenhall. com/roberts),** click on the *Online Portfolio Activities* module to continue your online portfolio supporting professional growth and development.

Companion Website
Also on the Companion Website at **www.prenhall. com/roberts,** you can measure your understanding of chapter content in the *Objectives* and *Self-Check* modules and apply concepts in the *Additional Applications Exercises* and *For Your Discussion* modules.

FOR FURTHER READING

Backes, C. R., and Backes, L. S. (1999). Making the Best of a Learning Experience. *Techniques: Making Education and Career Connections, 74*(5), 23–24.

Costa, A. L., and Garmston, R. L. (2002). *Cognitive Coaching: A Foundation for Renaissance Schools* (2nd ed.). Norwood, MA: Christopher-Gordon Publishers.

Cramer, G., and Hurst, B. (2000). *How to Find a Teaching Job: A Guide for Success.* Upper Saddle River, NJ: Merrill/Prentice Hall.

Danielson, C., and McGreal, T. (2000). *Teacher Evaluation to Enhance Professional Practice.* Alexandria, VA: Association for Supervision and Curriculum Development.

Danna, S. (2003, February/March). Pursuing National Board Certification. *Pi Lambda Theta Educational Horizons*, p. 5.

Good, T. L., and Brophy, J. E. (2003). *Looking in Classrooms* (9th ed.). New York: Addison Wesley/Longman.

Graham, P., et al. (Eds.). (1999). *Teacher/Mentor.* New York: Teachers College Press.

Hurst, C. O., and Otis, R. (2000). *Friends and Relations: Using Literature with Social Themes, Grades 3–5.* Greenfield, MA: Northeast Foundation for Children.

Kellough, R. D. (2001). *Surviving Your First Year of Teaching: Guidelines for Success* (2nd ed.). Upper Saddle River, NJ: Merrill/Prentice Hall.

Konrad, R. (2003, December 29). Business: Workplace. *The Sacramento Bee,* pp. D1, D4.

Lipton, L., and Wellman, B., with C. Humbard (2001). *Mentoring Matters: A Practice Guide to Learning-Focused Relationships.* Sherman, CT: MiraVia.

Minkel, W. (Ed.). (2003, June). Techknowledge. *School Library Journal,* pp. 28–30.

Minkel, W. (Ed.). (2003, November). Techknowledge: Rage against the Machine. *School Library Journal,* p. 34.

NASDTEC Manual 2000: Manual on the Preparation and Certification of Educational Personnel (5th ed., Table E-2). Dubuque, IA: Kendall/Hunt Publishing.

Oakley, K. (1998). The Performance Assessment System: A Portfolio Assessment Model for Evaluating Beginning Teachers. *Journal of Personnel Evaluation in Education 11*(4), 323–341.

Olson, R., and Meyer, R. (1995, September). News: Survey Says CD-ROMs Boost Reading Scores. *School Library Journal,* pp. 41, 99, 108.

Perry A. (2003, Summer). Tech versus the Human Touch: Teacher Affect Is More Effective. *Educational Horizons, 81*(4), 183–185.

NOTES

1. D. B. Martin, *The Portfolio Planner: Making Professional Portfolios Work for You* (Upper Saddle River, NJ: Merrill/Prentice Hall, 1999). See also G. Cramer and B. Hurst, *How to Find a Teaching Job: A Guide for Success* (Upper Saddle River, NJ: Merrill/Prentice Hall, 2000); the theme issue of *Teacher Education Quarterly, 25*(1) (Winter 1998); and the Internet at *www.teachnet.com.*

2. *Education Week* (Fall 2000) launched their test phase of a national online teacher job bank on which districts nationwide may post their job vacancies and on which job-seeking teachers can post their résumés. See *www.edweek.org.*

3. For additional suggestions for preparing for a teaching job interview, see Chapter 5 of Cramer and Hurst, *How to Find to Teaching Job,* note 1.

4. See Chapter 4, Creating a Professional Portfolio, in C. Danielson, *Enhancing Professional Practice: A Framework for Teaching* (Alexandria, VA: Association for Supervision and Curriculum Development, 1996), pp. 38–50.

5. The International Center for Information about New Teacher Mentoring and Induction at *www.teachermentors.com/MCenter%20Site/MCategoryList.html.* For additional information, see a description of California's Beginning Teacher Support and Assessment (BSTA) Program at *http//btsa.ca.gov/,* and T. L. Good and J. E. Brophy, *Looking in Classrooms,* 9th ed. (New York: Addison Wesley/Longman, 2003).

6. K. S. Shapiro and J. E. Clauses, Freshness in the Mountains, *Educational Leadership, 57*(8), 66–68 (May 2000).

7. The NEA and the AFT have merged in at least two states, Minnesota and Montana.

8. G. Cramer et al., *Teacher Study Groups for Professional Development* (Fastback 406) (Bloomington, IN: Phi Delta Kappa Educational Foundation, 1996).

9. A. Lieberman and M. Grolnick, Networks, Reform, and the Professional Development of Teachers, Chapter 10 (pp. 192–215) in A. Hargreaves (Ed.), *Rethinking Educational Change with Heart and Mind,* ASCD 1997 Yearbook (Alexandria, VA: Association for Supervision and Curriculum Development, 1997).

10. M. G. Sherin, Viewing Teaching on Videotape, *Educational Leadership, 57*(8), 39–41 (May 2000).

11. S. M. Goldberg and E. Pesko, The Teacher Book Club, *Educational Leadership, 57*(8), 39–41 (May 2000).

12. K. Chandler, Summer Sustenance, *Educational Leadership, 57*(8), 63–65 (May 2000).

13. R. Konrad, Business: Workplace, *The Sacramento Bee,* pp. D1, D4 (December 29, 2003).

14. W. Minkel (Ed.), TechKnowledge, *School Library Journal,* p. 34 (November 2003).

15. R. Olson and R. Meyer, New: Survey Says CD-ROMs Boost Reading Scores, *School Library Journal,* pp. 41, 99, 108 (September 1995).

Appendix

Hints for Short-Answer Response Questions: Praxis Warm-Ups

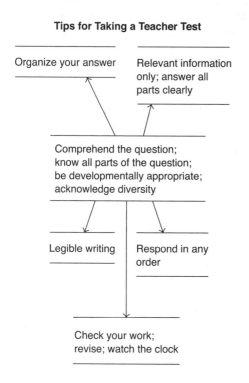

Tips for Taking a Teacher Test

Organize your answer

Relevant information only; answer all parts clearly

Comprehend the question; know all parts of the question; be developmentally appropriate; acknowledge diversity

Legible writing

Respond in any order

Check your work; revise; watch the clock

CHAPTER 1

Hints: You are asked to describe two different activities that you would use to help the children with learning problems who do not understand the ones, tens, and hundreds place-value arrangement in mathematics. You are asked how a teacher could also assess the children's understanding of ones, tens, and hundreds place-value arrangement. Consider what the children would be doing during the following two examples and write about each example; consider what assessment you would use and write about it.

Activity #1: Use of manipulatives

I would have the children use manipulatives (beans, chips, blocks, paper squares) of different colors and count different numbers of manipulatives separately to see ones, then a group of ten, then ten groups of ten to make one hundred. I would write the numeral that represents the number on the board so the children could see the numeral. I would have the children team up together as math partners and count manipulatives together; I would ask questions such as, "If I gave you two more (name the color) _____ ones, how many would you have? What is your total? I would have the partners combine their manipulatives, count, and recognize numerals, to participate in a cooperative learning activity.

Activity #2: Real-life example using popcorn

I believe that children learn best through hands-on learning and I would use a real-life example of popped popcorn as manipulatives. I would tell them that they have a kernel of popcorn to feed one to each bird that lives in the area near their home. I would have them announce the number of birds they have seen and have them hold the kernels of popcorn, one for each bird. I would tell them that they have just found out that two (three, four) other birds are flying in, and ask, what should they do? I would repeat this activity with different numbers so the children would understand the idea of basic facts (and one to one correspondence).

Assessment for both activities: To assess, I would look to see that all of the children are cooperating with the activity. I would notice who is listening to find out what to do. I would show numeral cards (or write the numerals on the board) and ask them to show the number of manipulatives that the numeral represents. I would ask questions such as, "If I have the numeral 2 in the tens space and 1 in the ones place, what number is it?" I would use observation as a major assessment tool. I would look for confusion. At the end of the activity, I would give a written problem and assess it to see if the students have improved in their understanding of the ones, tens, and hundreds place value arrangement.

CHAPTER 2

Hints: You are asked to describe two different activities that would help the fourth-grade students design and prepare graphs and give a justification of the activities for this age group. Consider explaining clearly two different activities that would help fourth-grade students prepare a graph; consider the cognitive (or social, emotional, physical) characteristics of these students to justify your choice of activities and write about it.

Activity #1: Favorite cookie graph
After a brief introduction to a line graph (perhaps pointing out to students that a line graph or bar graph is useful for showing differences in choices or showing changes over time), I would have the children play a graph game. To do this, I would divide the children into two groups. With input from the children, I would write the names of five favorite cookies on the board in a left-hand column.

Favorite Cookie Graph

Favorite Cookies	Total Tally
Chocolate chip	
Chocolate with vanilla filling	
Oatmeal-raisin	
Peanut butter	
Other	

Total Tally for Chocolate Chip

Team A	Team B

Total Tally for Chocolate with Vanilla Filling

Team A	Team B

I would have one student from each group, taking turns, go to the board to make a tally mark beside his or her favorite cookie or beside the term *Other*. I would continue this until all of the children have made their tally marks. Then, I would have one from

each group, on my signal, race to the board to write the total, adding the tallies for each cookie, i.e., one pair would race to the board to tally the total for the chocolate chip cookie. The group then counts the tallies for that cookie aloud to verify the addition. Another pair, on my signal, would race to tally the total for the next cookie, and so on. The first member of a team to tally a cookie's tallies correctly wins a point. The team with the highest number of points wins the game after all of the totals for all of the cookies have been added correctly. Discuss the use of a line graph and what information it can tell the children. If a student asks about a circle graph or pie graph, I will point out that it is best for showing the relationship between the whole and its parts, including information about comparing and contrasting.

Activity #2: Favorite ice cream graph
Discussing the use of a line graph, I would have the children repeat a favorite graph game. To do this, I would divide the children into two groups. With input from the children, I would write the names of five favorite flavors of ice cream on the board in a left-hand column.

Favorite Ice Cream Graph

Favorite Ice Cream	Total Tally
Chocolate	
Vanilla	
Strawberry	
Butter Pecan	
Other	

Total Tally for Chocolate

Team A	Team B

Total Tally for Vanilla

Team A	Team B

I would have one student from each group, taking turns, go to the board to make a tally mark beside his or her favorite flavor or beside the term *Other*. I would ask that if the student is a boy to make a tally mark with the letter B on top of it; if the student is a girl, then she should make a tally mark with a G on the top of it. I would continue this until all of the children have made their tally marks. Then, I would have one from each group, on my signal, race to the board to write the total adding the tallies for each flavor that the boys liked, then adding the tallies for each flavor that the girls liked; i.e., one pair would race to the board to tally the total of boys who liked the chocolate ice cream; the group then counts aloud the tallies for the boys who liked that flavor to verify the addition. Another pair, on my signal, would race to tally the total of girls who liked the chocolate ice cream and the group would count to verify the total. Another pair, on my signal, would race to the board to tally the total of boys who liked the next flavor, and so on. The first member of a team to count a flavor's tallies by boys/girls correctly wins a point. The team with the highest number of points wins the game after all of the totals for all of the flavors of ice cream liked by boys and by girls have been added correctly. I would discuss the use of this line graph and the information it can tell us (or the future owner of an ice cream store) about preferences that are similar or different between the boys and the girls in their choice of ice cream flavors.

Justification of activities for this age level: Fourth-grade students will become engaged in these two activities because students at this age level prefer active learning experiences; they like interaction with their peers and are willing to learn what they consider to be useful information. They like to use their skills to solve real-life problems (like determining the kind of ice cream flavors an owner should stock in his or her store if this fourth-grade class were to buy ice cream there). They can reason, judge, and apply their experiences and think about their own thinking. They want to be popular and have a sense of humor. They mature at varying rates and have individual differences. Physically, they have strong appetites and, socially, they want group acceptance.

CHAPTER 3

Hints: You are asked to describe two learning activities that you would use to help the third-grade students with learning problems in this class who do not fully understand the concept of transplanting. Activities could include making charts, diagrams, or drawing some planting maps about transplanting tasks. Some students could draw cartoons, tell stories, and make posters to show what they do when they transplant plants.

Other students could write invitations to a program they have planned about gardening/transplanting, draw advertisements, write invitations to members in another class, and plan a program that includes speeches about the value of transplanting, a script of a story about gardening, and a planned debate over what to do (or not to do) when considering transplanting a certain type of plant.

Still other students could write personal letters to one another about their transplanting experiences, or make daily entries in diaries or journals. For this question, you are to give examples of what the students would be doing and should explain how you would assess the two activities that you choose and the students' understanding of the concept of transplanting after they have completed the two activities.

Activity #1: Planting bean seeds
I would have the students plant three bean seeds—one each in three small clear plastic glasses—and water them frequently. When the beans have developed roots and the first two leaves, I would have the students transplant one of the seedlings into a small paper cup that they have decorated to give to different teachers as gifts. With hands-on learning in mind, I would have the students transplant a second seedling to a larger cup to take home and give to someone in the home.

Activity #2: Transplanting to the school campus
Considering the third seedling, I would have the students transplant it to a larger pot, and then eventually have the students transplant the seedlings to a place on the school campus where the students have determined that the transplanted seedlings will receive sunlight and water for future growth.

Assessment of both activities: To assess, I would look to see that all of the children are cooperating with the activity. I would notice who is listening to find out what to do. At the end of the activity, I would ask the students to demonstrate their understanding of the term *transplanting*. I would assess their responses to see if the students have improved their understanding of the term. As a group activity, I would ask them to demonstrate the meaning of the term in several ways: by reading the definition aloud from a dictionary, by reading some content about transplanting aloud from an information book, by showing an illustration about transplanting from a source of their choice, and by demonstrating with actions (similar to the game of charades) their understanding of the meaning of the word. With hands-on learning in mind, one assessment activity would be for a small group to take turns drawing from a deck of cards (whose faces show stick figure drawings of gardening tasks, i.e., raking leaves, pruning shrubs, cutting flowers) until they recognize two cards that show transplanting—one card that shows a plant in a pot and on the second card, a plant in the ground beside the same pot, which is now empty.

Another assessment activity would be to give each of the students one of the cards from the gardening deck and ask them to walk around the room until the two transplanting cards are found. I think it is very important for learning to be enjoyed by students so they will want to learn. If they don't enjoy the learning, I suspect some of the children will become disinterested and decide to turn their attention elsewhere. I believe that quite a few children need hands-on learning to further their comprehension.

CHAPTER 4

Hints: First, in the classroom vignette at the beginning of the chapter, you were asked to consider how the second-grade students, rather than the teacher, could accept the procedures and rules that the teacher suggested and also assume responsibility for their actions and make their classroom a community of learners. Next, in the Praxis Warm-Up at the end of the chapter, you were asked to take the role of a teacher working with older students and focus on rules and procedures. You were asked to begin a unit on the American Revolution for a fifth-grade class and plan one or two writing activities that will help your students pass along the information that they have learned about the need for laws/procedures/rules and will help organize their thinking about the idea that laws should be designed to equally support and value all members of a community, even a community in the time period of the American Revolution. As part of this instruction, you were then asked to give the purposes for and describe two writing activities that you might use in your unit on the American Revolution. Some of the activities (related to the letters in the word *activities*) that you can consider are the following:

A is for advertisements related to the period

C is for creating cartoons, making charts, stating comparisons

T is for telling stories

I is for invitations

V is for video programs

I is for individual letters

T is for telling predictions

I is for individual diaries and journals

E is for engaging in debates

S is for speeches and scripts

Consider giving the purposes of both of the writing activities and be sure to be clear about your specific writing examples.

Activity #1: Writing and purpose
I would select one of the following writing activities: asking the students to work in dyads to construct informational paragraphs about what was learned about rules in this unit of study with the *purpose* of developing an understanding of the particular concept of rules; or having the students each write a letter to a friend in the classroom to tell the friend what was learned with the purpose being to have the children use accurate information and apply it in another situation.

For a creative writing activity, I would ask the students to work together in pairs to write a response to the question "What do you think a colonist during the days of the American Revolution would say if transported to this time period and given a cell phone to communicate with others?" I understand that the letters in the word *purposes* will help me remember examples of the different purposes for learning activities for the students. I could focus on one of the following purposes for selected activities:

P particular concept selected (understanding of); to clarify thinking about a concept

U use of accurate information; to inform/advise

R requiring in-depth learning (to be applied); to record thoughts

P parts contribute to a whole situation (to see how the parts contribute to the whole); to persuade; to predict/hypothesize

O other situations (apply to); to compare to other situations

S synthesis and analysis (use of)

E expansion of the students' thinking

S stressing creativity; to entertain/amuse

Activity #2: Writing and purpose
I would engage the students in writing entries in their student learning journals for the *purpose* of expanding the students' thinking, to determine the students' understanding of the particular concept of *rules,* to note the use of accurate information, and to see the students' understanding of how parts (for instance, the making of rules) during the time period contributed to the whole situation of following someone's rules/not following someone's rules.

CHAPTER 5

Hints: You are asked, as a sixth-grade teacher, to describe two more writing activities (and the purposes) that you might use after a student brainstorming session about a language arts lesson on listening. And, you are to give examples for the students. Consider the following fanciful/creative and realistic kinds of writing activities.

Activity #1: Fanciful/creative writing and purpose

I would ask the students to assume that they had been assigned an alien writing partner and were going to be time travelers back to the time of the American Revolution to see the rules being used there. The student is to write a letter to the alien to explain what is going on. The alien, being from another planet, does not understand what rules are or what is going on. After the letters are written, the students can divide into small groups and take turns reading their letters or excerpts of their letters aloud and listening to one another. The *purposes* are to stress creativity, to use accurate information about the time period, to apply their learning to a different situation of letter correspondence, to display their listening skills, and to expand the students' thinking about ways to explain the topic to others.

Activity #2: Realistic writing and purpose

I would ask the students to consider writing an informational paragraph about an incident where rules were in evidence during this time period. After the informational paragraphs are written, the students can join together as partners and take turns reading the writing aloud and listening to one another. They can ask for feedback about their use of accurate information. The *purposes* would be to show the students' understanding of the particular concept of rules, to use accurate information, to expand the students' thinking, to demonstrate their listening skills, and to apply their learning to writing an informational-type paragraph.

CHAPTER 6

Hints: You are asked to take the role of a middle school teacher and draft two questions for the students to respond to in short-answer essays. You want the questions to give the students an opportunity to demonstrate their higher order thinking skills, which can include application, analysis, synthesis, and evaluation. You want to give them an opportunity to write about what they have learned on the subject of equality, so the main focus of the questions should be related to the concept of *equality* or the statement "All men/women are created equal." Tell which higher order thinking skills the questions would require the students to use and how the questions extend the students' knowledge about the topic.

Question #1: I would offer this question: "In what way can you apply what you have learned to a new situation and describe the effect of equality on peo-

ple in the _____ society where women and men are considered to be equal?"

Higher order thinking skills: The students would be required to use these higher order thinking skills: (a) application, i.e., they will use the knowledge that they have learned and apply that knowledge to a new situation (in this case, a different societal group); (b) analysis, i.e., the students will analyze the effect on people in a certain societal group so they can describe the effect in writing; and (c) evaluation, i.e., the students will make a judgment call about the concept that women and men were considered to be equal in the given society and give examples to support that view.

Question #2: I would offer this question: "In what way can you analyze what you have learned to describe the effect that a *lack* of equality had on the people in the _____ society?"

Higher order thinking skills: The students would be required to use these higher order thinking skills: (a) analysis, i.e., the students would use what they have learned to describe and consider/analyze the effect of the *lack* of equality on people in a society; (b) evaluation, i.e., the students will make a judgment call that there was a *lack* of equality in a particular situation and describe its effect on the people.

CHAPTER 7

Hints: You are asked to take the persona of a sixth-grade teacher who is teaching a humanities block that integrates language arts, reading, and social studies and list the steps that you would take to prepare your sixth graders to write a research report about a topic related to the concept of Manifest Destiny. You are asked to briefly explain each step.

Activity #1: Writing a research report

Here are the steps that I would take to guide the sixth-grade students through the writing of their research reports:

First, I would consider several prewriting activities that include discussing the topic, interviewing another person, researching information, taking notes when necessary, and brainstorming about the topic.

Second, I would consider the drafting process. I would encourage the students to record their ideas and at this step, would not have a great concern about spelling or the mechanics of the language.

Third, I would consider an editing step. I would engage the students in reading a draft aloud to a class partner for discussion and in trading drafts with partners for proofreading. At this step, I would encourage correcting and refining according to spelling and the mechanics of the language.

Fourth, I would consider a publishing step. I would have the students write a final copy and present the final work to others in small groups or to the whole group.

CHAPTER 8

Hints: You are asked to take the role of a kindergarten teacher who wants to make a smooth transition from one lesson to the next. You are asked to draft two questions that the students could respond to at the completion of a reading lesson that would help with the transition to the next lesson, a math lesson.

Question #1: Aiding Transition

I would offer this question: "In what way did the ending (or trick ending) make the story more interesting to you?"

Question #2: Aiding Transition

Then, second, I would offer this question: "Just as stories can be interesting to you, in what way can numbers make a math lesson interesting to you?"

CHAPTER 9

Hints: This chapter's teacher vignette was about real-life problem solving. The emphasis was on integrated learning and about looking at a problem or subject of study from the point of view of many separate disciplines. Related to this, you were asked to use a unit on reading newspaper articles related to a topic of interest to introduce students to the idea of public officials in the real world using knowledge from various disciplines to help solve one or more of their problems. After a week or two of reading newspaper articles, you discover that some of your students still don't understand a key principle of newspaper articles—the main idea. Describe two activities that might help these students identify main ideas in nonfiction prose. Give specific examples and explain the purpose of the activities.

Activity #1: What is this article really emphasizing?
I would have the whole group read an article on an overhead transparency and ask, "What is this article really emphasizing?" and "What do you think the main point is?" Record the students' responses and discuss.

Activity #2: Newspaper articles and the main point
I would clip brief articles from newspapers and clip off the accompanying headlines. I would have the students as pairs or triads, study one article, determine the main idea, and write the idea as a headline to later share with the whole group for discussion. I would repeat the activity with different news articles.

Purposes of the activities: The purposes of these activities are to develop an understanding of the particular concept of *main idea;* to clarify the students' thinking about a *main point* in an article; to use accurate information from a newspaper article; and to record their thoughts about a main idea.

CHAPTER 10

Hints: You are asked to explain the steps to guide the students through the writing process as they prepare to write a survival guide about natural disasters. Here are the steps that I would take to guide the students through the writing of a survival guide about natural disasters:

Step 1: I would plan several prewriting activities and have the students:

Discuss the topic
Interview another person to get information
Research information from sources
Take notes when necessary
Brainstorm about the topic.

Step 2: I would plan a drafting process and have the students:

Record their ideas
Basically ignore (for the moment) spelling/mechanics of the language and focus on writing their ideas.

Step 3: I would include an editing step and have the students:

Read their drafts aloud to a class partner for discussion/feedback/evaluation
Trade their drafts with partners for proofreading
After proofreading, start correcting and refining their drafts related to spelling/mechanics of the language.

Step 4: I would plan a publishing step and have the students:

Write a final copy
Present their final work to others in a group situation.

CHAPTER 11

Hints: You are asked to select a unit of study of your choice for students of a selected grade and age level. You are asked to describe an end-of-the-unit activity that would be an extension of the study. The activity should demonstrate your understanding of how children learn at this age and grade level.

Activity #1: End-of-the-unit activity

I have selected a unit of study about the American Revolution for fifth-grade students, usually ages 10/11. The end-of-the-unit activity that I would select as an extension of this study would be to let each student write his or her own informational narrative about what was learned and share it with the whole group in a culminating program that would extend the information about the topic to all of the students. If appropriate for the instructional time that I had, I would have the students prepare their informational narratives first by working in dyads to construct information paragraphs about what they learned, and then use the information as reference to support the writing of their narratives. As part of the culminating program on this topic, I would have them each write an informative letter to a friend in the class to tell the friend what he or she learned about the topic.

My understanding of how children learn at this age and grade level: Children in the fifth grade at the ages of 10 or 11 like interaction with their peers (such as participating in a culminating class program about the topic, or studying in dyads, or writing personal letters to class friends). They prefer active learning experiences (working with partners, writing letters to friends, preparing for a culminating program) and can use their skills in real-life situations (preparing for culminating programs, letter writing). Related to problems, they can reason, judge, and apply what they have experienced (working in dyads). They can think about their own thinking, i.e., metacognition: preassessing what they know through a K–W–L (known–want to know–learn strategy); asking what they want to know; and, still later, working in dyads or other types of groups to state/identify what they have learned.

Glossary

ability grouping The assignment of students to separate classrooms or to separate activities within a classroom according to their perceived academic abilities. This means matching instruction to the needs of students with similar abilities who are placed in groups; homogeneous grouping is the grouping of students of similar abilities, whereas heterogeneous grouping is the grouping of students of mixed abilities.

access mode A student-centered strategy that provides students with access to information gained by working with other students.

accommodation The cognitive process of modifying a schema or creating new schemata in response to one's experiences.

accountability Term that refers to the concept that an individual is responsible for his or her own behaviors and should be able to demonstrate publicly the worth of the activities carried out; a student can be asked to show that he or she has met specified standards; a teacher can be asked to demonstrate how he or she has been responsible for the students' performance.

achievement test See *standardized test*.

active learning Hands-on and minds-on learning.

advance organizer Preinstructional cues that encourage a particular mental set; used to enhance retention of materials to be studied.

advisor–advisee A homeroom or advisory program that provides each student with the opportunity to interact with peers about school and personal concerns and to develop a meaningful relationship with at least one member of the school staff.

affective domain The area of learning related to attitudes, feelings, interests, values, and personal adjustment.

aim The term sometimes used for the most general educational objectives.

aligned/authentic assessment An assessment that matches the instructional objectives.

aligned curriculum A curriculum in which teachers prepare specific objectives, teach toward them, and assess students' progress against them. Also known as *performance-based teaching* and *criterion-referenced measurement*.

alternative assessment Assessment of learning in ways that are different from traditional paper-and-pencil objective testing, such as direct examination of real-life tasks, a portfolio, *PowerPoint* presentation, project, or self-assessment. See also *authentic assessment*.

American Federation of Teachers (AFT) A national professional organization of teachers founded in 1916 and currently affiliated with the American Federation of Labor and Congress of Industrial Organizations (AFL–CIO).

analysis Dissecting information into its component parts to comprehend their relationships.

anchor assignment An ongoing assignment that students work on after they have finished their basic work. Also called *transitional activity* or *star activity*.

anticipatory set See *advance organizer*.

application Using information; one of the major categories (or levels) in Bloom's taxonomy of cognitive objectives.

articulation Term used when referring to the connectedness of the various components of the formal curriculum. *Vertical articulation* is used when referring to the connectedness of the K–12 curriculum; *horizontal articulation* refers to the connectedness across a grade level.

assessment A teacher's relatively neutral process of finding out what students are learning or have learned as a result of instruction. Helps a teacher make further decisions about teaching and the students' learning. See also *evaluation*.

assignments A statement telling the student what he or she is to accomplish as a follow-up to a lesson either as homework (responsibility papers) or as in-class work.

assimilation The cognitive process by which a learner integrates new information into an existing schema.

at-risk General term given to students who show a high potential for dropping out of formal education.

authentic assessment The use of evaluation procedures (usually portfolios and projects) that are highly compatible with the instructional objectives. Also referred to as *accurate, active, aligned, alternative, direct,* and *performance assessment*.

authentic learning Learning that occurs when students are actively (hands-on) and mentally (minds-on) engaged in skills and knowledge.

behavioral objective A statement describing what the learner should be able to do on completion of the instruction. It contains four ingredients: the audience (learner), the overt behavior, the conditions, and the degree (performance level). Also referred to as *performance* and *terminal objective.*

behaviorism A theory that equates learning with changes in observable behavior.

bias in tests, cultural This term refers to the bias that happens when the language of an item on a test hinders a response by a student of a particular ethnic or cultural background.

block scheduling The school programming procedure that provides large blocks of time (e.g., 2 hours) in which individual teachers or teacher teams can organize and arrange grouping of students for varied periods, thereby more effectively individualizing the instruction for students with various needs and abilities.

brainstorming An instructional strategy used to create a flow of new ideas, during which judgments of the ideas of others are forbidden; actions of students as they orally respond to a question and the teacher, a student, or classroom aide writes their responses on a board, chart, or transparency without making judgments about the responses.

broad questions Higher order thinking questions that require analysis, synthesis, or evaluation. Also known as *reflective, open-ended, thought,* and *divergent-thinking questions.*

CD–ROM (compact disc–read-only memory) Digitally encoded information permanently recorded on a compact disc.

character education Term that refers to the transmission of honesty and other values.

charter school Usually recognized as a school that is established within the provisions of state charter school laws that becomes an educational campus operating under a contract/charter that has been negotiated between the operators of the school and the sponsors who oversee the provisions of the contract/charter.

checklist Term that refers to a written description related to a topic that indicates an adequate demonstration/performance related to the topic.

classroom assessment Term that refers to a teacher's procedures that he or she uses to make decisions about the learning progress of the students; can include informal assessment strategies such as informal reading inventories, observations by the teacher, oral reports by students, performance samples, work in portfolios, and ongoing records.

classroom control The process of influencing student behavior in the classroom; includes all of a teacher's strategies related to maintaining a safe learning environment.

classroom management This is the teacher's system of establishing a climate for learning and includes his or her techniques used to prevent and respond to a student's misbehavior.

clinical supervision A nonevaluative collegial process of facilitating teaching effectiveness by involving a triad of individuals: the precredentialed teacher, the collaborating teacher, and the college or university supervisors/instructor/representative. Sometimes known as *effective supervision,* it includes (a) a preobservation conference between the supervisors and the precredentialed teacher to specify and agree on the specific objectives for an observation visit; (b) a data collection observation; and (c) a postobservation conference to analyze the data collected during the observation and to set goals for a subsequent observation.

closure In a lesson, the means by which a teacher brings the lesson to an end.

coached practice Providing individual attention to students by using in-class times to begin assignments.

coaching See *mentoring.*

cognition The process of thinking.

cognitive disequilibrium The mental state of not yet having made sense out of a perplexing (discrepant) situation.

cognitive domain The area of learning related to intellectual skills, such as retention and assimilation of knowledge.

cognitive experimentalism From this point of view, the main focus in teaching should be on facilitating the learner's gain of new perceptions that lead to desired behavioral changes which ultimately led to a more fully functioning individual. This view sees the learner as a neutral-interactive purposive individual in simultaneous interaction with the physical and biological environments.

cognitive psychology A branch of psychology devoted to the study of how individuals acquire, process, and use information.

cognitivism A theory that supports the idea that learning involves the construction or reshaping of mental schemata and that mental processes mediate learning; maintains that learners construct their own understanding of the topics they study. Also known as *constructivism.*

common planning time A regularly scheduled time during the school day when teachers who teach the same students meet for joint planning, parent conferences, materials preparation, and student evaluation.

compact disc (CD) A 4.72-inch disc on which a laser has recorded digital information.

comparative organizer An introduction that mentally prepares students for a study by helping them make connections with materials already learned or experienced. See also *advance organizer.*

competency-based instruction Instruction that is designed to evaluate student achievement against specified and predetermined behavioral objectives. The term also indicates instruction referred to as *outcome-based* and *results-driven instruction.*

comprehension A level of cognition that refers to the skill of *understanding.*

computer-assisted instruction (CAI) Instruction received by a student when interacting with lessons programmed into a computer system; can also refer to the management of information about the performance of students and selections of educational resources that can be prescribed and controlled for individual lessons.

computer literacy The ability at some level on a continuum to understand and use computers.

concept A general idea or thought that you have, based on your experiences, that classifies or categorizes information or phenomena that ranges from simple (objects) to complex (perhaps themes); also an abstraction (i.e., each person's concept about phenomena is an abstraction) that is unique to that person's experiences; refers to a group of facts or ideas that can have something in common.

conceptual misunderstanding   Faulty understanding of a major idea. See also *misconception*.

constructivism   See *cognitivism*.

continuous progress   Term that refers to the progress of a student who moves at his or her own pace through a sequence of lessons that make up the curriculum.

convergent-thinking question   Thinking that is directed to a preset conclusion.

cooperative learning group   A genre of instructional strategies in which small groups of students work together and help each other on learning tasks; emphasis is on support for one another rather than on competition.

core curriculum   Subject or discipline components of the curriculum considered absolutely necessary. Traditionally these are English/language arts, mathematics, science, and social science.

covert behavior   A learner behavior that is not outwardly observable.

criterion   A standard by which behavioral performance is judged.

criterion-referenced assessment   Assessment in which standards are established and behaviors are judged against preset guidelines, rather than against behaviors of others. Also referred to as *competency-based, performance-based, results-driven,* or *outcome-based measurement.*

criterion-referenced measurement   See *criterion-referenced assessment.*

critical thinking   The ability of a learner to recognize and identify problems and discrepancies, to propose and to test solutions, and to arrive at tentative conclusions.

cross-age coaching   An instructional strategy that places students, sometimes in different age groups, in a tutorial role in which one student helps one another learn.

cues   Hints or prompts that can produce student behaviors that a teacher wants to reinforce.

culminating activities   The activities that bring a unit of study to a natural close.

culminating presentation   A way in which students can apply what they have learned; a final presentation/activity that often includes an oral report, a hands-on item of some kind, and a written report.

curriculum   Originally derived from a Latin term referring to a race course for the chariots, the term still has no widely accepted definition. As used in this text, *curriculum* is that which is planned and encouraged for teaching and learning. This includes both school and nonschool environments, overt (formal) and hidden (informal) environments, and broad as well as narrow notions of content—its development, acquisition, and consequences.

curriculum standards   What students should know (content) and should be able to do (process and performance).

data input phase   The lowest level of questioning, i.e., gathering and recalling information.

data output phase   The highest level of questioning, i.e., to think intuitively, creatively, and hypothetically, and to use imagination.

data processing phase   The intermediate level of questioning, i.e., drawing relationships of cause and effect, to synthesize, to analyze, to summarize, to compare/contrast, and to classify data.

deductive learning   Learning that proceeds from the general (the whole, looking overall at a particular group, kind, class, topic) to the specific (a designation of the particular characteristics). See also *expository instruction.*

delivery mode   Manner in which information is delivered; often uses traditional strategies such as textbook reading, lecturing, questioning, and teacher-centered or teacher-planned discussions. Also known as the *didactic, expository,* or *traditional* style of instruction.

demonstration   Term that refers to a showing or exhibition of methods or reasoning.

developmental activities   Activities that make up the majority of the lessons and an ongoing unit.

developmental characteristics   A set of common intellectual, psychological, physical, and social characteristics that, when considered as a whole, indicate an individual's development relative to others during a particular age span.

developmental needs   A set of needs unique and appropriate to the developmental characteristics of a particular age span.

diagnostic assessment   Collecting data on a student's strengths/weaknesses in areas of identified skill sets.

didactic instruction   See *explicit* or *direct instruction.*

differentiated learning   Personalization of learning for students of various abilities; can include differentiated reading, flexible grouping, tiered assignments, and different tasks for special populations of students. Also a synonym for personalized instruction that reflects a concern for learners and a teacher's way of adjusting the teaching and learning environment to enhance the learning needs of individual students. See also *multireading approach, personalized instruction,* and *tiered instruction.*

differentiated/tiered instruction   Teacher insight of and use of varied methods and content of instruction according to individual student differences and needs. See also *differentiated learning* and *personalized instruction.*

direct experience   Learning by doing (applying) that which is being learned.

direct instruction   Teacher-centered expository instruction.

direct intervention   Teacher use of verbal reminders or verbal commands to redirect student behavior, as opposed to nonverbal gestures or cues.

discipline   The process of controlling student behavior in the classroom. This term has been largely replaced by the terms *classroom control* and *classroom management.* It is also used in reference to the subject taught (e.g., language arts, mathematics, social sciences).

discovery learning   This is learning that proceeds from identifying a problem, developing the hypotheses, testing the hypotheses, and arriving at a conclusion. See also *critical thinking.*

divergent-thinking question   Thinking that expands beyond original thought.

downshifting   Reverting to earlier learned, lower cognitive level behaviors.

early adolescence The developmental stage of young people as they approach and begin to experience puberty. This stage usually occurs between 10 and 14 years of age and deals with the successful attainment of the appropriate developmental characteristics for this age span.

eclectic Utilizing the best from a variety of sources.

effective school A school where students master basic skills, strive for academic excellence in all subjects, demonstrate achievement, and display good behavior and attendance. Known also as an *exemplary school.*

elective High-interest or special needs courses that are based on student selection from various options.

electronic teaching portfolio A collection of your professional work over periods of time that shows how your teaching has changed; can include reflections and feedback about your teaching.

elementary school Any school that has been planned and organized especially for children of some combination of grades kindergarten through six. There are many variations, though; for example, a school might house children of preschool through seven or eight and still be called an elementary school or *grade school.*

empathy The ability to understand the feelings of another person.

equality Considered to be the same in status or competency level.

equilibration The mental process of moving from disequilibrium to equilibrium.

equilibrium The balance between assimilation (integrating new information) and accommodation (modifying or creating a new schema).

equity Fairness and justice; impartiality.

essay Form of measurement that asks a student to write a response to a problem/question.

evaluation Like assessment, but includes making sense out of the assessment results by judging the worth of something, usually based on criteria or a scoring guide/rubric. Evaluation is more subjective than is assessment.

evaluative question A question that requires a student to place a value on something or to take a stance on some issue.

exceptional student A student who deviates from the average in any of the following ways: his or her ability to communicate, mental characteristics, multiple disabilities, neuromotor characteristics, physical characteristics, and social behavior. Also known as a *special needs student* and *special education student.*

exemplary school A school where students master basic skills, seek academic excellence in all subjects, demonstrate achievement, and display good behavior and attendance. Known also as an *effective school.*

explicit instruction Teacher-centered instruction, typically with the entire class, where the teacher controls student attention and behaviors as opposed to permitting students greater control over their own learning and behaviors. Also called *explicit teaching* and referred to as *explicit/direct instruction, expository teaching,* or *teacher-centered instruction.* This mode of instruction is different from implicit/indirect experiences.

exploratory course A course designed to help students explore curriculum experiences based on their felt needs, interests, and abilities.

expository instruction Classroom instructional approach that is usually presented in a sequence: Present the information to students, make a reference to selected examples, and apply the information to students' experiences.

expository organizer An introduction that mentally prepares students for a study by helping them see an arrangement of what is to be learned. See *advance organizer.*

extended-day school A school that has extended its daily schedule.

extended-year school Schools that have extended the school year calendar from a designated 180 number of days to a longer period, such as 210 days.

extrinsic motivators Rewards for learning such as certificates, gifts, grades, points, stickers, and teacher/parent/guardian expectations.

facilitating behavior Teacher behavior that makes it possible for students to learn.

facilitative teaching See *implicit teaching.*

family, educational See *school-within-a-school.*

feedback In interpersonal communication, this is information sent from the receiver to the originator that provides disclosure about the reception of the intended message.

flexible scheduling Organization of classes and activities in a way that allows for variation from day to day; contrast with the traditional fixed schedule that does not vary from day to day.

formative assessment Evaluation of learning in progress.

full inclusion A commitment to each special needs student to educate him or her to the maximum extent that is appropriate in the class, school, and district.

full-service community school A school that serves as a community center.

goal, course A broad generalized statement telling the expected outcomes of the course.

goal, educational A statement telling what the instructor intends to do that is often broad and general in scope; can reflect an expected educational outcome. Also known as an *instructional goal.*

goal indicators Term used to indicate performance objectives that are parts of larger educational goals that reflect the competencies that the students are expected to achieve.

goal, instructional See *goal, educational.*

goal, teacher A statement about what the teacher hopes to accomplish.

grade school See *elementary school.*

hands-on learning Learning by doing or active learning.

heterogeneous grouping A grouping pattern that does not separate students into groups based on their intelligence, learning achievement, or physical characteristics.

high-stakes testing Term that refers to some standardized tests that measure which standards are being met by the students; in some cases, is used to make a decision about a student being promoted to the next grade.

holistic learning Learning that incorporates emotions with thinking.

homogeneous grouping A grouping pattern that separates students into groups based on their intelligence, school achievement, or physical characteristics.

house (educational) See *school-within-a-school*.

implicit teaching Student-centered teaching using discovery learning and inquiry learning instructional strategies.

inclusion The commitment to the education of each special needs learner, to the maximum extent appropriate, in the school and classroom he or she would otherwise attend. See also *full inclusion*.

independent study An instructional strategy that allows a student to select a topic, set the goals, and work alone to attain them.

individualized education program (IEP) An instructional plan/program designed by general education teachers, special education teachers, parents/guardians, school/district resource professionals, and, in some cases, the student.

individualized instruction See *individualized learning*.

individualized learning Self-paced process whereby individual students assume responsibility for learning through study, practice, feedback, and reinforcement with appropriately designed instructional packages or modules.

inductive learning Learning that proceeds from the specific to the general.

informal assessment Informal and classroom-based assessment strategies that include informal reading inventories, observations by the teacher, oral reports, performance samples, portfolios, and ongoing records.

initiating activities The activities that start with a beginning lesson or start a unit into motion.

inquiry learning Instructional approach that is similar to discovery learning except that the learner designs the processes to be used in resolving a problem. Inquiry learning typically demands higher levels of mental operation than does discovery learning because the students themselves often gather the needed information and use it to investigate problems in real life.

in-service teacher Term used when referring to credentialed and employed teachers.

instruction Planned arrangement of experiences to help a learner develop understanding and to achieve a desirable change in behavior; experiences associated with methods facilitating student learning.

instructional components Denotes the arrangement of the procedures to be used in a lesson plan.

instructional module Any instructional unit that includes these components: rationale, objectives, pretest, learning activities, comprehension checks, post-test.

instructional objectives Statements describing what the student(s) will be able to do on completion of the instructional experience. Also called *learning objectives*.

integrated (interdisciplinary) curriculum Curriculum reorganization that combines subject matter traditionally taught separately. Also known as *integrated studies, thematic instruction,* and *multidisciplinary teaching*.

integrated thematic unit A unit that integrates multiple disciplines and is centered on a central theme.

interdisciplinary team An organizational pattern of two or more teachers representing different subject areas. The team shares the same students, schedule, areas of the school, and the opportunity for teaching more than one subject.

interdisciplinary thematic unit (ITU) A thematic unit that crosses boundaries of two or more disciplines.

intermediate grades Term sometimes used to refer to grades 4–6. An intermediate school, for example, is an elementary school that houses children of grades 4–6.

internalizing The extent to which an attitude or value becomes a part of the learner. That is, without having to think about it, the learner's behavior reflects the attitude or value.

intervention A teacher's interruption to redirect a student's behavior, either by direct intervention (e.g., by a verbal command) or by indirect intervention (e.g., by eye contact or physical proximity).

intramural program Organized activity program that features events between individuals or teams from within the school.

intrinsic motivation Term that indicates the motivation of learning through the student's internal sense of accomplishment.

introduction The section of a lesson plan that prepares the students mentally for the lesson. Also referred to as the *set* or *initiating activity*.

intuition Knowing without conscious reasoning.

I-search paper An approach to writing a research paper that differs from the traditional research paper approach and engages the students in listing information they would like to know, conducting a study to find information, keeping a log that is a process journal, and preparing a summary of their findings.

jigsaw An instructional approach to facilitate students' metacognitive development in which individual students or small groups of students are given responsibilities for separate tasks that lead to a bigger task or understanding. The students put together the separate tasks/parts to make a whole.

journals, student A record, diary, or account of daily learning that includes what students are studying, classroom interactions, free writing, or school events. Also called *process journals, response journals,* and *dialogue journals*.

knowledge Recognizing and recalling information.

learning A change in behavior resulting from experience.

learning activity Denotes *how* students will learn something.

learning center (LC) An instructional strategy that uses activities and materials located at a special place in the classroom and is designed to allow a student to work independently at his or her own pace to learn one area of content; types include direct-learning center, open-learning center, and skill center.

learning modality The way a person receives information. Four modalities are recognized: visual, auditory, tactile (touch), and kinesthetic.

learning objective Denotes what the students will learn as a result of the learning activity. Also called *instructional objectives.*

learning resource center The central location in the school where instructional materials and media are stored, organized, and accessed by students and staff.

learning station A learning center that is somehow linked or sequenced to another center where each incorporates a different medium or modality or focuses on a special aspect of the curriculum.

learning style The way a person learns best in a given situation.

learning targets Competencies that the students are expected to achieve. Also called *educational goals,* which can be divided into performance objectives and sometimes referred to as *goal indicators.*

lesson conclusion Denotes the section of the lesson that provides closure; the planned process of bringing the lesson to an end.

lesson development The section of a lesson plan that details the activities that occur between the beginning and the end of the lesson.

literacy Another term for English/reading/language arts in curriculum plans for multiple subjects.

locus of control This term refers to the location where the responsibility for the instructional outcomes is placed.

looping An arrangement in which a cohort of students and teachers remains together as a group for several years at a particular school. Also referred to as *multiyear grouping, multiyear instruction, multiyear placement,* and *teacher–student progression.*

magnet school A school that specializes in a particular academic area, such as the arts, international relations, mathematics, science, and technology. Also referred to as a *theme school.*

mainstreaming Placing an exceptional student in a regular classroom for all (inclusion) or part (partial inclusion) of his or her learning.

manipulatives Objectives that can be moved/used with the hands with the goal of demonstrating something.

mastery learning The concept that a student should master the content of one lesson before moving on to the content of the next.

mean The average score in a distribution of scores achieved by test takers.

measurement The process of collecting and interpreting data.

median The middle score in a distribution of scores achieved by test takers.

mentoring One-on-one coaching, tutoring, or guidance to facilitate learning.

metacognition The ability to think about, to understand, and to develop one's own thinking and learning.

middle grades This term reflects a movement in the 1980s that relied on research that indicated that the needs and interests of children in the seventh and eighth grades more closely resemble those of elementary schoolchildren than those of ninth graders, resulting in schools that typically house grades 5–8.

middle level education Any school unit between elementary and high school.

middle school A school that has been planned and organized especially for students of ages 10–14 and that generally has grades 5–8, with grades 6–8 being the most popular grade-span organization, although many varied patterns exist. For example, a school might include only grades 7 and 8 and still be called a middle school.

minds-on learning Learning in which the learner is intellectually active, thinking about what is being learned.

misconception Faulty understanding of a major idea or concept. Also known as a *naive theory* and *conceptual misunderstanding.*

mode The most frequent score in a distribution of scores achieved by test takers.

modeling A teacher's explicit/direct and implicit/indirect demonstration, by actions and by words, of the behaviors expected of students.

multicultural education A deliberate educational attempt to help students understand facts, generalizations, attitudes, and behaviors derived from their own ethnic roots as well as those of others. In this process the students should unlearn racism and biases and recognize the interdependent fabric of our human society, giving due acknowledgment for contributions made by all its members.

multilevel instruction See *multitasking.*

multimedia The combined use of sound, video, and graphics for instruction.

multiple intelligences A theory of several different intelligences, as opposed to just one general intelligence; other intelligences that have been described are verbal/linguistic, musical, logical/mathematical, naturalist, visual/spatial, bodily/kinesthetic, interpersonal, and intrapersonal.

multipurpose board A writing board with a smooth plastic surface.

multireading approach Teacher use of different reading and workbook assignments and supplementary sources; students work out of different books and do different exercises and can work toward the same or different objectives. See also *multitasking.*

multitasking The simultaneous use of several levels of teaching and learning in the same classroom with students working on different objectives or different tasks leading to the same objectives. Also called *multilevel instruction.*

naive theory See *misconception.*

narrow questions Lower order thinking questions, such as recall questions, that have single correct answers. Also called *convergent-thinking questions.*

National Education Association (NEA) The nation's oldest professional organization of teachers organized in 1857 as the National Teachers Association and changed in 1879 to its present name.

National Network of Partnership 2000 Schools An educational program where schools have membership and parents/guardians are included as partners; teachers and administrators strive to inform parents/guardians about their child's progress, about the school's family involvement policy, and about any programs in which family members can participate.

norm-referenced Assessment process in which an individual performance is judged relative to overall performance of the group. It is different from criterion-referenced assessment, which establishes preset standards and judges student behaviors against the preset standards rather than against the behaviors of other individuals.

norms Standardized test scores from a representative group of students nationally that were used to compare a single student's score in a particular testing situation; the term can also indicate the median (middle score) achievement of a large group.

organizing Placing values into a system of dominant and supporting values.

orientation set See *advance organizer.*

outcome-based education Instruction that is designed to evaluate the achievement of students against specified and predetermined behavioral objectives; the term also refers to instruction that is referred to as *competency-based, results-driven,* and *performance-based instruction.*

overlapping The teacher's ability to attend to several matters at once.

overt behavior A learner behavior that is outwardly observable.

paraprofessional An adult who is not a credentialed teacher but who works with children in the classroom with and under the supervision of a credentialed person.

partial inclusion Placement of special needs students in a regular education classroom for part of the day.

partners A student who works with another student in accomplishing a learning task.

peer teaching (PT) Clinical technique of preparing, implementing, and evaluating a teaching demonstration for a small group of peers.

peer tutoring An instructional strategy that places students in a tutorial role in which one student helps another learn.

percent A specified number of parts out of one hundred; can indicate the number of units in proportion to one hundred.

percentile Ranking that compares a child's score with the scores of all the other children who have taken the test. Also known as a *percentile rank* (PR or % rank).

performance assessment See *authentic assessment.*

performance-based instruction Instruction designed around evaluating student achievement against specified and predetermined behavioral objectives. The term also refers to *competency-based, outcome-based,* and *results-driven instruction.*

performance objective See *behavioral objective.*

personalized instruction A synonym for differentiated or tiered instruction that reflects a concern for learners and a teacher's adjustment in the teaching and learning environment to meet the learning needs of individual students. See *differentiated/tiered instruction.*

personalized learning Learning that reflects the point of view that all persons learn in their own ways and at individual rates and are influenced by learning styles and capacities, modality preferences, information-processing habits, motivational factors, and physiological factors.

plan B Denotes an addition to your lesson plan about what to do if you finish the lesson and time remains.

pod Term for a *school within-a-school;* sometimes, referred to as a cluster, family, house, or village. It is a teaching arrangement in which a team of teachers is assigned to work with the same group of about 125 students for a common block of time, for the entire school day, or, in some instances, for all the years those students are at that school.

portfolio assessment An alternative approach to evaluation that assembles representative samples of the student's work over time as a basis for assessment.

positive reinforcer A means of encouraging desired student behaviors by rewarding those behaviors when they occur.

postobservation conference A visit in which the student teacher/intern, the cooperating teacher, and the supervisor/principal discuss the classroom students' performances and the teaching performance.

practice Denotes the teacher's follow-up, i.e., ways in which the teacher intends to have students interact in the classroom such as individual practice, in dyads, or small groups, to receive guidance or coaching from each other or from the teacher.

Praxis teacher tests Tests required by some states for credentialing and licensing of teachers with the passing scores recommended by panels of educators; includes multiple-choice and constructed response-type questions.

preassessment Diagnostic assessment of what students know or think they know prior to the instruction.

preobservation conference A visit between student teachers/interns/teachers with supervisors/principals to discuss goals, objectives, teaching strategies, and the evaluation process.

preservice Term that refers to precredentialed teachers in training, as opposed to in-service teachers or teachers who are employed.

prior knowledge Earlier acquired facts, information, and ideas that comprise what a student knows before learning something else or before a lesson.

probationary teacher An untenured teacher; after a designated number of years in the same district (usually 3 years), the probationary teacher, upon rehire, receives a tenure contract.

procedure Statement that indicates to students a way to accomplish a task; it can also indicate the section of a teacher's lesson plan that outlines what a teacher and the students will do during the lesson. See *rules.*

professional logbook A diary-type journal that serves as documentation of specific professional contributions and activities and also as documentation of a teacher's breadth of professional experience.

project A relatively long-term investigation or study from which students produce their culminating presentations that show how the students apply what they have learned.

proportion The relation of one thing to another.

psychomotor domain Classification of learning loco-motor behaviors that include moving, manipulating, communicating, and creating.

realia Real objects, such as political campaign buttons, plants, and memorabilia, used as visual props in teaching.

receiving Being aware of the affective stimulus and beginning to have favorable feelings toward it.

reciprocal teaching A form of collaborative teaching in which the teacher and the students share the teaching responsibility and all are involved in asking questions, clarifying, predicting, and summarizing.

reflection The conscious process of mentally replaying experiences.

reflective abstraction See *metacognition*.

relaxed alertness A classroom environment that is perceived by the student as challenging and nonthreatening.

reliability In measurement, the consistency with which an item is measured over time.

responding Taking an interest in the stimulus and viewing it favorably.

results-driven instruction See *performance-based instruction*.

romanticism-maturationism From this point of view, the main focus in teaching is the addition of new ideas to a subconscious store of old ideas. Related to a theoretical position that indicates the learner's mind ranges from neutral-passive to good-active and key persons include Jean J. Rousseau and Sigmund Freud. Key instructional strategies include classic lecturing and rote memorization.

rubric A presented, prescribed, or established form or method for assessing a student's work; can also be an outline of the criteria for an accomplishment. See *scoring guide*.

rules In classroom management, rules/procedures are the standards of expectation for classroom behavior. See *procedure*.

sans penalty Without a negative consequence.

schemata (singular: schema) A mental construct by which the learner organizes his or her perceptions of situations and knowledge.

school-within-a-school Sometimes referred to as a house, cluster, family, house, pod, or village, it is a teaching arrangement in which one team of teachers is assigned to work with the same group of about 125 students for a common block of time, for the entire school day, or, in some instances, for all of the years those students are at that school.

scoring guide A method for assessing a student's work; can also be an outline of the criteria for an accomplishment. See also *rubric*.

self-contained classroom Commonly used in the primary grades, it is a grouping pattern in which one teacher teaches all or most all subjects to one group of children.

self-paced learning See *individualized learning*.

sequencing Arranging ideas in logical order.

simulation An abstraction or simplification of a real-life situation.

special needs student A special education student. See *exceptional student*.

standard unit A way to organize a unit into a series of activities built into lessons around a topic, major concept, or block of subject content; also known as a traditional or conventional unit.

standardized test A test that assesses students under specified conditions and scored under specified procedures.

stanine Shortened form of *standard nine;* indicates a student's standardized test performance based on a scale from 1 to 9 points as shown on a normal curve. This performance (stanine) is identified as a specific percentage of the normal curve (stanine score).

statement of mission A school's written philosophy or vision that often relates what the school means to the people within the school or district.

student teaching A classroom experience component of teaching preparation, often the culminating experience, in which the precredentialed teacher practices teaching students while under the supervision of a credentialed teacher, and in university programs, a university supervisor.

summative assessment Assessment of learning after instruction is completed.

synthesis Putting components of information together to generate new ideas.

teacher's logbook A diary-type journal that documents a teacher's teaching activities with dated entries.

teaching See *instruction*.

teaching observation A visit where the supervisor/ principal collects data on the classroom students' performance of objectives and performance of the teaching strategies.

teaching style The way a teacher teaches; includes the teacher's distinctive mannerisms complemented by his or her choices of teaching behaviors and strategies.

teaching team A team of two or more teachers who work together to provide instruction to the same group of students, either alternating the instruction or team teaching simultaneously.

teaching video A form of alternative authentic assessment that involves the teacher/student teacher/intern in the design and evaluation of teaching future lessons.

team teaching Two or more teachers working together to provide instruction to a group of students.

technology Related to elementary schools, this term includes the students' use of computers, the Internet, television, VCRs, DVD players, compact discs, CD-ROMs, electronic games, cell phones, personal digital assistants, and other high-tech items.

tenured teacher After serving a designated number of years in the same school district (usually three) as a probationary teacher, the teacher, upon rehire, receives a tenure contract, which means that the teacher is automatically rehired each year thereafter unless the contract is revoked by either the district or the teacher and for specific and legal reasons.

terminal behavior   The behavior that has been learned as a direct result of instruction.

thematic unit   A unit of instruction built on a central theme or concept.

theme school   See *magnet school.*

think time   See *wait time.*

tiered instruction   A teacher's insight about (and use of) varied methods and content of instruction according to individual student differences and needs; different levels of assignments.

timetable   A planning and implementation guide for a lesson plan.

total immersion program   A program in which all of the classroom instruction is in the target foreign language.

tracking   The practice of the voluntary or involuntary placement of students in different programs or courses according to their ability and prior academic performance.

traditional instruction   Teacher-centered explicit instruction, typically using teacher talk, discussions, textbooks, and worksheets.

transitions   In a lesson, the planned procedures that move student thinking from one idea to the next or that move their actions from one activity to the next; a change.

validity   In measurement, the degree to which an item or instrument measures that which it is intended to measure.

valuing   Showing a tentative belief in the value of an effected stimulus and becoming committed to it.

video teaching   Referring to the teacher/student teacher/intern, this is a form of alternative authentic assessment that involves the design and evaluation of teaching future lessons.

village   A *school-within-a-school;* sometimes, referred to as a house, cluster, family, or pod.

wait time   In the use of questioning, this is the period of silence between the time a question is asked and the inquirer (teacher) does something, such as repeats the question, rephrases the question, calls on a particular student, asks another question, or answers the previous question him- or herself.

whole-language learning   A point of view of teaching with a focus on seeking or creating meaning that encourages language production, risk taking, independence in producing language, and the use of a wide variety of print materials in authentic reading and writing situations.

with-itness   Term that refers to a teacher's ability to be aware of what is going on in the classroom and, if needed, to intervene and redirect a student's misbehavior in a timely manner.

year-round school   A school that operates on a traditional schedule, that is, with the district's designated number of school days, but the days are spread out over 12 months rather than the more traditional 10. Most common is a 9-weeks-on, 3-weeks off format.

young adolescent   The 9- to 14-year-old experiencing the developmental stage of early adolescence.

Children's Literature Index

Name Index

Subject Index